Protecting China's Interests Overseas

Protecting China's Interests Overseas

Securitization and Foreign Policy

ANDREA GHISELLI

OXFORD
UNIVERSITY PRESS

OXFORD
UNIVERSITY PRESS

Great Clarendon Street, Oxford, OX2 6DP,
United Kingdom

Oxford University Press is a department of the University of Oxford.
It furthers the University's objective of excellence in research, scholarship,
and education by publishing worldwide. Oxford is a registered trade mark of
Oxford University Press in the UK and in certain other countries

First Edition published in 2021

Impression: 1

Published in the United States of America by Oxford University Press
198 Madison Avenue, New York, NY 10016, United States of America

British Library Cataloguing in Publication Data
Data available

Library of Congress Control Number: 2020945985

ISBN 978-0-19-886739-5

Printed and bound in Great Britain by
Clays Ltd, Elcograf S.p.A.

Preface

Among the many Chinese sayings, there is one that, translated literally, describes this book best: "It is coincidence that makes a book" (无巧不成书). This study is the product of the many events that first brought me to study Chinese and then made me interested in Chinese affairs.

Coming from a small, quiet city in Italy's Emilia Romagna, between the Apennine Mountains and the Adriatic Sea, I did not have any special link with or interest in China or, in general, Asia. When I started studying the Chinese language in Venice in 2008, I had almost no clue about China. From then on, many things happened that made me spend a significant number of years in that country and write a book on its foreign policy.

Back then, relations between the West and China were far more relaxed than today. China, too, was different. Over the years, the situation has significantly changed and, today, we are told that we live in an era of great power competition.

One of the most significant products of this turn of events is that Chinese foreign policy is increasingly seen as an issue that can be only black or white. In my opinion, this is something that the world cannot afford, as confrontational narratives go hand in hand with similarly confrontational, but more dangerous policies.

Against this background, I believe that the mission of a so-called "China watcher," even one who became so by accident, is to provide a balanced and accurate analysis of the situation, especially when it comes to a subject like the expansion of China's interests overseas and its attempts to protect them.

There is no doubt that the analysis in the following pages has flaws. Yet I did my best and I hope the reader will appreciate my work.

Acknowledgments

This book could have not been written without the help and support of the many people whom I had the luck and privilege to meet over the years. The first person who ought to be thanked is my wife. My nocturnal writing habits and her much healthier need to sleep like normal people working outside academia were hard to reconcile with each other. This was especially true during the final and, to borrow from the Italian poet Giacomo Leopardi, "crazy and most desperate" days of writing. Despite this, she was always supportive and patient. My family has also provided me with great support and love which has kept me afloat in the most difficult moments. This book would not be here without them.

I think that research is not just about collecting data and writing during the many solitary hours that scholars spend in front of a laptop. Indeed, I would not have been able to write this book without the encouragement and the help of many other fellow scholars who helped me in different moments along the way.

This book originates from the doctoral dissertation that I wrote at the School of International Relations and Public Affairs of Fudan University. My then advisor, Professor Chen Zhimin, constantly exhorted me to be rigorous in the interpretation of the sources and cautious in my analysis, so as to truly shed light on a complex issue like that at the center of this study. Like a true mentor, he was supportive, patient, as well as very straightforward during the many hours that we spent talking about my work. Yet it goes without saying that any mistakes in this book can be attributed to me alone.

Heartfelt thanks also go to five other people whom I consider friends, first, and colleagues, second. The first two are Professor Enrico Fardella and Professor Giovanni B. Andornino. Their vision and inspirational leadership at the TOChina Hub and the ChinaMed Project had a tremendous influence on me and my research, pushing me to look at China's presence in North Africa and the Middle East. The third is Doctor Jean Christopher Mittelstaedt, who has never pulled punches in his feedback on my work and has always pushed me to do better. His German sense of humor, critical mind, and straightforwardness never allowed me to settle for work that was only "good enough." The fourth is Professor Ivan W. Rasmussen. Ivan offered me guidance and advice countless times, kindly sharing with me precious suggestions and funny moments. Professor Courtney J. Fung is the fifth person, who, with her ambition and incredible talent, is a model for every emerging scholar. Courtney has always been a source of inspiration for me, and her words of advice were very important from when I started working on this book.

Professor Rosemary Foot, too, deserves a special acknowledgment. Although we met only a few times, she has always been incredibly kind and supportive. She is also one of the scholars who took time to read and comment on the early drafts of different chapters of this book. I look forward to paying back the favor to her and to Professor Shaun Breslin, Ms. Yunnan Chen, Doctor Pippa Morgan, as well as Doctor Andrew Chubb for the same reason. While they gave me important suggestions on how to improve the analysis presented here, any error is, again, mine alone.

Others who pushed me in the right direction before, during, and after the writing of the manuscript are Doctor Andrew Scobell, Doctor Sean M. Lynn-Jones, Professor Geoffrey F. Gresh, and Professor Pascal Vennesson. This book is the proof that a few words of encouragement and a spot-on comment from a senior scholar can truly make a difference.

Finally, I am indebted to Mr. Dominic Byatt of Oxford University Press and the two anonymous reviewers who read the original draft of this book. Always clear and helpful, Dominic was a great guide throughout the process of publication, always ready to resolve any doubt that I had. The two reviewers provided important feedback, helping me to improve the structure of the book and clarity of my argument.

Contents

List of Illustrations

List of Tables

List of Abbreviations

AMS	Academy of Military Science
ASEAN	Association of Southeast Asian Nations
BRI	Belt and Road Initiative
CASS	Chinese Academy of Social Sciences
CCP	Chinese Communist Party
CCP CMC	Central Military Commission of the Chinese Communist Party
CCP CNSC	Central National Security Commission of the Chinese Communist Party
CCP FALSG	Foreign Affairs Leading Small Group of the Chinese Communist Party
CICIR	China Institutes of Contemporary International Relations
CMC	Central Military Commission
CNPC	China National Petroleum Corporation
CNSC	Central National Security Commission
GG	Go Global
MFA	Ministry of Foreign Affairs
MINUSMA	United Nations Multidimensional Integrated Stabilization Mission in Mali
MOD	Ministry of National Defense
MOFCOM	Ministry of Commerce
MOOTW	Military Operations Other Than War
MPS	Ministry of Public Security
NDRC	National Development and Reform Commission
NDU	National Defense University
NOC	national oil company
ODI	overseas direct investments
PAP	People's Armed Police
PLA	Chinese People's Liberation Army
PLA AMS	Academy of Military Science of the Chinese People's Liberation Army
PLA Daily	People's Liberation Army Daily
PLA NDU	People's Liberation Army National Defense University
PSC	Private Security Company
SASAC	State-Owned Assets Supervision and Administration Commission
SOE	state-owned enterprise
TEU	twenty-foot equivalent unit
UN	United Nations
UNAMID	United Nations-African Union Hybrid Operation in Darfur

UNMIS	United Nations Mission in Sudan
UNMISS	United Nations Mission in South Sudan
UNSC	United Nations Security Council
UNTAC	United Nations Transitional Authority of Cambodia
UNTAET	United Nations Transitional Administration in East Timor
WANA	West Asia and North Africa

Introduction

On March 2, 2011, just as the civil war was raging in Libya and Western countries were about to launch air strikes against Muammar Gaddafi's military, China completed the evacuation of some 36,000 of its nationals from the North African country. On March 15, the official newspaper of the Chinese People's Liberation Army (PLA), the *PLA Daily* (*People's Liberation Army Daily*), published an article arguing that the events in Libya marked a turning point for Chinese foreign policy: a crisis in a third country had never impacted Chinese interests abroad as much as this one. According to the military commentator, China's "interest frontiers"—the geographical space that is defined (and constantly redefined) by the evolution of China's interests and the threats to them—had never been so far from its geographical borders.[1] Suddenly, the need to protect them had become a powerful factor in the equation of Chinese foreign policy. In particular, this need caused the transformation of the Chinese foreign and security policy machine, thereby allowing for the expansion of China's security footprint overseas.

China's military presence outside Asia, in the Middle East and North Africa in particular, has never been larger than it is today. Over 2,600 Chinese "blue helmets" are deployed abroad in United Nations peacekeeping operations in ten countries. Since 1990, when China sent its first military observers abroad, China has deployed more than 30,000 peacekeepers (Gu 2016). At the same time, the PLA Navy has been patrolling the Gulf of Aden for more than ten years. China's first overseas military base was inaugurated in the East African country of Djibouti in August 2017. What was meant to be a simple logistics hub turned out to be a base capable of hosting armored vehicles and helicopters. Eight thousand Chinese troops have also started the necessary training to join the United Nations Peacekeeping Capability Readiness System, a newly formed rapid-deployment standby force. The number of employees of Chinese private security companies sent abroad has grown to the extent that, in 2016, they outnumbered the peacekeepers deployed by China (Bi 2017).

---

[1] In Chinese: 利益边疆 (Lìyì biānjiāng).

Protecting China's Interests Overseas: Securitization and Foreign Policy. Andrea Ghiselli, Oxford University Press (2021). © Andrea Ghiselli.
DOI: 10.1093/oso/9780198867395.001.0001

That protecting the interests overseas comprises a military component seems today part of the foreign policy consensus in Beijing. Zhou Ping (2016, 2018), a professor who works as an advisor to the State Council, wrote that China must extend its "strategic frontiers" to make them overlap with its interest frontiers by establishing a military presence there.[2] Hence, the expert in Middle Eastern affairs Liu Zhongmin (2018, 49), candidly wrote that "along with the continuous expansion of China's overseas interests and the increase in international responsibilities…we need to discuss what is an appropriate presence of our military forces abroad." China's top policymakers have indeed discussed this issue and, during the first meeting of the Central National Security Commission (CNSC) of the Chinese Communist Party (CCP), held on April 17, 2018, Chinese President and CCP General Secretary Xi Jinping declared that protecting China's overseas interests is an essential part of the efforts to defend the country's economic development and national security (People's Daily 2018).

That a country resorts to military means to protect its interest frontiers is not a new phenomenon in history. Balancing territorial defense and protecting interests in faraway regions, as Paul Kennedy's seminal study (1987) on the rise and fall of great powers shows, have always been two of the main challenges that all aspiring great powers have had to face. John Semple Galbraith (1960) analyzed the same problem in the case of the British Empire by, interestingly, using the term "turbulent frontiers," an expression very similar to that used by the Chinese commentator in the *PLA Daily*.

Yet this is not an obvious development for China. Besides cases like Taiwan and the protection of its own territorial integrity, the security and military dimension of China's foreign policy has long been suppressed in favor of a business-only approach to the world, especially outside Asia. Yitzhak Shichor (2005, 235) aptly described it as China's "Japanized" foreign policy. Hence, what is happening can clearly be understood as the beginning of a major change in China's international orientation (Hermann 1990). Therefore, how has the need to protect its interest frontiers influenced Chinese foreign and security policy? That is to say, how has the presence of Chinese nationals and assets abroad been framed as a security issue in the Chinese foreign and security policy debate? What parts of China's foreign and security policy machine were involved in such a process and, at the same time, shaped by it?

This book argues that, so far, what happened in China does not seem to differ significantly from what other scholars have noticed when other great powers have had to deal with the same problem. On the one hand, crises abroad put pressure on Chinese civilian and military elites to acknowledge

---

[2] In Chinese: 战略边疆 (Zhànlüè biānjiāng).

that protecting the life and assets of Chinese individuals and companies overseas had to be included in their understanding of national security and, therefore, new policies became necessary. On the other hand, uncertainty, lack of clear information and experience, and different interests within the bureaucracy have undermined the emergence of a well-thought-out strategy until very recently. Indeed, despite the obvious differences between today's China and the imperial powers of the past, such as the British Empire described by Galbraith, the vocabulary used by Chinese commentators to describe the problem is not the only similarity. Chinese policymakers share the same difficulties in devising a clear strategy and directing the vast and different agencies under their command to tackle the problem of defending the country's interest frontiers in a coordinated way. After all, China's policymaking process is rather fragmented, with a growing number of actors competing for influence and resources (Lampton 2001, Mertha 2009). At the same time, modern China has scant global experience and its elites have little understanding of what happens outside Asia and—until the arrival of Donald Trump at the White House—the United States. As a prominent Chinese scholar involved in the country's international aid program commented:

> When we go to a Southeast Asian country, we cannot understand their language, but we feel at home and find it easy to carry out projects with them. In Africa, everything is different, so it is hard to know how to proceed.
>
> (Stallings and Kim 2017, 24)

China, Its Interest Frontiers, and the Gaps in Our Knowledge

The problem of protecting the lives and assets of Chinese citizens abroad is a new one, not just for Chinese policymakers but also for foreign observers, especially when it comes to studying the role of the Chinese armed forces. Indeed, in spite of the global significance of this issue, most scholars and analysts in the English-speaking academic community have preferred to focus on hard uses of the Chinese armed forces. The few studies that revolve around the problems that China is encountering in protecting its interests overseas provide good background on this topic (Parello-Plesner and Duchâtel 2015, Rolland 2019). Yet, being mostly based on anecdotes and case studies, they are not enough to understand this important aspect of Chinese foreign policy and policymaking.

Current scholarship is dominated by three general and interconnected themes that heavily influence what is considered important, what is not important, what is asked, and what (or how it) is answered. The first theme is the inevitability of a future crisis or conflict with China. This is an old fear, both in the policy and academic world, especially in the United States. The perception of a future threat, caused by Chinese actions during the 1995-6 Taiwan Strait crisis, prompted Congress in October 1999 to authorize the preparation of classified and unclassified reports on Chinese military developments to be issued every year, up to at least 2021. Today, other countries, such as North Korea and Russia, are identified as immediate threats to American security. However, the American armed forces see China as the most important threat in the long term (United States Senate Committee on Armed Services 2017). Similarly, John J. Mearsheimer's classic argument (2001) about the inevitability of a clash between the current hegemonic power and the rising one is, almost twenty years since its first articulation, still used in many studies about the risks of war with China and how to avoid it (Coker 2014, Goldstein 2015, Allison 2017).

Second, China's military is a traditional security threat to Asian stability and, especially, American interests in that region. This argument has been popular since the early 1990s (Yang and Liu 2012). On the one hand, government officials, scholars, and journalists have produced an enormous quantity of reports, papers, and articles on China's quickly expanding military budget and the development of new weapons. On the other hand, events such as the 1995-6 Taiwan Strait crisis, the surfacing of a Chinese submarine not far away from the *Kitty Hawk* carrier in 2006, the 2009 *Impeccable* incident, the reported aiming of its targeting radar by a Chinese warship at a Japanese one in 2013, and the growing number of "unsafe encounters" between the Chinese PLA Air Force and its Japanese and American counterparts, have shown that the PLA is quickly learning how to put its new hardware to use.

Third, the Chinese military is essentially an Asian actor and Chinese leaders are concerned about domestic stability and protecting China's interests in the region. After all, they have to take care of disputes with neighboring countries, the emerging rivalry with the United States, the much-desired reunification with Taiwan, and the instability caused by the North Korean regime. Hence, as Andrew J. Nathan and Andrew Scobell (2012) concluded, the PLA is very unlikely to expand its operations outside Asia in a significant way, even in the case of reunification with Taiwan. Christina Lin pointed out that the fact that American foreign policy institutions still consider China mostly as an Asian power only is surely one of the main reasons why the American foreign policy community continues to hold the same Asian-centered approach (Ghiselli 2017, 2).

Combined together, these three factors produce a paradoxical result: Chinese military operations outside Asia are either seen as an attempt to establish spheres of influence, and thus a threat to American influence, or as operations of no significant value in terms of China's national security. Because of this, the necessity for China to protect its interest overseas has mostly been treated as an issue of international relations, in other words, how it shapes its relations with other countries, without paying, first, enough attention to it in terms of foreign policy, that is, how it emerged in China's foreign policy agenda and how it influences Chinese behavior. This is a serious problem. Indeed, this approach has had a rather negative influence on how we understand the dynamics behind operations overseas that the PLA has carried out so far, which, from peacekeeping to antipiracy patrols, all belong to the category of Military Operations Other Than War (MOOTW).

Since Chinese MOOTW overseas hardly fit with the dominant traditional security-centered approach, there has been no real systematic and comprehensive attempt to look at their origin, and this remains a significantly understudied topic. There are a few very well-researched works, like that of Erickson and Strange (2015) on Chinese antipiracy operations, or Fanie Herman (2016) on peacekeeping, but they focus solely on specific cases or operations. On the other hand, more general studies on the concept of MOOTW in China tend to be highly descriptive and have no ambition to explain its development and translation in operational terms (Kamphausen 2013, Clemens 2016). Other publications, instead, focus too much on the operational aspects of this issue (Scobell and Beauchamp-Mustafaga 2019). The evolution of Chinese MOOTW overseas, therefore, remains a complex phenomenon despite this lack of attention. The antipiracy missions in the Gulf of Aden carried out by the PLA Navy since late 2008 are a case in point and show how the lack of scholarly attention produced inconsistent and problematic interpretations.

Between 2008 and 2010, the PLA Navy deployed one Type 52C destroyer, one Type 52B destroyer, one Type 51 destroyer, one Type 54 frigate, nine Type 54A frigates, and three supply ships. The Type 52B/C and the Type 54A warships are the most advanced in the group and today form the backbone of the Chinese Navy. While the first two missions lasted for four months, subsequent ones were extended to six months. Usually, the naval groups are composed of one frigate, one destroyer, and a supply ship, or two frigates with a supply ship. In those years, the PLA Navy had only four Type 52B/C destroyers and six Type 54A frigates in total (O'Rourke 2017, 30–4). Even allowing for a shortened period of training after commissioning, these numbers mean that, at any time during those years, up to half of its fleet of modern destroyers and a third of its modern frigates were not available. At the same time, Chinese sailors had to follow limited rules of engagement while patrolling an area smaller than that of other navies, and could not do much to eliminate pirate threats (Lin-Greenberg 2010). Reportedly, the Chinese Navy arrested a pirate for the first time only in early 2017.

Because of the strict rules of engagement and its inexperience in sustaining these kinds of long-range deployments, many scholars pointed out that the PLA's war-waging capabilities benefit only in a marginal way from engagement in antipiracy missions and other MOOTW overseas (Fravel 2011, Chase and Gunness 2010, Erickson and Strange 2015, 23–44). From this point of view, these deployments represent a significant and overly onerous investment in terms of fighting capabilities for operations outside Asia, while tensions with the United States and other claimants in the East and South China Seas maritime disputes continue to grow. Yet other PLA watchers emphasize how those operations influence traditional security trends in Asia by providing new training opportunities to the PLA (McDevitt 2012, 81, Gill and Huang 2009, Johnston 2016, 36–8, Lai 2012). Others, instead, downplay the security motivations of those operations in favor of their diplomatic side (Allen 2015, Mastro 2015, 209, Fravel 2011, Strange 2012, Blasko 2012, 3). It is evident that there is a problem when it comes to understanding and explaining Chinese military operations that are clearly more than an attempt to establish a symbolic presence and, at the same time, are far from being a real challenge to American predominance in the Middle East and Indian Ocean.

At the same time, many scholars treat China as a monolithic unitary actor, thereby paying little attention to how domestic politics account for the definition of Chinese national interests and the role of the PLA in their pursuit. Moreover, most of the analyses pay little attention to the other actors within the Chinese foreign policy machine that are involved in protecting China's interest frontiers and, if necessary, supporting the PLA in doing so. The classic *The Making of Chinese Foreign and Security Policy in the Era of Reform (1978-2000)* edited by David M. Lampton is an obvious exception. Yet it is a unique and outdated one. Today, even the most recent attempts to shed light on the making of Chinese security strategy focus only on the PLA (Saunders and Scobell 2015), and not on all the other actors that play a role before or in the aftermath of a possible military intervention. Besides, one should not forget that, as several scholars (Johnston 2013, Jerdén 2014, Hirono and Suzuki 2014, Hayes 2015) have already pointed out, an extreme, if not exaggerated focus on the traditional security side of Chinese foreign policy is symptomatic of the dangerous politicization of academic work, which is responsible for the creation of an overly confrontational narrative and, potentially, policy that can hardly benefit anyone.

To conclude, it is crucial to understand how China approaches the protection of its interests overseas and, in that context, the role of its armed forces. It will be impossible to get the future of China's international relations right if we do not fill the gap in our knowledge pertaining to this crucial aspect of its foreign policy. The repercussions of failing to do so would go beyond the academic debate, especially as the world enters (again) a grim era of great power competition.

Studying China's Interest Frontiers and the Role of the PLA in Defending Them

Breaking with the narrow, traditional, security-centered, and often structuralist approach commonly used to study Chinese security strategy, this book analyses China's approach to its interest frontiers by looking at it from within the framework of securitization theory. Some, indeed, might have already noticed that the main research question and its two sub-questions, with "how" at the beginning and their focus on the policymaking process, are formulated according to the work of the so-called second-generation securitization scholars, especially Thierry Balzacq (2011a) and Stefano Guzzini (2011). Those scholars paid great attention to how to operationalize the ideas and concepts that were initially put forward by the Copenhagen School of security studies with Buzan, Wæver, and de Wilde's seminal book *Security: A New Framework for Analysis* (1998). In particular, they emphasize the necessity not only to connect speech acts with concrete actions, but also to understand and study securitization as a causal mechanism, thereby shedding light on the different dynamics that compose it. Ole Wæver (2011, 470–1) described securitization as an "idea theory . . . that clearly has one distinct concept at its center, and in which key concepts form a closely integrated constellation." Hence, within this framework, other elements from the vast and diverse literature of foreign policy analysis, from bureaucratic politics to civil-military relations, can be employed to explain the peculiar relations between the actors involved in the securitization process.

Securitization theory is based on an ontology that includes the realist assumption that security is essentially about survival but allows for the introduction of the ontological importance of language that is posited by post-structuralism (Wæver 1989). Hence, answering the above questions requires starting from the simple fact that the legitimacy, and thus the survival, of a government derives from its ability to provide its citizens with a set of basic public goods related to the concepts of both traditional and non-traditional security (Klosko 2005, 27). Clearly, such a general principle is open to different interpretations depending on how the members of a government understand the meaning of security (Security for whom? Security against what?). One must look at the world and the problems in it through the eyes of a certain actor if one wants to understand that actor's actions.

There is no space for definitions of security and threat imposed by external observers. It is necessary, therefore, to track the process of securitization of issues that became existential threats to the sources of legitimacy of the Chinese civilian and military leadership. In other words, the key is to understand how the Chinese government became aware of the threats to its interests abroad and, against this background, to shed light on the motivations of the actors involved, and the context within which they operate. Only then will it be possible to unveil the causal connection between the threats to the lives and assets of Chinese nationals overseas and the Chinese leadership's evolving definition of security, which together have fueled the rise in the Chinese policy agenda of the need to protect its interest frontiers, with the growth of Chinese overseas military deployments.

To do so in an effective and rational way, it is necessary to define the thematic and geographical scope of the study. The problems in the literature outlined above indicate how to do so; additionally, a quick overview of what Chinese officials and scholars say will point those interested in China's interest frontiers in the right direction. To begin with, it is necessary to reassess the importance of events outside Asia and their impact on Chinese foreign policy. If one looks at where major incidents involving the security of Chinese nationals and where the main ongoing Chinese military operations are taking place, it is clear that the geographical focus of the analysis must be the Middle East and North Africa. Of course, the definition of those two regions must be flexible because, as economic interests expand and new threats appear on the horizon, geographical borders are replaced by interest frontiers. Hence, the reader of this book must be aware that countries like Mali and Ethiopia, not usually counted among those of the two above-mentioned regions, are taken into consideration too (the complete list of the countries included is in Appendix 1). Of course, this does not mean that China does not have similar problems in other regions. However, the presence and evolution of the Chinese military in the Middle East and North Africa is outstanding in terms of quantity and quality. Therefore, its study offers the best opportunity to understand the dynamics behind China's approach to the defense of its overseas interests in those regions and, potentially in the future, other places around the world.

Second, non-traditional security must be put at the center of the analysis. As a leading Chinese scholar puts it, no country in the Middle East challenges China's territorial unity and sovereignty. They all adhere to the One China Policy and support China's position in maritime disputes in the

East and South China Seas. Yet this does not mean that Chinese security and foreign policy should not quickly adapt to threats in and from that region, such as the propagation of terrorism and attacks against Chinese nationals and companies there (Niu 2017). Indeed, even Chinese senior officials identify non-traditional security threats as a reason for China to deploy the PLA abroad (J. Yang 2018). PLA scholars, too, are very clear about the fact that the decision to carry out MOOTW abroad was born out of the necessity of dealing with non-traditional security issues (Guangming Daily 2010, Su 2017, Y. Wang 2015, 2).

It is within these theoretical, geographical, and thematic boundaries that this book begins its analytical assault on the black box of Chinese foreign policy. In every securitization process, there is an actor that leads the construction of a threat by describing an issue as detrimental to the security of a referent object. To have new measures taken against this new threat, the securitizing actor must convince a particular audience that can empower the actor to do so. Regardless of the political system, the securitizing actor and the empowering audience are different persons, usually belonging to different institutions of the state or groups within that society. In a democracy, the securitizing actors are the elected members of the government, while the empowering audience is the members of the parliament or congress. In modern China, we have the civilian members of the CCP and the soldiers of the PLA.

The Top Leadership and the Chinese People's Liberation Army

The most important actors in the making of Chinese foreign and security policy are the CCP General Secretary, acting as Chairman (to date this post has always been held by a man) of the Central Military Commission of the CCP, and his fellow military members in the Commission. Despite the impressive work of scholars like James Mulvenon (Hoover Institution), the Commission remains impenetrable to external observers; it is impossible to know who convinced whom, who the securitizing actor is, and who belongs to the empowering audience. However, for the purposes of this book, there are good theoretical and practical reasons to take the civilian leaders as the securitizing actors and the PLA as the empowering audience. To begin with, the securitizing actor is usually recognized as having a higher level of institutional authority than its audience. By promoting the professionalization of the PLA through the reforms that began in the 1980s, the civilians essentially pushed the soldiers out of the decision-making process. Over time, the military's influence in policy areas other than security has markedly declined, along with its representation in key organs for policymaking (Swaine 2012).

Today, China's top civilian and military leaders follow different career paths and have limited opportunities to interact with each other until they attain positions in Beijing, or are elected to positions in the CCP Central Committee (Hague 2004, 220–1). In the past, especially under Mao, disunity of the civilian leadership created room for the military to wield substantial influence in non-military affairs and vice versa (Fravel 2019). This was not because the PLA necessarily wanted that but, rather, because it became prey to factional politics within the party. Hence, the just-outlined developments were crucial in creating an institutional framework that further reduces the possibility that the military can be involved or drawn into policy debates that are not related to security policy. The Chinese civilian leadership effectively has what Huntington (1957) defined as objective control of the armed forces (Miller 2015).[3] Chapter 1, therefore, focuses on how the civilian leaders view non-traditional security and the role of the PLA in the context of China's security and foreign policy. In those pages, it is possible to see how the connection between non-traditional security issues overseas, China's interests abroad, and the role of the PLA in foreign policy became increasingly strong in the foreign and security policy agenda of Jiang Zemin, Hu Jintao, and Xi Jinping.

At the same time, the securitizing actor always tries to convince as broad an audience as possible in order to preserve the actor's legitimacy. Rumors about the PLA "going rogue" and high-profile acts of disobedience have been largely and convincingly debunked (Chubb 2013, Fravel 2015, Swaine 2015, Mattis 2015). In general, there is a solid consensus among scholars about the fact that the CCP makes the major decisions and is able to impose its will on the PLA without significant problems (Saunders and Scobell 2015, Mulvenon 2001, Scobell 2017). However, this does not mean that the PLA cannot develop its own preferences regarding its role in foreign policy to speed up or slow down the securitization process. The literature on civil-military relations suggests that civilians and soldiers have different preferences about both the missions the armed forces should take on and the level of violence that should be used. On the one hand, civilians are more open to what Peter D. Feaver and Christopher Gelpi (2004) categorized as "interventionist" uses of force, and they prefer low levels of violence. Peacekeeping and counterterrorism/counterinsurgency operations can be considered classic "interventionist" missions. On the other hand, soldiers prefer "realpolitik" missions and being free from

---

[3] In essence, objective control implies a division of work between civilians and soldiers. Civilians recognize an autonomous military professionalism and soldiers give up their role as decision-makers in the life of the country.

civilian interference regarding the level of violence used. They see the use of force as necessary to resolve interstate problems that represent a substantial threat to national security and to the nation's core interests. The identity of the soldiers as professionals tasked with defending the country is pivotal in the development of such different approaches. Accordingly, Andrew Scobell (2003) and David Shambaugh, and Ren Xiao (2012) have pointed out that PLA officers in general prefer hawkish policies for traditional national defense, and have a clear position on these kinds of issues. However, PLA officers appear less interested in other situations in which they might be called upon to intervene. Chapter 2, therefore, revolves around the PLA's point of view on its role beyond traditional "realpolitik" missions and, in particular, on the defense of China's interest frontiers.

Other Actors and a New Environment

The dialogue between the securitizing actor and the empowering audience does not take place in a vacuum. Some elements in the background of the attempted securitization act might propel the argument of the securitizing actor further, as well as potentially undermining it. Therefore, one cannot but investigate the facilitating conditions of the securitization process, that is, the origin and the main features of what is framed as a threat to the referent object (Buzan, Wæver, and de Wilde 1998, 31–3). Moreover, it is important to look at the role of other actors, known as "functional actors" in the context of securitization theory, that can influence the dynamics of the securitization process without being the referent object or the actor calling for security on behalf of the referent object (Buzan, Wæver, and de Wilde 1998, 36).

Therefore, Chapter 3 looks at the steady expansion of China's human and economic presence abroad. It begins with an overview of the major decisions of the Chinese government and the twists and turns in the evolution of the legal and institutional framework that regulates the behavior of Chinese companies in their endeavor to explore the world in search of business opportunities and strategic resources. It then shows how the Chinese presence in the Middle East and North Africa developed, diversified, and coalesced around a handful of countries whose stability is crucial to the safety of Chinese interests. The chapter concludes with an analysis of how China's interest frontiers emerged when the Arab Spring broke out and Chinese companies found themselves unprepared to cope with the challenge.

Once the nature and the origin of China's interest frontiers is clear, it is time to look at how the Chinese foreign policy bureaucracy and community of experts looked at them and at their protection, and whether they were in a position to help their leaders to make well-informed decisions. Chapter 4 shows that this was largely not the case. This is what emerges by looking at the development of the Chinese diplomatic system in terms of regional expertise, personnel, resources, and political standing. As for the specialists in area studies in Chinese universities and think tanks, it seems that they lacked either the necessary skills or the influence to warn the government about the risks brewing in the Middle East and North Africa. It was their colleagues in the more influential community of international relations who were able to shape the government's response to the crises in those regions, but only after the crises had taken place.

Although it is not as decisive a factor as it is in Western liberal democracies, the space for Chinese public opinion to influence foreign policy has grown over the years thanks to greater access to the Internet, diversification of the media landscape, and the simple fact that today's Chinese leaders are not revolutionary heroes who can ignore what the population think (Hao and Lin 2007). While public opinion cannot influence the country's foreign policy on issues related to China's "core interests"—the CCP's commanding role and the country's territorial integrity and sovereignty (Chubb 2018)—the situation is different when the discussion is of less sensitive matters. Chinese strategy in the Middle East and North Africa is one of those topics (J. Wang 2012). At the same time, other studies have already shown that Chinese public opinion seems in favor of the use of military means to defend Chinese interests (Chen Weiss 2019). Hence, Chapter 5 looks at how Chinese public opinion reacted to crises overseas and how the government calibrated its narrative to deal with the growing attention paid by Chinese citizens to each new foreign policy issue.

China Moves to Protect Its Interest Frontiers

Securitization echoes in the actions of policymakers under the form of regulatory and capacity tools. Regulatory tools, in a self-explanatory way, regulate practices that already exist, to limit liabilities rather than to eliminate any threat against the referent object. This is the case with laws that force companies investing abroad to improve their risk-assessment capabilities and invest more in security. At the same time, regulatory tools often provide the framework for the use of capacity tools. Capacity tools are the "specific modalities for imposing external discipline upon individuals and groups," that is, to neutralize a perceived threat by following procedures and regulations previously created (Balzacq 2011b, 17).

Hence, Chapter 6 focuses on the regulatory tools developed by the party, the state, and the PLA. It shows how the growing concerns of civilian leaderships led to increasingly broader changes in the laws and institutions that regulate the actions of the agencies belonging to the State Council and the PLA. The chapter begins by looking at the attempts of the Ministry of Foreign Affairs and Chinese companies, especially state-owned ones, to adapt to the orders coming from Zhongnanhai (the central headquarters of the Communist leadership). Hence, Chapter 6 discusses the role of the CCP CNSC and new laws aimed at improving inter-agency coordination and providing stronger legal foundations for the use of the military overseas. The Chinese armed forces, which include the Chinese People's Armed Police, are then put at the center of the analysis to observe how they adapted to the evolving situation.

Chapter 7 looks at China's capability tools, in other words, how the operations that the Chinese armed forces have carried out overseas since the 1990s have evolved as the Chinese government has gradually become more aware of the importance of protecting the country's interests in faraway regions. The chapter shows how a Chinese security architecture has steadily emerged over the years despite some significant problems. During this process, the presence of Chinese soldiers changed from being country to subregion-focused and from being single to multipurpose. China has also tried to expand its room for diplomatic maneuvering and has striven to have the land, sea, and air components of its armed forces all available for deployment when necessary.

The Conclusion to the book discusses the findings and their implications for how we understand Chinese foreign policy, its making, and its implementation. In particular, it focuses on the role of the impact of crises in pushing Chinese policymaking forward; the centripetal and centrifugal forces that shape relations between Chinese policymakers and policy-implementing institutions; and the effectiveness of China's approach to defending its interest frontiers and its future challenges. The chapter concludes with some final considerations about what China's need to protect its interests overseas means for foreign policymakers.

Bibliography

Allen, Kenneth. 2015. "The Top Trends in China's Military Diplomacy." *China Brief* 15 (9): 10–14.

Allison, Graham Tillet. 2017. *Destined for War: Can America and China Escape Thucydides's Trap*. Boston, MA: Houghton Mifflin.

Balzacq, Thierry. (ed.) 2011a. *Securitization Theory: How Security Problems Emerge and Dissolve*. London: Routledge.

Balzacq, Thierry. 2011b. "A Theory of Securitization." In Thierry Balzacq (ed.), *Securitization Theory*, 1–30. London: Routledge.

Bi, Yuchan. 2017. "中国保安服务企业的国际化进程 [The Process of Internationalization of the Chinese Private Security Industry]." *Modern World Police* 12: 21–4.

Blasko, Dennis J. 2012. *The Chinese Army Today*. London: Routledge.

Buzan, Barry, Ole Wæver, and Jaap de Wilde. 1998. *Security: A New Framework for Analysis*. London: Lyenne Rienner Publishers.

Chase, Michael S., and Kristen Gunness. 2010. "The PLA's Multiple Military Tasks: Prioritizing Combat Operations and Developing MOOTW Capabilities." *China Brief* 10 (29): 5–7.

Chen Weiss, Jessica. 2019. "How Hawkish Is the Chinese Public? Another Look at 'Rising Nationalism' and Chinese Foreign Policy." *Journal of Contemporary China* 28 (119): 679–95.

Chubb, Andrew. 2013. "Propaganda as Policy? Explaining the PLA's 'Hawkish Faction' (Part Two)." *China Brief* 13 (6): 12–16.

Chubb, Andrew. 2019. "Assessing Public Opinion's Influence on Foreign Policy: The Case of China's Assertive Maritime Behavior." *Asian Security* 15 (2): 159–79.

Clemens, Morgan. 2016. "PLA Thinking on Military Operations Other Than War." In Joe McReynolds (ed.), *China's Evolving Military Strategy*, 298–333. Washington DC: Jamestown Foundation.

Coker, Christopher. 2014. *The Improbable War: China, the United States and the Logic of Great Power Conflict*. New York: Oxford University Press.

Erickson, Andrew S., and Austin M. Strange. 2015. *Six Years at Sea…and Counting: Gulf of Aden Anti-Piracy and China's Maritime Commons Presence*. Washington DC: Jamestown Foundation.

Feaver, Peter D., and Christopher Gelpi. 2004. *Choosing Your Battles: American Civil-Military Relations and the Use of Force*. Princeton, NJ: Princeton University Press.

Fravel, M. Taylor. 2011. "Economic Growth, Regime Insecurity, and Military Strategy: Explaining the Rise of Noncombat Operations in China." *Asian Security* 7 (3): 177–200.

Fravel, M. Taylor. 2015. "The PLA and National Security Decisionmaking: Insights from China's Territorial and Maritime Disputes." *PLA Influence on China's National Security Policymaking*, ebook position 5749–6409. Stanford, CA: Stanford University Press.

Fravel, M. Taylor. 2019. *Active Defense: China's Military Strategy since 1949*. Princeton, NJ: Princeton University Press.

Galbraith, John Semple. 1960. "The 'Turbulent Frontier' as a Factor in British Expansion." *Comparative Studies in Society and History* 2 (2): 150–68.

Ghiselli, Andrea. 2017. "Reflecting on China's Presence in the Mediterranean Sea." *T.note* 2.

Gill, Bates, and Chin-Hao Huang. 2009. "China's Expanding Role in Peacekeeping." *SIPRI Policy Paper* 25.

Goldstein, Lyle. 2015. *Meeting China Halfway: How to Defuse the Emerging US-China Rivalry*. Washington DC: George Washington University Press.

Gu, Zhenqiu. 2016. "Spotlight: China Makes Great Contributions to UN Peacekeeping Operations." *Xinhua*. July 29. Accessed December 13, 2017. http://news.xinhuanet.com/english/2016-07/29/c_135547791.htm.

Guangming Daily. 2010. "国防大学专家谈"非战争军事行动":兵今天怎么用 [NDU Experts Discuss MOOTW: How to Use the Military Today]." *Guangming Daily*. May 5. Accessed January 4, 2018. http://www.ce.cn/xwzx/gnsz/gdxw/201005/26/t20100526_21447514.shtml.

Guzzini, Stefano. 2011. "Securitization as a Casual Mechanism." *Security Dialogue* 42 (4–5): 329–41.

Hague, Elizabeth. 2004. "PLA Leadership in China's Military Regions." In Andrew Scobell and Larry Wortzel (eds), *Civil-Military Change in China: Elites, Institutes, and Ideas after the 16th Party Congress*, 219–56. Carlisle Barracks, PA: United States Army War College.

Hao, Yufan, and Su Lin. 2007. 中国外交决策: 开放与多元的社会因素分析 [*Chinese Foreign Policymaking: An Analysis of Societal Forces*]. Beijing: Social Sciences Academic Press.

Hayes, Jarrod. 2015. "Securitization Forum: Three Challenges to Securitization Theory in the U.S." *Duck of Minerva*. September 21. Accessed December 1, 2017. http://duckofminerva.com/2015/09/securitization-forum-three-challenges-to-securitization-theory-in-the-u-s.html.

Herman, Fanie. 2016. *China's African Peacekeeping Decision-Making in the Hu Jintao Era*. New Delhi: Vij Books India.

Hermann, Charles F. 1990. "Changing Course: When Governments Choose to Redirect Foreign Policy." *International Studies Quarterly* 34 (1): 3–21.

Hirono, Miwa, and Shogo Suzuki. 2014. "Why Do We Need 'Myth-Busting' in the Study of Sino-African Relations?" *Journal of Contemporary China* 23 (87): 443–61.

Hoover Institution. n.d. *Biography: James Mulvenon*. Accessed December 13, 2017. https://www.hoover.org/profiles/james-mulvenon.

Huang, Kunlun. 2011. "全球化时代的国家利益观 [Outlook on the National Interests in a Globalized Era]." *People's Liberation Army Daily*. March 15.

Huntington, Samuel P. 1957. *The Soldier and the State: The Theory and Politics of Civil-Military Relations*. Cambridge, MA: Harvard University Press.

Jerdén, Bjorn. 2014. "The Assertive China Narrative: Why It Is Wrong and How So Many Still Bought into It." *The Chinese Journal of International Politics* 7 (1): 47–88.

Johnston, Alastair Iain. 2013. "How New and Assertive is China's New Assertiveness?" *International Security* 37 (4): 7–48.

Johnston, Alastair Iain. 2016. "The Evolution of Interstate Security Crisis-Management Theory and Practice in China." *Naval War College Review* 69 (1): 28–71.

Kamphausen, Roy. 2013. "China's Military Operations Other Than War: The Military Legacy of Hu Jintao." *The Hu Jintao Decade in China's Foreign and Security Policy (2002–12): Assessments and Implications.* Stockholm: SIPRI. Accessed October 14, 2020. https://silo.tips/download/china-s-military-operations-other-than-war-the-military-legacy-of-hu-jintao.

Kennedy, Paul. 1987. *The Rise and Fall of Great Powers.* New York: Random House.

Klosko, George. 2005. *Political Obligations.* New York: Oxford University Press.

Lai, David. 2012. "The Agony of Learning: The PLA's Transformation in Military Affairs." In Roy Kamphausen, David Lai, and Trevis Tanner (eds), *Learning by Doing: The PLA Trains at Home and Abroad,* 337–84. Carlisle, PA: United States Army War College Press.

Lampton, David M., ed. 2001. *The Making of Chinese Foreign and Security Policy in the Era of Reform, 1978–2000.* Stanford, CA: Stanford University Press.

Lin-Greenberg, Erik. 2010. "Dragon Boats: Assessing China's Anti-Piracy Operations in the Gulf of Aden." *Defense & Security Analysis* 26 (2): 213–30.

Liu, Zhongmin. 2018. "在中东推进"一带一路"建设的政治和安全风险及应对 [The Political Risks and Security Threats of the Belt and Road Construction in the Middle East and Countermeasures]." *International Review* 2: 36–50.

McDevitt, Michael. 2012. "PLA Naval Exercises with International Partners." In Roy Kamphausen, David Lai, and Trevis Tanner (eds), *Learning By Doing: The PLA Trains at Home and Abroad,* 81–126. Carlisle, PA: United States Army War College Press.

Mastro, Oriana Skylar. 2015. "A Global Expeditionary People's Liberation Army: 2025–2030." In Roy Kamphausen and David Lai (eds), *The Chinese People's Liberation Army in 2025,* 207–34. Carlisle Barracks, PA: United States Army War College Press.

Mattis, Peter. 2015. *China's Military Is not Going Rogue.* January 6. Accessed December 2, 2017. http://nationalinterest.org/feature/chinas-military-not-going-rogue-11976.

Mearsheimer, John J. 2001. *The Tragedy of Great Power Politics.* New York: W. W. Norton.

Mertha, Andrew. 2009. " 'Fragmented Authoritarianism 2.0': Political Pluralization in the Chinese Policy Process." *China Quarterly* 200: 995–1112.

Miller, Alice L. 2015. "The PLA in the Party Leadership Decisionmaking System." In Phillip C. Saunders and Andrew Scobell (eds), *PLA Influence on China's National Security Policymaking,* ebook position 1292–764. Stanford, CA: Stanford University Press.

Mulvenon, James. 2001. "China: Conditional Compliance." In Muthiah Alagappa (ed.), *Coercion and Governance: The Declining Political Role of the Military in Asia*, 317–35. Stanford, CA: Stanford University Press.

Nathan, Andrew J., and Andrew Scobell. 2012. *China's Search for Security*. New York: Columbia University Press.

Niu, Xinchun. 2017. ""一带一路"下的中国中东战略 [China's Middle East Strategy within the 'One Belt One Road' Framework]." *Foreign Affairs Review* 4: 1–25.

O'Rourke, Ronald. 2017. "China Naval Modernization: Implications for U.S. Navy Capabilities." *Congressional Research Service*. September 18. Accessed January 5, 2018. https://www.fas.org/sgp/crs/row/RL33153.pdf.

Parello-Plesner, Jonas, and Mathieu Duchâtel. 2015. *China's Strong Arm: Protecting Citizens and Assets Abroad*. London: Routledge.

People's Daily. 2018. "指导新时代国家安全工作的强大思想武器—学习《习近平关于总体国家安全观论述摘编》 [A Powerful Ideological Weapon to Guide the National Security Work in the New Era—Learning from 'Xi Jinping's Excerpt on the Overall National Security Concept']." *People's Daily*. May 4. Accessed May 6, 2018. http://paper.people.com.cn/rmrb/html/2018–05/04/nw.D110000renmrb_20180504_1-06.htm.

Rolland, Nadège, ed. 2019. *Securing the Belt and Road Initiative: China's Evolving Military Engagement along the Silk Roads*. Washington DC: National Bureau of Asian Research.

Saunders, Phillip C., and Andrew Scobell. 2015. *PLA Influence on China's National Security Policymaking*. Stanford, CA: Stanford University Press.

Scobell, Andrew. 2003. *China's Use of Military Force: Beyond the Great Wall and the Long March*. New York: Cambridge University Press.

Scobell, Andrew. 2017. "Civil-Military 'Rules of the Game' on the Eve of China's 19th Party Congress." *The National Bureau of Asian Research*. October 11. Accessed January 3, 2018. https://www.nbr.org/publication/civil-military-rules-of-the-game-on-the-eve-of-chinas-19th-party-congress/.

Scobell, Andrew, and Nathan Beauchamp-Mustafaga. 2019. "The Flag Lags but Follows: The PLA and China's Great Leap Outward." In Phillip C. Saunders, Arthur S. Ding, Andrew Scobell, Andrew N. D. Yang, and Joel Wuthnow (eds), *Chairman Xi Remakes the PLA: Assessing Chinese Military Reforms*, 171–202. Washington DC: National Defense University Press.

Shambaugh, David, and Ren Xiao. 2012. "China: The Conflicted Power." In Henry R. Nau and Deepa M. Ollapally (eds), *Worldviews of Aspiring Powers*, ebook position 767–1459. New York: Oxford University Press.

Shichor, Yitzhak. 2005. "Decisionmaking in Triplicate: China and the Three Iraqi Wars." In Andrew Scobell and Larry M. Wortzel (eds), *Chinese National Security Decisionmaking under Stress*, 191–228. Carlisle Barracks, PA: United States Army War College Press.

Stallings, Barbara, and Eum Mee Kim. 2017. *Promoting Development: The Political Economy of East Asian Foreign Aid*. Singapore, SG: Palgrave.

Strange, Austin M. 2012. *Non-Combat Operations of China's Armed Forces in the 21st Century: Historical Development, Current Drivers and Implications for Military Projection*. Williamsburg, VA: College of William & Mary.

Su, Yuyao. 2017. ""非战争军事行动"写入政府工作报告意味着什么? [MOOTW Have Entered in the Report of the Government: What Does It Mean?]." *PLA Daily*. March 9. Accessed December 20, 2017. http://www.81.cn/byyd/2017–03/09/content_7520823.htm.

Swaine, Michael D. 2012. "China's Assertive Behavior—Part Three: The Role of the Military in Foreign Policy." *China Leadership Monitor* 36. Accessed October 14, 2020. https://www.hoover.org/research/chinas-assertive-behavior-part-three-role-military-foreign-policy.

Swaine, Michael D. 2015. "The PLA Role in China's Foreign Policy and Crisis Behavior." In Phillip C. Saunders and Andrew Scobell (eds), *PLA Influence on China's National Security Policymaking*, ebook position 3071–636. Stanford, CA: Stanford University Press.

United States Senate Committee on Armed Services. 2017. "Hearing to Consider the Nomination of General Joseph F. Dunford, Jr., for Reappointment to be Chairman of the Joint Chiefs of Staff." *U.S. Senate Committee on Armed Services*. September 26. Accessed October 1, 2017. https://www.armed-services.senate.gov/imo/media/doc/17-80_09-26–17.pdf.

Wæver, Ole. 1989. *Security, the Speech Act: Analysing the Politics of a Word*. Copenhagen: Centre for Peace and Conflict Research.

Wæver, Ole. 2011. "Politics, Security, Theory." *Security Dialogue* 42 (4–5): 465–80.

Wang, Jing. 2012. "伊拉克战争与公众参与中国中东外交政策制定 [The Iraq War and Public Participation in China's Middle East Policy]." *Arab World Studies* (4): 95–111.

Wang, Yongming. 2015. 多种能力-提高非战争军事行动 [*Various Capabilities: Improving MOOTW Capabilities*]. Beijing: Changzheng Publishing House.

Yang, Jiechi. 2018. "Working Together to Build a World of Lasting Peace and Universal Security and a Community with a Shared Future for Mankind." *PRC Ministry of Foreign Affairs*. July 14. Accessed August 2, 2018. http://www.fmprc.gov.cn/mfa_eng/zxxx_662805/t1577242.shtml.

Yang, Yi Edward, and Xinsheng Liu. 2012. "The 'China Threat' through the Lens of US Print Media: 1992–2006." *Journal of Contemporary China* 21 (76): 695–711.

Zhou, Ping. 2016. "周平：中国应该有自己的利益边疆 [Zhou Ping: China Should Have Its Own Interst Frontiers]." *Aisixiang*. June 11. Accessed November 1, 2019. http://www.aisixiang.com/data/75426-2.html.

Zhou, Ping. 2018. "如何认识我国的边疆 [How to Understand the Borders of Our Country]." *Qiushi*. January 21. Accessed December 1, 2019. http://www.qstheory.cn/llqikan/2018-01/21/c_1122290581.htm.

1

The Chinese Government, the Idea of Security, and Foreign Policy

There are a number of civilian actors involved in foreign and security policy-making in China. Naturally, the General Secretary of the Chinese Communist Party (CCP) is the most important actor, setting the general direction of the country's foreign policy. Party, military, and state institutions have to interpret such indications. How, then, has the perception of new threats to Chinese interests overseas evolved among Chinese top leaders—the key securitizing actors in the country—and their foreign policy advisors? What solutions have they proposed?

To answer these questions, this chapter looks at the concept of security proposed by the Chinese civilian leadership over time, its components, and the role of the armed forces in relation to it. It has already been mentioned in the Introduction of this book that non-traditional security issues have played a key role in making Chinese policymakers aware of the existence of their country's interest frontiers. This chapter shows it more clearly. Special attention is paid to the idea of non-traditional security and how it evolved and acquired new meanings in Chinese official discourse. The chapter wants to present this growing awareness as part of a broader and gradual evolution of Chinese foreign and security policy.

The chapter tells a story of continuity that began with the turbulent end of the Mao era and Deng Xiaoping imposing his agenda of economic development after the economic and societal destruction of the Great Leap Forward and the Cultural Revolution. Deng Xiaoping's reforms created the basic pre-conditions for China's interest frontiers to emerge. On the one hand, the new imperative of economic reconstruction and growth translated into, among other things, the easing of state control over every aspect of the economic and social life of the country. As Chinese society began diversifying, the state also started to become more responsive to the diverse needs of its citizens. On the other hand, the reforms started the engine of the Chinese economy. During the seminal third session of the 11th CCP Central Committee of late December 1978, Deng Xiaoping started the countdown to the day Chinese

Protecting China's Interests Overseas: Securitization and Foreign Policy. Andrea Ghiselli, Oxford University Press (2021). © Andrea Ghiselli. DOI: 10.1093/oso/9780198867395.001.0001

companies could go abroad looking for natural resources and markets (Chapter 3).

The reforms sowed the seeds of Chinese overseas interests and, consequently, of China's interest frontiers. The story of what happened since those fateful days of 1978 is divided into three parts. While the first covers a large period, that is, until end of the second term of Jiang Zemin as General Secretary of the CCP in 2002, the other two focus on Hu Jintao's and Xi Jinping's administrations, respectively. As appears in an increasingly clear way towards the end of the chapter, continuity in the securitization process of non-traditional security issues has not always been a voluntary choice for Chinese leaders. In particular, the evacuation from Libya of around 36,000 Chinese nationals in 2011 was a watershed moment, one that most likely left Xi Jinping no choice but to speed up the development and implementation of measures aimed at boosting protection of China's overseas interests. The interested reader can find comments and information about the sources used in this chapter in Appendix 1.

From National Security to the New Security Concept

As pointed out by Yu Xiaofeng and Wei Zhijiang (2015, 213), the idea of national security was, of course, already present in Chinese political discourse before Deng's coming to power, but it was clearly subordinated to that of political security.[1] However, as Hua Guofeng's interregnum ended during the 12th Party Congress of September 1982, Deng Xiaoping and his allies brought a new set of ideas to the center of Chinese policymaking. The first appearance of the term "national security" in a Chinese official document, the "Report on the Work of the Government" delivered by Premier Zhao Ziyang in June 1983 (PRC Central Government), was symptomatic of that change.

The term "security" was used in three different ways in Chinese documents published in the 1980s.[2] To begin with, the frequent references in the reports on the work of the government to international events like the Soviet invasion of Afghanistan and other crises produced by competition between the American and the Soviet superpowers were partially connected with China's own national security as they were seen as "a threat to world peace

[1] In Chinese: 国家安全 (Guójiā ānquán) and 政治安全 (Zhèngzhì ānquán).
[2] In Chinese: 安全 (Ānquán).

and the security of every country." However, these references were usually put in the paragraphs of the reports describing the international situation rather the drivers of China's military modernization (PRC Central Government 1984). The modernization of the Chinese People's Liberation Army (PLA) and the Chinese People's Armed Police (PAP), instead, seemed justified, if only to protect the geographical borders that separated China's domestic economic development from the chaos outside. The term "security" became "national security" solely in that case. Finally, the focus on economic development led to more frequent use of the term "security" in statements related to economic production and development.

Although the emergence of national security as an important concept can be seen as part of the broader process leading to the decision to create some sort of separation between party and state announced during the 13th Party Congress (People's Daily 1987), Chinese scholars have pointed out that "national security" and "political security" remained very similar ideas (Yu and Wei 2015, 214). At the same time, each of these ways to use the term "security" reflected different concerns of the Chinese leaders and were disconnected from each other. The instruments to address them were also very different and presented in a separated way: the PLA was not meant to prepare for anything beyond an invasion, or a short, local conflict to defend China's borders; economic planning focused on domestic policies to promote internal development; Chinese diplomacy served to create a safe international environment for the country's economic development and not to expand or protect its interests overseas. For example, China's decision to start casting votes regarding peacekeeping missions at the United Nations (UN) and financially supporting those missions in 1981 and 1986, respectively, had no significant implications for the PLA.

The end of the 1980s and the beginning of the 1990s, with the tragic events of Tiananmen Square in June 1989 and the fall of the Soviet Union in 1991, saw the Chinese Communist regime under great pressure, both domestically and internationally. According to Bates Gill (2007, 1–20), the combination of internal and external turmoil in those years created a sense of deep insecurity among the Chinese elite. Intense internal debate among different factions led to the decision to try avoiding isolation and rebuilding relations with the external world. The Chinese leadership had already started to formulate a regional strategy in the 1980s in order to both prevent potential threats arising on the borders and to get closer to the newly industrialized countries in the region in order to better study their economic model. Hence, neighboring countries became a major target of Chinese diplomacy, as they also showed some degree of support for Beijing.[3] For example, Singapore and Indonesia decided to establish (resume, in the case of Indonesia) diplomatic relations with China in 1990. Sino-Vietnamese relations also normalized in the same year. For a few years, however, the Chinese leaders focused on addressing the immediate internal political and economic challenges that emerged by the end of the 1980s and culminated in the widespread demonstrations of spring and summer 1989. Foreign policy was essentially limited to small steps aimed at repairing the damage suffered by the country's international image and reducing the isolation that followed international outrage about the events of Tiananmen. By 1992, when Russian president Boris Yeltsin made his first official visit to China, it became clear that relations between China and Russia were moving in a positive direction. It seemed that a new chapter in Chinese diplomacy was about to open. Yet the 1995-6 Taiwan Strait crisis and the strong, albeit waning influence of Deng Xiaoping until his very last few years prevented Jiang Zemin's ideas from fully and officially emerging.

Although Jiang had already served as General Secretary of the CCP for eight years and there had been major leadership changes at the 14th Party Congress in 1992, it is appropriate to consider the 15th Party Congress (the first party conclave since Deng Xiaoping's death) in 1997 as the real beginning of the Jiang Zemin era. As pointed out by Avery Goldstein (2001), by that time, China had, apparently, concluded that accepting the constraints that come with working in multilateral settings was preferable to the risk of isolation and encirclement, and could help foster a reputation for responsible international behavior. In 1998, Jiang himself told Chinese ambassadors that:

> all major countries rely on regional organizations for their own development and try to use multilateral contexts to achieve what they cannot accomplish through bilateral means. We need to place greater emphasis on this, guide our actions according to circumstances, and seek advantages while avoiding disadvantages.
>
> (CCP Central Literature Editing Committee 2011, 201)

The creation of the Shanghai Five, along with the signing of the Treaty on Deepening Military Trust in Border Regions in Shanghai on April 26, 1996, by China, Kazakhstan, Kyrgyzstan, Russia, and Tajikistan and the decision to become a full Dialogue Partner of the Association of Southeast Asian Nations

---

[3] Zhao Suisheng (1999) offers a clear and precise account of this shift.

(ASEAN) the same year were key manifestations of this new approach. The idea of China shouldering international responsibilities started to develop in Chinese foreign policy circles in those years as well (Li 2008).[4]

Beijing's embrace of multilateral diplomacy, especially in Asia, was more than a symbolic change. Indeed, it is in that context that the New Security Concept emerged.[5] The New Security Concept was not an initiative of the military (Finkelstein 2003, 197-203). Chinese strategists started to revise China's security strategy around 1993, and Chinese diplomats officially introduced it to a foreign audience at the ASEAN Regional Forum conference on confidence-building measures held in Beijing in March 1997 (Thayer 2003, 89-90). Over the years, its content became clearer. On July 31, 2002, the Chinese delegation to the ASEAN Regional Forum clarified the meaning of the New Security Concept by presenting the ad hoc position paper, *China's Position Paper on the New Security Concept* (PRC MFA 2002a). The same year, China and ASEAN signed a memorandum of understanding aimed at building cooperation on non-traditional security issues (PRC MFA 2002b).

The New Security Concept started to appear in China's defense documents as well. After the 1998 defense white paper hinted at it, the 2000 white paper stated that China's defense policy had to be based on "mutual trust, mutual benefit, equality and cooperation" and that:

> the UN Charter, the Five Principles of Peaceful Coexistence and other uni-versally recognized principles governing international relations should serve as the political basis for safeguarding peace while mutually beneficial cooperation and common prosperity serve as its economic guarantee. To conduct dialogue, consultation and negotiation on an equal footing is the right way to solve disputes and safeguard peace. Only by developing a new security concept and Li establishing a fair and reasonable new international order can world peace and security be fundamentally guaranteed.
>
> (PRC State Council's Information Office 2000)

The New Security Concept, thus, was the answer to the need to boost the country's diplomatic standing and economic prowess while advancing the view of a multipolar world order in response to American global dominance, especially after the bombing of the Chinese embassy in Belgrade by American

---

[4] Reportedly, this concept was developed further into the term "responsible great power" (负责任大国, Fùzérèn dàguó) over the years by borrowing from the diplomatic language used by the Clinton and Bush administrations to integrate China in the international system (Shichor 2007, 107).

[5] In Chinese: 新安全观 (Xīn ānquán guān).

aircraft in 1999 made many in the top Chinese civilian and military leadership fear the advent of a new era of American unilateralism.

As Jiang's power reached its apex, and the policy fruits of his ideas started to mature, three interconnected trends can be identified as characteristics of his administration. First, national security consolidated its position in the Chinese policy debate as the key driver of the modernization of the Chinese armed forces. Li Peng and Zhu Rongji consistently used terms like "national security" or "security of the motherland" in statements related to national defense and military modernization in all the reports they delivered (Figure 1).[6] Importantly, the same words were not used in other contexts.[7] In foreign policy terms, this confirms that China had adopted a state-centric, military-based approach to security. Consistently, its armed forces' main external task was

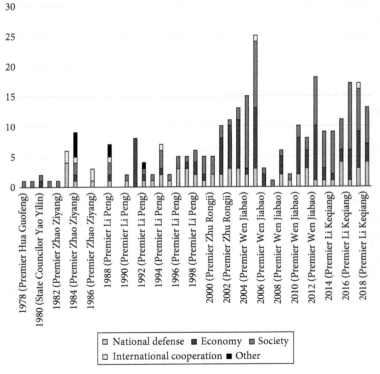

Figure 1 The word "security" in reports of the Chinese government
Source: PRC Central Government. Compiled by the author.

[6] In Chinese: 祖国安全 (Zǔguó ānquán).
[7] The numbers refer to the number of times that the word "security" (安全, Ānquán) was used in statements concerning national defense, economic development, social stability and social issues, general statements about Chinese diplomacy and relations with other countries, and other topics not directly related to China.

to protect China against other countries' attacking troops. Second, non-traditional security threats started to be considered important factors in international affairs. This idea was made explicit for the first time in 2002, in Jiang's speech at the 16th Party Congress (People's Daily 2002). Whether they were actual threats to China, however, is a more ambiguous issue. For instance, they were not mentioned in statements about national defense but, usually, in the section of speeches and reports about the international situation. None of Jiang's speeches to the members of the CCP Central Military Commission (CMC) of reported in his *Selected Works* mentions non-traditional security threats. Actually, the assessment of the impact of the 9/11 terrorist attack on China's security situation suggests that non-traditional security threats were seen as "non-traditional security opportunities." According to the 2002 (PRC State Council's Information Office) defense white paper:

> major countries, while cooperating with and seeking support from each other, are, nonetheless, checking on and competing with one another. But since the terrorist attacks against the United States on September 11, 2001, they have stepped up their coordination and cooperation.

The rise of international terrorism was not a completely negative situation for Chinese diplomacy. Third, the emergence of the New Security Concept created the rhetorical and diplomatic platform for Chinese soldiers to engage in operations outside China's borders, although the initial level of this engagement was limited to small delegations of high-ranking officials and military observers.

Chinese leaders conceived this move as a diplomatic one aimed at boosting the country's image in the region, rather than addressing direct threats to China's national security. Indeed, the power asymmetry existing between China and its partners in the context of China-ASEAN relations turned the institutionalization of cooperation on non-traditional security issues mostly into a vehicle to enhance China's standing as a regional leader (Arase 2010). However, this also proved to be a crucial factor of change in the years that followed because the civilian leadership attached great importance to those operations. That taking part in UN-led peacekeeping operations was moved from the "International Security Cooperation" chapter of the defense white paper of 1998 to becoming one of the guidelines of China's national defense policy in all the white papers beginning with that released in 2000 is quite telling (PRC State Council's Information Office 1998, 2002).

In line with this, China formally joined the UN Class-A stand by arrangements system in January 2002 and offered an engineering battalion

(525 troops), a medical unit (thirty-five troops), and transport companies (160 troops in total) deployable within ninety days after the request from the UN. According to Major General Du Nongyi (2015, 149), Jiang Zemin's emphasis on engaging in international affairs to promote global stability is one of the main drivers of the sudden increase in Chinese contributions to peacekeeping in the mid-2000s, when Jiang still maintained his role of Chairman of the CCP CMC. Chapter 7 provides a more detailed analysis of China's engagement in peacekeeping operations in those years.

It is important to point out that Jiang was not a radical innovator, and, at least from a rhetorical point of view, he built on the words uttered by Deng Xiaoping in September 1982 during the opening of the 12th Party Congress (People's Daily 1982). Back then, Deng called on the party to "speed up the modernization of socialism, fight to achieve reunification with Taiwan, oppose hegemonism, and protect world peace." In November 2001, and then during the 16th Party Congress of 2002, Jiang Zemin used almost the same words to describe the Three Historical Duties of the Communist government (People's Daily 2002).[8] The difference lies in the implementation of those instructions as the two leaders brought with them different life experiences and faced different domestic and international challenges.

Governing for the People

The veteran China watcher, Li Cheng, (2016, 251-6) describes Hu Jintao as one of the main leaders of the "populist faction" of Chinese elite. According to him, that faction "draws its name from the well-known political rhetoric of 'putting people first' and, consequently, orients its policies toward economic equality, social justice and more balanced regional development." This coalition competes against the "elitist coalition" which was born with Jiang Zemin and is composed of a mix of leaders who rose through the ranks by governing in the rich coastal provinces of Eastern China and of leaders born into the families of Communist revolutionaries or other high-ranking officials, like Jiang himself and Xi Jinping. Yet, just as Jiang built upon the ideas first outlined by Deng, so Hu used Jiang's concepts to formulate his own policies.[9] In

---

[8] In Chinese: 三个历史任务 (Sān gè lìshǐ rènwù).

[9] There are different opinions about who exercised real authority between Jiang Zemin and Hu Jintao during the 2002–5 period, when Jiang preserved his position as Chairman of the CCP CMC, although Hu was the CCP General Secretary. For example, Alice Miller (2011) and Joseph Fewsmith (2003) each reached totally different conclusions. Miller stated that Hu was surprisingly quick to push

particular, it is crucial to see the nexus existing between Jiang's Three Represents and Hu's Governing for the People.[10]

The Three Represents theory was first put forward by Jiang Zemin in 2000 during an inspection tour in Guangdong Province. It became part of the Constitution of the CCP at the 16th Party Congress and of the Constitution of the People's Republic of China two and four years later, respectively. The Three Represents are the rhetorical instrument that Jiang used to enlarge the support base of the party and the pool of new members, especially including private entrepreneurs, by arguing that the CCP represents "the development trend of China's advanced productive forces, the orientation of China's advanced culture and the fundamental interests of the overwhelming majority of the Chinese people." Jiang enlarged the group of those eligible to contribute to the party and China's political life, thereby expanding the role of society in the policymaking process. Jiang was largely forced to do so because the reality of Chinese society had drastically changed through the decades of economic reform and the party was looking for ways to regain at least part of the legitimacy lost in Tiananmen Square. Jiang's move, thus, was reactive and inward-looking because it essentially aimed at changing the political settings within China.

Hu's Governing for the People continued the process of inclusion of China's society as an important factor in Chinese policymaking. Yet, unlike Jiang's Three Represents, it had far deeper and omnidirectional effects, including over China's understanding of security as Hu enlarged the scope of policymaking beyond a purely state-centric approach. According to party sources (People's Daily 2012a), the concept of Governing for the People was first outlined by Hu in December 2002, even before the exposition of other concepts, like that of Scientific Outlook on Development and Harmonious Society, which later became signatures of his administration.[11] At least in theory, this concept puts the common citizen at the very center of the government's action, since "the people are the foundation" of everything, including the legitimacy

---

forward his own initiatives immediately after the 16th Party Congress; while Fewsmith prognosticated that a meaningful political succession remained at least five years away. Since we will probably never know what kind of relationship existed back then between the two men, this book stands by Kiselycznyk and Saunders's assessment that "despite periodic reports about conflicts between political factions loyal to Jiang Zemin and Hu Jintao and about differences in policy lines, whatever tensions existed have remained manageable" (2010, 7). Had Hu no intention to continue the path outlined by Jiang, the situation would have been different.

[10] In Chinese: 三个代表 (Sān gè dàibiǎo) and 执政为民 (Zhízhèng wèi mín).
[11] In Chinese: 科学发展观 (Kēxué fāzhǎn guān) and 和谐社会 (Héxié shèhuì).

of the party.[12] To ensure that the government could protect the people's interests, boosting the party's "governance capability" became a top priority for Hu's leadership (Fewsmith 2004).[13]

It is against this background that defense against non-traditional security threats became part of the overall preparations to improve national defense. Indeed, the Central Committee of the CCP approved a document that included that instruction in September 2004 (PRC Central Goverment). The defense white paper published in December 2004 (PRC State Council's Information Office) stated that China planned to enhance its "national strategic capabilities by using multiple security means to cope with both traditional and non-traditional security threats so as to seek a comprehensive national security in the political, economic, military and social areas."

As the idea of Governing for the People started to float in Chinese political debate, China suddenly became the epicenter of the outbreak of the SARS epidemic. That crisis sparked an intense debate on the concept of human security in China, thereby probably pushing the government to continue the development of more people-centered policies (Breslin 2015). China had been impermeable to that idea before. Indeed, human security was not part of the definition of non-traditional security that China used in the context of China-ASEAN cooperation (Arase 2010). Yet the situation changed and, as pointed out by Chinese scholars, the evolution from New Security Concept to Comprehensive National Security should be seen as an acknowledgment of the importance of expanding the understanding of the concept of security to include the security of the people and not just that of the state.[14]

The basic assumption behind this change is that "the security of the people is the core of national security" (Zhang 2004, 9). Tellingly, along with statements about the fact that "traditional and non-traditional security issues are intertwined," the Chinese Premier promised to increase efforts to "vigorously protect the lives and legitimate rights and interests of Chinese nationals living abroad" already in 2005 (PRC Central Government). As the security of the citizen became an important part of China's understanding of national security, and addressing non-traditional security issues was rising in the security agenda as well, the connection between them started to become evident and to echo in the order given by the Chinese civilian leadership to the Ministry of Foreign Affairs (MFA) and the military.

During the 10th Conference of Chinese Diplomatic Envoys Stationed Abroad of 2004, Hu made it clear to senior diplomats that protecting Chinese

[12] In Chinese: 以人为本 (Yǐ rén wéi běn).   [13] In Chinese: 执政能力 (Zhízhèng nénglì).
[14] In Chinese: 综合国家安全 (Zònghé guójiā ānquán).

nationals abroad against non-traditional security threats was one of their most important tasks (People's Daily 2004). Hu's words came only a month after the MFA established the Department of External Security Affairs to complement the work of the Department of Consular Affairs, which was already tasked with offering assistance to Chinese citizens abroad (Chapter 6 sheds further light on the development of the Chinese consular protection system). On July 6, 2004 (*Xinhua*), Zhang Qiyue, the then MFA spokesperson, stated that the decision to establish the new department was born out of the acknowledgement that non-traditional security issues were becoming more prominent in international affairs, and Chinese interests were also affected by them. Indeed, Chinese nationals were the victims of numerous small-scale incidents around the world that year, from robberies in the United States to being arrested as for illegal fishing by the Peruvian Coastguard, and the killing of eleven of them in Afghanistan.

A few months later, the State Council created the ministerial-level Small Group for Coordination on External Emergencies, led by the then Minister of Foreign Affairs, Li Zhaoxing. The group was tasked with the important role of protecting China's overseas interests (Zhang 2007, 258). During the Central Conference on Work Relating to Foreign Affairs of August 21, 2006, Hu stated that consular assistance had to be strengthened, along with the creation of a quick-reaction mechanism to crises involving the security of Chinese citizens and companies abroad (CCP Central Literature Editing Committee 2016a, 513–19). According to Wan Xia (2007), a professor of international law at the China Foreign Affairs University, these institutional developments should be seen as the most evident manifestations of the new direction for Chinese diplomacy set by the top leadership. It is important to point out that this is not the first organization created to address non-traditional security threats, but it was the first to do so with regard to external threats. Indeed, in 2001 the Chinese leadership created the National Anti-Terrorism Coordination Small Group, which later became the National Anti-Terrorism Leading Small Group (PRC MPS 2013). In his speech at the first meeting of the group on October 23, 2001, Hu Jintao, who was the leader of the group, talked about fighting domestic and international terrorist organizations, but his words indicate rather clearly that the focus was overwhelmingly on operations within China's borders (CCP Central Literature Editing Committee 2016a, 512–15).

While it seems that the MFA received rather direct and precise orders, Hu took the long road to express his thinking in military terms. During a meeting of the CCP CMC that was held immediately after he became chairman of the same commission in late 2004, Hu Jintao presented for the first time the

New Historic Missions as a translation in security terms of the concept of Scientific Outlook on Development (Jia, Li, and Cao 2008).[15] The new missions, officially spelled out in the defense white paper published in 2006 (PRC State Council's Information Office), included:

> providing an important guarantee of strength for the party to consolidate its ruling position; providing a strong security guarantee for safeguarding the period of important strategic opportunity for national development, providing a powerful strategic support for safeguarding national interests; and playing an important role in safeguarding world peace and promoting common development.[16]

James Mulvenon (2009) argues that this new set of missions should be seen as an adjustment that Hu Jintao proposed in the face of new requirements and challenges created by China's increasingly global interests and entanglements. Indeed, Hu was very explicit at that meeting of the CCP CMC, when he stated that "the [economic] development of the country has, over time, gradually pushed the national interests beyond the traditional territorial water, and air space borders, towards the oceans, the space, and the electromagnetic space" (CCP Central Literature Editing Committee 2016a, 259). The PLA "must be careful to protect not only the country's survival interests but also the country's development interests" (p. 259). Moreover, participation in UN peacekeeping operations became a symbol of China's pledge to use its growing military power only for global security and not to bully other countries during its period of "peaceful development" (PRC State Council's Information Office 2011).[17] The pressure on the PLA to prepare for overseas operations, therefore, was increasing from both a security and a diplomatic perspective.

The securitization of non-traditional security issues overseas brought about the emergence of a new term—"development interests"—to describe the referent object of the new threats that the Chinese leadership saw on the horizon.[18] It appeared in a public document for the first time in the 2004 defense white paper (PRC State Council's Information Office 2004a). Two key elements that comprise the concept of "development interests" must be highlighted. First, for the first time, the Chinese leadership acknowledged the

---

[15] In Chinese: 新的历史使命 (Xīn de lìshǐ shǐmìng).
[16] The original set of "historic missions" are promoting modernization, completing reunification with Taiwan, and promoting world peace.
[17] In Chinese: 和平发展 (Hépíng fāzhǎn).   [18] In Chinese: 发展利益 (Fāzhǎn lìyì).

existence of important components of national security—Chinese companies and nationals going abroad looking for economic opportunities—outside the country's geographical borders. However, this does not mean that it is possible to talk about proper overseas interests because there is no reference to other countries in the official statements of those years. Rather, the term "development interests" seems to be pointing to the process of expansion of Chinese interests, as the references to outer space and the oceans in the texts specifically indicate. However, it is not clear if the Chinese leadership had anything specific, such as the security of the oceanic lines of communications, in mind. For example, although the story of Hu Jintao talking about the "Malacca dilemma" quickly became famous after the *China Youth Daily* reported it (Shi 2004), Peking University's Zha Daojiong found that the person who created that term was not the Chinese president but "a person who participated in a conference that was chaired by President Hu" (Glaser 2016).[19] Second, the addition of "development interests" as separate from "survival interests" officially signaled for the first time that the PLA was ordered to operate abroad, not only to carry out military diplomacy but also to defend China's interests as an extension of its traditional mission of defending the survival of the state and the country.[20] Indeed, according to the defense white paper of 2006, the modernization of the PLA was justified and necessary because it was consistent not only with the trends of the new global revolution in military affairs and the necessity of guarding China's national security, but also with the need to protect the country's "development interests" (PRC State Council's Information Office 2006). Not fulfilling Hu's New Historic Missions, thus, meant partially delegitimizing the modernization of the armed forces and the investment of growing resources in that endeavor.

It is upon this basis that Hu Jintao and his top aides continued to elaborate on what the threats to China's interests were and what must be done to address them. In this regard, the defense of the national interest and the promotion of China's international standing became common themes in the statements of civilian officials. For example, celebrating sixty years of Chinese diplomacy with an article in *Qiushi*, Yang Jiechi (2009), who at that time was serving as Minister of Foreign Affairs, insisted that the role of the people as the fulcrum of China's foreign policy had to be preserved. The protection of the Chinese people and the nation's overseas interests had to continue ranking high among the tasks of government. According to him, sovereignty, security, and

---

[19] In Chinese: 马六甲困境 (Mǎliùjiǎ kùnjìng).   [20] In Chinese: 存在利益 (Cúnzài lìyì).

development interests were "organically united."[21] Former State Councilor, Dai Bingguo, stated that China planned to use its growing hard power in support of its development strategy through a more active engagement in cooperation over non-traditional security issues, from natural disasters and energy security to international peacekeeping (2010).

That the military had to play a more active role became clearer too. During the fourth session of the 10th National People's Congress, on March 4, 2006, Hu Jintao told the PLA delegation that the armed forces had to prepare to respond to "diverse kinds of threats" (Guo 2010, 1).[22] He repeated this order in his speech during the 17th National Party Congress of October 2007 and added that the PLA had to improve its ability to carry out "diversified military missions" to neutralize the new threats (People's Daily 2007).[23] It is difficult to say why a new term—"diverse kinds of threats"—was introduced. A possible explanation is that, while it is a synonym for non-traditional security threats, it better expresses the diversification of the threats to the security of Chinese interests than the term "non-traditional security threats," which was, and still is, used in defense white papers to describe the international security environment in general. Moreover, the coupling of "diverse kinds of threats" with "diversified military missions" makes sense in the context of Chinese political language, which pays great attention to slogans that are used both to motivate the intended audience and to summarize the content of a specific policy (Shambaugh 2013, 217).

During a meeting of the CCP CMC on December 28, 2007, Hu also provided a more detailed description of the referent object of his call to expand the understanding of security and, consequently, the PLA's missions: a stable supply of energy, safe strategic lines of communications, and the security of Chinese investment projects and Chinese nationals abroad (CCP Central Literature Editing Committee 2016b, 37). Hu also mentioned the concept of Military Operations Other Than War as the operational bridge between the expansion of Chinese interests and the growing non-traditional security threats against them (CCP Central Literature Editing Committee 2016b, 41). The term "Military Operations Other Than War" appeared in a public document for the first time in the defense white paper published in January 2009 (PRC State Council's Information Office). This was also the first time that a document of this kind, which usually offers much more general and less

---

[21]   In Chinese: 有机统一 (Yǒujī tǒngyī).
[22]   In Chinese: 多种安全威胁 (Duō zhǒng ānquán wēixié).
[23]   In Chinese: 多样化军事任务 (Duōyàng huà jūnshì rènwù).

technical descriptions of what the PLA does, discussed a specific doctrinal concept. The civilian leadership surely wanted to emphasize the importance and depth of the change.

While the second term of Hu Jintao was getting closer to its end, the wind of revolution started to blow in North Africa. It has been shown above that the Chinese leadership was aware of the fact that the growing presence of Chinese companies and citizens abroad had to be added to the national security equation. However, it was not prepared for the sudden need to evacuate some 36,000 Chinese nationals from Libya, where protestors and security forces started to clash as early as the first days of February 2011, and where several Western countries were about to intervene with bombers and cruise missiles (Chapter 3 further illustrates how the Arab Spring endangered Chinese interests in North Africa and the Middle East). It was the largest evacuation of Chinese citizens ever conducted and, as Chapters 2 and 5 show, it had an unprecedentedly deep impact on how the Chinese military and public opinion viewed defending the country's overseas interests militarily.

The Chinese government reacted to this crisis by establishing an ad hoc emergency command center led by the then Vice Premier Zhang Dejiang (Zhang 2011). The government could not but feel the urgency to press, once again and more explicitly, the military to develop a systematic response to the rising threats overseas in order to protect the country's development interests. By then, that was not just a general statement in official documents; rather, it had become the faces of the Chinese nationals being evacuated from North Africa. In his last report as Party General Secretary, Hu put further pressure on the PLA to follow his orders regarding the protection of the lives and assets of Chinese citizens and companies abroad (People's Daily 2012b). He stated that China was facing "existential problems" and "development problems" caused by traditional and non-traditional security issues.[24] Consequently, the party required the PLA and the whole national defense establishment to achieve "a great development" as part of its modernization process.[25] In comparison with the report delivered in 2007, the PLA was explicitly required to play an active role during peacetime while improving the level of war readiness. While Hu denounced the problem, it was up to the new leader, Xi Jinping, to find a solution for the protection of China's faraway interest frontiers.

---

[24] In Chinese: 生存安全问题 (Shēngcún ānquán wèntí) and 发展安全问题 (Fāzhǎn ānquán wèntí).
[25] In Chinese: 一个大的发展 (Yī gè dà de fā zhǎn).

Xi Jinping and the Libyan Pandora's Box

The transition from Hu Jintao to Xi Jinping was very different from that which brought Jiang Zemin and Hu Jintao to power, because they both had to wait before officially assuming the leadership of the party, the PLA, and the state. On the other hand, Xi probably had already sidelined Hu inside the party-PLA-state machine before the official transition of power. Indeed, he was immediately able to launch a still-ongoing aggressive anti corruption campaign throughout the party and state bureaucracy and, at the same time, to start a sweeping reform of the PLA. By late 2016, Xi became the "core" of the Chinese leadership, a title that his predecessor could not boast to have held.[26] In foreign policy, he has quickly built his reputation as a leader determined to take China on "the road to national rejuvenation" and has stressed the importance of the PLA becoming an army ready to fight and win on the battlefield.[27] His call to improve war readiness was most likely a reference to the need to eliminate corruption as a major obstacle to the PLA's modernization and as a corrosive factor in party-PLA relations (Lam 2013), rather than explicitly giving a warning about the possibility of fighting a war. An army capable of winning real wars is, in any case, undoubtedly also one of the pillars of his assertive foreign policy, which has made the more traditional security side of his security and military agenda stand out in the eyes of external observers.

After all, Xi inherited a desperate situation as Chinese leader. On the one hand, according to sources of the Hong Kong-based *South China Morning Post*, he witnessed how the two vice chairmen of the CCP CMC, Xu Caihou, and Guo Boxiong, isolated Hu Jintao and challenged his authority (Chan 2015). On the other hand, Obama's Pivot to Asia was picking up steam. While the air-sea battle became officially part of American military doctrine in 2010, many Asian countries and the United States supported the idea of moving on with talks for the expansion of the Trans-Pacific Partnership and its transformation into a regional free-trade bloc based on American standards. But that was not all: Xi also inherited the task of finding a solution to the many problems that emerged from the Libyan Pandora's Box. In line with this, references to protecting Chinese citizens and legal persons overseas started to appear regularly in reports on the work of the government delivered by Premier Li Keqiang in the following years (Figure 2).

The urgency of addressing this issue can be seen in the comparison of the first two defense white papers published on Xi's watch. Like Hu before him,

---

[26] In Chinese: 核心 (Héxīn).   [27] In Chinese: 复兴之路 (Fùxīng zhī lù).

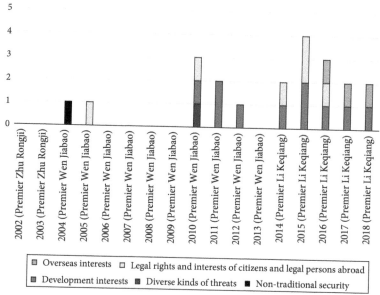

Figure 2 References to China's overseas interests and the threats to them in the reports on the work of the government under Hu Jintao and Xi Jinping
Source: PRC Central Government. Compiled by the author.

Xi's approach to security strategy has been composed of two steps: the formulation of a new concept and the description of what the PLA is meant to do in operational terms. Yet it is the 2015 white paper, not that issued in 2013, that introduced Xi's new security concept. The titles of the two documents are telling in both their content and priorities: *The Diversified Employment of China's Armed Forces* and *China's Military Strategy* (PRC State Council's Information Office 2013, 2015). The first chapter of the 2013 defense white paper, which is entitled "New Situation, New Challenges and New Missions," describes a worrisome scenario. On the one hand, "some country has strengthened its Asia-Pacific military alliances, expanded its military presence in the region, and frequently makes the situation there tenser" and, on the other hand, "the security risks to China's overseas interests are on the increase."

Yet, while the instructions for the PLA to confront "some country" are rather vague, the white paper encouraged "active planning for the use of armed forces in peacetime, dealing effectively with various security threats and accomplishing diversified military tasks," and referred to "strengthening overseas operational capabilities such as emergency response and rescue, merchant vessel protection at sea and evacuation of Chinese nationals, and providing reliable security support for China's interests overseas" (PRC State Council's

Information Office 2013). As Chapter 7 further discusses, that same year, China deployed its first contingent of combat troops who were officially part of UN peacekeeping missions.

For the first time, the term "overseas interests" appeared in an official defense-related document.[28] By referring to "overseas interests" as an extension of "development interests," the Chinese leadership clarified what the new target of the government's actions and policies beyond traditional state/ regime survival was. Consequently, the PLA was called on to make the necessary preparations. Although the terms "development interests" and "maritime interests" had been used for many years, and entail the possible deployment of the PLA abroad for naval escorts, the creation of the term "overseas interests" marked an important change.[29] Indeed, this term has been officially used only since the publication of the 2013 defense white paper, four years after the launch of the antipiracy missions in late 2008. Moreover, while "maritime interests" are usually associated with "maritime rights," which initially referred to protecting China's territorial waters and, only later, international waterways, the protection of Chinese nationals and legal persons overseas implies the possibility of the PLA operating in a foreign country.[30] This also clearly entails a far more flexible interpretation of the noninterference principle, thus signaling the new level of priority attached to the nation's interests abroad.

It took two more years to see the emergence of Xi Jinping's new concept of security. As Wang Duo (2018), a professor at the PLA National Defense University, wrote, it was necessary to summarize and "systematize" the different aspects of security that emerged over the years.[31] According to him, this was the first—and a necessary—step in reorganizing China's understanding of security and its security strategy as "domestic and external factors became increasingly more complex." Hence, Xi Jinping introduced the idea of Holistic National Security, during the first meeting of the CCP Central National Security Commission (CNSC) on April 15, 2014 (CCP Central Literature Research Center 2018, 3–5).[32] During that first meeting, Xi declared that a new understanding of national security that has "the security of the people as compass, political security at its roots, economic security as its pillar, military security, cultural security, and social security as its protections, and that relies on the promotion of international security" was necessary (People's Daily 2014).

[28] In Chinese: 海外利益 (Hǎiwài lìyì). [29] In Chinese: 海洋利益 (Hǎiyáng lìyì).
[30] In Chinese: 海洋权利 (Hǎiyáng quánlì). [31] In Chinese: 系统化 (Xìtǒng huà).
[32] In Chinese: 总体国家安全观 (Zǒngtǐ guójiā ānquán guān).

According to official party publications, Holistic National Security is now composed of "political security," "territorial integrity," "military security," "economic security," "cultural security," "social stability," "technological security," "cybersecurity," "ecological security," "resource security," "nuclear security," and "overseas interests security" (CCP Central Literature Research Center 2018, 17–223). At the same meeting of the CCP CNSC where he outlined the concept of Holistic National Security, Xi Jinping declared that protecting China's overseas interests is an essential part of the efforts to defend the country's economic development and national security (People's Daily 2018). In his statement, he also pointed out that this was a particularly pressing issue, as Chinese human and economic presence abroad was expanding along with the implementation of the Belt and Road Initative, a multibillion-dollar plan to integrate the economic and logistic networks of the Eurasian continent.

The concept of Holistic National Security, therefore, further consolidated the position of the lives and the assets of Chinese citizens and companies abroad as being among the most important referent objects of China's security strategy. This evolution took place along with the more general acknowledgment that parts of China, that is, its companies and citizens, lay well beyond the country's geographical borders, closer to events and phenomena that had little to do with China's national security until recently. This is why the concept of Holistic National Security aims at balancing internal and external, traditional and non-traditional security, and protecting both China's existence and her development interests (PRC State Council's Information Office 2015).

Liu Yuejin (2014a, 2014b), a professor at the University of International Relations and a research fellow with the Council for National Security Studies, wrote that this attempt to balance different aspects of security means that the Chinese government is moving towards a concept of security where distinctions between external and internal, traditional and non-traditional, and so on are simply disappearing. After all, as Xi Jinping himself stated, national security "is entirely for the people, and relies entirely on the people" in order to "prevent and neutralize every kind of security risk and constantly improve the people's sense of security" (People's Daily 2016). As Tsinghua University's Wang Zhenmin (2016) emphasized, it was the growing seriousness of non-traditional security threats that prompted the expansion of the Chinese leadership's understanding of national security to include outer space, international waters, and other new areas of security as well as protecting the security of China's overseas interests. In 2016, two years after it was spelled out for the first time, the People's Publishing House published the *Cadre Manual of the Holistic National Security Concept*, thereby officially starting the systematic process of dissemination of the new concept among party, PLA, and government officials (Xinhua 2016).

Xi did not create a new term, such as Hu's "diverse kinds of threats," to describe the threats against Chinese overseas interests. Rather, official documents and reports on Xi's statements are straightforward in identifying the threats, a likely sign of the urgent need to neutralize them. Reportedly, during an "important meeting" with the military in December 2012, Xi stated that international and regional instability, piracy, terrorism, and natural disasters were the main threats to China's expanding overseas interests (M. Liu 2017, 38).[33] While the 2013 defense white paper is less specific in this regard, the 2015 *China's Military Strategy* highlighted that Chinese interests and national security are:

> vulnerable to international and regional turmoil, terrorism, piracy, serious natural disasters and epidemics, and the security of overseas interests concerning energy and resources, strategic sea lines of communication, as well as institutions, personnel and assets abroad, has become an imminent issue.
>
> (PRC State Council's Information Office 2015)

At another meeting held in February 2016, Xi further emphasized that Chinese nationals and organizations overseas faced an increasingly serious terrorist menace (M. Liu 2017, 38). The 2019 defense white paper, entitled *China's National Defense in the New Era*, added that Chinese diplomatic missions, too, are in danger and that "overseas interests are a crucial part of China's national interests" (PRC MOD 2019).

Against this background, the 2015 *China's Military Strategy* white paper lists for the first time the protection of overseas interests as a "strategic task" and explains clearly what was then expected from the PLA:

> A holistic approach will be taken to balance war preparation and war prevention, rights protection and stability maintenance, deterrence and war fighting, and operations in wartime and employment of military forces in peacetime. . . . To realize China's national strategic goal and implement the holistic view of national security, new requirements have been raised for innovative development of China's military strategy and accomplishing military missions and tasks. . . . China's armed forces will work harder to

---

[33] According to the newspaper *Epoch Times* (2015), the term "important meeting" (一次重要会议, Yī cì zhòngyào huìyì) refers to meetings related to the sweeping reforms of the armed forces carried out by Xi Jinping. More generally, it seems to be a term used for important meetings focused on the structure and organization of the PLA (*Shanghai Observer* 2018).

create a favorable strategic posture with more emphasis on the employment of military forces and means, and provide a solid security guarantee for the country's peaceful development. . . . In response to the new requirement coming from the country's growing strategic interests, the armed forces will actively participate in both regional and international security cooperation and effectively secure China's overseas interests.

(PRC State Council's Information Office 2015)

The 2019 white paper repeated that the protection of China's interests overseas is one of the "fundamental goals of China's national defense in the new era" (PRC MOD 2019).

As far as publicly available sources show, Xi has not been so specific during important meetings with the civilian arm of the Chinese foreign policy machine. For example, he simply stated the importance of protecting the country's overseas interests during the Central Conference on Work Relating to Foreign Affairs of late November 2014 (PRC MFA 2014). Reportedly, he did not mention the nature of the threats or specific ways to address them. It is difficult to find a clear reason for this difference. However, it is possible to put forward a credible hypothesis based on the words of scholars affiliated with China's diplomatic system. Although Zhang Lili (2011), a professor at the Diplomatic Studies Institute of the Foreign Affairs University, praised the work of Chinese diplomats in Libya in 2011, Xia Liping (2015), another scholar at the same university, pointed out that the MFA was not fully prepared to deal with crises of that scale. For example, the MFA officially knew that only 6,000 (one-sixth of the total evacuees) Chinese nationals—those who had registered on the official list of the MFA—were in Libya in 2011. Moreover, the MFA issued a warning to travelers to Libya, the first of this kind, only on February 22, 2011. Although there might be other reasons, a mix of the rising level of threat and the difficulties met by MFA in protecting Chinese nationals abroad (see Chapter 6) probably pushed the top Chinese leaders to look at the military as the necessary instrument for protecting China's interest frontiers. At the same time, Xi Jinping had been a strong supporter of China's involvement in international peacekeeping. In 2015, in front of the UN General Assembly, China pledged USD 100 million to the African Union standby force and USD 1 billion to establish the UN Peace and Development Trust Fund. These commitments were followed by a pledge to build a peacekeeping standby force of 8,000 troops from the Chinese armed forces. Therefore, diplomatic considerations, too, continued to make the PLA even more central to China's peacetime foreign policy.

Conclusion

This chapter has shown how the concept of security changed in China over the last forty years until the inclusion of the protection of the country's overseas interests has become one of its key components. This process is composed of three interconnected and clearly identifiable trends.

The first is continuity despite different leadership styles. Jiang Zemin, Hu Jintao, and Xi Jinping each came to power under very different circumstances. Their personalities and personal backgrounds are very different too. Yet, if one compares the three different national security concepts that Jiang, Hu, and Xi put forward, one can notice a gradual but steady enlargement to make space for non-traditional security threats. Of course, it was not necessarily a continuity of choice. For example, Hu was probably never fully free from the underlying influence of Jiang before he had to make room for Xi, beginning as early as 2007, when the latter started being groomed as the next top leader. Xi himself, regardless of his preferences, had little choice but to continue the work of Hu with regard to the expansion of the PLA's role in foreign policy beyond traditional national defense. As described above, the 2011 Libyan crisis had a deep and clear impact on the process of formulating a new security concept.

Therefore, it is possible to identify two factors behind the continuity. The first is the tradition of expanding on, rather than destroying and rebuilding, the concepts and policies of past leaders. The original impulse given by Deng to better integrate China in world affairs was fundamental in sowing the seeds of a larger role for the PLA as a tool of statecraft, and it has not weakened over time. Indeed, the importance of military diplomacy was never questioned by any leader. Even today, despite the presence of combat troops as part of the Chinese peacekeeping contingents deployed in Mali and South Sudan, peacekeeping is still seen as part of the activities belonging to international cooperation and military diplomacy.

The second factor is the growing number and seriousness of incidents where Chinese nationals or companies were involved (Chapters 3 and 5 will shed light on the origins of those incidents and the reaction of Chinese public opinion to them). Hu's preference, genuine or not, for people-centric policies was certainly important, but kidnappings of Chinese workers or sailors were not that infrequent. The isolated and extremely specific reference to the "legal rights and interests of Chinese citizens and legal persons abroad" in the report delivered by Wen Jiabao in 2005 can hardly be a coincidence. Yet the Libyan crisis was simply a much more serious and, thus, more influential event. The reversal of the usual from-concept-to-policy process that took place with the publication of the 2013 defense white paper speaks loudly about the sudden urgent need to address a problem that had never emerged before in such a clear and unmistakable way.

The second trend is the transformation of non-traditional security issues from diplomatic opportunities to representing a specific set of security threats. For a long time, China joined other countries in the effort to deal with non-traditional security issues more for the sake of being part of the group than to actually neutralize those threats. The expansion of the understanding of security proceeded along with a clarification of what threats China actually faced. Jiang Zemin's New Security Concept brought non-traditional security issues into the picture of Chinese national security and foreign policy, but they were distant and abstract. The state was the referent object of the New Security Concept and, therefore, what was not a threat to the state was not viewed as a threat at all. This is why non-traditional security issues outside Chinese borders ended up being framed more as opportunities than threats. The case of the 9/11 attack is extremely telling about this very pragmatic approach. Between the early 1990s and the early 2000s, the referent object was still the state's survival. The Chinese government saw in military operations related to non-traditional security issues a way to improve China's diplomatic network and strengthen its relations with other countries in order to ensure a beneficial environment for the country's much-needed economic development. The nature of the issue, thus, was not that important.

Yet the appearance of new terms to better describe both the referent object and threats was symptomatic of a change in how events taking place outside China's geographical borders started to be seen as undermining Chinese interests. The importance of protecting the lives and assets of Chinese citizens abroad became a priority on a par with boosting China's international image. The clearer this became, the more precise was the way the Chinese government identified the threats that needed to be eliminated, which is a typical sign of progressing securitization. It would be wrong to say that Chinese citizens became a more important referent object than the state. Rather, as was well-summarized by Shaun Breslin (2015), the nature of the Chinese state makes it particularly easy to transform certain issues into strategic objectives to be pursued by the state as long as the top leaders decide that the survival of a new referent object is necessary for the survival of the state and the regime. The protection of China's interest frontiers, thus, became part of the efforts to protect the regime, and the state changed its approach accordingly (Chapter 6 further explores the institutional and legal changes that took place over the years). Hence, the diplomatic value of dealing with non-traditional security threats did not wane and the final goal of the state's action did not change. This explains why China's growing interests in protecting its overseas interests and its international image merged into the election of the UN as the main channel of expression for Chinese activism in foreign policy (Foot 2014). This was a choice that has had significant implications for China's military presence on the verge of its interest frontiers (Chapter 7).

The third trend is the evolution of the tools of foreign policy statecraft toward an increasingly militarized response to non-traditional security threats. The recognition that non-traditional security issues not only provided opportunities to boost China's international standing, but that they are also threats to the safety of the country's overseas interests, prompted the Chinese leadership to reassess thoroughly the role of the PLA in peacetime foreign policy. In particular, once the threatening nature of non-traditional security issues abroad started to become evident in the mid-2000s, the Chinese government opted for strengthening the civilian institutions instead of addressing militarily the new threats right away. Indeed, Hu Jintao's New Historic Missions envisioned a larger role for the PLA in this regard, but what Chinese soldiers were called to do was still unclear, as was the specific meaning of "development interests." Nonetheless, as the seriousness of the threat and the identity of their referent object became clearer, so did the new task bestowed on the PLA: actively striving to neutralize the new threats. Naturally, Chinese diplomats remain fundamental actors in the protection of China's interest frontiers, and the missions that the Chinese leadership described in the white papers and in the speeches of its top representatives are far from indicating that a military-only option even exists. However, the change is clear and is extremely significant not only because of the expansion of the military dimension of Chinese foreign policy, but also because of the influential role of the PLA in the policymaking process. The PLA itself, thus, is at the center of Chapter 2.

Bibliography

Arase, David. 2010. "Non-Traditional Security in China-ASEAN Cooperation: The Institutionalization of Regional Security Cooperation and the Evolution of East Asian Regionalism." *Asian Survey* 50 (4): 808–33.

Breslin, Shaun. 2015. "Debating Human Security in China: Towards Discoursive Power?" *Journal of Contemporary Asia* 45 (2): 243–65.

CCP Central Literature Editing Committee. 2011. *Selected Works of Jiang Zemin.* Vol. II. Beijing: Foreign Language Press.

CCP Central Literature Editing Committee. 2016a. 胡锦涛选文 [*Selected Works of Hu Jintao*]. Vol. II. Beijing: People's Publishing House.

CCP Central Literature Editing Committee. 2016b. 胡锦涛选文 [*Selected Works of Hu Jintao*]. Vol. III. Beijing: People's Publishing House.

CCP Central Literature Research Center. 2018. 习近平关于总体国家安全观论述摘编 [*Excerpts of Xi Jinping's Discussions Related to the Comprehensive National Security Concept*]. Beijing: Central Party Literature Press.

Chan, Minnie. 2015. "Hu Jintao's Weak Grip on China's Army Inspired Xi Jinping's Military Shake-Up: Sources." *South China Morning Post*. March 11. Accessed January 2, 2018. https://www.scmp.com/news/china/article/1734663/hu-jintaos-weak-grip-chinas-army-inspired-president-xi-jinpings-military.

Dai, Bingguo. 2010. "戴秉国: 坚持走和平发展道路 [Dai Bingguo: Insisting on the Path of Peace and Development]." *PRC Ministry of Foreign Affairs*. December 6. Accessed January 16, 2018. http://www.fmprc.gov.cn/ce/ceit/chn/zl/yjjj/gjldrjh/t806659.htm.

Du, Nongyi. 2015. 新中国军事外交与国际维和研究 [*Military Diplomacy of New China and International Peacekeeping*]. Beijing: PLA National Defense University Press.

Epoch Times. 2015. "陆媒披露习近平的'次重要会议' [Mainland Media Reveal Xi Jinping's 'Important Meetings']." *Epoch Times*. November 27. Accessed February 1, 2018. http://www.epochtimes.com/gb/15/11/27/n4583204.htm.

Fewsmith, Joseph. 2003. "The Sixteenth National Party Congress: The Succession that Didn't Happen." *China Quarterly* 173: 1–16.

Fewsmith, Joseph. 2004. "Promoting the Scientific Development Concept." *China Leadership Monitor* 11.

Finkelstein, David M. 2003. "China's 'New Concept of Security,'" In Stephen J. Flanagan and Micheal E. Marti (eds), *The People's Liberation Army and China in Transition*, 197–210. Washington DC: National Defense University Press.

Foot, Rosemary. 2014. "'Doing Some Things' in the Xi Jinping Era: The United Nations as China's Venue of Choice." *International Affairs* 90 (5): 1086–100.

Gill, Bates. 2007. *Rising Star*. Washington DC: Brookings Institution Press.

Glaser, Bonnie S. 2016. "China's Energy Security: A Conversation with Zha Daojiong." *Center for Strategic and International Studies*. December 20. Accessed February 12, 2018. https://www.csis.org/podcasts/chinapower/china%E2%80%99s-energy-security-conversation-zha-daojiong.

Goldstein, Avery. 2001. "The Diplomatic Face of China's Grand Strategy: A Rising Power's Emerging Choice." *China Quarterly* 168: 835–64.

Guo, Jingyan. 2010. "新世纪新阶段科学建军强军的重大方略 [Fundamental Strategy for Scientific Building of a Powerful Army in the New Stage in the New Century]." *China Military Science* 6: 1–8.

Jia, Yong, Xuanliang Li, and Zhi Cao. 2008. "强军之路 [The Path to a Strong Army]." *Xinhua*. December 22. Accessed October 16, 2017. http://paper.people.com.cn/rmrbhwb/html/2008-12/22/content_161881.htm.

Kiselycznyk, Michael, and Phillip C. Saunders. 2010. "Civil-Military Relations in China: Assessing the PLA's Role in Elite Politics." *China Strategic Perspectives* 2.

Lam, Willy. 2013. "Commander-in-Chief Xi Jinping Raises the Bar on PLA 'Combat Readiness.'" *China Brief* 7 (2): 2–4.

Li, Cheng. 2016. *Chinese Politics in the Xi Jinping Era*. Washington DC: Brookings Institution Press.

Li, Nan. 2008. "'中国的国际责任观' 研讨会综述 [Summary of the 'China's International Responsibility Concept' Seminar]." *Journal of Contemporary Asia-Pacific Studies* 6: 150–5.

Liu, Mingfu. 2017. *习近平打造第三代解放军 [Xi Jinping Building the Third Generation of the People's Liberation Army]*. New York: American Academic Press.

Liu, Yuejin. 2014a. "论总体国家安全观的五个'总体' [On the Five Components of the 'Overall National Security Concept']." *Frontiers* 6: 14–20.

Liu, Yuejin. 2014b. "非传统的总体国家安全观 [Non-Traditional Concept of Overall National Security]." *Journal of International Security Studies* 6: 3–25.

Miller, Alice. 2011. "The Politburo Standing Committee under Hu Jintao." *China Leadership Monitor* 35.

Mulvenon, James. 2009. "Chairman Hu and the PLA's 'New Historic Missions.'" *China Leadership Monitor* 27.

People's Daily. 1982. "中国共产党第十二次全国代表大会开幕词 [Opening Ceremony of the 12th National Congress of the CCP]." *People's Daily*. September 1. Accessed November 12, 2017. http://cpc.people.com.cn/GB/69112/69113/69684/69696/4949905.html.

People's Daily. 1987. "赵紫阳在中国共产党第十三次全国代表大会上的报告 [Zhao Ziyang's Report at the 13th National Congress of the Communist Party of China]." *CPC News*. December 25. Accessed September 15, 2017. http://cpc.people.com.cn/GB/64162/64168/64566/65447/4526369.html.

People's Daily. 2002. "在中国共产党第十六次全国代表大会上的报告 [Report at the 16th National Congress of the CCP]." *People's Daily*. November 8. Accessed December 26, 2017. http://cpc.people.com.cn/GB/64162/64168/64569/65444/4429116.html.

People's Daily. 2004. "Chinese President Calls on Diplomats to Better Serve Country." *People's Daily*. August 30. Accessed November 15, 2017. http://en.people.cn/200408/30/eng20040830_155249.html.

People's Daily. 2007. "胡锦涛在中国共产党第十七次全国代表大会上的报告 [Hu Jintao's Report at the 17th National Congress of the Communist Party of China]." *People's Daily*. October 15. Accessed December 5, 2017. http://cpc.people.com.cn/GB/64093/67507/6429852.html.

People's Daily. 2012a. "胡锦涛同志提出, 权为民所用、情为民所系、利为民所谋 [Comrade Hu Jintao Proposed that Power Should Be Used for the People, Love for the People, and Profit for the People]." *People's Daily*. October 28. Accessed January 3, 2018. http://theory.people.com.cn/n/2012/1028/c350808-19413195.html.

People's Daily. 2012b. "胡锦涛在中国共产党第十八次全国代表大会上的报告 [Hu Jintao's Report to the 7th Plenary Session of the 18th National Congress of the CCP]." *People's Daily*. November 19. Accessed October 18, 2017. http://cpc.people.com.cn/n/2012/1118/c64094-19612151-1.html.

People's Daily. 2014. "习近平：坚持总体国家安全观 走中国特色国家安全道路 [Xi Jinping: Upholding a Holistic National Security Concept Taking the Path of Security with Chinese Characteristics]." *People's Daily*. Edited by Zihui Wang. April 16. Accessed December 16, 2017. http://cpc.people.com.cn/n/2014/0416/c64094-24900492.html.

People's Daily. 2016. "习近平在首个全民国家安全教育日之际作出重要指示 [Xi Jinping Makes an Important Comment during the First Annual National Security Education Day]." *People's Daily*. April 15. Accessed November 23, 2017. http://cpc.people.com.cn/n1/2016/0415/c64094-28278100.html.

People's Daily. 2018. "指导新时代国家安全工作的强大思想武器—学习《习近平关于总体国家安全观论述摘编》 [A Powerful Ideological Weapon to Guide the National Security Work in the New Era—Learning from Xi Jinping's Excerpt on the Overall National Security Concept]." *People's Daily*. May 4. Accessed June 4, 2018. http://paper.people.com.cn/rmrb/html/2018-05/04/nw.D110000renmrb_20180504_1-06.htm.

PRC Central Government. 1983. "1983年政府工作报告 [Report on the Work of the Government of 1983]." *PRC Central Government*. June 6. Accessed December 1, 2018. http://www.gov.cn/premier/2006-02/16/content_200823.htm.

PRC Central Government. 1984. "1984年国务院政府工作报告 [Report on the Work of the Government of 1984]." *PRC Central Government*. May 15. Accessed December 2, 2018. http://www.gov.cn/premier/2006-02/16/content_200834.htm.

PRC Central Government. 2004. "中共中央关于加强党的执政能力建设的决定 [The CCP's Central Committee Decision on Strengthening the Party's Governance Capabilities]." *PRC Central Government*. September 26. Accessed December 3, 2017. http://www.gov.cn/test/2008-08/20/content_1075279.htm.

PRC Central Government. 2005. "2005年国务院政府工作报告 [Report on the Work of the Government of 2005]." *PRC Central Government*. March 5. Accessed December 2, 2018. http://www.gov.cn/premier/2006-02/16/content_201218.htm.

PRC MFA. 2002a. "China's Position Paper on the New Security Concept." *PRC Ministry of Foreign Affairs*. July 31. Accessed November 2, 2017. http://news.xinhuanet.com/zhengfu/2002-08/06/content_512599.htm.

PRC MFA. 2002b. "Joint Declaration of ASEAN and China on Cooperation in the Field of Non-Traditional Security Issues." *PRC Ministry of Foreign Affairs.* November 4. Accessed December 15, 2017. http://www.fmprc.gov.cn/nanhai/eng/zcfg_1/t26290.htm.

PRC MFA. 2014. "The Central Conference on Work Relating to Foreign Affairs Was Held in Beijing." *PRC Ministry of Foreign Affairs.* November 29. Accessed December 15, 2017. https://www.fmprc.gov.cn/mfa_eng/zxxx_662805/t1215680.shtml.

PRC MOD. 2019. "China's National Defense in the New Era." *PRC Ministry of National Defense.* July 24. Accessed July 25, 2019. http://eng.mod.gov.cn/news/2019-07/24/content_4846443.htm.

PRC MPS. 2013. "国家反恐怖工作领导小组成立 郭声琨兼任组长(简历) [The National Anti-Terrorism Leading Small Group Has Been Established; Guo Shengyu Is the Leader (Cv)]." *The Observer.* August 28. Accessed December 27, 2017. https://www.guancha.cn/politics/2013_08_28_168666.shtml.

PRC State Council's Information Office. 1998. "China's National Defense." *China. org.* July. Accessed December 5, 2017. http://www.china.org.cn/e-white/5/index.htm.

PRC State Council's Information Office. 2000. "China's National Defense in 2000." *China.org.* October 16. Accessed December 4, 2017. http://www.china.org.cn/e-white/2000/20-2.htm.

PRC State Council's Information Office. 2002. "China's National Defense in 2002." *China.org.* December. Accessed December 3, 2017. http://www.china.org.cn/e-white/20021209/index.htm.

PRC State Council's Information Office. 2004a. "2004年中国的国防 [China's Defense in 2004]." *PRC State Council's Information Office.* December 27. Accessed January 29, 2018. http://www.scio.gov.cn/zfbps/ndhf/2004/Document/307905/307905.htm.

PRC State Council's Information Office. 2004b. "China's National Defense in 2004." *China.org.* December 27. Accessed September 7, 2017. http://www.china.org.cn/e-white/20041227/II.htm.

PRC State Council's Information Office. 2006. "2006 年中国的国防 [China's Defense in 2006]." *PRC State Council's Information Office.* December 29. Accessed December 24, 2017. http://www.gov.cn/zhengce/2006-12/29/content_2615760.htm.

PRC State Council's Information Office. 2009. "China's National Defense in 2008." *China.org.* January 20. Accessed January 14, 2018. http://www.china.org.cn/government/whitepaper/node_7060059.htm.

PRC State Council's Information Office. 2011. "China's Peaceful Development." *PRC State Council.* September 6. Accessed November 28, 2017. http://english.gov.cn/archive/white_paper/2014/09/09/content_281474986284646.htm.

PRC State Council's Information Office. 2013. "The Diversified Employment of China's Armed Forces." *China Daily*. April 16. Accessed December 15, 2017. http://www.chinadaily.com.cn/china/China-Military-Watch/2013-09/09/content_16953672.htm.

PRC State Council's Information Office. 2015. "China's Military Strategy." *PRC Ministry of National Defense*. May 26. Accessed December 3, 2017. http://www.mod.gov.cn/auth/2015-05/26/content_4586723.htm.

Shambaugh, David. 2013. *China Goes Global: The Partial Power*. New York: Oxford University Press.

Shanghai Observer. 2018. "中央军委的重要会议提出哪些要求？ [What Necessities Were Raised in the Important Meetings of the Central Military Commissions?]." *Shanghai Observer*. August 20. Accessed November 4, 2017. https://www.shobserver.com/news/detail?id=100890.

Shi, Hongtao. 2004. "中国的'马六甲困局' [China's 'Malacca Dilemma']." *China Youth Daily*. June 15. Accessed February 3, 2018. http://zqb.cyol.com/content/2004-06/15/content_888233.htm.

Shichor, Yitzhak. 2007. "China's Darfur Policy." *China Brief* 7.

Thayer, Carlyle A. 2003. "China's 'New Security Concept' and Southeast Asia." In David W. Lovell (ed.), *Asia-Pacific Security: Policy Challenges*, 89–107. Camberra: Australia National University Press.

Wan, Xia. 2007. "海外公民保护的困境与出路-领事保护在国际法领域的新动向 [Protection of Overseas Citizens: Predicament and Solutions—New Trends in Consular Protection in International Law]." *World Economics and Politics* 5: 37–42.

Wang, Duo. 2018. "十九大报告为什么在'国家安全观'前面加了'总体'二字，有何深意？ [Why the Word 'Holistic' Was Added before 'National Security' at the 19th Party Congress]." *Shanghai Observer*. January 30. Accessed March 1, 2018. https://www.shobserver.com/news/detail?id=78457.

Wang, Zhenmin. 2016. "树立总体国家安全观 [Establishing a Comprehensive National Security Concept]." *People's Daily*. May 31. Accessed December 12, 2017. http://paper.people.com.cn/rmrb/html/2016-05/31/nw.D110000renmrb_20160531_4-07.htm.

Xia, Liping. 2015. "十八大以来" 外交为民 "理念与实践的新发展 [Practice and Development of 'Diplomacy for the People' since the 18th Party Congress]." *People's Daily*. February 6. Accessed February 23, 2018. http://cpc.people.com.cn/n/2015/0206/c187710-26521276.html.

Xinhua. 2004. "外交部新增涉外安全事务司 [The MFA Establishes the Department of External Security Affairs]." *China.com*. July 6. Accessed December 15, 2017. http://www.china.com.cn/chinese/kuaixun/603744.htm.

Xinhua. 2016. "'总体国家安全观干部读本' 出版发行 [The Publication of 'The Cadre Manual of the Holistic National Security Concept' Begins]." *Xinhua*.

April 16. Accessed January 25, 2018. http://www.xinhuanet.com/politics/ 2016-04/16/c_1118642552.htm.

Yang, Jiechi. 2009. "维护世界和平促进共同发展-纪念新中国外交60周年 [Protecting Peace Promoting Common Development-Commemorating 60 Years of Diplomacy for the People]." *Qiushi* 19: 22–4.

Yu, Xiaofeng, and Zhijiang Wei. 2015. 非传统安全概论 [*Non-Traditional Security*]. Beijing: Peking University Press.

Zhang, Lantao. 2004. "关于" 和平崛起 "与新安全观的理论思考 [Theoretical Thoughts about 'Peaceful Rise' and the New Security Concept]." *Journal of the University of International Relations* 5: 6–9.

Zhang, Lili. 2007. 外交决策 [*Diplomatic Decisions*]. Beijing: World Knowledge Press.

Zhang, Lili. 2011. "中国全力从利比亚大撤侨分析 [Analysis of China's Great Efforts in Evacuating Nationals from Libya]." *People's Daily*. April 21. Accessed September 28, 2017. http://cpc.people.com.cn/GB/68742/187710/191095/ 14448336.html.

Zhao, Suisheng. 1999. "China's Periphery Policy and Its Asian Neighbors." *Security Dialogue* 30 (3): 335–46.

2

The Chinese Armed Forces and the Challenges of Globalization

The Chinese military has been in the process of modernizing and transform-ing for more than thirty-five years. Military modernization, the last of Deng Xiaoping's Four Modernizations, was subordinate to national economic development throughout the 1980s and 1990s.[1] This ranking was a rational strategic decision for a nation starting from a low economic base during a period of relatively low external threat. The different ranking of the elements of the Four Modernizations was central to the thinking of paramount leader Deng Xiaoping, who justified a long-term approach to military moderniza-tion by announcing that the danger of a major world war was far off. In 1985, the Central Military Commission (CMC) of the Chinese Communist Party (CCP), led by Deng, declared that the most likely military contingency China faced was no longer an "early, major and nuclear war" as foreseen by Mao, but rather a "local, limited war." After a parenthesis of intense political training as commanded by Jiang Zemin's Five Statements in the aftermath of the events of Tiananmen Square, the Chinese leadership started to push the Chinese People's Liberation Army (PLA) to become a more professional and modern military.[2] Such a call from the top leadership found fertile ground within the PLA, which was deeply shocked by the spectacular defeat of the Iraqi armed forces—a heavily Soviet-based force like the PLA—at the hands of the United States in 1991, and was keen to close the gap with the best fighting force in the world (Ka 2005, 99–100; D. Cheng 2011).

It is against this background that the analysis of how the PLA, the main empowering audience of the Chinese top civilian leaders, reacted to the securi-tization of non-traditional security issues and started to look at the defense of China's interest frontiers begins. This chapter shows that the PLA's path

---

[1] In Chinese: 四个现代化 (Sì gè xiàndàihuà).
[2] Jiang's Five Statements (五句话, Wǔ jù huà) commanded the PLA to be "politically qualified and militarily competent, have a fine style of work, maintain strict discipline and be assured of adequate logistical support" (政治合格、军事过硬、作风优良、纪律严明、保障有力, Zhèngzhì hégé, jūnshì guòyìng, zuòfēng yōuliáng, jìlù yánmíng, bǎozhàng yǒulì).

Protecting China's Interests Overseas: Securitization and Foreign Policy. Andrea Ghiselli,
Oxford University Press (2021). © Andrea Ghiselli.
DOI: 10.1093/oso/9780198867395.001.0001

toward the inclusion of the protection of China's overseas interests among its missions was not a smooth one. This is because "the PLA obeys the Party, but the Party does not tell the PLA what to do" (Scobell 2017, 5). This chapter shows the tortuous process that began in the 1990s by dividing it into three parts. The first shows how deeply skeptical the PLA was until the late 2000s about the necessity of operating abroad, potentially cooperating with foreign militaries to tackle non-traditional security threats. During the short second period, until the early 2010s, signs of change started to appear in the thinking of some PLA scholars. Yet the majority still thought that it was up to the MFA and civilian institutions in general to deal with non-traditional security issues that could affect China's security environment. The situation changed drastically after 2011. Senior officers suddenly and fully accepted the idea that the PLA could and should turn into an organization capable of dealing with both traditional security threats and non-traditional security ones. Yet a strong state-centric approach remained a defining feature of the PLA's approach to missions other than war. Interested readers can find comments and information about the sources used in this chapter in Appendix 1.

New Era, Old Threats

Foreign militaries have always been an important source of inspiration for the PLA (see Figure 3). Indeed, Chinese scholars did not miss the main trends of the time regarding the changes that were taking place in other countries. Wang Zhenxi, a high-ranking military scholar who served as military attaché abroad and worked at both the Academy of Military Science (AMS) of the PLA and the PLA National Defense University (NDU), summarized how

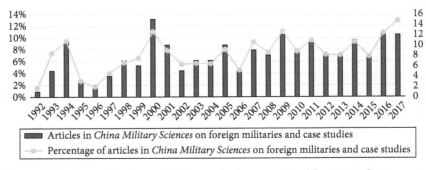

Figure 3 Studies on foreign militaries and other countries' foreign policy

Note: See Appendix 1 for a complete description of the categories used to classify the articles published in *China Military Science*.

Source: China Military Science, various years. Compiled by the author.

Western militaries were changing and being used as follows: on the one hand, a transition from quantity to quality was clearly taking place in the midst of decreasing defense budgets. Therefore, the potential military threat from the West, and the United States in particular, was not decreasing (Wang 1992). Rather, the lethality of Western armies was increasing. On the other hand, regional and international organizations were being set up and used to cement Western hegemony around the world (Wang 1994; Yu 1995). Wang and others admitted that the United Nations (UN) was beginning to play a larger role in international affairs again, especially through peacekeeping missions, but Western countries were using their financial, diplomatic, and military power to promote missions that were most beneficial to their own interests.

The growing frequency, the higher level of violence, and the broader scope of peacekeeping missions in those years were taken as worrying signs that further prevented the PLA from looking at peacekeeping operations as something different from a traditional threat to other countries' sovereignty (Li 1997). Therefore, China had to keep preparing to fight a local war, not only because that was still a highly probable event, but also because UN-led peacekeeping operations were not politically viable. Consequently, activities beyond traditional national defense found very limited space, even in the context of military diplomacy. In a 1994 study authored by the then Director of the former General Staff Department's Foreign Affairs Bureau, Fu Jiaping (1994), the PLA's engagement with foreign forces was limited to dialogue and exchanges.[3] Although China had been participating in UN-led missions since late 1989, peacekeeping simply was not mentioned.

Skepticism turned into outright refusal to see UN-led operations as something different from instruments of military interventionism when the war in Kosovo broke out in 1999. Notwithstanding the bombing of the Chinese embassy in Belgrade on May 7, 1999, PLA scholars were impressed by the NATO intervention. In particular, they studied its implications for international security and what that conflict meant in terms of trends in military affairs and in the conduct of war. While emphasizing how the forces of the former Federal Republic of Yugoslavia lost because of the loss of the initiative in battle and their technological inferiority (Huang 1999), many in the PLA saw the conflict in Kosovo as a lethal blow to the slowly recovering authority of the UN (Peng 1999; Ren 1999). As the West was accused of neo-interventionism, PLA Navy's Zhang Wei (1999) argued that the war in Kosovo and the

---

[3] The PLA General Staff Department was reorganized as the PLA Joint Staff Department of the CCP CMC in January 2016.

resulting weakness of international organizations were going to negatively affect the security environment in Asia. According to Zhang, future American unilateral moves in the Taiwan Strait and the Korean Peninsula were to be expected soon. No study of ethnic and racial tensions in the Balkan Peninsula and their importance in triggering the war was published in the PLA AMS's flagship journal *China Military Science*. Essentially, the war in Kosovo further convinced Chinese scholars that the use of military force remained strictly connected to hard politics.

PLA scholars were just as skeptical about cooperation with foreign navies within the UN framework as they were about peacekeeping. In a 1997 article penned by the Director of the China Naval Research, Liu Zhenhuan, the role of the navy was limited to deterring other countries involved in maritime disputes in the East and South China Seas from infringing on China's sovereignty, and to avoiding escalation in case of an armed conflict. This is because, while peacekeeping was seen as a potential threat, the UN Convention on the Law of the Sea was regarded as inefficient and weak. According to Liu, the convention does not provide effective conflict resolution mechanisms and, at the same time, risks expanding disputes by drawing in other countries, even if they have no reason to be involved in a dispute between China and the other claimants. Distrust of international organizations and international law ran deep in the PLA. Yu Zhengshan (1999, 2000), a professor from the Xi'an Institute of Political Science, summarized this idea by arguing that international laws and organizations were not useless, but simply too weak to constrain the great powers. His suggestion, therefore, was to keep on focusing on developing military muscle and, later, to learn how to make the best use of international law and organizations to defend China's interests. Finally, cooperation in Asia, including jointly tackling non-traditional security threats, was undermined by the perception that China's neighbors were modernizing their naval forces. Hence, the priority for the PLA Navy, and the PLA at large, was preparing for conventional military clashes (Fang 1999).

As the new millennium began, the situation did not change substantially: non-traditional security issues continued being either ignored or treated superficially. During that time, the scholars who expressed the clearest position on the role of the PLA in peacetime and non-traditional security were General Yao Youzhi (an important figure in the debate about military strategy and the man behind the 2001 edition of the *Science of Military Strategy*) and General Zhao Xide (2001). Those high-ranking officers saw no connection between the use of military force in peacetime and non-traditional security.

Deterrence and war preparation were the only focuses of the PLA's activities in times of peace. This point of view was extremely popular. For example, Major General Cao Bingjin (2000), the Deputy President of the PLA National University of Defense Technology, and two other researchers from the same institution argued that although non-traditional security issues were becoming a growing threat for China's national security, the PLA's main business was preparing for a war. It was, if necessary, up to other organs of the state to deal with non-traditional threats abroad. A similar position was put forward by Ren Xiangqun (2001), a colonel at the PLA AMS, and Ret. Major General Li Jijun (2004), a senior officer who served as head of the CCP CMC's general office and Deputy President of the PLA AMS. An even more extreme example of lack of interest in non-traditional security issues can be found in an interview with Hong Bing, the Director of the PLA AMS Department of Strategic Studies' 3rd Division (Xia 2001). Instead of focusing on what kind of policies were necessary to confront the rising threat of international terrorism in the aftermath of the 9/11 attack, the fight between terrorists and anti-terrorism forces was framed as a study of the efficacy of asymmetric warfare against more numerous and better-equipped forces, a hot topic for military debate in China.

While some officers were explicit about their not being keen on expanding the role of the PLA to taking care of non-traditional security threats in foreign policy, other officers simply ignored the issue. For example, during a lecture about the goals and trends of Chinese defense policy for senior officers at the PLA NDU in December 1999, the then Deputy Chief of the General Staff Department, Xiong Guangkai (2000), made no reference to non-traditional security and missions other than national defense. Similarly, reviewing the 2001 edition of the *Science of Military Strategy*, the President of the PLA AMS, Lieutenant General Ge Zhenfeng, and other senior PLA AMS scholars completely ignored non-traditional security among the issues touched upon in the text (Deng 2001).

Some scholars did show some interest in exploring the relationship between the PLA and non-traditional security in times of peace. However, their approach underscored a regional-level, mostly maritime engagement which was still greatly framed from a traditional security point of view. Two professors from the PLA Navy Command College offered a tentative analysis of what the navy could do in peacetime through naval diplomacy and, in a strong Mahanian tone, protect the sea lines of communication (Feng and Zhang 2001). While it is clear that the scope of the operations that they envisioned was essentially regional, with little or no details of what threats the

PLA Navy should defend against in peacetime, conventional deterrence against others was mentioned as the main goal of the proposed operations. Similarly, a Chinese officer commenting in the *PLA Daily* on the impact of the 9/11 attack wrote that international terrorism was on the rise and a threat to world peace. Yet, given the leading role of the People's Armed Police in domestic anti-terrorism, it is not clear from his words what the PLA was supposed to do beyond "strengthening theoretical research and summarizing domestic and foreign experiences" (Chen 2002). Such vagueness in defining the threats and the focus on the traditional side of the security issue was reflected in the writings of other military scholars who, implicitly most of the time, described dealing with non-traditional security threats as an excuse to receive more funding (Niu and Wu 2003; He, Zou, and Lai 2005; Wan 2005).

Very few officers called for China's national security to be redefined beyond traditional national defense. The clearest articulation of such an idea came from Major General Ma Ping (2005, 2006), who directly referred to securitization theory to argue that the dominating narrow interpretation of the concept of military security had to be expanded and adjusted to China's changing interests and level of development. Tian Bingren (2007), Political Commissar of the PLA Army Command College, and PLA NDU's Jin Yinan (2006) also wrote in favor of a more flexible role for the PLA at home and abroad in order to respond to growing non-traditional security threats to the authority of the party. None of them, however, offered clear examples of what those threats are. Major General Chen Yong (2006), the head of the PLA Army Command College, claimed in 2006 that China's security interests included territorial integrity as well as the interests of its citizens abroad. Yet training to fight, protecting the country's territorial integrity, fighting terrorists at home, and preserving social stability are the four main duties of the PLA that he listed. Only during an interview with the *PLA Daily* did Chen add that the PLA should keep on engaging in peacekeeping, disaster relief operations abroad, joint exercises with foreign armies, and international anti-terrorism cooperation (Zhang 2006). However, he framed these missions as not necessary to boosting China's own security; rather, they were to provide a more general contribution to regional peace. It is, thus, possible to see that Chinese military scholars ended up referring to traditional missions for the PLA, even when the intellectual will to consider an expansion of the role played by the PLA in foreign policy was there.

In the years that followed, PLA scholars did not deny that non-traditional security issues could turn into threats for national security, but they also believed that the PLA had little to do with them. According to two PLA AMS researchers, Wang Guifang (2006) and Kang Wuchao (2007), China's national security is based on the protection of a variety of interests. The "core interests" (sovereignty and territorial integrity) are the top priority, "development interests" (world order, energy supply, and fighting the "three evils") rank below them, and "normal interests" (cybersecurity, international crime, health security) remain at the bottom.[4] The lower the ranking, the smaller the role, and the less time the PLA should spend on protecting them. Indeed, Kang argues that achieving reunification with Taiwan and being able to deter and fight wars against other countries are the real tasks of the PLA. As Wang Guifang (2008) further elaborates in another article, the PLA cannot be deployed for every emergency, but only in extreme situations. After all, the PLA has much to worry about, even during peacetime, because no international law or agreement can stop states from competing and attacking each other (Zheng 2006; Zheng and Zheng 2009). Therefore, the PLA has to be ready. At most, the PLA's operations should be confined to China's neighborhood, either to build trust with Central Asian countries (Chen 2006) or to patrol the East and South China Seas and defend the country's interests there through peaceful and, if necessary, "non-peaceful" means (Tang, Ye, and Wang 2006).[5]

In summary, until the mid-2000s, Chinese officers were rather consistent in their skepticism about the expansion of their missions and the inclusion of non-traditional threats among the issues that they should take care of. Few scholars specified the geographical scope of the non-traditional security threats they mentioned in their articles, or whether the threats were within Chinese borders. Similarly, almost no one was able to give clear examples of those threats. Despite their growing relevance, they argued, it was up to civilian institutions to respond to them. At the same time, distrust of international law and organizations caused a sincere sense of frustration, if not anxiety. Therefore, non-war operations in peacetime were to be aimed at securing China's external environment through either military diplomacy or deterrence, especially in its neighborhood. Defending the Communist regime and the state against external, traditional threats was not simply the core of the PLA's duty: it was its only mission.

Signs of Change

"Traditional [security threats] decrease, non-traditional [security threats] grow," wrote the *PLA Daily* in late July 2008 (Che 2008). These words reflected

---

[4] In Chinese: 核心利益 (Héxīn lìyì), 发展利益 (Fāzhǎn lìyì), and 一般利益 (Yībān lìyì).
[5] In Chinese: 非和平手段 (Fēi hépíng shǒuduàn).

an important change in how the PLA looked at non-traditional security issues and, as shown in Chapter 6, at the concept of Military Operations Other Than War (MOOTW). Yet this change mainly took place in how the PLA saw its role within Chinese borders, not outside. Indeed, the *PLA Daily* published those words just a month after the Wenchuan earthquake caused the death of almost 87,000 people in China's Sichuan Province. The impact on how the PLA thought about its role in foreign policy was much more superficial. Non-traditional security issues did become something the PLA started being more aware of in foreign policy, but they were not considered as serious threats yet or, as David Lai called them (2012, 367), something that could be transformed into a "battle laboratory" to test new hardware or gain experience.

Nonetheless, the debate evolved in an interesting way. First of all, scholars belonging to the air force and especially the navy, which published in *China Military Science* in those years, clearly understood that non-traditional security issues offered important opportunities for their services. For example, Rear Admiral Tian Zhong (2008) and Xu Ping (2010), Director of the then PLA Navy Headquarters' General Office, listed a number of potential operations, from the fight against pirates and smugglers to international disaster relief and other overseas missions, in order to show the PLA Navy's ability to adapt to China's evolving security needs. Scholars from the Air Force Command College, too, argued that the PLA Air Force "must leave the gates of our country behind and walk towards the world outside" in order to counter a variety of threats ranging from terrorism to hostile hegemonic powers and natural disasters (Shang et al. 2010, 12).

However, it seems that most of them had little interest in the actual targets of those operations. As pointed out by Toshi Yoshihara and James R. Holmes (2010), Chinese sailors have been avid readers of Alfred Thayer Mahan's work on sea power since the early 2000s. His influence has already been mentioned above. However, it is at this point that Chinese navy officers fully embraced Mahan's grammar of sea power in their arguments in favor of a larger role for the PLA Navy (Lin 2010; Zuo 2010). According to them, China should build an ocean-faring naval force because it is sea power that transforms nations into great powers capable of shaping history (Wang 2010). PLA NDU scholars, too, supported this argument (Liang 2010; Zhang 2010). Non-traditional security issues, therefore, appear more like an excuse to operate abroad rather than something the officers of the PLA Navy considered a threat. This is not surprising. The "PLA Navy lobby" has played an important role in Chinese security policymaking since the late 1980s, advocating larger naval budgets and promoting policies that emphasize the national importance of Chinese maritime interests and naval capabilities (Yung 2015).

The officers in the PLA Ground Forces too started to discuss non-traditional security issues, albeit with more uncertainty than their colleagues in the navy, and mostly thinking about these new threats in domestic terms (Xu 2008; H. Zhang 2008; Fan and Lou 2009). Indeed, while they did not write where and how the PLA Ground Forces should join international operations, they were explicit in pointing out the priority of military modernization (G. Wang 2008; Zhang 2009). The contribution that carrying out missions abroad could give to the modernization of the PLA Ground Forces was a contested issue. Major General Du Nongyi (2007), the Director of the PLA International Relations Academy's Research Department, and another scholar from the same institution praised peacekeeping missions as opportunities to improve China's international reputation and make Chinese soldiers gain some much-needed experience. However, Zhan Yu (2007), President of the Shijiazhuang Mechanized Infantry Academy, and other officers argued that while activities like peacekeeping are important, they belong to military diplomacy. Others also wrote about missions abroad, especially peacekeeping and non-traditional security issues overseas as "platforms" for the PLA to boost China's soft power (Peng 2009; Tian, Chen, and Ding 2010).[6] Peacekeeping operations "are not simply military in nature; they are more political-diplomatic operations," declared the Director of the Peacekeeping Affairs Bureau of the Ministry of National Defense (Li and Gao 2011).

The superficiality of the interest of PLA scholars in overseas operations can be seen in the way they studied events in the Middle East and Africa, the center of gravity of Chinese antipiracy and peacekeeping operations. *China Military Science* rarely publishes articles on specific events, especially if they take place in faraway regions. This surely explains to a significant extent why no article on Africa has ever been published in it, and events in the Middle East too have received little attention. The peak of the attention on the Middle East was in 2003, when the journal published a collection of analyses of the American invasion of Iraq. As in the case of the 1999 Kosovo war, PLA scholars were more interested in the latest tactical and technological innovations displayed by Western armies and how Soviet-style forces were painfully defeated. Unsurprisingly, they wanted to learn lessons to increase the PLA's chances of survival in a potential war against the United States and its allies, rather than understand the dynamics of the region where those conflicts took place. *China Military Science* published an article on the

---

[6] In Chinese: 平台 (Píngtái).

Middle East again in late 2010. The author, a researcher in the PLA AMS Research Department, highlighted several trends in Middle Eastern security affairs, from the rising level of social instability to the persistent interest of Western countries in shaping the region, and the large quantity of modern weapons available to non-state actors (Zhu 2010). The article was submitted in July 2010, when the turmoil of the so-called Arab Spring and the subsequent massive evacuation of Chinese citizens from Libya were just a few months away. Yet it makes no reference to the potential risks for Chinese companies and nationals in the region.

The bloody revolutions and civil wars that began shortly after the publication of the article caught many in the West off guard; so, Chinese military scholars certainly cannot be blamed for not having seen them coming. What happened in those regions was not yet seen as potentially dangerous for China's security and, therefore, relevant to the PLA. It is, of course, possible that someone in the PLA was aware of the risks for Chinese overseas interests, and a single article can hardly represent the entire Chinese military machine. However, there is little doubt that the PLA had almost no interest in non-traditional security issues abroad. In keeping with this wrote Wang Guifang (2009), the PLA should not ignore threats to Chinese interests outside Asia, such as terrorism and political instability in other countries, but its core missions in foreign policy remained preventing Taiwan's independence and other countries from interfering in China's affairs. Of those writing in *China Military Science* in those years, the only one clearly in favor of a larger role for the PLA against non-traditional security threats to China's overseas interests was the then Senior Colonel Chen Zhou (2009). At the time, he probably represented a minority inside the PLA, but his foresight allowed him later to become one of the hundred most important and influential contributors to Chinese military thinking (Sina 2011).

Military Crises and Military Threats

In the early 2010s, support for expanding the role of the PLA in Chinese foreign policy strengthened decisively, especially due to a reassessment of the concept of national security and of non-traditional security as a fundamental part of it. Compared to previous years, the change was radical. The Libyan crisis was clearly at the root of it. References to the evacuation from the North African country in Chinese military publications are numerous. As the *PLA Daily* journalist Huang Kunlun wrote in 2011, the Libya evacuation signaled an irreversible expansion of the scope of China's interest frontiers beyond its territorial borders. That event must become a source of lessons for the PLA on how to protect China's overseas interests, wrote another commentator in the *China National Defense Daily* (Dong 2011). Likewise, Liu Jixian (2013), the former Vice President, PLA AMS, argued that the PLA must be able to deal with other crises abroad, like the 2011 Libya evacuation, when some 36,000 Chinese citizens were rescued.

Against this background, Wang Guanzhong (2013), then a PLA Deputy Chief of Staff, during the first session of the 18th National Party Congress of November 2012 emphatically endorsed the decision to transform the PLA into a more global force in order to protect Chinese citizens living abroad and the nation's development interests. Subsequently, the number of references to the protection of the lives and assets of Chinese citizens abroad as part of the missions of the PLA multiplied in Chinese military publications (Y. Liu 2013; Ren 2016). The main reason for this was the establishment of an intellectual connection between that mission and the survival of the ruling CCP. For example, the Director of the Army Building Research Office of the PLA AMS, Major General Zhang Qindong (2014), argued that everything threatening the supreme authority of the CCP, as well as China's military and economic interests and social stability must be included in the concept of military security. According to another scholar belonging to the Political Work Department of the PLA AMS, successful operations overseas against non-traditional security threats not only boost China's international image as a responsible power, but also boost support for the government and the PLA among Chinese citizens at home and abroad (Li 2014).

The change in the thinking of PLA scholars was not superficial. Rather, it seems that the Libyan incident prompted a profound reassessment of how the PLA understood China's national security and its role in guaranteeing it. According to Song Dexing (2010, 2012), the head of the International Strategy Research Centre of the Nanjing PLA Institute of International Relations, the world was entering a new "age of anxiety."[7] Non-state actors and other non-traditional security threats have become serious challenges to the security of the state. At the same time, while traditional interstate conflicts are economically and diplomatically too expensive, non-military crises can easily lead to inter-state conflicts. Therefore, it is possible and necessary to counter them militarily, if needed. Suddenly, the point of view of Chen Zhou, who had been promoted to the rank of Major General and Director of the Policy

---

[7] In Chinese: 焦虑的时代 (Jiāolǜ de shídài).

Research Center of the PLA AMS by then, became mainstream. Major General Cheng Jiangguo (2012) of the PLA Nanjing Political College, and the Director of the China Foundation for International and Strategic Studies, Zhang Tuosheng (2011), expressed this position clearly in articles published in *China Military Science*. They argued that the distinction between traditional and non-traditional security had become an impediment to the formulation of an effective defense strategy and the development of the PLA.

Consequently, international deployments were not only useful for improving China's international image, as had been the case in the past (L. Liu 2012), but also necessary for responding to security crises. Although traditional security naturally remains more important than non-traditional security (Fu, Wei, and Wang 2012), a series of articles on Hu Jintao's military thinking identified the occurrence of "sudden emergencies" as the link between traditional and non-traditional security in the eyes of the PLA (Guo 2012; Li 2012).[8] For example, large-scale environmental crises, such as the scarcity of water, can be at the heart of interstate wars (Du 2015). Other scholars, like the Director of the PLA NDU Research Department Qin Tian (2013) and the PLA International Relations Academy's Liu Chaoxing (2012), reformulated this idea by saying that in today's world it is important to consider both "military crises" caused by non-military issues and traditional "military threats" from other states.[9]

Caution is always necessary in the deployment of the PLA abroad, but the armed forces must be prepared to face all possible dangers. While traditional crises are mostly expected in Asia (Wu and Wang 2012), expanding the deployments of troops outside the region was beginning to be seriously considered as something the PLA had to be prepared to do. Consequently, consensus on the importance of a military presence overseas was reached quickly. Interestingly, maybe to further justify the support for the change of mind that was taking place, a report prepared by a research group of the Strategic Research Department of the PLA AMS (2016) argued that many other great powers in the past used the military to protect their interests abroad during their rise. Thus, the issue for China was not whether or not to do the same, but how to do it without scaring other countries. The level of interest in exploring this new path was enough to make not only scholars from the PLA NDU Logistic and Equipment Research Center (Chen and Zhang 2012), but also the then CCP CMC member and leader of the PLA General Logistics

---

[8] In Chinese: 突发事件 (Tú fā shìjiàn).
[9] In Chinese: 军事危险 (Jūnshì wéixiǎn) and 军事威胁 (Jūnshì wēixié).

Department, Zhao Keshi (2013), write in favor of exploring possible ways to establish military outposts overseas. Despite the worsening of the security environment in Asia in those years caused by the unresolved maritime disputes and growing American military presence in the region, the Deputy Director of the PLA Strategic Planning Department proposed the acceleration of the rebalancing process within the armed forces in order to make the PLA Navy and PLA Air Force truly global forces (Zhang 2014). They had to be capable of winning wars and defending China's overseas interests. According to Ma Xiaotian (2015), the then PLA Air Force Commander and CCP CMC member, the Chinese air force must become capable of long-range strikes, space warfare, and supporting the PLA in peacetime through strategic airlift capabilities. Another heavyweight in the Chinese military world, the CCP CMC member and Minister of Defense Chang Wanquan (2014) stated his support for pushing the internationalization of the PLA's operations with a clear focus on non-traditional security while also building up defenses in Asia. Although some such as the PLA NDU's Major General Yang Yi (2012) called for limiting military engagement abroad and a very traditional understanding of security, such strong support from the top probably brought the debate on the role of the PLA with regard to non-traditional security and China's foreign policy to an end.

Conclusion

Chapter 1 showed that the Libyan incident had a deep impact on the thinking of Chinese civilian leaders but they were already open to adding the protection of Chinese interest frontiers to the existing duties of the PLA. In comparison, this chapter has shown that the PLA's march towards the inclusion of the protection of China's interest frontiers among its missions was not so linear and smooth. If one considers how long it took for the PLA to fully toe the line, it is evident that the civilian leadership, especially the Hu administration, failed at least to some extent to convince the military of the necessity of including in their remit countering non-traditional security threats overseas. The PLA, like other military bodies around the world (Feaver and Gelpi 2004), has always held a traditional, state-centric approach to security. Even when Chinese military scholars included the security of ordinary citizens among the reasons for the PLA's overseas operations, they did so by linking the successful neutralization of non-traditional threats to them with the support and legitimacy of the regime. The inclusion of non-traditional missions in the duties of the PLA did not take place by eliminating the conceptual barrier between traditional and non-traditional security threats, as the civilian leadership did. Rather, non-traditional missions were accepted largely because their ultimate goal was "traditionalized" by building a conceptual bridge—the relationship between "military threats" and "military crises"—between non-traditional threats and the much more classic survival of the state and the regime. Therefore, the PLA's approach to overseas operations and the protection of China's interests overseas was essentially a crisis-driven one. The radical impact of the events in Libya of early 2011 is clear evidence of this.

While they were all similar in their state-centric approach to security, the various military services probably carried out different cost–benefit analyses regarding operating overseas. Not surprisingly, officers from the navy were the most interested in discussing the expansion of PLA duties during peacetime. After all, the PLA Navy has been trying to grow into a blue-water force for years now, an ambition actively cultivated by promoting a strong "naval culture."[10] Two articles penned by Tong Haibin (2012), the then Director of the Navy Command College's Political Work Department, and Duan Zhaoxian (2013), Deputy Chief of the PLA Navy Staff, are exemplary. According to them, a global and powerful naval force is the true symbol of a country's power. It was time for the navy to think beyond the waters surrounding China and, consequently, to convince the leadership to prioritize investment in the navy. Promoting the expansion of missions that the PLA Navy can perform was the next natural step. As highlighted above, navy officers became very vocal about this issue, especially in the late 2000s, when the navy had already started to deploy task forces for the Gulf of Aden, rather than earlier, despite the fact that Hu Jintao promoted commanders of the PLA Navy and Air Force to become members of the CCP CMC in 2004.

From this point of view, it is also possible to see that the PLA Navy probably was receptive to the idea of "development interests" to a significant extent because of its own organizational interests. Similarly, some officers belonging to the PLA Ground Forces made the argument in the mid-2000s that their service could contribute to neutralizing unspecified non-traditional security threats, but they were most likely trying to defend the still-dominant position of their service within the PLA. History and pride also played an important, albeit not critical role in the argument made by PLA intellectuals. The study of historical precedents set by other great powers has always been one of the favorite topics of Chinese scholars, both civilian and military. Given China's pride as one of the oldest still-existing civilizations, and its

---

[10] In Chinese: 海军文化 (Hǎijūn wénhuà).

vision of its progress in making a comeback on the stage of history, it is not surprising that Chinese military scholars used a thinly veiled "manifest destiny" argument in their support for building an ocean-faring naval force, or swiftly changing their position and supporting the establishment of some sort of military presence abroad.

It is important to note that almost none of the officers mentioned here paid much attention to the idea that overseas operations could provide opportunities to test new equipment and allow soldiers to gain experience. This might be particularly surprising if one considers that the further back one goes, the wider the gap between Chinese and Western forces was. However, the significant gap might actually be one of the reasons for the PLA's lack of interest in overseas deployments related to non-traditional security. Indeed, while for some cooperation means reducing the costs associated with resolving a common problem and improving mutual trust through openness, the situation changes radically if, as dictated by interstate conflict-centered Chinese strategic culture (Ghiselli 2018), international law and organizations are seen as tools that states use against each other. The discussion among PLA officers on MOOTW that will be analyzed in Chapter 6 further confirms this approach. Therefore, it would not be surprising if many thought that the risks from supporting those institutions far outweighed the benefits that the PLA might have enjoyed in terms of experience. This belief was surely strengthened by the Kosovo War and the American invasion of Iraq. Moreover, as argued in Chapter 6, many in the PLA were aware that their armed forces lacked sufficient skilled officers to join international efforts such as UN peacekeeping. Some could have even thought that showing those deficiencies to foreign militaries might have undermined Chinese security. Therefore, the weaker the PLA perceived itself, the less forthcoming it would have been in participating in missions abroad to counter non-traditional security threats. On the other hand as the results of modernization began to appear, not only could the PLA have become more comfortable making its presence abroad more visible as a way of showing its newly found strength, but it might also have started to appreciate the opportunities to test its new equipment, thereby also becoming gradually more receptive to the securitization act initiated by the civilian leadership.

Bibliography

Cao, Bingjin, Decai Li, and Zili Zhu. 2000. "关于国家安全战略的几点思考 [Views on National Security Strategy]." *China Military Science* 6: 111–16.

Chang, Wanquan. 2014. "亚太安全与中国国防建设 [Asia-Pacific Security and China's National Defense Building]." *China Military Science* 6: 1–3.

Che, Hua. 2008. "世界新军事变革加速战争形态演进 [The New Revolution in Military Affairs Accelerates the Evolution of War]." *People's Liberation Army Daily*.

Chen, Yigong, and Zonghui Zhang. 2012. "国际军事合作后勤初探 [An Exploration of International Military Cooperative Logistics]." *China Military Science* 6: 101–8.

Chen, Yong. 2006. "全球化背景下的军队历史使命 [Army Historic Mission on the Background of Globalization]." *China Military Science* 1: 15–21.

Chen, Yutian. 2002. "把反恐怖斗争纳入军队的职责范围 [Adding Antiterrorism to the Missions of the Armed Forces]." *People's Liberation Army Daily*, March 23.

Chen, Zhou. 2009. "试论新形势下中国防御性国防政策的发展 [On the Development of China's National Defense]." *China Military Science* 6: 63–71.

Cheng, Dean. 2011. "Chinese Lessons from the Gulf Wars." In Andrew Scobell, David Lai, and Roy Kamphausen (eds), *Chinese Lessons from Other People's Wars*, 153–200. Carlisle, PA: Strategic Studies Institute United States Army.

Cheng, Jianguo. 2012. "开放与包容一个具有重要时代价值的战略理念 [Openness and Tolerance: A Strategic Concept with Important Values of the Times]." *China Military Science* 1: 49–57.

Deng, Hui, ed. 2001. "构建中国军事战略管理新体系 [Constructing a New System of Chinese Military Strategic Theory]." *China Military Science* 6: 1–5.

Dong, Wentao. 2011. "'利比亚撤离行动对国防动员的启示 [The Important Lesson from the Evacuation of Chinese Nationals from Libya for the National Defense Staff in the New Century]." *China National Defense Daily* 5: 31–2.

Du, Chao. 2015. "未来战争与环境安全问题探析 [An Exploration of Future Warfare and Environmental Security Issues]." *China Military Science* 4: 84–9.

Du, Nongyi, and Tao Wang. 2007. "维护外交新世纪新阶段军事外交的旅律 [Peacekeeping Diplomacy: Main Theme of Military Diplomacy in the New Phase of the New Century]." *China Military Science* 4: 106–13.

Duan, Zhaoxian. 2013. "论建设海洋强国的战略目标 [On Strategic Objectives for Building China into a Maritime Power]." *China Military Science* 3: 12–15.

Fan, Zhenjiang, and Yaoliang Lou. 2009. "新世纪新阶段军事战略指导研究 [A Study of Military Strategic Guidance in the New Period in the New Century]." *China Military Science* 3: 36–44.

Fang, Yonggang. 1999. "论中国海军对外军交往 [On Military Contacts of the PLA Navy with Foreign Armies]." *China Military Science* 1: 123–6.

Feaver, Peter D., and Christopher Gelpi. 2004. *Choosing Your Battles: American Civil-Military Relations and the Use of Force*. Princeton, NJ: Princeton University Press.

Feng, Liang, and Xiaolin Zhang. 2001. "论和平时期海军的战略使用 [The Strategic Application of the Navy in Peacetime]." *China Military Science* 3: 77–84.

Fu, Guangming, Xiaohui Wei, and Xi Wang. 2012. "胡锦涛关于军队参与处置国家重大突发事件重要论述研究 [A Study of Hu Jintao's Important Expositions on Participation of the Armed Forces in Handling Serious Emergencies]." *China Military Science* 5: 36–45.

Fu, Jiaping. 1994. "轮和平与发展形势下的国防外交 [On Foreign Affairs in National Defense in the Situation of Peace and Development]." *China Military Science* 4: 55–60.

Ghiselli, Andrea. 2018. "Revising China's Strategic Culture: Contemporary Cherry-Picking of Ancient Strategic Thought." *China Quarterly* 233: 166–85.

Guo, Jingyan. 2012. "胡锦涛关于形势下国防和军队建设重要论述的时代特色 [Characteristics of the Time in Hu Jintao's Important Expositions on National Defense Building under the New Situation]." *China Military Science* 5: 1–9.

He, Jiacheng, Fang Zou, and Zhijun Lai. 2005. "国际军事安全形势及我国的国防经济发展战略 [Situation of International Military Safety and the Development Strategy of China National Defense Economy]." *Military Economic Research* 1: 10–14.

Huang, Jialun. 1999. "科索沃战争的启示 [Inspirations from the Kosovo War]." *China Military Science* 4: 116–22.

Jin, Yinan. 2006. "新安全观下的中国战略 [China's Strategy within the Framework of the New Security Concept]." *Bridge of Century* 1: 80–3.

Ka, Po Ng. 2005. *Interpreting China's Military Power*. New York: Frank Cass.

Kang, Wuchao. 2007. "试析国家利益与战略方向 [Analysis of National Interests and Strategic Orientation]." *China Military Science* 2: 84–90.

Lai, David. 2012. "The Agony of Learning: The PLA's Transformation in Military Affairs." In Roy Kamphausen, David Lai, and Trevis Tanner (eds), *Learning by Doing: The PLA Trains at Home and Abroad*, 337–84. Carlisle, PA: Strategic Studies Institute United States Army.

Li, Jijun. 2004. "全球化时代的中国国家安全思考 [Reflection on China's National Security in the Era of Globalization]." *China Military Science* 2: 38–43.

Li, Qinggong. 1997. "试论冷战后世界军事格局的演变 [Views on the Evolution of the Post-Cold War World Military Pattern]." *China Military Science* 1: 112–9.

Li, Quan. 2012. "胡锦涛关于树立综合安全关重要论述研究 [A Study of Hu Jintao's Important Expositions on Establishing Comprehensive Security Concepts]." *China Military Science* 5: 26–35.

Li, Xueyong, and Jiquan Gao. 2011. "一次维和处突的成功探索—访国防部维和事务办公室负责人 [A Successful Exploration of Peacekeeping—Interview with the Director of the Peacekeeping Affairs Bureau of the Ministry of National Defense]." *People's Liberation Army Daily*, September 17.

Li, Zufa. 2014. "试论军事软实力 [A Study of Military Soft Power]." *China Military Science* 1: 70–7.

Liang, Fang. 2010. "海洋强国争夺和控制海上战略通道规律探析 [An Analysis of the Laws of Sea Power Contending for and Controlling Strategic Maritime Passages]." *China Military Science* 5: 135–42.

Lin, Dong. 2010. "制濒海权 控制海土的地缘制权 [Command of the Waters along the Coast: Geographical Command of Waters Territory]." *China Military Science* 5: 143–9.

Liu, Chaoxing. 2012. "中国参与国际军事安全机制刍议 [A Discussion of China's Participation in International Military Security Mechanism]." *Journal of Jiangnan Social University* 14 (1): 11–14.

Liu, Jixian. 2013. "深化对强军目标的认识与实践 [Deepen the Understanding of the Objectives of Strengthening the Military and Its Practices]." *China Military Science* 4: 11–20.

Liu, Linzhi. 2012. "对推进中国军事公共外交的基点思考 [Views on Promoting Military Public Diplomacy in China]." *China Military Science* 5: 104–13.

Liu, Yuejun. 2013. "论和平时期军事力量的运用 [On the Employment of Military Force in Peacetime]." *China Military Science* 5: 42–51.

Ma, Ping. 2005. "国家利益与军事安全 [National Interests and Military Security]." *China Military Science* 6: 61–72.

Ma, Ping. 2006. "军事安全与国家利益 [Talking about Military Security and National Interests]." *National Defense* 6: 16–18.

Ma, Xiaotian. 2015. "论建设空天一体,攻防兼备的强大人民空军 [On Building a Powerful People's Air Force with Integrated Airspace Capabilities and Capable of Both Defenses and Offenses]." *China Military Science* 3: 1–5.

Niu, Li, and Jifeng Wu. 2003. "试论21世纪中国军事战新观念 [On the New Concepts of Chinese Military Strategy in the 21st Century]." *China Military Science* 2: 85–90.

Peng, Guanqian. 1999. "科素沃战争与当代国际战略格局 新干涉主义 本刊记者方军事科学研究人员 [Kosovo War and International Strategic Pattern Today an Analysis of New Interventionism—Interviews with the AMS Researchers]." *China Military Science* 2: 15–17.

Peng, Yuhua. 2009. "善用军事软实力 [Making Good Use of Military Soft Power]." *People's Liberation Army Daily*, October 22.

PLA AMS Strategic Research Department. 2016. "军事因素与大国崛起—主要从世界近现代史角度的研究 [Military Factor and the Rise of Big Powers—From a Perspective of Modern and Contemporary History]." *China Military Science* 1: 71–8.

Qin, Tian. 2013. "中国和平发展进程中的军事阿全分析及对策思考 [An Analysis of and Countermeasures for China's Military Security in the Process of Peaceful Development]." *China Military Science* 2: 57–64.

Ren, Xiangqun. 1999. "从冷战工具到世界宪兵—北约50年评说 [From a 'Cold War Tool' to 'World Military Police'—A Review of NATO in the Past 50 Years]." *China Military Science* 2: 26–30.

Ren, Xiangqun. 2001. "国际战略发展趋势对中国安全的影响 [The Implications of the Trends of International Strategic Development for the Security of China]." *China Military Science* 6: 17–21.

Ren, Zhiqiang. 2016. "我国武装力量整体功能优化问题研究 [A Study on the Optimization of Overall Capabilities of China's Armed Forces]." *China Military Science* 6: 47–56.

Scobell, Andrew. 2017. "Civil-Military 'Rules of the Game' on the Eve of China's 19th Party Congress." *The National Bureau of Asian Research.* October 11. Accessed February 17, 2018. https://www.nbr.org/publication/civil-military-rules-of-the-game-on-the-eve-of-chinas-19th-party-congress/.

Shang, Jinsuo, Zhen Li, Liguang Li, and Pingping Wang. 2010. "新世纪新阶段人民空军建设发展的科学理论指南 [A Scientific Theoretical Guide for the Development of the People's Air Force in the New Stage in the New Century]." *China Military Science* 6: 9–16.

Sina. 2011. "中央军委给陈舟记一等功表彰其国防科研成果 [The Central Military Commission Gave Chen Zhou a First-Class Commendation for His National Defense Scientific Research Achievements]." *Sina Military.* October 22. Accessed January 3, 2018. http://mil.news.sina.com.cn/2011-10-22/0336670359.html.

Song, Dexing. 2010. "国际关系中的力量运用-侧重于中国方面的分析 [Use of Force in International Relations—Analysis of the Chinese Case]." *Foreign Affairs Review* 6: 66–75.

Song, Dexing. 2012. "试论后冷战时代战略制定的诺干趋向 [Trends in Establishing Strategies in the Post-Cold War Era]." *China Military Science* 2: 60–6.

Tang, Fuquan, Xinrong Ye, and Daowei Wang. 2006. "中国海洋维权战略初探 [On the Strategy of Defending Chinese Sea Rights]." *China Military Science* 6: 56–67.

Tian, Xiang, Yongqiang Chen, and Jun Ding. 2010. "军事软实力视野下我军形象力建设探析 [An Analysis of PLA's Image-Building from the Perspective of Military Soft Power]." *China Military Science* 4: 116–24.

Tian, Zhong. 2008. "海军非战争军事行动的特点,类型及能力建设 [Characteristics, Categories and Capability Development of Naval Non-War Military Operations]." *China Military Science* 3: 25–30.

Tien, Bingren. 2007. "新世纪新阶段我军历史使命的科学拓展 [Scientific Expansion of the PLA Historic Missions in the New Phase in the New Century]." *China Military Science* 5: 21–7.

Tong, Haibin. 2012. "海军文化建设的价值理念和精神追求 [Values and Morals for Development of Naval Culture]." *China Military Science* 6: 17–25.

Wan, Dongcheng. 2005. "On Coordinated Development of China's National Defense and Economic Construction in the Current Stage." *China Military Science* 3: 96–104.

Wang, Guanzhong. 2013. "努力建设与我国国际地位相移,与国家安全和发展利益相适应的巩固国防和强大军队 [Strive to Build Strong National Defense and Powerful Armed Forces Commensurate with China's International Standing, National Security, and Development Interests]." *China Military Science* 1: 3–10.

Wang, Guifang. 2006. "国家利益与中国安全战略选择 [National Interests and Choices of China Security Strategies]." *China Military Science* 1: 76–83.

Wang, Guifang. 2008. "非传统安全与国家安全战略 [Non-Traditional Security and State Security Strategy]." *China Military Science* 1: 120–6.

Wang, Guifang. 2009. "试析中国安全利益发展的基本特征与现实途径 [An Analysis of the Basic Features of and Approaches to the Development of China's Security Interests]." *China Military Science* 6: 21–5.

Wang, Guosheng. 2008. "对我军历史使命的认识与思考 [Understanding and Thinking of the PLA Historical Missions]." *China Military Science* 5: 63–70.

Wang, Jinghai. 2010. "海洋强国争夺和控制海上战酪通道规律探析 [An Analysis of the Laws of Sea Power Contending for and Controlling Strategic Maritime Passageways]." *China Military Science* 5: 135–42.

Wang, Zhenxi. 1992. "外军质量建设面面观 [A Look at the Promotion of Quality in Foreign Militaries]." *China Military Science* 2: 44–54.

Wang, Zhenxi. 1994. "冷战后动荡继续 条横期沉浮未卜 [After the Cold War Chaos Continues Adjusting to the Unpredictable Ups and Downs]." *China Military Science* 1: 89–92.

Wu, Qingli, and Pengfei Wang. 2012. "试论根据国家未来安全需求建设军事力量体系 [On the Building of a Military Force Structure in Accordance with Future National Needs]." *China Military Science* 5: 73–8.

Xia, Zhengnan (ed.) 2001. "理性认识 恐怖战 与 反恐怖战 [A Rationalist Understanding of Terrorist War and Anti-Terrorism War]." *China Military Science* 6: 138–40.

Xiong, Guangkai. 2000. "中国的国防政策 [China's National Defense Policy]." *China Military Science* 5: 17–22.

Xu, Fenlin. 2008. "在军队建设中牢固树立安全发展历年 [Consolidating the Idea of Security Development in Army Building—Understanding on Studying Hujintao's Important Idea of Security Development]." *China Military Science* 1: 36–42.

Xu, Ping. 2010. "胡锦涛关于完成多样化军事任务战略思想研探 [A Tentative Analysis of Hu Jintao's Strategic Thinking on Accomplishing Diversified Military Tasks]." *China Military Science* 2: 85–92.

Yang, Yi. 2012. "国家战略能力的建设与运用 [Construction and Use of National Strategic Capabilities]." *Expanding Horizons* 3: 31–5.

Yao, Youzhi, and Xide Zhao. 2001. "战略的泛化，守恒与发展 — 夜谈树立科学的战略观 [The Generalization, Conservation, and Development of 'Strategy']." *China Military Science* 4: 120–7.

Yoshihara, Toshi, and James R. Holmes. 2010. *Red Star over the Pacific: China's Rise and the Challenge to U.S. Maritime Strategy.* Annapolis, MD: Naval Institute Press.

Yu, Qifen. 1995. "90年代国际军事形势的回顾与展望 [Review and Prospects of International Military Trends in the 1990s]." *China Military Science* 1: 50–8.

Yu, Zhengshan. 1999. "国际法于当代归家安全 [The Law of Nations and National Security in the Contemporary Era]." *China Military Science* 3: 58–65.

Yu, Zhengshan. 2000. "在军事斗争中运用国际法的几点探讨 [Views on Applying International Law to Military Struggle]." *China Military Science* 4: 109–14.

Yung, Christopher D. 2015. "The PLA Navy Lobby and Its Influence over China's Maritime Sovereignty Policies." In Phillip C. Saunders and Andrew Scobell (eds), *PLA Influence on China's National Security Policymaking*, 274–99. Stanford, CA: Stanford University Press.

Zhan, Yu. 2007. "关于党的国防和军队建设科学发展理论 [A Study on Scientific Development Theory of the Party's Defense and Army Building]." *China Military Science* 5: 10–20.

Zhang, Hui. 2008. "国际恐怖主义威胁与军队的新职责 [International Terrorist Threat and New Missions of the Armed Forces]." *China Military Science* 3: 14–24.

Zhang, Ming. 2014. "对新形势下几个战略问题的思考 [Reflections on Several Strategic Issues in the New Situation]." *China Military Science* 2: 17–23.

Zhang, Qindong. 2014. "科学防范重大安全文体的理性思考 [Rational Consideration on Scientifically Preventing Serious Security Incidents]." *China Military Science* 2: 82–90.

Zhang, Shiping. 2010. "和平发展的中国呼唤海权 [Peacefully Developing China Appeals for Sea Power—Rational Thinking on China's Sea Power]." *China Military Science* 3: 109–15.

Zhang, Shiquan. 2009. "我军性质，宗旨和职能思想的创新发展 [Creative Development of the Thought of the Nature, Tenets and Functions of the PLA]." *China Military Science* 5: 100–13.

Zhang, Tuosheng. 2011. "中国国际军事安全危机行为研究 [On China's Behavior in Dealing with International Military Security Crises]." *World Economics and Politics* 4: 103–21.

Zhang, Wei. 1999. "从科索沃危机的处理看过健全机制的走向及其影响 科索沃战争于国际形势的变化趋势 [Views of the Trend and Influence of the International Security Mechanism for the Settlement of the Crisis of the Kosovo War]." *China Military Science* 3: 76–80.

Zhang, Xinyang. 2006. "提高维护国家利益的战略能力 [Boosting the Capablities to Protect National Interests]." *People's Liberation Army Daily*, March 13.

Zhao, Keshi. 2013. "新形势下加快我军后勤现代化的战略思考 [Strategic Thoughts on Accelerating Modernization of PLA Logistics in the New Situation]." *China Military Science* 4: 1–10.

Zheng, Guoliang. 2006. "新作战空间军事对抗的国际法问题研究 [The Issue of Internaional Law in the New Operational Dimension]." *China Military Science* 6: 101–6.

Zheng, Guoliang, and Ming Zheng. 2009. "网络战的国际法问题研究 [A Study of Network Warfare in Terms of International Law]." *China Military Science* 5: 130–5.

Zhu, Xiaoli. 2010. "试析中东地区形势的未来发展 [An Analysis of the Future Development of the Situation in the Middle East Region]." *China Military Science* 5: 129–34.

Zuo, Liping. 2010. "关于维护国家海洋利益发展的战略思考 [Strategic Thinking on Safeguarding the Development of National Maritime Interests]." *China Military Science* 3: 8–14.

3
From Deng's Reforms to Libya

As Kerry Brown (2008, 30–1) pointed out, if one looks at China's position in the world economy today and compares it with that of the eighteenth century, one will notice both one significant similarity and one crucial difference. On the one hand, just as it was before its painful encounter with the West, China is today once again the largest holder of foreign currency reserves in the world. Two hundred years ago, China enjoyed an important surplus in trade with the West. It was the "ultimate sink" of the world's money, as most of the silver mined in South America ended up in the Chinese imperial coffers (Frank 1998).[1] According to some accounts, the surge in Ming China's demand for silver, resulting from the demise of paper money in the fifteenth century, and its decrease around 1640, played a significant role in the rise and fall of the Spanish Empire (Flynn and Giráldez 1996). Today, despite the decline experienced in recent years (Figure 4), China's reserves of foreign currency give it an almost equally formidable influence over the fortunes of the world economy. On the other hand, in the words of Ching Kwan Lee (2017, 1–30), there is "a specter haunting the world—the specter of 'global China.'" After three decades of sustained growth, overcapacity, falling rates of profit, underconsumption, shrinking demand from traditional export markets, and scarcity of strategic resources are major imbalances that have compelled Chinese corporations, workers, and entrepreneurs to go abroad in search of new opportunities. According to the *World Investment Report* published by the Investment and Enterprise Division of the United Nations Conference on Trade and Development (2018), as of 2017, China was the world's third-largest investor. The Chinese economic and human footprint has never been so great outside the country's territorial borders.

China's interest frontiers exist because its economy went global. They exist because Chinese capital and companies went to some of the most unstable regions of the world, such as North Africa and the Middle East. The focus of this

---

[1] For a fascinating and compelling analysis of the causes and effects of that situation, the curious reader can read Giovanni Arrighi's *Adam Smith in Beijing* (2007).

Protecting China's Interests Overseas: Securitization and Foreign Policy. Andrea Ghiselli, Oxford University Press (2021). © Andrea Ghiselli.
DOI: 10.1093/oso/9780198867395.001.0001

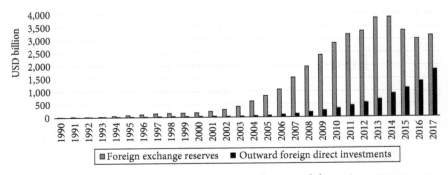

Figure 4 Chinese foreign exchange reserves and outward direct investments
Source: PRC State Administration of Foreign Exchange and PRC Ministry of Commerce. Compiled by the author.

chapter is to show that the growth of China's interests in dangerous parts of the world is, as mentioned at the beginning of Chapter 1, one of the outcomes of Deng's decision to make China open its doors to the world. It is from there that Chinese capital, companies, and workers flowed out, supported by the continuously strong political push from the leaders in Zhongnanhai. It seemingly was a disorderly process, as the system meant to oversee it grew fragmented and, interestingly, even limited its own power to control it. Hence, the first section of the chapter tracks the evolution of the policies enacted by the Chinese government to make Chinese enterprises go overseas, and the consequent expansion of China's human and economic presence abroad. The second section focuses on the shape that China's interest frontiers took in the Middle East and North Africa. It shows both how Chinese interests grew and diversified and where they coalesced. It does so by looking at five different indicators: trade and shipping, energy, investments, contracts signed by Chinese companies, and Chinese workers present in the countries taken into consideration. The third section demonstrates how the trends outlined in the previous two sections combined and clashed in 2011 in Libya. It also shows how they did not affect each other, thereby laying the foundations for continuous pressure on China's interest frontiers.

To Go Global

If one had to identify the precise moment the process that led to the emergence of Chinese interest frontiers started, one would say that everything began on August 13, 1979. That day, the State Council indicated for the first time that Chinese capital could be used to set up companies abroad. Regardless of the size of the investment, all applications had to be approved by the State Council. Moreover, only state-owned enterprises (SOEs), along with provincial and municipal economic and technological cooperation enterprises under the State Economic and Trade Commission (now part of the National Development and Reform Commission, or NDRC), were allowed to invest abroad. However, the real policy work to lay the foundations for Chinese overseas investments took place between 1982 and 1985. On the one hand, the Ministry of Foreign Trade merged with the Ministry of Foreign Economic Liaison, the State Import and Export Regulation Commission, and the State Foreign Investment Regulation Commission, and became the Ministry of Foreign Economic Relations and Trade in early 1982. It had the task of overseeing the approval process of Chinese companies' investments overseas. The newly created institution moved quickly to issue the Notice on the Authorization and Principle of the Approval of the Establishment of Non-Commercial Overseas Enterprises and the Trial Regulation on the Approval Procedure and Administration of Establishing Non-Commercial Overseas Enterprises, in 1984 and 1985, respectively.

The passage from the 1980s to the 1990s was not smooth. Chinese overseas direct investments (ODI) were starting to pick up but the lack of experience and supervision led to investments in unfeasible projects and key personnel escaping abroad with the money. These failures happened against the background of growing economic instability due to the overheating of the economy and, more seriously, the tragic events of Tiananmen Square, which threatened to close down the Chinese economy that Deng had opened up a decade earlier. However, Deng's final enterprise, the famous Southern Tour of 1992, succeeded in putting China back on course for deeper integration with the world economy.

The process of examination and approval for overseas investments was reformed too. The Ministry of Foreign Economic Relations and Trade was renamed the Ministry of Foreign Trade and Economic Cooperation in 1993 and put in charge of the administration of overseas enterprises and ODI-related policies with the help of the State Planning Commission, which was responsible for the feasibility studies of proposed ODI. The same year, the Ministry of Foreign Trade and Economic Cooperation was also authorized to establish its own offices in embassies and consulates to support Chinese companies abroad (PRC MOFCOM 1993). At the same time, in 1988, the State Council established the State-Owned Assets Management Bureau to coordinate the management of all state-owned assets. That agency operated under the guidance of the Ministry of Finance.

In 1990, the State Council (2016) issued the Notice on Strengthening the Management of State-Owned Assets. In this notice, the principle of state-owned asset management was described as "unified guidance, decentralized management," thereby recognizing the SOEs' increased management autonomy within the boundaries set by the national economic strategy.[2] These were the first two steps towards the creation of the State-Owned Assets Supervision and Administration Commission (SASAC). The financial position of SOEs was further strengthened by the dividend policy enacted by central government. Before 1993, SOEs were required to turn over dividends to the state. However, the tax reform in 1994 removed this dividend payment requirement and SOEs were only required to pay taxes to the state.

Over the next decade, many policies and guidelines were issued in order to push state offices to think of the firms under their jurisdiction as assets to be managed according to market principles. The central government also began to emphasize the notion of listing large SOEs on foreign stock exchange markets. In 1998, a backlash against what some saw as a "selling out" led the then Premier, Zhu Rongji, to order the merger of the State-Owned Asset Management Bureau with the Finance Ministry System. Fifteen industrial ministries were abolished, a move leading to the creation of state-owned giants like the China National Petroleum Corporation (CNPC). CNPC took over all onshore exploration and production of oil and gas, while the China National Offshore Oil Corporation was formed in 1982 to handle offshore production. Sinopec, founded in 1983, focused on refining and petrochemical production. This division of labor has largely disappeared today.

At the same time, the Asian financial crisis of 1997–8 added further pressure to reform the regulatory framework of SOEs' investments overseas (Yang 2004). The management of state assets was shared by five separate ministries or commissions with different responsibilities: the Ministry of Finance was responsible for overseeing revenue and profit; the Central Work Committee on Large Enterprises of the Chinese Communist Party (CCP) for the appointment of the top management of the largest firms; the State Economic and Trade Commission for making industry policies and restructuring; the State Planning Commission for investment; and the Labor Ministry for the approval of the overall wage bill. In particular, the CCP Central Work Committee on Large Enterprises, responsible for nominations for top positions in large enterprises and supervised directly by the State Council, played an important role in this new management model.

---

[2] In Chinese: 统一领导、分级管理 (Tǒngyī lǐngdǎo, fēnjí guǎnlǐ).

The giant SOEs of the oil sector had already started their own process of expansion overseas by exploiting both their superior technical knowledge of the domestic and international energy market and the weak control that the State-Owned Assets Management Bureau could exercise upon them (Downs 2000). However, in the late 1990s, the Chinese leadership felt ready to officially begin the effort not only to bring foreign companies to China, but also to push Chinese companies to go abroad. Indeed:

> Not only do we need to actively attract foreign enterprises to invest and set up factories in China, we also need to actively guide and organize strong domestic enterprises to go global by investing and building factories in foreign countries and making use of their markets and resources. . . . The key is to provide leadership and progressively organize and support a number of leading, large and medium-sized SOEs to go global and become the first wave in the opening of foreign markets to Chinese investment abroad. This is a major strategy for both opening up and our economic development

said Jiang Zemin on December 24, 1997, to the delegates at the National Foreign Investment Affairs Meeting (CCP Central Literature Editing Committee 2011, 92). This is when the Go Global (GG) strategy started to emerge.

Jiang had just consolidated his own position a few months earlier at the 15th Party Congress, and a number of daunting challenges were ahead of him. After decades of rapid and sometimes chaotic transformation, the Chinese leaders had to achieve three interconnected goals if they wanted to keep the country's export-oriented economic engine running. First was to consolidate China's position in the international trade system and push domestic economic reforms forward through accession to the General Agreement on Tariffs and Trade (which later became the World Trade Organization). Second was to gain access to new foreign markets by enhancing the competitiveness of a few national champions through the continuous reform of the state-owned part of the economy. Third was to secure the supply of strategic natural resources. After all, China began to import crude petroleum from Oman in 1983, originally as a temporary measure for dealing with domestic transportation bottlenecks in moving crude petroleum from northern China to refineries located along the upper stretches of the Yangtze River. The volume of China's crude petroleum exports peaked in 1985, reaching 30 million metric tons, and, from 1988, Chinese imports of crude and processed fuels began to rise rapidly. In 1993, China became a net importer of oil products, and in 1996 it became a net importer of crude

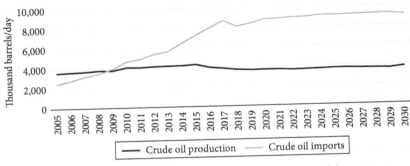

Figure 5 China's crude oil production and imports, present and future
Source: IHS Markit. Compiled by the author.

petroleum. Imports of crude oil surpassed its domestic production in 2009 (Figure 5).

According to Alice Miller (2011), it was during the 9th National People's Congress of March 1998 that Jiang Zemin started the political processes needed to achieve those goals. The Congress approved another round of sweeping reforms of the ministries and institutions belonging to the State Council. The overarching purpose was to break the longstanding linkages between State Council ministries and their corresponding industrial bureaus in provincial and local governments, on the one hand, and the SOEs they administered, on the other. The Congress also elected Zhu Rongji as Premier of the State Council, which led to a renewed push by Beijing to negotiate the accession to the World Trade Organization after years of domestic resistance, led by Zhu's predecessor, Li Peng, and other, older leaders who retired at about the same time. The results of this new push materialized between 2001 and 2003, in the wake of the agreement reached by Jiang Zemin and Bill Clinton regarding China joining the World Trade Organization during their two-hour-long meeting in Auckland in September 1999.

That success not only boosted significantly the contribution of trade to China's wealth and propelled it to become the world's largest exporter (Figure 6), but also provided Jiang and Zhu with the political capital they needed to counter those who were against their economic policies after the failure of Zhu's trip to Washington in April 1998. Hence, shortly before becoming the 143rd member of the World Trade Organization on December 11, 2001, the delegates to the fourth session of the 9th National People's Congress approved the 10th Five Year Plan (2001–5) on March 5, 2001. The plan mentioned the GG strategy in an official Chinese policy document for the first time (People's Daily 2001). Jiang's speech at the 16th Party Congress further cemented the position of the GG in the Chinese foreign economic discourse (People's Daily 2002).

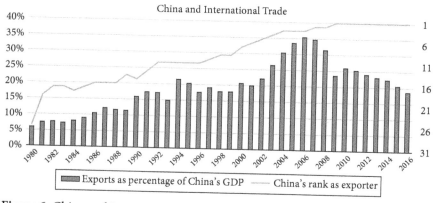

Figure 6 China and international trade
Source: Department of Trade and External Economic Relations Statistics, National Bureau of Statistics of China (various years). Compiled by the author.

Finally, while the Ministry of Foreign Trade and Economic Cooperation was renamed the Ministry of Commerce (MOFCOM), the establishment of SASAC in March 2003 marked the end of a period of creative destruction in which the main thrust of state enterprise reform had been the disruption of protected bureaucratic relationships and the dramatic downsizing of the state sector.

As Naughton (2015, 48) pointed out, the gigantic SOEs created after the dismantling of different ministries in 1998 had been operating without a real owner, as prey to bureaucratic interests, and with poor fiscal discipline under the weak supervision of the State-Owned Asset Management Bureau. SASAC, with the support of the NDRC, was meant to rationalize the reform process of SOEs and improve their corporate governance by creating highly profitable companies ready to be listed on the stock market and by stripping them of burdensome liabilities, such as social services and debts. Its full ministerial rank and relatively large personnel allocation reflected the leading role that Hu Jintao assigned it (Leutert 2018). SASAC retained control over 196 large SOEs, while ownership of the remaining more than 100,000 smaller companies was passed to provincial and lower-level governments. SASAC's elite firms are not at the cutting edge of technological innovation. Rather, they are meant to provide a stable supply of energy, power, transport, and communication services, and industrial materials, which is "by far the most powerful strand of the 'go international' policy." (Naughton 2015, 63) Most of the SOEs operating in those sectors, therefore, are considered "important backbone state-owned enterprises."[3] The data released by MOFCOM, indeed, say that activities for the extraction of

[3] In Chinese: 重要骨干国有企业 (Zhòngyào gǔgàn guóyǒu qǐyè).

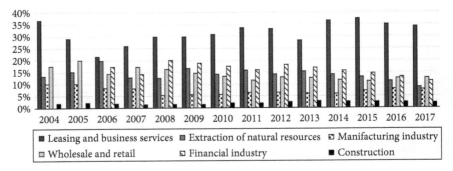

Figure 7 Main economic sectors abroad targeted by Chinese investments

Note: Unfortunately, the Ministry of Commerce does not provide a clear explanation of what "leasing and business services" are.

Source: PRC MOFCOM, National Bureau of Statistics of China, and PRC State Administration of Foreign Exchange (2017). Compiled by the author.

natural resources abroad have long been the second or third most important targets of Chinese ODI (Figure 7).

The institutional framework that has emerged is complex. It is composed of MOFCOM in charge of supervising and facilitating the operations of Chinese investors, both private and state-owned abroad; the NDRC sets the strategic priorities and approves the projects for investments put forward by Chinese companies; SASAC owns the large central SOEs and pushes for their profitability; SINOSURE offers insurance products such as export credit insurance; the Export-Import Bank of China and the China Development Bank provide loans (mostly to SOEs and large private companies); the State Administration of Foreign Exchange takes care of currency issues; the Ministry of Foreign Affairs (MFA) coordinates with MOFCOM in order to ensure that Chinese investments do not damage China's international image and foreign policy goals; the State Administration of Taxation regulates the fiscal aspect of Chinese overseas commercial operations; and, finally, the State Council is in charge of ensuring coordination between these different agencies and intervenes in particular cases, either because of an emergency or because the proposed investment is exceptional in scale. Above these institutions of the state, the CCP Central Leading Small Group on Financial and Economic Affairs (now CCP Central Financial and Economic Affairs Commission), the CCP Central Leading Small Group on Foreign Affairs (now the CPP Central Foreign Affairs Commission), and—paying special attention to the SOEs since 2013—the CCP Central Leading Group for Comprehensively Deepening Reforms supervise everything. The most recent ministerial reshuffle in early 2018 led to the creation of the China International Development Cooperation

Agency, which took over most of MOFCOM's and MFA's aid-related responsibilities, supposedly to end the longstanding competition between the two ministries. However, a recent analysis suggests that this new vice-ministerial agency will not significantly help interagency coordination to improve (Rudyak 2018).

Although support for the GG strategy remained strong under Hu Jintao, it is with Xi Jinping that the policy received a further impulse under the form of the Belt and Road Initiative (BRI). Announced in late 2013, the BRI is not a grand scheme formulated by Xi alone but, rather, the result of the evolution of Chinese domestic economic development and foreign policy (Johnson 2016, 2–10). Against the backdrop of a domestic economic slowdown and the consequent efforts of economic rebalancing, China is searching for a new engine of economic growth. In particular, the government is looking for a way to reduce economic imbalance among Chinese provinces, one of the negative legacies left by Deng Xiaoping's landmark reforms. Domestically, the BRI has become key to this, by bringing together and reframing China's diverse regional development and revival programs, such as the West Development Strategy and the Raising the Central Region and Revitalizing the Old Northeast Industrial Bases Plan.[4] Externally, the BRI adopts an ambitiously holistic approach that aggregates industry, investment, aid, trade, security, and foreign policy along the Silk Road Economic Belt and the 21st-Century Maritime Silk Road. Whether or not Wang Jisi's famous idea about "marching West" really influenced Chinese leadership (Wang 2012), the BRI does not simply encourage Chinese companies to go overseas but, somehow more precisely, it points to the Eurasian continent including East Asia, Southeast Asia, Central Asia, the Middle East, and Eastern Europe.[5] The BRI also puts the emphasis on the idea of connectivity, thereby officially adding the construction of big logistic infrastructures to the list of the primary goals of China's economic activities abroad. It is important to point out, however, that projects that began before 2013 and/or in other regions, especially in Europe and Africa, are usually rebranded as part of the BRI. The BRI, thus, expands and elaborates upon the foundations of the GG strategy rather than supplanting it.

In 2014, the BRI led to the creation of the Asian Infrastructure Investment Bank and the Silk Road Fund, with an initial firepower totaling USD 140 billion. In 2017, Xi Jinping announced an additional contribution of USD 100 billion to the Silk Road Fund. While the significance of these new institutions

---

[4] In Chinese: 西部大开发 (Xībù dà kāifā) and 振兴东北老工业基地 (Zhènxīng dōngběi lǎo gōngyè jīdì).

[5] In Chinese: 西进 (Xī jìn).

cannot be denied, discussion of their functioning is beyond the scope of this chapter. Rather, it is more important to point out that the BRI brought the idea of China going global to the core of Chinese foreign policy. This process took place between early 2015 and late 2017. The first step was the issuing of the Vision and Actions on Jointly Building Silk Road Economic Belt and 21st-Century Maritime Silk Road in March 2015 by the NDRC and the MFA (2015), which laid out China's internal and external priorities within the BRI framework. The second step linked the BRI in a firmer and more precise way to China's economic planning by inserting it in the 13th Five-Year Plan covering the period between 2016 and 2020 (Xinhua 2016). Finally, the 19th Party Congress of late October 2017 approved the enshrinement of the BRI in the constitution of the CCP (CCP Central Organization Department 2017). According to a scholar belonging to the China Foreign Affairs University, the success of the BRI, and therefore of China's GG strategy, has never been so important to the political survival and legacy of a Chinese leader, even in the face of rising tensions in the South China Sea (Nie 2016).

While more political capital was invested in strengthening the ties between China and the world economy, and consistently expanding its human and economic presence abroad, other key changes happened beneath the surface. The first was the shrinking of the already limited authority of state institutions in favor of those of the CCP both in policymaking and in policy management (Link 2013, 251–3). On the one hand, the BRI has increased the relative authority of the NDRC vis-à-vis other state agencies of the Chinese state by making it the home institution of the CCP Leading Small Group for Advancing the Development of the One Belt One Road—the task force of high-level state and party officials assigned to oversee the implementation of the BRI. However, the absolute authority of the NDRC, and thus that of the other state institutions, significantly decreased under the political weight of the leading small group (Yu 2018). On the other hand, it seems that the Party Central Organization Department has been exercising more influence than before in the appointment of top managers of SOEs, who are both high-ranking state officials working under the directive of SASAC and party members. By making either the figure of Party Secretary overlap with that of General Manager or President, and by forcing top managers to rotate in leading positions in other SOEs, the party ensures a better grip on those companies through the Central Commission for Discipline Inspection and prevents top managers from creating their own factions in the companies they lead (Leutert 2018).

Somehow, the same happened inside private and foreign companies in China too. Although China's company law has always mandated the creation of party cells inside every company operating in China (National People's

Congress 2013), this rule remained unapplied until the Party Central Organization Department (2012) issued the Provisional Opinions on Reinforcing and Improving the Work of Party Construction in Non-State-Owned Enterprises in 2012. Later, in September 2017, the State Council and the Party Central Committee (2017) jointly issued the New Opinions on Promoting the Entrepreneurship and Giving Better Play to Their Roles, thereby ordering the creation of party cells inside foreign-invested joint ventures and strengthening the role of the party in managing the decisions of the SOEs and private companies. This move of the CCP, however, is mostly aimed at influencing the behavior of companies functioning within China's border, rather than outside. It should be seen as part of Xi Jinping's signature anticorruption campaign after many high-level arrests within the armed forces and state institutions, including that of the former security tsar and CNPC top manager, Zhou Yongkang. Indeed, if one is to draw insights from recent cases of SOEs severely damaging Chinese foreign policy while pursuing their own economic objectives, as in the case of the Myitsone hydropower dam project in Myanmar (Lee and Zou 2017), it seems that even stronger party institutions inside companies have little restraining power over the behavior of top managers when it comes to launching troublesome projects.

The second key change, which is of extreme relevance if one wants to understand the expansion of China's human and economic presence in dangerous regions, is how the NDRC and MOFCOM, and other agencies as well, have largely limited their control over non-financial investments abroad. Between 2001 and 2017, different agencies and ministries of the State Council issued several "measures," "decisions," "notices," "opinions," and "announcements" in order to regulate and support Chinese investments abroad (see Appendix 2).[6] Importantly, the simplification of those regulations proceeded along two lines. First, MOFCOM and the NDRC now only take care of the largest investments. While only projects worth USD 30 million or more need the approval of the NDRC in Beijing, those below that sum must be taken care of by its provincial offices (PRC NDRC 2017). Only when an investment is in the arms industry does the NDRC in Beijing intervene, regardless of the sum involved. In comparison, the previous regulations also mandated that investments above USD 10 million in activities related to "resource development," such as mining and the extraction of oil and natural gas, had to be approved by officials in Beijing (PRC NDRC 2011).[7] Given the importance of those activities, both in policy terms and in scale of investment, as well as the interests of provincial authorities

---

[6] In Chinese: 办法 (Bànfǎ), 决定 (Juédìng), 通知 (Tōngzhī), 意见 (Yìjiàn), and 公告 (Gōnggào).
[7] In Chinese: 资源开发 (Zīyuán kāifā).

in promoting the development of the companies based within the territory under their jurisdiction, this is not a small detail. Similar limitations were lifted in 2014 in the case of MOFCOM (2014).

At the same time, there has been a clear transfer of responsibility for the potential risks associated with investing in dangerous countries from the state to the investor. On the one hand, MOFCOM (2014) and its provincial branches retain the power to "approve or reject" a project after a thorough vetting of the proposal for investment in countries that have no diplomatic relations with China or that are under sanctions by the United Nations.[8] At the time of writing, the total number of "sensitive countries" is around twenty (PRC MFA Consular Affairs Office 2018).[9] The same holds true when it comes to investments in "sensitive industries," which include the arms industry, activities related to transboundary water resources, the media, and a few other sectors (PRC MOFCOM 2018).[10] Mining and the energy industry are not included in that list. The opinion of MOFCOM's overseas offices, too, must be taken into account in those investments. In all other cases, however, MOFCOM "records" and releases a certification within three workdays of the online submission of the proposal.[11] The investor has to present his or her own business license and fill a form self-certifying that his or her project does not involve sensitive countries and/or industries.

Although the MFA and MOFCOM are called on to evaluate the feasibility of overseas investments and assess the risks associated with participating in bids for, and potentially carrying out, projects overseas, Chinese companies have been repeatedly told that they are responsible for the safety of the workers they send abroad according to the principle of "[he or she] who sends personnel abroad is responsible for them."[12] This was made clear in 2005 in a notice issued by MOFCOM, the MFA, and SASAC (2005) combined to clarify the meaning of the National Overseas Emergency Response Plan approved by the State Council the same year. Chapter 6 further shows how measures inspired by that principle affected relations between Chinese companies and the nascent Chinese private security industry.

China's Interests in the Middle East and North Africa

As the Chinese economy grew, so did the quantity of Chinese products being transported daily by sea to faraway countries. In terms of both Chinese goods being transported and vessels owned by Chinese shipping companies, the

---

[8] In Chinese: 核准 (Hézhǔn). [9] In Chinese: 敏感国家 (Mǐngǎn guójiā).
[10] In Chinese: 敏感行业 (Mǐngǎn hángyè). [11] In Chinese: 备案 (Bèi'àn).
[12] In Chinese: 谁派出, 谁负责 (Shéi pàichū, shéi fùzé).

growing importance of maritime trade has fueled the expansion of China's maritime presence, especially on the routes connecting Asia with Europe, passing through the Indian Ocean, the Suez Canal, and the Mediterranean Sea. Between 1990 and 2017, the size of the Chinese-owned fleet grew from 1,547 vessels to 5,206, and the average deadweight, that is, how much a ship can carry when fully loaded, grew from 16,222.5 to 31,776.8 tons (UNCTAD 2018, 2000). At the same time, the importance of North Africa and the Middle East has significantly increased over the years thanks to a number of inter-connected factors, some related to Chinese policies and some related to broader trends in the global shipping industry.

The most important China-specific factor is the growing penetration of Chinese products in Middle Eastern and North African countries thanks to their lower prices (Figure 8). Albeit still absorbing a small share of Chinese exports (6.5%, USD 146.4 billion), those markets are located en route to the most lucrative European ones. Since more than 90 percent of the trade between China and the European Union has always been ship-borne (Hillman 2018), this means that between a fifth and a fourth of China's exports (4.3% of China's GDP in 2016) passes over the oceans and the seas mentioned above. Every year, more than 1,000 Chinese ships transport goods of every kind, from oil to home appliances and grain, sailing along the China-Indian Ocean-Suez Canal-Europe route (Pan 2018).

Beyond China, the 2008 financial crisis caused a significant decline in global trade and in the quantity of goods transported by sea, and their path of expansion has not yet returned to the pre-crisis level (SRM 2017, 45). Technological developments in the shipping industry have led to the launch of increasingly larger vessels that encourage their operators to create economies of scale. These

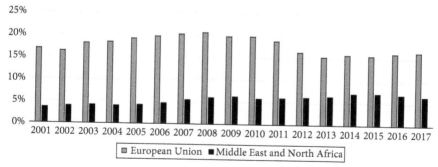

Figure 8 Percentage of Chinese exports to Europe, the Middle East, and North Africa

Source: ITC Trade Map. Compiled by the author.

factors pushed shipping companies, including Chinese ones, to seek higher market concentration through a large number of big mergers and acquisitions, as well as alliances and cooperation agreements, in order to rationalize routes, improve rates of loading, and reduce competitive pressure on freight rates (SRM 2017, 49). In China's case, one can see the result of this process by looking at the recent history and the fleet of the giant SOE China COSCO Shipping. This company is the result of the merger between COSCO and China Shipping in April 2016. The same month, COSCO Shipping signed a memorandum of understanding with CMA CGM, OOCL, and Evergreen Line to form the Ocean Alliance (Knowler 2016). COSCO is currently completing the procedures to acquire OOIL, the parent company of OOCL (Shipping Technology 2018), thereby creating the third-largest container operator in the world, with a total capacity of 2.4 billion TEU[13] (11.6% of the world total). The composition of COSCO Shipping's own fleet reflects the technological trends in the shipping industry; while its bulk is made up of medium-size vessels (below 10,000 TEU) acquired throughout the 2000s, megaships (above 10,000 TEU) constituted 30 percent of the new acquisitions between 2011 and 2013 and more than 50 percent from 2013 to late 2018 (COSCO Shipping 2018). The maximum profit from a megaship can be gained only by making it stop in as many deepwater ports as possible during each trip.

The natural result of the convergence between China-specific and shipping industry-specific factors is that the Ocean Alliance, particularly the COSCO-OOCL conglomerate, has not only focused on the East Asia-Mediterranean Sea route to serve the European and the increasingly important Middle Eastern and North African markets, but has also extended its reach to ports on the Atlantic coast of the United States (SRM 2016, 130, Panaro and Ferrara 2018, 10). Since the owners of terminals and ports can determine the priority in onload and offload for the ships, thereby cutting the downtime for those vessels and improving their economic efficiency, the massive investments by COSCO and other Chinese companies in those facilities in the Gulf (Abu Dhabi), around the Suez Canal (Suez Canal Container Terminal and Djibouti), and the Mediterranean Sea (Haifa, Algeciras, Piraeus, Ambarli, and Vado) further prove the growing scale of China's interests in those waters.

Of course, China's booming economy and exports would not have been possible without a stable supply of raw materials, especially oil. Indeed, as mentioned above, securing stable energy supplies has been a key driver of China's outward expansion even before the GG strategy was officially unveiled.

---

[13] The 20-foot equivalent unit (TEU) is a unit of cargo capacity often used to describe the capacity of container ships and container terminals. It is based on the volume of a 20-foot-long (6.1 m) intermodal container, a standard-sized metal box which can be easily transferred between different modes of transportation, such as ships, trains, and trucks.

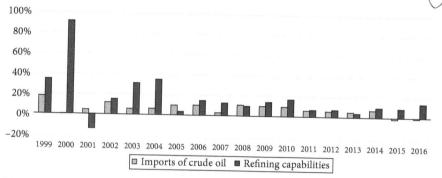

Figure 9 Yearly variations in China's imports of crude oil and refining capabilities
Source: British Petroleum. Compiled by the author.

The key to understanding the foreign policy side of China's approach to energy security abroad, especially in the case of crude oil, is to look at its refinery capabilities (Kim 2016). After all, if a country is not capable of refining the oil from oilfields owned by its national oil companies (NOCs), those investments will have little value in terms of energy security. This is why, as Figure 9 shows, China has been building up its refining capabilities since the late 1990s in order to ensure that increases in oil imports could be properly processed. In particular, those efforts were devoted to adding units for the refinement of sour crude (sulfur content > 1.0%/weight) after the supplies of sweet crude (sulfur content < 0.5%/weight) in China and neighboring countries started to become tight, either because of the natural decline of production or because the boom of Asian economies made regional producers like Indonesia sell more oil in their domestic markets.

The reason for China investing significant sums in developing new refining capabilities is that only Middle Eastern countries, which mostly produce sour crude, are able to provide China with the quantity of oil its economy requires. Indeed, the gradual expansion of refinement capabilities and China's soaring demand for oil have greatly contributed to cementing the central position of countries like Saudi Arabia, Iran, Iraq, and Kuwait (Figures 10 and 11) in China's energy strategy after a transitional period that saw African producers supplying significant quantities of sweet crude, which is similar to that produced by Chinese oilfields (Downs 2006). Inviting Middle Eastern governments to invest in China's downstream industry has further strengthened the energy ties between China and the region. Indeed, Saudi and Kuwaiti investments in Chinese refineries are based on the long-term supply of crude produced by those same countries, thereby ensuring both a market for the producers and a stable source for China (Gamal 2018, Hussain 2011). Similar arrangements, albeit in a reversed way, can be

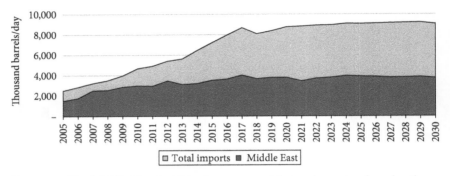

Figure 10 The Middle East in China's present and future imports of crude oil
Source: IHS Markit. Compiled by the author.

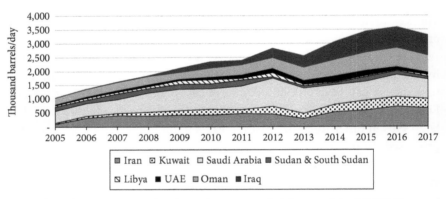

Figure 11 China's main crude oil suppliers in North Africa and the Middle East
Source: IHS Markit. Compiled by the author.

found in resource-backed loans from the Chinese government to resource-rich countries where cooperation over the construction of infrastructure is linked to the provision of oil or other raw resources.

NOCs have always had the monopoly on technical knowledge, and Chinese officials are usually inclined to believe that state control of strategic resources (including their extraction, transportation, and processing) is a safer strategy than relying on their purchase in international markets (Liou 2009, Downs 2000, Erickson and Collins 2007). Against this background, Chinese leaders tasked the NOCs with acquiring downstream and, especially, upstream assets abroad. Yet, as many scholars have pointed out, while the expansion of refining capabilities allows China to use a larger variety of crude to produce strategic products like diesel and jet fuel and thereby enhance its energy security, possessing overseas oilfields provides almost no practical economic and security benefit (Leung, Li, and Low 2011, Breslin and Zha 2010). For example, on the economic side, in 2007, CNPC and Sinopec preferred to export the products of their refineries in China rather than sell them in the domestic market, because the returns were higher. As fuel started being rationed and private gas stations in Guangdong Province were shut down, the situation was resolved only when central government allowed fuel prices to increase by 8 percent, thereby minimizing the losses of the two NOCs (Liou 2009, 678–9).

On the security side, besides the fratricidal fight between Sinopec and CNPC to outprice each other, their deep involvement in the Sudanese oil industry—USD 4.3 billion invested between 1996 and 2007 (Suliman and Badawi 2010)—played a significant role in the process leading to the deployment of Chinese peacekeepers in 2008 (Norris 2016, 78–80). Moreover, studies have also highlighted the fact that SOEs, not just Chinese ones, that operate in the energy and mining sector also tend not only to pay higher prices than their private counterparts to acquire upstream assets, but also to prefer to continue to operate in countries where they have previous experience (Bass and Chakrabarty 2014). This may explain why, for example, Chinese assets in Sudan and South Sudan, which are most likely entirely owned by SOEs, started to grow again every time their value dropped, regardless of the ongoing fraught situation in those countries (Figure 12).

While the trade in oil and other goods was pivotal in the creation of China's "development interests" at sea, it also laid the foundations for the expansion of its "overseas interests" on land through the construction of harbors, which usually also required the construction or the upgrade of the logistic, industrial, and social infrastructures around them. Moreover, the SOEs working in the construction sector, like the China State Construction Engineering Corporation, have always been pushed to expand their operations abroad to capture shares

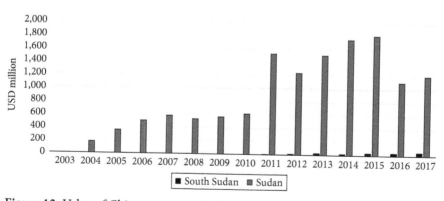

Figure 12 Value of Chinese assets in Sudan and South Sudan

Source: PRC MOFCOM, National Bureau of Statistics of China, and PRC State Administration of Foreign Exchange (various years). Compiled by the author.

of those markets, especially in the developing world, by taking full advantage of the opportunities created by the mix of international bids, aid programs, and preferential loans to those countries, and the easy credit from Chinese banks. China is not new to building infrastructure in places like Africa, but the real boom in construction and engineering companies going abroad dates back to 1999. That year, the Ministry of Foreign Trade and Economic Cooperation relaxed the regulations for those kinds of companies, and more than 400 obtained a license to operate overseas. Despite the shortage of qualified managers and the constant competition against each other (Xiao 2000), almost 2,800 Chinese companies working in that sector have assets overseas today (PRC MOFCOM, PRC NBS, and PRC SAFE 2018, 43).

Market share does not always mean profits. Indeed, Liou (2014) has pointed out that Chinese construction companies often sacrifice their profit margins for the sake of gaining a market share. Since Chinese companies usually outprice their foreign and local competitors, they are also often engaged in wars against each other. Moreover, it has also been noted that Chinese construction companies occasionally take on non-profitable projects in an attempt to gain the favor of local governments so that they are possibly chosen for future, more lucrative contracts (Brautigam 2009, 143–8). Nonetheless, it is important to highlight the fact that the Middle East and North Africa stand out as relatively lucrative markets for the Chinese construction and engineering sectors. While the contracts signed by Chinese companies in those regions are only a fraction of the total, their total value can make up one-third of the total of those signed around the world (Figure 13). This is why the Middle East and North Africa are of great interest to Chinese companies. Egypt, Iran, Iraq, Saudi

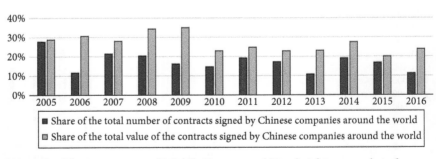

Figure 13 The importance of Middle Eastern and North African markets for Chinese construction companies

Source: Department of Trade and External Economic Relations Statistics, National Bureau of Statistics of China (various years). Compiled by the author.

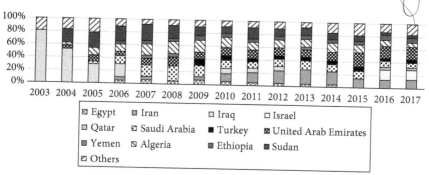

Figure 14 Main recipients of Chinese ODI (stock) in the Middle East and North Africa

Source: PRC MOFCOM, National Bureau of Statistics of China, and PRC State Administration of Foreign Exchange (various years). Compiled by the author.

Arabia, Turkey, the United Arab Emirates, Algeria, Ethiopia, Libya, and Sudan are the countries where Chinese companies have signed particularly numerous and often very lucrative contracts for many years.

While Chinese companies are busy building assets for other countries, their own appear limited. Indeed, the share of Chinese ODI stock in the Middle East and North Africa is hardly significant. Unfortunately, although the data published by MOFCOM are helpful in identifying the main recipients of Chinese ODI in the region (Figure 14), there is virtually no way of knowing in a comprehensive way which sectors have been the main targets in those countries, nor what role private companies and SOEs played. Previous studies on the different investment strategies pursued by Chinese SOEs and private actors show that the former pay little attention to the size of the market of the target country and prefer investing in either natural-resource-rich developing countries, even if those resources are still not developed for export, or in technologically advanced developed countries (Hurst 2011). Moreover, as mentioned above, SOEs that work in the engineering and construction sectors are, at least to some extent, politically motivated to seek market shares. On the other hand, much like their foreign counterparts, Chinese private companies are more attracted by large and affluent markets, thereby following a more conventional location strategy (Amighini, Rabellotti, and Sanfilippo 2012). While some of the countries considered here are extremely rich in natural resources, mostly oil and gas, they are not technologically advanced.

Therefore, it can be hypothesized that the vast majority of Chinese investors in the Middle East and North Africa are SOEs. Private companies are most likely found in countries that, like Turkey and the monarchies of the Gulf, can offer a large market for Chinese goods or that are hubs for regional traders. Large private enterprises like Huawei and ZTE, however, often compete for international bids to build telecommunications infrastructure and have access to the credit provided by Chinese state-owned banks. For example, a quick search online can easily reveal that Huawei is active in countries like Oman, Sudan, Ethiopia, Algeria, Egypt, and others working within specific diplomatic frameworks agreed between China and the host country, as well as for international organizations, and deals on its own with foreign governments and customers.

China's overseas interests are not an intangible flow of money or the goods and the energy resources shipped to and from the Middle East and North Africa. Rather, China's overseas interests are the Chinese nationals who live and work there. The fact that the "SOEs are the vanguard and main army"[14] of Chinese economic engagement in the countries at the center of this book means that Figure 15 (Li 2017), which represents the number of Chinese workers there for labor services and construction projects, presents a fairly realistic picture of the evolution of the situation since 2002. While most of the workers in Jordan and Israel belong to the first category, most of the other countries host or hosted Chinese workers employed on both kinds of contracts.

As Figure 16 shows, the countries in those regions absorb an important proportion of Chinese workers sent abroad every year. If, as is most probable, the situation of most of the countries taken into consideration here is like that

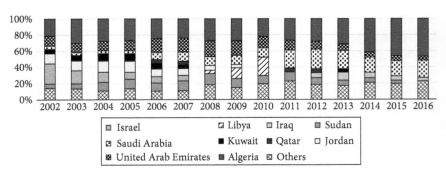

Figure 15 Largest communities of Chinese workers in the Middle East and North Africa

Note: The data presented here refer only to workers employed for labor services and engineering projects. For further information, see Appendix 3.

Source: Department of Trade and External Economic Relations Statistics, National Bureau of Statistics of China (various years).

---

[14] In Chinese: 国企是先锋和主力军 (Guóqǐ shì xiānfēng hé zhǔlì jūn).

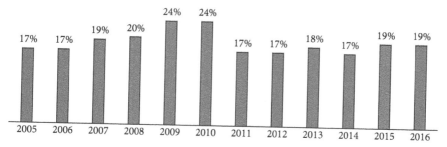

Figure 16 Share of Chinese workers in North Africa and the Middle East

Note: The data presented here refer only to workers employed for labor services and engineering projects. For further information, see Appendix 3.

Source: Department of Trade and External Economic Relations Statistics, National Bureau of Statistics of China (various years).

in Africa, the presence of Chinese citizens building roads and other big infrastructure projects is not imposed on local governments as it might be in the case of Chinese products and machinery when it comes to concessional loans. Most of the time, it is Chinese companies that push to have their own workers, who are often deemed better-performing (Brautigam 2009, Kernen and Lam 2014, Alden and Davies 2006). This is usually true during the initial phase of a project, as the Chinese contractor works to tight deadlines, especially when the project is part of a larger set of deals signed by the Chinese and the host governments, and there is little time to train local workers (Tang 2010). At first, the Chinese skilled workers supervise or work together with local workers until the latter become independent. The degree of localization of construction workers tends to increase proportionally with the duration of the work although some Chinese workers, usually mid- and high-level managers, are always retained.

The Chinese government encourages Chinese companies to hire local workers, because localizing the workforce is conducive to improving relations with local governments and communities. This is particularly true in the post-Arab Spring era, as local governments needed to show progress in developing their national economy, and China wanted to dispel rumors in the Western media about its colonialist ambitions. It is a very sensitive issue because in countries where the presence of Chinese workers is significant, such as Algeria, local media often publish articles arguing that Chinese workers are stealing local jobs. In these cases, the fact that China is also one of the main suppliers of cheap goods further undermines China's image (Haddouche 2017). In other countries, such as Israel, the presence of Chinese workers in place of worship or areas which are populated by conservative religious groups, has created significant friction (Gazit 2018). An alternative, as happened in Saudi Arabia, is to force the Chinese to convert to another religion so that they can be accepted (Emirates 24/7 2010). For these reasons, Chinese companies usually follow local regulations that mandate the hiring of up to 80 percent of the workforce from the local community. This, for example, was the case with Zhenghua Oil in the development of part of the East Baghdad field in Iraq (Rai al-Youm 2017).

When Chinese companies want to bring in more Chinese workers than regulations would otherwise allow, anecdotal evidence shows that they will usually do this in negotiation with the local authorities. For example, the government of the Ningxia Hui Autonomous Region has been negotiating with its Omani counterparts about the possibility of lowering the minimum share of local workers that must be hired in the China-Oman Industrial Park in Duqm to 10 percent (China Council for the Promotion of International Trade 2017). This, however, is a very particular and rare case that does not change the broader picture. That said, there have been cases of Chinese workers brought overseas illegally. In Algeria, a group of Chinese nationals were seen protesting on the streets because the local company that had hired them to build a residential compound had not been paying them (Zhang 2018). However, since they had been working without the necessary work permits, their rights could not be protected. Hence, since Chinese companies are forced to localize their workforce relatively quickly for a variety of reasons, the large and constant local presence of Chinese workers over the years can be seen as indicative of the growing economic importance of North Africa and the Middle East for China.

Table 1 shows the countries where the Chinese economic and human footprint was the largest between 2004 and 2016. While Saudi Arabia, the United Arab Emirates, Algeria, Sudan, and South Sudan clearly stand out, Iraq, Ethiopia, and, especially, Libya cannot be overlooked either. Each of them was among the five countries that annually hosted the largest communities of Chinese workers and/or where the value of Chinese assets was the highest and/or had the largest market for Chinese engineering companies. Those Chinese workers and companies represent the foundation of China's interest frontiers.

While the case of Libya is analyzed in greater detail in the next section of this chapter, it is useful here to look at the nature of the economic relations between China and the other countries in Table 1 and how China's presence there developed. Unsurprisingly, most of those countries derive a significant portion of their wealth from the export of natural resources, which is usually employed to finance other infrastructural projects. In Iraq's case, the continuous flow of American aid and the exclusion of American, German, French, and Russian companies from bids to rebuild the country's oilfields and infrastructure in the aftermath of the 2003 invasions laid the foundations for the

Table 1 The development of China's human and economic presence in North Africa and the Middle East

	2004	2005	2006	2007	2008	2009	2010	2011	2012	2013	2014	2015	2016
Iraq	ODI (USD 434.87 million)	ODI (USD 434.87 million)	ODI (USD 436.18 million)						Workers (8,736)	Workers (15,562), Contracts (USD 5,246.2 million)	Workers (11,769), Contracts (USD 6,384.16 million)	Workers (10,584)	Workers (8,148), Contracts (USD 5,528.58 million)
Israel	Workers (10,585)												ODI (USD 4,229.88 million)
Jordan	Workers (11,734)	Workers (13,132)	Workers 1,156	Workers (11,883)	Workers (8,737)								
Kuwait		Workers (8,680)											
Qatar								Workers (6,684)					
Saudi Arabia		Contracts (USD 1,268.91 million)	Workers (1,0519), ODI (USD 272.84 million), Contracts (USD 1,725.86 million)	Workers (16,121), ODI (USD 404.03 million)	Workers (16,245), ODI (USD 620.68 million), Contracts (USD 3,557.42 million)	Workers (20,898), ODI (USD 710.89 million), Contracts (USD 5,933.31 million)	Workers (23,257), ODI (USD 760.56 million), Contracts (USD 6,651.56 million)	Workers (30,606), ODI (USD 883.14 million), Contracts (USD 4,512.54 million)	Workers (35,579), ODI (USD 1,205.86 million), Contracts (USD 3,988.3 million)	Workers (35,325), ODI (USD 1,747.06 million), Contracts (USD 6,371.57 million)	Workers (32,508), ODI (USD 1,987.43 million), Contracts (USD 9,468.36 million)	Workers (37,977), ODI (USD 2,434.39 million), Contracts (USD 6,072.21 million)	Workers (42,069), ODI (USD 2,607.29 million)

(Continued)

Table 1 (Continued)

	2004	2005	2006	2007	2008	2009	2010	2011	2012	2013	2014	2015	2016
United Arab Emirates	Workers (9,803), ODI (USD 46.56 million), Contracts (USD 502.82 million)	Workers (11,969), ODI (USD 144.53 million), Contracts (USD 805.85 million)	Workers (20,302), ODI (USD 144.63 million), Contracts (USD 1,672.32 million)	Workers (23,826), ODI (USD 234.31 million), Contracts (USD 2,479.9 million)	Workers (29,453), ODI (USD 375.99 million), Contracts (USD 6,198.41 million)	Workers (34,066), ODI (USD 440.29 million)	Workers (28,584), ODI (USD 764.29 million), Contracts (USD 2,120.04 million)	Workers (16,817), ODI (USD 1,174.5 million)	Workers (14,257), ODI (USD 1,336.78 million)	Workers (12,999), ODI (USD 1,514.57 million)	Workers (11,648), ODI (USD 2,333.45 million)	Workers (11,662), ODI (USD 4,602.84 million)	Workers (10,075), ODI (USD 4,888.3 million)
Algeria	Workers (23,478), ODI (USD 34.49 million), Contracts (USD 986.31 million)	Workers (25,554), ODI (USD 171.21 million), Contracts (USD 1,832.14 million)	Workers (28,923), ODI (USD 247.37 million), Contracts (USD 8,057.77 million)	Workers (33,450), ODI (USD 393.89 million), Contracts (USD 3,257.77 million)	Workers (39,795), ODI (USD 508.82 million), Contracts (USD 3,486.33 million)	Workers (49,631), ODI (USD 751.26 million), Contracts (USD 4,045.89 million)	Workers (45,208), ODI (USD 937.26 million), Contracts (USD 4,821.37 million)	Workers (36,562), ODI (USD 1,059.45 million), Contracts (USD 6,458.47 million)	Workers (40,537), ODI (USD 1,305.53 million), Contracts (USD 5,036.96 million)	Workers (48,679), ODI (USD 1,497.21 million), Contracts (USD 7,006.84 million)	Workers (71,542), ODI (USD 2,451.57 million), Contracts (USD 9,750.92 million)	Workers (91,212), ODI (USD 2,531.55 million), Contracts (USD 6,895.85 million)	Workers 91,596, ODI (USD 2,552.48 million), Contracts (USD 5,848.15 million)
Ethiopia								Contracts (USD 6,010.6 million)	Contracts (USD 5,230.87 million)	Contracts (USD 3,583.27 million)	Workers (14,078), Contracts (USD 5,075.62 million)	Workers (9,973), Contracts (USD 4,672.93 million)	Workers (9,883), Contracts (USD 8,354.05 million)

	C1	C2	C3	C4	C5	C6	C7	C8	C9	C10	C11	C12
Libya	Workers (8,689), ODI (USD 171.61 million)	Workers (11,035), ODI (USD 351.53 million)	Workers (11,860), ODI (USD 497.13 million)	Contracts (USD 3,272.16 million)	Contracts (USD 10,023.97 million)	Workers (24,155), Contracts (USD 5,862.65 million)	Workers (46,744)					
Sudan and South Sudan				Workers (16,904), ODI (USD 574.85 million)	Workers (20,335), ODI (USD 528.25 million)	Workers (20,538), ODI (USD 563.89 million)	Workers (20,295), ODI (USD 613.36 million)	Workers (15,406), ODI (USD 1,530.62 million)	Workers (12,505), ODI (USD 1,247.5 million), Contracts (USD 6,270.42 million)	Workers (10,450), ODI (USD 1,533.51 million)	ODI (USD 1,766.38 million)	ODI (USD 1,845.34 million)
Egypt				ODI (USD 131.6 million)								
Iran			ODI (USD 46.68 million)		ODI (USD 715.16 million)		ODI (USD 1,351.56 million)	ODI (USD 8,022.2 million)	ODI (USD 2,851.2 million)	ODI (USD 3,484.15 million)	Contracts (USD 3,463.12 million), ODI (USD 2,949.19 million)	Contracts (USD 8,022.2 million), ODI (USD 3,330.81 million)
Turkey						ODI (USD 386.17 million)						
Yemen		ODI (USD 77.77 million)		ODI (USD 140.54 million)								

(Continued)

Table 1 (Continued)

	2004	2005	2006	2007	2008	2009	2010	2011	2012	2013	2014	2015	2016
Oman	Contracts (USD 202.28 million)												

Note: Among the countries taken into consideration in this book, those in the table are those that, at least once from 2004 to 2016, were among the top five markets for Chinese companies (measured in terms of the total value of the contracts signed by Chinese engineering companies) and/or hosted one of the five largest communities of Chinese contract workers employed to carry out engineering projects and to perform labor services and/or were among the top five destinations for Chinese investments (measured in terms of the stock value of Chinese assets).

Source: PRC MOFCOM, National Bureau of Statistics of China, and PRC State Administration of Foreign Exchange (various years), Department of Trade and External Economic Relations Statistics, National Bureau of Statistics of China (various years). Compiled by the author.

long-term presence of Chinese companies. As Yitzhak Shichor (2005) argues, this was the result of careful diplomatic balancing by Beijing as its experience in how to deal with events in the Middle East grew side by side with its energy interests there. The important Chinese presence in Saudi Arabia, too, is largely due to China's thirst for oil and expanded on the basis of China's successful diplomatic positioning before and after the American invasion of Iraq (Olimat 2013, 138, Al-Shaifi 2015).

In the case of Sudan, China's deep and long-standing involvement in the country since the late 1990s resulted from a mix of factors somehow similar to those at play in Iraq. On the one hand, oil is the main driver and pillar of the expansion of China's presence. On the other hand, the exclusion from the Sudanese economy of Western competitors, although, in this case, due to American sanctions, allowed Chinese companies to consolidate their dominant position. As politics and economy influence each other, Sudan has repeatedly requested enormous loans to finance the building of infrastructure, thereby further fueling the penetration of Chinese companies in the local economy. Being a newborn country, with its well-documented security problems, it is no surprise that the data available describe an extremely limited Chinese human and economic presence in South Sudan. However, China's presence there was already well-established before it became an independent country because a large share of the oilfields operated by Chinese companies in Sudan happened to be within South Sudanese borders after 2011. Consequently, their presence in that country has never disappeared (Vasselier 2016). It is dormant.

As shown by COSCO's 2016 investment of more than USD 700 million for the thirty-five-year concession agreement with Abu Dhabi Ports to develop and operate the second container terminal port of Khalifa, the United Arab Emirates is one of the main hubs for Chinese trade in the region. About 60 percent of the Chinese exports to the Middle East and North Africa go through this Arab country (Olimat 2013, 164). The fifty-year agreement between Jiangsu Provincial Overseas Cooperation & Investment Company and Abu Dhabi Ports to take a lease on 2.2 square kilometers at the Khalifa Industrial Zone Abu Dhabi is further proof of this. Indeed, most Chinese companies operate within the free trade zones around the country. The relationship between China and the United Arab Emirates has always been fairly stable, thanks to a shared interest in the smooth trade in oil, and the country's business-friendly environment. Many large Chinese companies established their regional headquarters in Dubai more than ten years ago; hence, they have been deeply involved in the construction of the country's logistic infrastructure and residential buildings.

Algeria is somehow different from the other countries because its diplomatic relations with China date back to the late 1950s and, at least rhetorically, were forged in the common anti-imperialist struggle. Moreover, although Algeria is significantly dependent on its export of crude, China has never been a significant buyer of it. Strong Western competition limited the penetration of Chinese NOCs in this North African country. Nonetheless, there is a large Chinese economic and human footprint related to Algeria's oil (Zoubir 2019). Indeed, it is revenue from oil that allowed the Algerian government to finance policies like the Economic Support and Recovery Plan and the Complementary Growth Support Program, which included the construction of large infrastructural projects as well as measures to force foreign companies selling products such as cars in Algeria to localize part of the production. Chinese companies were among the major winners of that oil-fueled spending spree (Calabrese 2017). Algeria has hosted the largest community of Chinese workers in North Africa and the Middle East since 2003 (more than 91,000 at the end of 2016).

Finally, a number of economic and political factors have made China's presence in Ethiopia boom, especially over the last decade (Gessese 2019). First, Ethiopia is the second most populous country in Africa (after Nigeria) with a population close to 190 million people, which makes it a leading investment destination for Chinese products and companies. Second, Ethiopia is strategically located in the Horn of Africa, where it plays a stabilizing and bridging role in reaching other countries in the continent. Hence, China is the number one foreign investor in Ethiopia. There are currently 1,238 registered Chinese companies, of which 90 percent are privately owned. The total capital of these companies is more than USD 2.2 billion. China is also one of Ethiopia's main foreign lenders. As of 2019, the total amount of Ethiopia's loans has reached USD 50 billion, of which USD 24 billion is from domestic creditors and USD 26 billion from foreign creditors. The latter portion equates to 30 percent of its GDP. Among foreign creditors, China is ranked third after the World Bank and the African Development Bank, lending a little under USD 8 billion.

Heaven Is High and the Emperor Is Far Away

As mentioned in Chapter 1, Chinese nationals were victims of robberies and other kinds of attacks well before 2011. Equally, countries hosting large communities of Chinese workers and receiving significant Chinese ODI are not located solely in the Middle East and North Africa. However, there is no other place in the world where interests of this scale combine with diffuse and persistent high-level threats, including political instability, terrorism, piracy, and war. Therefore, it was natural that China's interest frontiers would emerge here rather than elsewhere. Yet what made them emerge in a disruptive way was the unpreparedness of Chinese companies to deal with the threats to their assets and workers. This is mostly the result of the trends outlined above: institutional fragmentation, transfer of responsibility for the success and safety of overseas investments from state institutions to individual companies, and strong and sustained political support for the expansion of the activities of Chinese companies abroad, especially in developing countries. It has already been said that the significant degree of freedom enjoyed by Chinese companies, either because of their influence over the institutions that should control them or because of the difficulty that those institutions have in tracking them, has sometimes translated into significant diplomatic damage for China. In the case of the Middle East and North Africa, however, they were the first to suffer because of this.

Chapters 1 and 2 showed clearly that the 2011 Libyan crisis was a turning point for China's thinking about the defense of its interest frontiers. Unsurprisingly, Libya is on the list of countries where Chinese interests—and the presence of workers in particular—were particularly significant (Table 1). The evacuation from Libya of some 36,000 Chinese nationals was an exceptional event, both because the number of people rescued was six times more than during all the previous ten years and because of the difficult conditions under which the evacuation took place. While the impact on Chinese public opinion is discussed in Chapter 5, what matters here is the damage caused by the Libyan civil war to Chinese companies in the North African country and beyond.

Before the unrest broke out, seventy-five Chinese companies—thirteen large SOEs among them—were operating in Libya's telecommunications, energy, and construction sectors. At the end of 2010, China's National Bureau of Statistics reports that 46,744 Chinese workers were in Libya (Figure 17). The rapid growth in the number of Chinese workers in the country began in 2007, the same year companies like China State Construction Engineering Corporation, China Civil Engineering Construction Corporation, Gezhouba Group, and China Metallurgical Group Corporation started to accumulate contracts worth more than USD 13 billion for the construction of railroads, roads, residential compounds, university facilities, and so on (Lu 2011). Chinese media reported that the companies involved in the crisis not only lost contracts worth USD 18.8 billion in total, but also suffered losses of up to USD 1.5 billion in

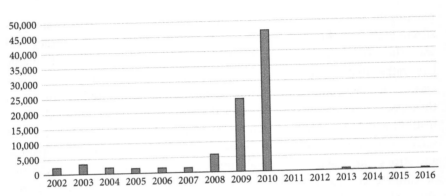

Figure 17 Chinese workers in Libya

Note: The data presented here refer only to workers employed for labor services and engineering projects. For further information, see Appendix 3.

Source: Department of Trade and External Economic Relations Statistics, National Bureau of Statistics of China (various years). Compiled by the author.

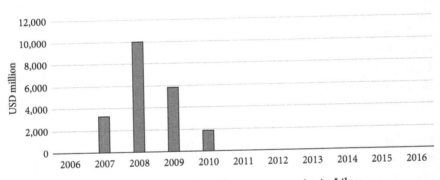

Figure 18 Value of contracts signed by Chinese companies in Libya

Note: Contracts for labor services and design and consulting services are not taken into consideration because the relevant data are only partially available. For further information, see Appendix 3

Source: Department of Trade and External Economic Relations Statistics, National Bureau of Statistics of China (various years). Compiled by the author.

machinery and facilities destroyed or damaged during the clashes and Western air raids (Southern News Network 2011). The data of the National Bureau of Statistics actually indicate that the total value of contracts signed by Chinese companies was slightly more than USD 21 billion (Figure 18).

In an attempt to minimize the scale of the problem, MOFCOM officials wrote articles in the newspapers arguing that the media were wrong to consider the halted contracts as real losses. According to Mei Xinyu (2011), a researcher at the MOFCOM's Chinese Academy of International Trade and Economic Cooperation, the Libyan government, which was the main customer of Chinese companies, had probably already paid part of the sum to the companies that had already started to work, and that it was legally responsible for paying the rest after the end of the unrest. Mei also stated that, in any case, the companies were going to be assisted by the insurance sold by SINOSURE and other insurance companies. Yet, while it is not clear if and which of the two currently existing governments in Libya will have to pay the remaining sum for the contracts, Chinese companies were in a far worse situation than Mei described. Indeed, a number of Chinese ambassadors with experience in the Middle East and North Africa told *Southern News Network* journalists (2011) that the extreme unpreparedness of Chinese companies to deal with political risks was far from being a mystery. According to Qin Hongguo, a former ambassador to Kuwait, this problem "has existed for more than 20 years" because Chinese companies are deaf to the warnings sent out by the MFA. Huang Shijiao, another former Chinese ambassador, commented that if the companies in Libya had gotten in touch with the Chinese embassy in a timely manner, the damage would have been far less.

Besides, although SINOSURE was quick to provide assistance to its customers, only a handful of the seventy-five companies involved had bought insurance against political risks. *Elite Reference* reported that only 5.68 percent, or USD 17.3 billion, of the USD 304.75 billion of the total Chinese ODI was insured in 2010. In the case of Libya, only USD 3.5 billion of the USD 18.8 billion lost was covered by some kind of insurance (Lu 2011). Moreover, as pointed out by a journalist on the *China Economic Weekly*, although at least some of the SOEs had bought export credit insurance from SINOSURE, the fact that both the insured and the insurer are state-owned entities means that the state was simply moving the loss from one entity to the other without actually limiting the enormous damage (Leng 2011).

According to a study published by the Academy of Macroeconomic Research—the main think tank inside the NDRC—99 percent of Chinese companies active abroad had never purchased export credit insurance before 2011 (Economic Information Daily 2016). More generally, studies on the relationship between Chinese investments and political risk suggest that Chinese companies are not particularly sensitive to political risks in the countries in which they operate. Indeed, while some studies find that Chinese investors are responsive to such dangers (Duanmu and Guney 2009), others find that they are not or, even, that Chinese investments abroad are positively correlated with political risks (Buckley et al. 2007, 510, Quer, Claver, and Rienda 2012,

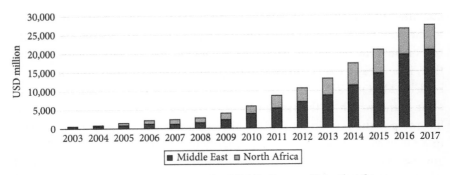

Figure 19 Value of Chinese assets in the Middle East and North Africa

Source: PRC MOFCOM, National Bureau of Statistics of China, and PRC State Administration of Foreign Exchange (various years). Compiled by the author.

Ramasamy, Yeung, and Laforet 2012). Apparently, the situation has not changed much since 2011. As a Chinese security consultant lamented in 2015, Chinese medium-sized and small private companies still often underestimate risks abroad, investing very little in risk assessment or other measures to protect their assets and employees abroad (Deng 2015). According to him, many companies usually dedicate only 1 percent of their budget to security. More generally, a statistical analysis of the relationship between local security conditions in North Africa, the Middle East, and the Horn of Africa and the number of Chinese contract workers there between 2004 and 2017 shows that Chinese companies are responsive to the occurrence of violent events but much less good at anticipating them, even if warned (Ghiselli and Morgan 2020). This has not changed since the Arab Spring.

In keeping with these findings, the changes in the patterns of Chinese presence in these regions after 2011 are not significant. The expansion of China's economic and human presence in North African and Middle Eastern countries has continued. Equally, the value of Chinese assets in those regions has continued to grow in value (Figure 19). The total value and the number of the contracts allocated to Chinese companies has also remained largely unchanged (Figure 20). Even more interestingly, in 2016 North Africa had almost the same number of Chinese workers as were there on the eve of the Arab Spring (Figure 21). In other words, there were 123,233 and 112,400 at the end of 2010 and 2016, respectively. Among those employing workers in this area, were a Mr. Qiang and a Mr. Wei who were later named and shamed by the MFA for investing in a steel mill in Libya and hiring workers from Hubei, Sichuan, and Hunan despite the security warning issued by the Chinese government (PRC MFA Consular Affairs Office 2017).

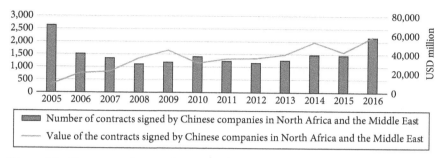

Figure 20 Changes in the number and value of the contracts signed by Chinese companies in North Africa and the Middle East

Note: Contracts for labor services and design and consulting services are not taken into consideration because the relevant data are only partially available. For further information, see Appendix 3.

Source: Department of Trade and External Economic Relations Statistics, National Bureau of Statistics of China (various years). Compiled by the author.

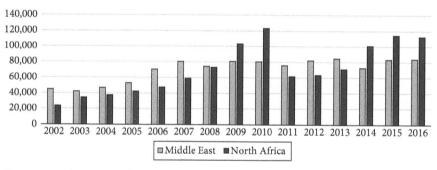

Figure 21 Chinese workers in North Africa and the Middle East

Note: The data presented here refer only to workers employed for labor services and engineering projects. For further information, see Appendix 3.

Source: Department of Trade and External Economic Relations Statistics, National Bureau of Statistics of China (various years). Compiled by the author.

Conclusion

The emergence of China's interest frontiers was the result of the explosive and chaotic transformation that began with Deng's reform and culminated in early 2011 in Libya. It is a story of failure for both the Chinese state and, especially, Chinese companies, as the former focused on the domestic effects of China's integration into the world economy, and the latter did their best to exploit the spaces created by a fragmented and decentralized system to maximize their interests overseas. What is most surprising is that the different actors did not subsequently change their course of action in any significant way. This is particularly true as Xi Jinping's BRI continued to provide fresh political support to Chinese public and private entrepreneurs to go abroad, despite having an obvious interest in avoiding Libya-like crises.

Two interrelated elements are worthy of the attention of the reader. First, the focus on economic development and the need/will to present itself as a rising power without hegemonic ambitions have long driven China's business-only approach to North Africa, the Middle East, and other developing regions. Yitzhak Shichor (2005, 215) aptly described this as the "Japanization" of China's foreign policy in regions outside Asia. Yet, while in the past the Chinese government preferred not to get involved in security issues far from China's national borders, the emergence of the interest frontiers in 2011 destroyed the intellectual barriers that prevented China from doing so outside Asia. Now, as Chapter 1 showed, it seems that Chinese leaders have no intention of rebuilding those barriers since their approach to national security has made them receptive to the idea of securitizing events in faraway regions that could threaten the country's overseas interests. Indeed, it seems that, after the Libyan crisis brought to light the problem of defending their interest frontiers, the Chinese government focused on finding a way to increase the protection of the lives and assets of its citizens abroad rather than scaling back its global ambitions. While this does not mean that Chinese leaders have imperialist goals, it cannot be denied that, somehow—as the words of the navy officers mentioned in Chapter 2 indicate—a deep belief in the historical necessity of China's return to its dominant place, at least in world economic affairs, permeates the expansion of China's overseas interests as much as it is fueled by business motivations. This, coupled with a rather fragmented institutional system, might help to explain why state and party agencies have usually been slow in intervening to stop projects officially carried out in the name of national wealth and glory, but practically and pragmatically implemented to pursue corporate interests.

Second, as the political will to expand Chinese economic presence in BRI countries—which are mostly developing ones—remains strong, the onus to make that happen is on the SOEs. Chinese private investors are, in fact, avoiding those countries (Joy-Perez and Scissors 2018). This, therefore, puts SOE managers in an increasingly difficult position, as they have to follow discordant, yet equally strong imperatives. It also transforms them into figures somehow similar to those of the British viceroys described by Galbraith (1960) in his study on British imperialism in India. Indeed, the SOEs operating on the border of China's interest frontiers are both the almost exclusive agents of the expansion of Chinese economic activities and the most immediate victims of security threats there. The top managers of the SOEs cannot command troops to secure their assets as the British viceroys could. However, the combination of a growing vulnerability to security threats with the holding of a ministerial position in the state and party hierarchies gives them both reason and tools to try to influence the way a Chinese security presence evolves on its interest frontiers. While Chapter 6 looks at that issue, Chapter 4 takes into consideration the voices of foreign policy professionals, like the diplomats mentioned above, who work inside and very close to the Chinese foreign policy machine to understand why some knew about the risks and yet the Libyan crisis still happened.

Bibliography

Alden, Chris, and Martyn Davies. 2006. "A Profile of the Operations of Chinese Multinationals in Africa." *South African Journal of International Affairs* 13 (1): 83–96.

Al-Shaifi, Haider Hamood Radhi. 2015. "CNPC, CNOOC and Sinopec in Iraq: Successful Start and Ambitious Cooperation Plan." *Journal of Middle Eastern and Islamic Studies (in Asia)* 9 (1): 78–98.

Amighini, Alessia, Roberta Rabellotti, and Marco Sanfilippo. 2012. "Do Chinese SOEs and Private Companies Differ in Their Foreign Location Strategies?" *EUI Working Paper* (27).

Bass, Eric, and Subrata Chakrabarty. 2014. "Resource Security: Competition for Global Resources, Strategic Intent, and Governments as Owners." *Journal of International Business Studies* 45: 961–79.

Brautigam, Deborah. 2009. *The Dragon's Gift: The Real Story of China in Africa.* Oxford: Oxford University Press.

Breslin, Shaun, and Daojiong Zha. 2010. "Energy Security and China's International Relations." In Shaun Breslin (ed.), *Handbook of China's International Relations*, 64–75. London: Routledge.

Brown, Kerry. 2008. *The Rise of the Dragon: Inward and Outward Investment in China in the Reform Period 1978–2007.* Oxford: Chandos Publishing.

Buckley, Peter J., L. Jeremy Clegg, Hinrich Voss, Adam R. Cross, Xin Liu, and Ping Zheng. 2007. "The Determinants of Chinese Outward Foreign Direct Investment." *Journal of International Business Studies* 38 (4): 499–518.

Calabrese, John. 2017. *Sino-Algerian Relations: On a Path to Realizing Their Full Potential?* October 31. Accessed March 12, 2018. http://www.mei.edu/publica-tions/sino-algerian-relations-path-realizing-their-full-potential

CCP Central Committee and PRC State Council. 2017. "关于营造企业家健康成长环境弘扬优秀企业家精神更好发挥企业家作用的意见 [New Opinions

on Promoting the Entrepreneurship and Giving Better Play to Their Roles]."
Xinhua. September 8. Accessed February 8, 2018. http://www.xinhuanet.com/
politics/2017-09/25/c_1121722103.htm.

CCP Central Literature Editing Committee. 2011. *Selected Works of Jiang Zemin.*
Vol. I. Beijing: Foreign Language Press.

CCP Central Organization Department. 2012. "中共中央办公厅印发《关于
加强和改进非公有制企业党的建设工作的意见（试行）》 [Provisional
Opinions on Reinforcing and Improving the Work of Party Construction in
Non-State-Owned Enterprises]." *CCP Organization Department*. May 24.
Accessed February 1, 2019. http://fuwu.12371.cn/2013/01/07/ARTI13575282
47407449.shtml.

CCP Central Organization Department. 2017. "中国共产党章程 [Constitution
of the Communist Party of China]." *CCP Central Organization Department*.
October 24. Accessed January 12, 2018. http://www.12371.cn/2017/10/28/
ARTI1509191507150883.shtml.

China Council for the Promotion of International Trade. 2017. "各方合力 多措
并举 中阿产业园圆梦有方 [All Parties Work Together to Interpret Properly
the Dream of the Chinese-Arab Industrial Park]." *China Trade News*.
December 28. Accessed January 30, 2018. http://www.chinatradenews.com.
cn/epaper/content/2017-12/28/content_50059.htm.

COSCO Shipping. 2018. "Vessels." *COSCO Shipping*. Accessed January 14, 2019.
http://lines.coscoshipping.com/home/Services/ship/0.

Deng, Yancai. 2015. "'中国民营安保公司'出海'记 [Memories of a Chinese
Security Company Abroad]." *Xinhua—International Leader Herald*. December 2.
Accessed June 14, 2018. http://www.xinhuanet.com//herald/2015-12/02/c_
134877677.htm.

Department of Trade and External Economic Relations Statistics, National
Bureau of Statistics of China. Various years. 中国贸易外径统计年鉴
[*China Trade and External Economic Statistical Yearbook*]. Beijing: China
Statistics Press.

Downs, Erika. 2000. *China's Quest for Energy Security*. Santa Monica, CA: RAND
Corporation.

Downs, Erika. 2006. "Brookings Foreign Policy Studies Energy Security Series:
China." *Brookings Institution*. December 1. Accessed March 16, 2018. https://
www.brookings.edu/research/brookings-foreign-policy-studies-energy-
security-series-china/.

Duanmu, Jing-Lin, and Yilmaz Guney. 2009. "A Panel Data Analysis of Locational
Determinants of Chinese and Indian Outward Foreign Direct Investment."
Journal of Asia Business Studies 3 (2): 1–15.

Economic Information Daily. 2016. "中国信保助力"带一路" 项目卸下风险包袱 [SINOSURE to Help the 'Belt and Road' Projects to Limit the Risks]." *Economic Information Daily*. April 29. Accessed April 3, 2018. http://silkroad.news.cn/ Company/Cases/zjqd/11.shtml.

Emirates 24/7. 2010. "1,600 Chinese Workers Embrace Islam in Saudi." *Emirates 24/7*. September 12. Accessed November 13, 2017. https://www.emirates247. com/1-600-chinese-workers-embrace-islam-in-saudi-2010-09-12-1.289733.

Erickson, Andrew S., and Gabe Collins. 2007. "Beijing's Energy Security Strategy: The Significance of a Chinese State-Owned Tanker Fleet." *Orbis* 51 (4): 665–84.

Flynn, Dennis, and Arturo Giráldez. 1996. "China and the Spanish Empire." *Revista de Historia Economica—Journal of Iberian and Latin American Economic History* 14 (2): 309–38.

Frank, Andre Gunder. 1998. *ReOrient: Global Economy in the Asian Age*. Berkely, CA: University of California Press.

Galbraith, John Semple. 1960. "The 'Turbulent Frontier' as a Factor in British Expansion." *Comparative Studies in Society and History* 2 (2): 150–68.

Gamal, Rania E. 2018. "Exclusive: Saudi Aramco Eyes Partnerships as It Expands Refining, Petrochems." *Reuters*. June 12. Accessed July 14, 2018. https://www.reuters.com/article/us-saudi-aramco-downstream-exclusive/ exclusive-saudi-aramco-eyes-partnerships-as-it-expands-refining-petrochems- idUSKBN1J81M9.

Gazit, Amitai. 2018. *The Chinese Embassy Asked to Send a Representative to Oversee the Ultra-Orthodox Demonstration against the Light Rail Work during the Sabbath*. September 18. Accessed Juy 14, 2018. https://www.calcalist.co.il/ Ext/Comp/ArticleLayout/CdaArticlePrint1280/0,16492,3746357,00.html.

Gessese, Maadin Sahleselassie. 2019. "A Glimpse View on China-Ethiopia Relations in Recent Times." In Enrico Fardella and Andrea Ghiselli (eds), *ChinaMed Report 2019: China's New Role in the Wider Mediterranean Region*, 63–8. Turin: Torino World Affairs Institute—ChinaMed Project.

Ghiselli, Andrea, and Pippa Morgan. 2020. "A Turbulent Silk Road: China's Vulnerable Foreign Policy in the Middle East and North Africa." *China Quarterly*.

Haddouche, Hassan. 2017. "L'Algérie veut 'rééquilibrer' ses relations économiques avec la Chine [Algeria Aims to 'Rebalance' Its Economic Relations with China]." *TSA Algerie*. October 12. Accessed July 14, 2018. https://www.tsa- algerie.com/lalgerie-veut-reequilibrer-ses-relations-economiques-avec-la- chine/.

Hillman, Jonathan E. 2018. "The Rise of China-Europe Railways." *Center for International and Strategic Studies*. March 6. Accessed February 1, 2019. https:// www.csis.org/analysis/rise-china-europe-railways.

Hurst, William. 2011. "Comparative Analysis of the Determinants of China's State-Owned Outward Direct Investment in OECD and Non-OECD Countries." *China & World Economy* 19 (4): 74–91.

Hussain, Emran. 2011. "Kuwait-China Make US$9bn Refinery Project Official." *Refining & Petrochemicals.* March 17. Accessed Janury 16, 2018. https://www.refiningandpetrochemicalsme.com/article-8639-kuwait-china-make-us9bn-refinery-project-official.

Investment and Enterprise Division, United Nations Conference on Trade and Development. 2018. "World Investment Report." *United Nations Conference on Trade and Development.* June 6. Accessed January 15, 2019. https://unctad.org/en/pages/PublicationWebflyer.aspx?publicationid=2130.

Johnson, Christopher K. 2016. "President Xi Jinping's 'Belt and Road' Initiative." *Center for Strategic and International Studies.* March. Accessed December 25, 2017.https://www.csis.org/analysis/president-xi-jinping%E2%80%99s-belt-and-road-initiative.

Joy-Perez, Cecilia, and Derek Scissors. 2018. "Be Wary of Spending on the Belt and Road." *American Enterprise Institute.* November 14. Accessed January 15, 2019. https://www.aei.org/publication/be-wary-of-spending-on-the-belt-and-road/.

Kernen, Antoine, and Katy N. Lam. 2014. "Workforce Localization among Chinese State-Owned Enterprises (SOEs) in Ghana." *Journal of Contemporary China* 23 (90): 1053–72.

Kim, Inwook. 2016. "Refining the Prize: Chinese Oil Refineries and Its Energy Security." *The Pacific Review* 29 (3): 361–86.

Knowler, Greg. 2016. "Container Shipping's New Ocean Alliance Is Born." *The Journal of Commerce.* April 20. Accessed November 24, 2018. https://www.joc.com/maritime-news/container-lines/ocean-alliance/container-shipping%E2%80%99s-new-ocean-alliance-born_20160420.html.

Lee, Ching Kwan. 2017. *The Specter of Global China: Politics, Labor and Foreign Investment in Africa.* Chicago, IL: Chicago University Press.

Lee, Jones, and Yizheng Zou. 2017. "Rethinking the Role of State-Owned Enterprises in China's Rise." *New Political Economy* 22 (6): 743–60.

Leng, Xinyu. 2011. "利比亚危机，中国损失怎么办？[The Libyan Crisis, How Can China Deal with the Losses?]." *China Economic Weekly.* May 23. Accessed October 16, 2017. http://www.ceweekly.cn/html/Article/2011052356386947758.html.

Leung, Guy C. K., Raymond Li, and Melissa Low. 2011. "Transitions in China's Oil Economy, 1990–2010." *Eurasian Geography and Economics* 52 (4): 483–500.

Leutert, Wendy. 2018. "Firm Control: Governing the State-Owned Economy under Xi Jinping." *China Perspectives* 1–2: 27–36.

Li, Lihui. 2017. "国企走出去 风险如何防 [The State-Owned Companies Go Abroad: How to Defend against Dangers?]" *People's Daily.* August 10. Accessed March 13, 2018. http://paper.people.com.cn/zgjjzk/html/2017-08/14/content_1798485.htm.

Link, Perry. 2013. *An Anatomy of Chinese: Rhythm, Metaphor, Politics.* Cambridge, MA: Harvard University Press.

Liou, Chih-Shian. 2009. "Bureaucratic Politics and Overseas Investment by Chinese State-Owned Oil Companies: Illusory Champions." *Asian Survey* 49 (4): 670–90.

Liou, Chih-Shian. 2014. "Rent-Seeking at Home, Capturing Market Share Abroad: The Domestic Determinants of the Transnationalization of China State Construction Engineering Corporation." *World Development* 54: 220–31.

Lu, Ma. 2011. "中国在利比亚损失了什么 [What Has China Lost in Libya?]" *Elite Reference.* June 10. Accessed January 17, 2018. http://qnck.cyol.com/html/2011-06/10/nw.D110000qnck_20110610_1-01.htm.

Mei, Xinyu. 2011. "梅新育：中国在利比亚的损失没那么多 [Mei Xinyu: China's Losses in Libya Are Not so Big]." *Global Times.* June 9. Accessed January 13, 2018. http://finance.huanqiu.com/roll/2011-06/1745727.html.

Miller, Alice L. 2011. "Dilemmas of Globalization and Governance." In Roderick MacFarquhar (ed.), *The Politics of China,* 528–600. New York: Cambridge University Press.

National People's Congress. 2013. "Company Law of the People's Republic of China (Revised in 2013)." *Invest in China.* December 28. Accessed April 23, 2018. http://www.fdi.gov.cn/1800000121_39_4814_0_7.html.

Naughton, Barry. 2015. "The Transformation of the State Sector: SASAC, the Market Economy, and the New National Champions." In Barry Naughton and Kellee S. Tsai (eds), *State Capitalism, Institutional Adaptation, and the Chinese Miracle,* 46–74. New York: Cambridge University Press.

Nie, Wenjuan. 2016. "Xi Jinping's Foreign Policy Dilemma: One Belt, One Road or the South China Sea?" *Contemporary Southeast Asia: A Journal of International and Strategic Affairs* 38 (3): 422–44.

Norris, William J. 2016. *Chinese Economic Statecraft: Commercial Actors, Grand Strategy, and State Control.* Ithaca, NY: Cornell University Press.

Olimat, Muhamad S. 2013. *China and the Middle East: From Silk Road to Arab Spring.* London: Routledge.

Pan, Shanju. 2018. "中国海军为何10年护航不停歇？这名海军专家告诉你背后缘由 [Why Did the Chinese Navy Patrol for 10 Years without Stopping? This Naval Expert Tells You the Reason behind It]." *Sohu.* December 26. Accessed February 12, 2019. http://www.sohu.com/a/284749547_161795.

Panaro, Alessandro, and Olimpia Ferrara. 2018. "Gli investimenti cinesi, la nuova centralità del Mediterraneo e il ruolo dell'Italia [Chinese investments, the new centrality of the Mediterranean and Italy's role]." *OrizzonteCina* 9 (1): 8–14.

People's Daily. 2001. "国民经济和社会发展第十个五年计划纲要 [Outline of the 10th Five-Year Plan for National Economic and Social Development]." *People's Daily*. March 15. Accessed June 19, 2018. http://theory.people.com.cn/GB/40557/54239/54243/3783806.html.

People's Daily. 2002. "在中国共产党第十六次全国代表大会上的报告 [Report at the 16th National Congress of the CCP]." *People's Daily*. November 8. http://cpc.people.com.cn/GB/64162/64168/64569/65444/4429116.html.

PRC MFA Consular Affairs Office. 2017. "再次提醒中国公民暂勿前往利比亚等海外安全高风险国家和地区 [Warning for Chinese Nationals against Traveling to Libya and Other High-Risk Countries and Regions]." Consular Affairs Office, PRC Ministry of Foreign Affairs. December 19. Accessed April 15, 2018. http://cs.mfa.gov.cn/gyls/lsgz/lsyj/t1520598.shtml.

PRC MFA Consular Affairs Office. 2018. "未建交国代管馆名单 [List of the Countries without Official Diplomatic Ties]." Consular Affairs Office, PRC Ministry of Foreign Affairs. August 21. Accessed January 14, 2019. http://cs.mfa.gov.cn/zlbg/bgzl/qtzl/t1094257.shtml.

PRC MOFCOM. 1993. "对外经济贸易部关于驻外使（领）馆经济、商务机构合并及统一机构名称的通知 [Notice of the Ministry of Foreign Trade and Economic Cooperation on the Merger of Economic and Business Institutions and the Name of the Unified Agency of the Embassies (Consulates) Overseas]." *PKU Law*. March 24. Accessed May 1, 2018. https://www.pkulaw.cn/fulltext_form.aspx?Db=chl&Gid=a15a197e0071ce6abdfb&keyword=&EncodingName=&Search_Mode=&Search_IsTitle=0.

PRC MOFCOM. 2014. "境外投资管理办法 [Measures for Foreign Investment Management]." PRC Ministry of Commerce. September 6. Accessed June 13, 2018. http://www.mofcom.gov.cn/article/b/c/201409/20140900723361.shtml.

PRC MOFCOM. 2018. "境外投资敏感行业目录 [List of Sensitive Industries for Overseas Investments]." PRC Ministry of Commerce. Accessed May 15, 2018. http://www.ndrc.gov.cn/gzdt/201802/W020180211608651590809.pdf.

PRC MOFCOM, National Bureau of Statistics of China, and PRC State Administration of Foreign Exchange. Various years. "中国对外直接投资统计公报 [Statistical Bulletin of China's Outward Foreign Direct Investment]." Beijing. http://hzs.mofcom.gov.cn/article/date/201512/20151201223578.shtml.

PRC MOFCOM, PRC MFA, and PRC SASAC. 2005. "国务院办公厅转发商务部等部门关于加强境外中资企业机构与人员安全保护工作意见的通知 [Opinion on Strengthening the Safety Protection of Chinese Enterprises and Personnel in Overseas Chinese Enterprises]." PRC Central Government. October 8. Accessed May 8, 2018. http://www.gov.cn/zwgk/2005-10/19/content_79807.htm.

PRC MOFCOM, PRC NBS and PRC SAFE. 2018. "中国对外直接投资统计公报 [Statistical Bulletin of China's Outward Foreign Direct Investment]." Department of Outward Investment and Economic Cooperation, PRC Ministry of Foreign Affairs. September 28. Accessed December 11, 2018. http://hzs.mofcom.gov.cn/article/date/201809/20180902791492.shtml.

PRC NDRC. 2011. "国家发展改革委关于做好境外投资项目下放核准权限工作的通知 [Notice Improving the Decentralization of the Approval of Overseas Investment Projects]." PRC National Development and Reform Commission. February 14. Accessed May 10, 2018. http://www.mofcom.gov.cn/aarticle/b/g/201109/20110907760681.html.

PRC NDRC. 2017. "企业境外投资管理办法 [Measures for the Administration of Overseas Investment of Enterprises]." *PRC National Development and Reform Commission.* December 26. Accessed March 28, 2018. http://www.ndrc.gov.cn/zcfb/zcfbl/201712/t20171226_871560.html.

PRC NDRC and PRC MFA. 2015. "Vision and Actions on Jointly Building Silk Road Economic Belt and 21st-Century Maritime Silk Road." PRC National Development and Reform Commission. March 28. Accessed March 23, 2018. http://en.ndrc.gov.cn/newsrelease/201503/t20150330_669367.html.

PRC SASAC. 2016. "国务院关于加强国有资产管理工作的通知 [Notice on Strengthening the Management of State-Owned Assets]." *PRC Central Government.* October 19. Accessed May 1, 2018. http://www.gov.cn/zhengce/content/2016-10/19/content_5121652.htm.

Quer, Diego, Enrique Claver, and Laura Rienda. 2012. "Political Risk, Cultural Distance, and Outward Foreign Direct Investment: Empirical Evidence from Large Chinese Firms." *Asia Pacific Journal of Management* 29 (4): 1089–104. doi:https://doi.org/10.1007/s10490-011-9247.

Rai al-Youm. 2017. "Iraq and China Sign a Deal to Develop an Oilfield Eastern in Baghdad." *Rai al-Youm.* December 24. Accessed January 1, 2018. http://www.raialyoum.com/?p=800791.

Ramasamy, Bala, Matthew Yeung, and Sylvie Laforet. 2012. "China's Outward Foreign Direct Investment: Location Choice and Firm Ownership." *Journal of World Business* 47 (1): 17–25. doi:https://doi.org/http://dx.doi.org/10.1016/j.jwb.2010.10.016.

Rudyak, Marina. 2018. "Through the Looking Glass: The Institutions behind Chinese Aid." *East Asian Forum.* November 2. Accessed December 1, 2018. http://www.eastasiaforum.org/2018/11/02/through-the-looking-glass-the-institutions-behind-chinese-aid/.

Shichor, Yitzhak. 2005. "Decisionmaking in Triplicate: China and the Three Iraqi Wars." In Andrew Scobell and Larry M. Wortzel (eds), *Chinese National Security Decisionmaking under Stress*, 191–228. Carlisle Barracks, PA: United States Army War College Press.

Shipping Technology. 2018. "COSCO Shipping Receives US Approval to Buy OOIL." *Shipping Technology*. July 10. Accessed December 12, 2018. https://www.ship-technology.com/news/cosco-shipping-receives-us-approval-buy-ooil/.

Southern News Network. 2011. "中国企业在利比亚资产达188亿美元 损失难估量 [Chinese Companies Lost Contracts Worth USD 18 Billion, It Is Difficult to Assess the Damage]." *Global Times*. April 24. Accessed February 2, 2018. http://finance.huanqiu.com/roll/2011-03/1584398.html.

SRM. 2016. *Suez and Panama: New Global Routes Increasing the Centrality of the Mediterranean Basin*. Naples: Giannini Editore.

SRM. 2017. *The Mediterranean as New Key Crossroads: Outlooks, Geomaps and Italy's Role on the Silk Road*. Naples: Giannini Editore.

Suliman, Kabbashi M., and Ahmed A. A. Badawi. 2010. "An Assessment of the Impact of China's Investments in Sudan." *Africa Portal*. Accessed October 19, 2016. http://dspace.africaportal.org/jspui/bitstream/12345.6789/32436/1/Sudan-China-FDI-relations.pdf?1.

Tang, Xiaoyang. 2010. "Bulldozer or Locomotive? The Impact of Chinese Enterprises on the Local Employment in Angola and the DRC." *Journal of Asian and African Studies* 45 (3): 350–68.

UNCTAD. 2000. "Review of Maritime Transport." United Nations Conference on Trade and Development. December 5. Accessed April 4, 2018. https://unctad.org/en/pages/PublicationArchive.aspx?publicationid=1609.

UNCTAD. 2018. "Review of Maritime Transport." United Nations Conference on Trade and Development. October 3. Accessed November 30, 2018. https://unctad.org/en/pages/PublicationWebflyer.aspx?publicationid=2245.

Vasselier, Abigaël. 2016. "Chinese Foreign Policy in South Sudan: The View from the Ground." *China Brief* 16 (12): 15–19.

Wang, Jisi. 2012. "王缉思 : '西进', 中国地缘战略的再平衡 [Wang Jisi: 'Marching West', China's Geostrategic Rebalance]." *Global Times*. October 17. Accessed September 4, 2017. http://opinion.huanqiu.com/opinion_world/2012-10/3193760.html.

Xiao, Cifang. 2000. "发展对外承包工程的体制性矛盾与对策 [Systemic Contradictions and Countermeasures for the Development of Foreign Contracted Engineering Projects]." *Forum* 12: 7–9.

Xinhua. 2016. "中华人民共和国国民经济和社会发展第十三个五年规划纲要 [Outline of the 13th Five-Year Plan for the National Economic and Social Development of the People's Republic of China]." *Xinhua*. March 17. Accessed February 27, 2018. http://www.xinhuanet.com//politics/2016lh/2016-03/17/c_1118366322.htm.

Yang, Dali L. 2004. *Remaking the Chinese Leviathan: Market Transition and the Politics*. Stanford, CA: Stanford University Press.

Yu, Jie. 2018. "The Belt and Road Initiative: Domestic Interests, Bureaucratic Politics and the EU-China Relations." *Asia Europe Journal* 16 (3): 223–36.

Zhang, Chenjing. 2018. 阿尔及利亚中国工人抗议：拖欠工资、暴力驱逐 [Chinese Workers in Algeria Protest: Wage Arrears, Violent Expulsion]. July 28. Accessed August 13, 2018. https://m.guancha.cn/internation/2018_07_28_465960.shtml?s=wapzwybjwzb.t

Zoubir, Yahia H. 2019. "Les Relations del la Chine avec les pays du Maghreb: La place prépondérante de lAlgérie [Relations between China and the Maghreb Countries: Algeria's Centrality]." *Confluences Méditerranée* 2: 91–103.

4

The Problems of Knowledge in Policymaking

The securitization process does not happen in a vacuum. Key functional actors can play a very important role in helping the securitizing actor and the empowering audience to understand the nature of the threat to the referent object. In foreign policy, this is particularly true when policymakers are not familiar with the issue at hand and, therefore, there is ample room for other actors to influence them. Since the coming of Jiang Zemin to power, Chinese presidents have traveled to the Middle East and North Africa a number of times, mostly visiting Egypt and Saudi Arabia, but not in a regular way. They paid no visit to those regions between 2009 and 2016.[1] The patterns of the state visits by Chinese premiers, who usually travel less and privilege taking care of economic affairs over matters relating to foreign policy, are similar, at least in the fact that Egypt has been the most visited country.[2] Hence, it is up to China's community of foreign policy experts and practitioners to provide correct information about what is happening and what might happen, especially in the least-visited countries. In the last part of Chapter 3, it was mentioned that the unpreparedness of Chinese companies in those regions was not a secret, at least for some in the foreign policymaking machine. Yet the government, the companies, and, as shown in Chapter 5, the Chinese public were all caught off guard in relation to the events of 2011 in the Arab world.

A reader who is familiar with the recent literature on the Chinese community of foreign affairs professionals, including both diplomats and analysts in think tanks and universities, will be aware that it is very difficult to understand how knowledge is produced and channeled to policymakers. This is because

---

[1] 1996 (Egypt, Ethiopia, Mali), 1999 (Algeria, Morocco, Saudi Arabia), 2000 (Israel, Palestine, Egypt, Turkey), 2002 (Iran, Tunisia, Libya), 2004 (Egypt, Algeria), 2006 (Saudia Arabia, Morocco), 2007 (Sudan), 2009 (Mali, Saudi Arabia), 2016 (Saudi Arabia, Egypt, Iran), 2018 (United Arab Emirates).

[2] 1991 (Egypt), 1995 (Morocco), 2002 (Turkey, Egypt, Algeria, Morocco), 2003 (Ethiopia), 2006 (Egypt), 2009 (Egypt), 2012 (Qatar, United Arab Emirates, Saudi Arabia), 2014 (Ethiopia).

Protecting China's Interests Overseas: Securitization and Foreign Policy. Andrea Ghiselli,
Oxford University Press (2021). © Andrea Ghiselli.
DOI: 10.1093/oso/9780198867395.001.0001

both the fragmentation of the policymaking system and the pluralization of the actors involved have increased since the 1980s (Lampton 2001; Sutter 2012, 27). Moreover, it is not surprising that very little is known about the training and the background of the Chinese "soldiers in plainclothes," that is, the diplomats posted overseas.[3] On the basis of their personal experience at the Ministry of Foreign Affairs (MFA), Lu Ning (1997) and Liu Xiaohong (2001) wrote about the recruitment and training process of Chinese diplomats before the 1990s.[4] The brief study prepared by Michael Deegan and Joel Keralis (2017) is the only recent attempt to gain a more general understanding of the MFA's situation and tradition. The Chinese language literature is quite limited as well (Zhang and Zhao 2011; Zhang 2013; Wang and Li 2017; Liu 2018). This is all the truer when it comes to those parts of the Chinese academic, policy, and diplomatic community, either working in North African and Middle Eastern countries or on issues related to them. At most, Susan Shirk (2007, 109–10) praised individual diplomats like Wang Yi and Fu Ying many times when they served in the Asian Affairs Department of the MFA.

This chapter, therefore, argues that experts in Middle Eastern and North African affairs, both inside what Zhao Quansheng (2012, 134) defined as the "inner circle" (key policymaking individuals and organizations in the party and the government) and in the "outer circle" (the news media, universities, and think tanks), faced a number of challenges in either transmitting or producing precious information to policymakers. However, they probably did— and will increasingly—play a role in shaping Chinese foreign policy due to the growing demand for high-quality analyses and ideas necessary for improving the protection of China's interests overseas. This chapter first discusses the influence of the MFA within the Chinese foreign policymaking machine, and the professionalization and area expertise of its top officials posted in Middle Eastern and North African countries. The second section takes into consideration the Chinese community of both regional experts and generalist international relations scholars who work in "outer circle" institutions, assessing their expertise and ability to influence foreign policymaking.

---

[3] This expression was used by Zhou Enlai. In Chinese: 外交队伍是文装的解放军 (Wàijiāo duìwǔ shì wén zhuāng de jiěfàngjūn).
[4] Lu Ning served in the Chinese MFA as an analyst and assistant to a vice minister. Liu Xiaohong was a diplomat who worked in the Western European Affairs Department of the MFA between 1977 and 1997.

More Professional but Not More Influential

The world has transformed greatly, and China and its diplomats with it. Today's diplomats are the most professional and the most numerous that the People's Republic of China has ever had. This is mostly the result of historical trends rather than recent decisions taken by the Chinese leadership. Hence, it is important to review briefly the history of China's diplomatic corps, which can be divided into three main eras according to the number of the serving diplomats and the training they received.

The first, roughly from 1949 to the mid-1960s, is the era of the "general ambassadors." The first Chinese ambassadors sent abroad were high-ranking officials from the Chinese People's Liberation Army (PLA). Although many could not speak any foreign languages, and were not very used to Western etiquette and manners, China had to send its envoys to the first countries that recognized the infant People's Republic. Twelve of the first fifteen ambassadors were PLA generals, and many of the 700 diplomats sent to the seventeen Chinese embassies abroad during those early years had a military background.

The second period—also known as that of the "interpreter ambassadors"—spans the years from the mid-1960s to the 1990s. As China's diplomacy expanded after the Conference of Geneva and the Bandung Conference, Zhou Enlai, who was also the foreign minister, proposed the "three-three system."[5] That was the first institutionalized system for the recruitment and management of Chinese diplomats. According to it, while one-third of the diplomats were abroad, the two other thirds would be working at the headquarters in Beijing and undergoing specialized training. Hence, the MFA launched the Twenty-Year Program for Diplomatic Cadres Training in 1955 and the Seven-Year (1956–62) Program for Diplomatic Cadres Training.[6] At the same time, thousands of students were selected to be sent abroad to study foreign languages.

Between 1954 and 1966, China had seventy-seven ambassadors and only a third of them still belonged to the group of "general ambassadors." Probably as a result of the importance attached to professionalism and an awareness that the Chinese diplomatic machine still had to be organized in order to meet the significant challenges that any new country faces in the

---

[5] In Chinese: 三三制 (Sān sān zhì).
[6] In Chinese: 培养外交干部二十年规划 (Péiyǎng wàijiāo gànbù èrshí nián guīhuà) and 培养外交干部七年 (1956–62) 规划 (Péiyǎng wàijiāo gànbù qī nián (1956–62) guīhuà).

aftermath of its foundation, significant space for maneuvering was given to ambassadors to shape the organization of the ministry. For example, the discussion about splitting the Department of African and West Asian Affairs and creating a new one in charge of the Middle East and North Africa was already going on in the early 1960s within the MFA.[7] During Zhou Enlai's visit to Africa between 1963 and 1964, the then Chinese ambassador to the United Arab Republic Chen Jiakang officially submitted to the MFA a proposal to carry out such reform as one way to improve diplomatic work relating to Arab countries. His move, together with the Chinese government's growing interests in the Middle East as one of the main fronts of the global struggle between the capitalist and the socialist camps (Shichor 1979, 49–50), played an important role kickstarting the process that led to the creation of the Department of West Asian and North African (WANA) Affairs of the MFA in 1964 (Zheng and Long 2011).

Unfortunately, the Cultural Revolution disrupted not only Chinese diplomacy, also symbolized by the occupation of the MFA building by the Red Guards during the first half of 1967,[8] but also the quantitative and qualitative growth of the MFA. Some departments, such as that in charge of Middle Eastern and North African affairs, were even temporarily disbanded and/or absorbed by others as the scope of Chinese foreign policy shrank (Shichor 1979, 147–8). Many Chinese diplomats in Beijing and abroad were accused of being revisionists, reactionaries, and agents of foreign powers. Between 1966 and 1967, all the Chinese ambassadors—except Ambassador Huang Hua in Egypt—and about one-third of the staff of the Chinese embassies abroad were recalled to Beijing (Eisenman 2018).[9] Less experienced but more ideologically radical cadres were sent abroad to spread the Maoist message.

According to Daniel Tretiak (1980), while more than 80 percent of the ambassadors managed to return to a diplomatic career, probably because of

[7] The Department of African and West Asian Affairs was created in 1956, immediately after the Bandung Conference. Before then, the Department of West European and African Affairs was in charge of African affairs.

[8] The interested reader can find a more detailed account of events in Gurtov (1969).

[9] Probably, Huang was not recalled for three reasons. First, Egypt was a key country for Chinese diplomacy within those countries that formed Mao's "intermediate zone." Second, the embassy in Cairo played a key role in coordinating China's support for revolutionary movements in both Africa and the Middle East. Third, Huang, who joined the CCP after he went to Yan'an with Edgar Snow in the 1930s, was one of the most brilliant members of the party's international relations and propaganda machine. His value to the Chinese leadership is further proved by the fact that he later became the Chinese ambassador to the United Nations in 1971. As foreign minister, he accompanied Deng Xiaoping in his groundbreaking visit to the United States in 1972.

the protection that Zhou Enlai guaranteed to the MFA and its high-ranking officials, some 40 percent of the staff based in Beijing and counselor-level diplomats were not able to enjoy such protection and disappeared during those years. At the same time, the MFA was not able to hire qualified personnel either during or immediately after the Cultural Revolution because of the interruption of university courses. Therefore, in order to avoid sending diplomats abroad with no language skills at all, many of the ambassadors who were sent back after 1969 to the countries from which they had been recalled remained in service there for more than ten years (Wang and Li 2017).

In the early 1980s, the MFA started to replace ambassadors who were aged over 60 years old, and many retired during the years that followed. However, the third era really started in the 1990s, with the MFA being part of the efforts of the Chinese bureaucracy to achieve the "four-way transformation of the cadres" into a more revolutionary, younger, better-educated, and more technically specialized group.[10] The salaries of the diplomats was raised to exceed those of same-level public officials in order to attract high-quality recruits. However, this happened only after 30 percent of the officials aged below 30 had left the MFA as a result of the 1993–4 reform of the salary system in the public administration. According to Chinese media, the basic salary of a junior diplomat is slightly under RMB 7,000 (about USD 1,100) per month (Zhao 2016).

At the same time, the hiring process and career path of Chinese diplomats were standardized and regulated. From 2006, aspiring diplomats have had to go through the general exam that all those who want to become public servants have to take (People's Daily 2005). The candidates, usually from China's top universities, are sometimes recommended by their teachers to the MFA, which might also give quotas to those universities to fill (Loh 2019). Only those with the highest grades are allowed to sit the MFA-only professional test. In 2010, the Chinese government approved a new law aimed at clarifying the requirements, duties, and benefits for diplomats. As a comment of Zha Peixin, a member of the Standing Committee of the 11th National People's Congress and Vice Chairman of its Foreign Affairs Committee shows, one of the main changes that the 2010 Law of the People's Republic of China on Diplomatic Personnel Stationed Abroad introduced was that the minimum age for diplomats assigned to the embassies and consulates abroad was raised

---

[10] In Chinese: 干部四化 (Gànbù sì huà).

from 17 to 23 in order to ensure that virtually all the candidates hold at least a college degree (PRC NPC 2009b).

Yet, while today's diplomats are the most educated and professional in Chinese history, there are still problems in their skillset caused by the breathtaking speed of China's expansion of global interests and the fierce competition for talent between government institutions and business organizations. To begin with, the issue of professionalization seems, surprisingly, still a contested one despite the constant push in that direction throughout the history of the MFA. Indeed, the publicly available records of the discussion on the 2010 law show that there was no consensus over making explicit the goal of creating a professional class of diplomats. Although some argued that it was necessary to specify that Chinese diplomats must professionalize (PRC NPC 2009a), the law ended up requiring only "high-quality" diplomats for training (PRC NPC 2011).[11]

At the same time, the opportunity to earn more in the corporate world than in the embassies and consulates around the world remains one of the main reasons for the insufficient number of high-quality recruits. This is especially true when it comes to those skills that are extremely useful in an age of growing threats to Chinese interests in North Africa and the Middle East, but that do not improve career prospects in the MFA. Indeed, as the profile of current and past high-ranking officers shows, diplomats from the WANA Affairs Department rarely reach the rank of minister, vice minister, or assistant minister.[12] However, working in the Asian Affairs, North American and Oceanian Affairs, and European Affairs departments, and their affiliated embassies, greatly improves the chances of being promoted to the top positions in the MFA. For example, both the current minister, Wang Yi, and his predecessor, Yang Jiechi, are experts in Asian and American affairs, with long experience of service in those countries. This imbalance grows out of China's diplomatic priorities and has a deep impact on the career development of Chinese diplomats.

First, only the ambassadors to France, Germany, the United States, the United Kingdom, Brazil, Russia, India, North Korea, and Japan can hold the rank of

---

[11] In Chinese: 高素质 (Gāo sùzhì).

[12] Those who did are Chen Xiaodong (assistant foreign minister 2017-); Zhai Jun (assistant foreign minister 2006–9; Vice Minister 2009–14); Lu Guozeng (assistant foreign minister 2003–6, vice minister 2006–11); Wang Changyi (assistant foreign minister 1993–5); Wen Yezhan (vice minister1982–4); He Ying (vice minister 1975–82).

vice minister while serving abroad. Hence, they are also better positioned to move further up in the hierarchy of the state and party. The comparison between Zhai Jun, the current special envoy of the Chinese government to the Middle East and Wang Yi is telling.[13] They are close in age, as they were born in 1953 (Wang) and 1954 (Zhai), respectively. They also graduated, having majored in foreign languages from two of China's best language schools, the Beijing International Studies University and the Beijing Foreign Studies University. While Zhai studied Arabic, Wang learnt Japanese. Yet their career paths differ. Zhai joined the MFA in 1975, seven years earlier than Wang, and quickly rose through the ranks of the WANA Affairs Department by alternating periods in Beijing with periods in the Middle East. In 1997, the 43-year-old Zhai Jun became the youngest ambassador in the MFA's history and was given charge of the embassy in Libya. By the same year, Wang had also served abroad, although not as ambassador, and had already become the head of the Asian Affairs Department. Wang, therefore, was already better positioned to be promoted assistant foreign minister, as indeed happened in 1998. From that moment on, Wang moved on to higher positions both within the MFA and the party. His ambassadorship to Japan between 2004 and 2007, after promotion to the rank of vice minister in 2001, was simply one of the steps on the path that led him to become minister and state councilor. In comparison, Zhai became the director of the WANA Affairs Department and then assistant foreign minister only in 2003 and 2006, after a brief stint as a member of the Party Standing Committee of Zhenjiang, in Jiangsu Province, between 2000 and 2001. After five years as vice minister, from 2009 to 2014, Zhai was sent to France as ambassador.

Within the MFA, that was probably the only possible step forward for him. As a journalist from the *Shanghai Observer* commented, Zhai's vice-ministerial rank made it difficult to imagine what else he could have been assigned to, had the position in Paris not been available (Ruo 2014). In early 2019 he was nominated special envoy of the Chinese government, thereby returning to take care of Middle Eastern affairs instead of moving up in the hierarchy of the ministry. The differences between Wang's and Zhai's careers confirms the general pattern of promotion within the MFA: while capable diplomats from departments like the Asian/North American/European Affairs Department can aspire to become ministers or state councilors, those from other departments are more likely to become special envoys.

---

[13] In Chinese: 中国政府特使 (Zhōngguó zhèngfǔ tèshǐ).

Besides the extensive traveling, it is a position that does not seem to differ significantly from that of a normal ambassador and their office is, indeed, hosted by the same department of the MFA to which they previously belonged.

Second, the study of "non-common languages" has long received relatively scant support from the government.[14] Even a number of senior scholars and administrators at Beijing Foreign Studies University complained that the government should do more to encourage the study of languages like Arabic and Turkish because demand from ministries and private companies for people who can speak those languages has expanded significantly in recent years, while supply has remained extremely low (*International Herald Leader* 2015). Finding foreign language speakers is still a priority for the MFA. That means that it has to compete with other state and private institutions which can often offer higher salaries.

At the same time, probably because of the still-dominant focus on foreign languages, the MFA has to "borrow" officials from other ministries because its own diplomats do not always have the necessary technical skills. As pointed out by Wang Yizhou and Li Xinda (2017), the problem lies in the fact that the embassies suffer from expertise gaps when the rotation of these "borrowed" officials is interrupted by their home ministries. According to suggestions put forward by Xue Li (2012), director of the influential Department of International Strategy, Institute of World Economics and Politics of the Chinese Academy of Social Sciences (CASS), the lack of diplomats with previous working experience in the private sector and the limited off-the-job training and exchanges with the academic community are problems that still plague the Chinese diplomatic corps. As another observer pointed out, the lack of diversity, combined with very strict discipline enforced within the MFA ranks, is sometimes an obstacle for Chinese diplomats when it comes to socializing and working with their foreign counterparts (Qiu 2017).

All these factors are likely to contribute to limiting the influence of a group of diplomats within the MFA's WANA Affairs Department, which has grown increasingly experienced and knowledgeable over the years. Their growth in terms of regional expertise and familiarity with the policymaking related to those countries is evident if one compares them with, for example, their colleagues in European capitals (Table 2). To begin with, all but two of the ambassadors in North African and Middle Eastern countries over the last fifteen years are career diplomats. Of those two, one was actually

---

[14] In Chinese: 非通用语 (Fēi tōngyòng yǔ).

Table 2 Career and regional expertise of Chinese diplomats

	WANA (2004–17)	Europe (2004–17)
Average number of assignments abroad before becoming ambassador to a WANA/European country	3.5	2.7
Average number of countries in the WANA or Europe where the diplomat was posted before becoming ambassador to a WANA/European country	2.1	0.8
Percentage of ambassadors who were posted only to WANA/European countries before becoming ambassador to a WANA/European country	47.8%	21.2%
Percentage of ambassadors who rose through the ranks of the WANA/ European Affairs Department of the MFA before becoming ambassadors to WANA/European countries	54.3%	13.5%

Note: See Appendix 4 for further details on the data used for this table.

Source: Websites of Chinese embassies. Compiled by the author.

"borrowed" from the 3rd Department of the Chinese Communist Party (CCP)'s Central International Liaison Department, which is responsible for North African and Middle Eastern affairs.

The vast majority of them had already worked in embassies and consulates in those regions during earlier stages of their careers. Many top Chinese diplomats in WANA countries served only in other countries in the same region before becoming ambassadors. On average, a Chinese ambassador in a WANA country has already worked in two other countries of the region. The most notable exceptions are the ambassadors to Israel and francophone countries like Algeria. They, however, are often not selected randomly because at least some of them have worked in the United States (in the case of the ambassadors to Israel), and in France or other francophone countries. They, therefore, are familiar with the policies of local and external actors that can significantly affect China's relations with the country where they are posted. Hence, many of the Chinese ambassadors to North Africa and the Middle East, in theory, can count on significant knowledge of the region and a pre-existing network of local and foreign officials they met there previously. An interesting case is that of the current ambassador to Saudi Arabia, Chen Weiqing, who led China's "hawza[15] diplomacy" in Iraq, where he was previously posted, to get to know better the leaders of local religious communities, who can be important allies in the fight against Islamist terrorism in the region as well as at home (Al-Sudairi 2019). The ambassadors who serve, and served, in

---

[15] Hawzas are seminaries where Shi'a Muslim clerics are educated.

Egypt, Saudi Arabia, the United Arab Emirates, Syria, Libya, Yemen, Sudan, and South Sudan worked almost only in countries in North Africa and the Middle East and, sometimes, went back to countries where they had already served when they were younger.

At the same time, slightly more than half of the ambassadors in North African and Middle Eastern countries have risen through the ranks of the WANA Affairs Department of the MFA. Many reached the position of department director or deputy director before being promoted to an ambassadorship. The growing institutionalization of the career paths of these diplomats suggested by the data has several implications. First, it is very likely they have undergone intensive language training to perfect skills that most of them had already acquired by graduating from schools like the Beijing Foreign Studies University. Second, they are extremely familiar with Chinese policy in relation to the region. Third, they can transmit their knowledge to junior colleagues and keep up to date with the countries they are likely to be sent to. Therefore, they contribute to the accumulation and retention of precious expertise within the MFA.

The situation differs drastically in the case of Chinese ambassadors in Europe. To begin with, a small number of them were selected from the bureaucracy of provincial governments. This is the case, for example, of Cui Zhiwei. After a life spent in the government of Sichuan Province, Cui served from 2011 to 2014 as ambassador to Northern Macedonia. Ye Wei is now the ambassador in Albania after having held the same position in Slovenia. However, he worked for more than thirty years in the government of Nanjing before joining the MFA. There are also a few cases of ambassadors coming from the corporate world. It is not unusual for diplomats with experience of serving in other regions to be promoted to head embassies and consulates in Europe. This is often a sort of reward for many years of service in far less comfortable places. The above-mentioned case of Zhai Jun is just one of many. Moreover, many ambassadors certainly have some knowledge of European affairs and can read European newspapers without the level of training required to do the same in North Africa and the Middle East. Therefore, it is not surprising to see that, although some have been posted to the same European country many times, many of the top Chinese diplomats in Europe have never served there before their promotion. Under 20 percent of them come from the Department of European Affairs. The rest come from either other departments of the MFA or other institutions of the Chinese state. Moreover, as Table 2 shows, it seems that, on average, ambassadors in Europe also have less experience of working abroad than their counterparts in North Africa and the Middle East.

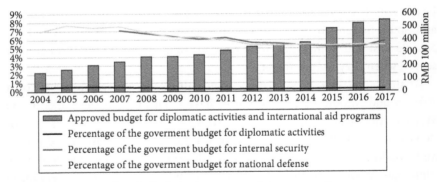

Figure 22 Putting China's diplomatic expenses into perspective

Notes: In order of magnitude, China's diplomatic expenses include those for international aid, support for international organizations, the activities of embassies and consulates abroad, and other general management costs. The costs for internal security in the tables of the Ministry of Finance include the budget of the Chinese People's Armed Police.

Source: PRC Ministry of Finance. Compiled by the author.

Nonetheless, these well-trained and experienced diplomats work in an institution that appears to be overstretched. Indeed, the MFA suffers from a mismatch between the growing number and complexity of the tasks assigned and the resources at its disposal. This problem is particularly acute in areas that are not perceived as central to Chinese diplomacy. Indeed, according to Li Wentao (2018), the deputy director of the Institute of African Studies of the China Institutes of Contemporary International Relations (CICIR), China's security engagement in Africa and the Middle East is undermined by the fact that China spends the vast majority of its "diplomatic resources" on its relationship with the United States and with its neighbors in Asia.[16] This fact, he argues, limits investment in diplomatic activities and intelligence gathering in Africa and other regions where Chinese interests are increasingly threatened by instability and terrorism.

Li's observation should also be put in the context of the broader evolution of the budget of the Chinese central government. China's expenses for diplomatic activities have been rising steadily over the years, although the proportion they take up of the total government budget has slightly decreased (Figure 22). Since the budget approved for the PLA and internal security activities has also decreased in terms of share of the total expenses of the Chinese state, the evolution of the MFA's budget can be read in two ways. On

---

[16] In Chinese: 外交资源 (Wàijiāo zīyuán).

the one hand, the similarity of patterns of defense and diplomatic expenses means that the MFA has not been left behind. On the other hand, however, it is surely not a sign of prioritization in the face of a significant increase in diplomatic ambitions. Either way, as a scholar from Nankai University pointed out, the gap between what the ministry has to do and can do seems to be growing rather than shrinking, risking a corresponding reduction in the quality of the diplomatic work (Dong 2016). A comparison with other countries' diplomatic budgets helps to clarify this fact: China's USD 7.5 billion in 2017 is an extremely low budget in comparison with the United States' USD 31.3 billion or Germany's USD 16.2 billion. Chapter 6 further shows how this lack of resources has influenced the work of China's consular protection system.

At the same time, although the MFA remains the leading institution in policy implementation in China, there is a large number of actors that can shape the environment in which Chinese diplomats work abroad, as well as the channels of communication between the ministry and the top policymakers. During the Hu Jintao administration, one could notice the growing distance between the minister of foreign affairs and the top leadership. Indeed, from the days of Zhou Enlai in the 1950s to those of Li Zhaoxing fifty years later, the influence of the MFA has reduced (Sun 2017). This is particularly clear if one looks at the diminished rank of its minister within the party hierarchy, and at the position that the official took after his tenure as leader of the MFA (Table 3). On the one hand, both Tang Jiaxuan and Li Zhaoxing did not make it into the Politburo of the CCP as their predecessors, Qian Qichen and Wu Xueqian, did. Moreover, while Tang, at least, became state councilor, which can still be considered a downgrade compared to the vice premiership of Wu and Qian, Li was sent to head the Foreign Affairs Committee of the National People's Congress.

It was Dai Bingguo who emerged as the foremost and highest-ranking figure in Chinese foreign policy in the Hu Jintao administration. Dai, an expert in Russian affairs, rose through the ranks of the MFA and became vice minister in 1993. Later, when he became the deputy head and then head of the CCP Central International Liaison Department, he earned Hu's confidence by accompanying the soon-to-be president and party secretary general on his trips abroad (Li 2016, 57). Thanks to his skills and the trust of the top leader, Dai went back to the MFA as chief of the CCP Committee of the Ministry, from 2003 to 2007. In 2008, he was promoted to state councilor with the foreign affairs portfolio. As director of the General Office of the CCP Foreign

Table 3 Top party and state positions of Chinese ministers of foreign affairs

Name	Tenure as minister of foreign affairs	Highest position in the party/government/ military
Zhou Enlai	1949–58	CCP Politburo Standing Committee member (1956–76); premier (1949–76)
Chen Yi	1958–72	CCP Politburo (1956–67); vice premier (1965–75); marshal of the PLA (1955–74)
Ji Pengfei	1972–3	CCP Central Committee (1973–82); vice president of the National People's Congress (1978–83)
Qiao Guanhua	1973–6	CCP Central Committee (1973–7); purged after the Cultural Revolution
Huang Hua	1976–82	CCP Central Committee (1973–87); vice premier (1976–82)
Wu Xueqian	1982–8	CCP Politburo (1987–92); vice premier (1988–93)
Qian Qichen	1988–98	CCP Politburo (1992–2002); vice premier (1993–2003)
Tang Jiaxuan	1998–2003	CCP Central Committee (1997–2007); state councilor (2003–8)
Li Zhaoxing	2003–7	CCP Central Committee (2002–7); Foreign Affairs Committee of the National People's Congress (2008–13)
Yang Jiechi	2007–13	CCP Politburo (2017–present); state councilor (2013–18)
Wang Yi	2013–present	CCP Central Committee (2007–present); state councilor (2018–present)

Source: Compiled by the author.

Affairs Leading Small Group, from 2005 until his retirement in 2013, Dai remained closer to the top leadership than both Li Zhaoxing and Yang Jiechi.

Being an experienced career diplomat himself, Dai's presence surely did not mean that there was a deficit of diplomatic expertise at the top of the Chinese polity. However, it added one more gatekeeper with his own preferences and priorities in a crucial position in the chain of command, thereby risking further deprioritizing information coming from certain regions, or increasing the reaction time to a crisis. A real change in the situation took place with the promotions of Yang Jiechi and Wang Yi, between late 2017 and early 2018. Yang, who has been the director of the Central Foreign Affairs Commission Office since 2013, became a member of the powerful Politburo of the CCP. Wang Yi rose to the rank of state councilor while also keeping the title of minister of foreign affairs. It is necessary to point out that Wang's double title is remarkable as only the heads of the Ministry of National Defense and the Ministry of State Security were allowed to do that in the past. Their promotions represent an important improvement for Chinese diplomats. On the one hand, Wang's new administrative rank puts the MFA in a higher position compared to those of other ministries of the State Council. Being one of the state councilors, Wang is part of the Standing Committee of the State Council and, therefore, has much easier access to the core of Chinese policymaking. The state counsellorship should also further strengthen his position within the CCP Central Foreign Affairs Commission as head of the lead department. On the other hand, Yang can better represent the interests of the diplomatic corps within one of the highest decision-making bodies of the CCP. Dai never reached that position. Moreover, Yang's influence is further strengthened by his membership of the National Security Commission of the CCP Central Committee.

Within the State Council, the MFA has also to deal with the influence of other important actors in shaping China's foreign economic engagement. The Ministry of Commerce (MOFCOM) is a fierce competitor of the MFA in countries and regions where investments and trade are the main drivers of Chinese foreign policy. Tellingly, a former Chinese ambassador to an African country told Lucy Corkin (2011, 74) that "It is only when problems occur that the Chinese companies contact me; otherwise, they do not see me at all." It is also important to emphasize how the National Development and Reform Commission (NDRC) too has increased its influence vis-à-vis the MFA in the aftermath of the launch of the Belt and Road Initiative (BRI). The BRI has strengthened the NDRC's capacity to shape China's foreign policy in the numerous countries involved in that initiative, including those in North Africa and the Middle East. While the initial meetings for the drafting of the BRI were co-chaired by Wang Yi and the former NDRC vice chairman, Xu Shaoshi, the NDRC has steadily strengthened its position thanks to its authority in setting the strategic priorities for Chinese investments abroad and, together with MOFCOM and (probably) the new China International Development Cooperation Agency, in approving them (Zhang 2016, 14).

Reportedly, officers from the NDRC were already taking the lead during the eighth meeting of the CCP Financial and Economic Leading Small Group (now CCP Central Financial and Economic Affairs Commission of the CCP Central Committee) in November 2014, when they briefed Xi Jinping, Li Keqiang, Liu Yunshan, and Zhang Gaoli on the key initiatives that were going to form the BRI, from the launch of the Asian Infrastructure Investment Bank to the establishment of the Silk Road Fund (Zhang 2016, 15). Shortly after that meeting, the NDRC also became the host institution of the general office of the CCP Leading Small Group for Advancing the Development of the One

Belt One Road, thereby becoming the agency in charge of the daily work of the high-level task force of state and party officials in charge of the implementation of the BRI. Yang Jiechi is one the four deputy chairs of that leading small group, together with Hu Chunhua, Xiao Jie, and He Lifeng. Although it is true, as Yu Jie (2018) argues, that it is not possible to say that the NDRC has a monopoly in the BRI, there is no doubt that China's top diplomat is less in control of it than if the NDRC were not involved so prominently. Naturally, it is likely that other agencies related to China's foreign policy, especially MOFCOM, have increased their influence as a result of the further prioritization of economic engagement with foreign partners envisaged by the BRI.

While the BRI mostly affected the standing of Chinese diplomats at a ministerial level, the growing use under Xi Jinping of high-ranking officials without a diplomatic background, such as presidential special envoys, also contributes to watering down the influence of Yang Jiechi and Wang Yi at a personal level when it comes to certain specific issues. Between 2013 and 2015, at least thirty-two officials, including ministers and deputy national leaders, met with foreign leaders at home and abroad on behalf of Xi Jinping. Without a shadow of doubt, the most interesting and powerful of them is Vice President Wang Qishan. Wang is a close ally of Xi Jinping and is his most trusted troubleshooter. During Xi Jinping's first term, Wang led the massive anticorruption campaign that, so far, has led to the arrest of more than 100,000 officials, including five former Politburo members. Despite his retirement from the Standing Committee of the Politburo, Wang still attends the meetings of that all-powerful party institution and of the CCP Central Foreign Affairs Commission. The title of vice president used to be largely ceremonial, but now it gives Wang the opportunity to have frequent meetings with foreign leaders without causing upheaval in the Chinese institutional setting, which is already stretched by the fact that he is nominally just one of the many party members without an official role in the party hierarchy.

The *People's Daily* pointed out that it seems there is a relationship between the visits of presidential special envoys, China's expanding overseas interests and, interestingly, the non-traditional security threats against them (Jia 2015). While Wang went on a tour in the Middle East in summer 2018, the former minister of Public Security and former secretary of the Central Political and Legal Affairs Commission of the CCP, Meng Jianzhu, visited Iran, Egypt, and Turkey in 2014, and England and Germany in 2015 on behalf of Xi Jinping in order to boost antiterrorism and security cooperation with countries where Chinese citizens are threatened, or which have expertise against those kinds of threats. This development, too, contributes to limiting the influence of Chinese ambassadors as well as top diplomats like Yang Jiechi and Wang Yi on non-economic foreign policy issues.

Outside the "Inner Circle" of Foreign Policymaking

The discussion among foreign and Chinese scholars about the role and influence of Chinese think tanks has been going on since the early 2000s as part of the general debate over the evolution of Chinese foreign policymaking. The maturation and development of the Chinese diplomatic machine since the 1980s greatly benefited from, and was heavily influenced by, the growing synergy between top government officials and the academic world (Zhao 1992; Gong, Men, and Sun 2009). For example, in the early 1990s, Jiang Zemin often received advice from scholars at Shanghai-based institutions such as Fudan University and the East China University of Political Science and Law. In 2006, at the First Forum on China's Think Tanks, held in Beijing, the Chinese authorities designated the top ten think tanks in the country for the first time in the history of the People's Republic.[17] At the same time, "revolving door" mechanisms between government agencies and research centers and the return of foreign-educated scholars have contributed to improving the quality of the research and expertise of those institutions that lay outside the "inner circle" of Chinese foreign policymaking (Zhu and Xue 2007; Li 2009). On the basis of her interviews with Chinese scholars in universities and other research institutions, Bonnie Glaser (2012) wrote that meetings between them and increasingly curious government officials have become more frequent and more effective platforms for discussing ideas about national security and foreign policy. Large businesses, such as SOEs with global interests, are also among the main "customers" of Chinese research institutions. Therefore, it is important to understand what and how the Chinese community of Middle Eastern and North African affairs experts could do to influence and warn policymakers about the threats to China's interest frontiers.

---

[17] The ten top think tanks are: CASS, the Development Research Center of the State Council, the Academy of Military Sciences, the China Institute of International Study, the China Institute of Contemporary International Relations, the China National Committee for Pacific Economic Cooperation, the China Association for Science and Technology, the China International Institute of Strategic Society, the Shanghai Institute for International Studies, and the Chinese Academy of Sciences.

The study of Middle Eastern and North African affairs and languages in China was created to support Chinese diplomacy. After the Bandung Conference in 1955, Zhou Enlai embarked on three tours to Asian and African countries. Before leaving for the third one in late 1963, he submitted a proposal to Mao Zedong about strengthening the study of foreign languages and international affairs. The proposal was approved and became Central Document No. 886 of 1963 (Zhao 2005), thereby giving a significant boost to the research and teaching of area studies, including Middle Eastern and North African affairs and languages. Those types of studies were already being conducted in the foreign language and history departments of a few schools such as Peking University (since 1954), the University of International Business and Economics (since 1954), and the China Foreign Affairs University (since 1958). However, it was in the 1960s that their institutionalization began, thanks to the creation of new teaching programs at the Shanghai International Studies University (1960), the Beijing Foreign Studies University (1961), the CCP Central International Liaison Department (1961), the Beijing Foreign Studies University (1962), the Beijing International Studies University (1964), the Beijing Language and Culture University (1964), the Northwest University (1964), the Yunnan University (1964), CASS (1964), and the PLA Foreign Language School in Luoyang (1964).

While some institutions had both language courses and classes on political, economic, social, and cultural trends in North African and Middle Eastern countries, the majority had only one of the two. Nonetheless, they were all meant to train personnel for the party, the state, and the military. After the Cultural Revolution, during which language schools were partially protected by Zhou Enlai, Deng Xiaoping's reform created a more relaxed environment and favorable conditions for the deepening and diversification of research (Wang 2010, 41). Indeed, the number of publicly available publications boomed, and in 2009 the number of articles and books looking at the Middle East and North Africa from a variety points of view totaled 11,000 and 1,200, respectively (Zhou 2010). The research carried out by Chinese scholars has been driven by both endogenous and exogenous factors (Yang 2010; Cheng 2010). On the one hand, China's growing energy needs and commercial expansion are behind many of the studies on the economies of the countries in North Africa and the Middle East. On the other hand, events like the Iranian Revolution, the First Gulf War, the 9/11 attack, and Iran's nuclear program inspired the publication of a significant number of books and articles.

It is difficult to assess the impact of scholars on Chinese foreign policy-making because even successful bottom-up input rarely receives feedback, and the leadership style of the top policymakers can create, as well as reduce, the room for such information (Jakobson and Manuel 2016). Nonetheless, a review of how Middle Eastern and North African affairs scholars in China look at their own community reveals that their ability to influence the dynamics of the "inner circle" of foreign policymaking is rather limited due to two main issues (Lin 2012; Fan 2013; Zhang 2017; Pu and Li 2018).

The first is the difficulty of those in the "outer circle" in communicating with policymakers. Chinese scholars can (try to) communicate with government officials at different levels through eight different channels. First is joining brainstorming meetings with government officials from the ministries and agencies of the State Council and top leadership figures. Second is exploiting personal connections with officials in state or party institutions. Third is writing reports and studies commissioned by government departments. Fourth is writing reports on trips abroad. These reports can be either solicited by the government or submitted on the scholar's own initiative. Fifth is joining the delegations of government officials for trips abroad. Sixth is writing internal non-solicited reports. Seventh is publishing in academic and media outlets. Eighth is serving as a diplomat and/or advisor to an ambassador/consul for a short period of time in an embassy or consulate abroad. However, the number of scholars who can actually hope to have their words heard or read by government and party officials is extremely limited. On the one hand, not many experts have personal relationships with "inner circle" officials. On the other hand, only a limited number of scholars, usually former diplomats, government officials, and PLA officers, work in institutions that have strong institutional channels for submitting their reports to government agencies.

The second problem is the low number of high-quality studies. Chinese scholars ascribe this problem to many interrelated factors. First, the Chinese academic community is dominated by international relations generalists, and area studies are, therefore, underdeveloped and mostly carried out in history and foreign language departments. Second, too few researchers received language training. This is probably because most of those who have received it work for the MFA or the private sector, where demand and pay are higher than in academia. Third, there is a lack of creativity and critical perspective. With limited or no access to original-language open and classified sources, many scholars can only rely on information and analyses produced abroad. Fourth, many recycle themselves as experts on whatever issue is most popular or write studies that simply repeat and support the policies of the government. Unfortunately, but not surprisingly, only unsolicited reports and studies deemed to be of sufficiently high quality by the heads of research institutions and by officers in the general office of the receiving institution are submitted for distribution to specific offices in the government bureaucracy and, possibly, to the top leadership.

These problems are not uncommon in Chinese research institutions working on foreign policy issues (Zhang and Fang 2018). However, it seems that they are particularly acute when it comes to North African and Middle Eastern affairs. Hence, the number of Chinese scholars who can write unsolicited reports or expect to be called on regularly to provide policy advice on those topics is small. Most frequently, they are based at the Institute of WANA Studies of CASS, the Shanghai Institute of International Studies, CICIR, or the China Institute of International Studies. Among the institutions that operate outside of ministries, party organizations, and the PLA, these think tanks are recognized by Chinese scholars as the most influential in the field of international relations (Appendix 5). They all have well-known relations with government organs—CASS with the State Council, the Shanghai Institute of International Studies with the Shanghai government, CICIR with the Ministry of State Security, and the China Institute of International Studies with the MFA—and, at the same time, carry out a broad range of activities, such as engaging with the media and training graduate students, which in-house think tanks do not do. To date, nineteen scholars in those institutions have received college-level Arabic/Turkish/Farsi/Hebrew language training or served for brief stints in embassies or consulates in North Africa and the Middle East (two are former ambassadors) or are members of centers specializing in Middle Eastern and African studies. Most of them are at CICIR and the China Institute of International Studies. However, according to the information reported on their profiles online, only seven share all three features mentioned above. The number goes up to nine if we include the two former ambassadors at the China Institute of International Studies, who, being over 80 years old, are probably less engaged than their younger colleagues. Exceptions exist and other scholars outside those four institutions are certainly consulted by the government or are capable of producing high-quality research, but the community of Middle Eastern and North African experts is still clearly in its early stages of development, and its capacity to provide cautionary advice to Chinese policymakers is likely to be limited.

The growing demand for analysis of political, ethnic, and religious trends in the Middle East and North Africa from the CCP leadership might provide the necessary impetus for the improvement in the quality of the research done by Chinese scholars and the subsequent channels of communication with the government (Appendix 6). Until then, however, there is little doubt that the factors outlined above place Chinese scholars—who, much like their Western counterparts, did not see the Arab Spring coming (Fan 2013)—in a weak position in terms of providing any warning of possible threats to China's interest frontiers. A great number of the known cases of scholars contributing to changes in Chinese foreign policy are mostly related to specific events. For example, a classic scenario could be one expert providing the correct analysis of how the elections in a certain country might go or how another country might react to specific Chinese actions (Glaser 2012).

Yet, in light of the current state of the community of Middle Eastern and North African studies scholars, it is more probable that it was the general debate on China's engagement in international security affairs and the protections of its interests overseas that influenced the development of the attitude of the government regarding the use of the military abroad. Indeed, while specific country/region-expertise resides in the "inner circle" of policymakers, more general intuitions and ideas can be more easily developed outside strictly disciplined state institutions. The intellectual debate in the "outer circle" can offer new ways to use the superior technical expertise of officials in the "inner circle" and point to new solutions to the problems they face.

Against this background, one of the studies that set the tone for the study of non-traditional security and Chinese foreign policy is authored by Peking University's Wang Yizhou (1998), who at the time was the deputy director of the Institute of World Economics and Politics of CASS and is now widely acknowledged to be one of the most influential scholars in China. He argues that globalization forces every country to abandon the highly state-centric approach that dominated international affairs until the end of the Cold War. Security, he points out, is no longer only about war and peace between countries, but also about tackling "low politics" threats that are closely related to the life of the people and develop in a world where the boundary between domestic and foreign policy is becoming less clear.[18] Wang's ideas were shared by other scholars in influential think tanks, such as CICIR's Vice President Fu Mengzi (1999), and those in universities, such as Wang Yong (1999) in Peking

---

[18] In Chinese: 低级政治 (Dījí zhèngzhì).

University. Wang Yong, in particular, argues that China's public opinion pays significant attention to non-traditional security issues.

Over time, the importance of addressing non-traditional security threats in foreign policy continued to grow in the eyes of Chinese scholars. In a review of the understanding of non-traditional security within the context of China's foreign policy, CICIR's Zhai Kun (2003) argues that the process leading to placing traditional and non-traditional security on an equal footing can be divided into three phases. The first ended in 1997, when Jiang Zemin's New Security Concept started to make room for non-traditional security issues in foreign policy. Between 1997 and 2001, non-traditional security became more important but was seen as clearly separate from traditional security. The 9/11 attack opened the third phase and made clear how non-traditional threats can be dangerous for the security of the state. In keeping with this, Zhai points out that, while international cooperation was the key to addressing these new issues, it was important to consider the use of traditional and non-traditional soft and hard means to eliminate them. After Wang Yizhou's 1998 article, another study, which became one of the most frequently mentioned studies in the debate, was published by Nanjing University's Zhu Feng (2004). Zhu argues that, while traditional security remains at the core of state security, the development of means of guarding against non-traditional security threats was the natural development of the post-Cold War international security environment. By influencing global trends, those issues can affect the security of countries in other parts of the world, including China. This is why, he wrote, it was imperative for the Chinese academic community to continue studying how global problems can undermine the security of the state and of the individual.

In line with this, the number of publications on non-traditional security issues, international affairs, and Chinese foreign policy have continued to grow. At the same time, an increasing number of scholars have started to see new threats developing alongside the growth of China's interests abroad. In particular, three topics started to be connected with each other: non-traditional security issues, Chinese overseas interests, and China's engagement in international security affairs. For example, Zhao Lei (2007), a peacekeeping expert from the CCP Central Party School, emphasizes how growing engagement in peacekeeping operations not only helps African people but also boosts the defense of China's developing interests there. Therefore, he writes, deploying troops in a timely manner should not be seen as interventionism as long as those countries ask for help. He then suggested establishing coordination mechanisms between the Chinese troops deployed for peacekeeping and the embassies and consulates in the target country, while also becoming more familiar with the regulations of the United Nations and the situation in Africa. In this way, China could become more capable of intervening when necessary. Interestingly, Chinese peacekeepers and embassies abroad have indeed recently set up coordination mechanisms like those described by Zhao (Chapter 7).

These types of studies were published in parallel with others that highlight how instability overseas threatens Chinese interests. One of them was written by Peking University's Zhao Daojiong (2006). He writes very clearly that at that time instability in Sudan was already affecting the operation of Chinese oil companies, and that China's international image and position vis-à-vis other great powers could be significantly undermined by adopting a careless approach to the problems in that country. In the years that followed, as the academic community became more vocal in expressing doubts regarding the sustainability of the principle of noninterference in the internal affairs of other countries, the call for the military to play a greater role within the context of China's "peaceful rise" grew increasingly stronger (Chen and Huang 2009).[19] The real issue at the center of the debate was not *whether* but *how* to intervene, reconciling both the need to preserve China's peaceful image and the use of the military instrument when necessary. *Foreign Affairs Review* and *World Economics and Politics*, two of the most prestigious and insightful academic journals in China, published by CASS and the MFA-affiliated China Foreign Affairs University, respectively, published a number of articles on this topic in the late 2000s (Su 2009; Zhang 2009; Men and Zhong 2009).

The consensus that emerged in those years was further strengthened after the Libyan crisis, with terms like "creative intervention" and "constructive intervention"[20] being increasingly used. While Wang Yizhou (2011)'s *Creative Involvement: A New Direction in China's Diplomacy* is probably the most famous and most representative of the publications of the post-Libyan crisis period, many other scholars in Chinese universities and think tanks wrote about the need to develop a military solution to non-traditional security problems abroad. For example, Fudan University's Zhao Huasheng (2011) too argues that Chinese diplomacy had to change in the face of the threats that political instability in other countries posed to Chinese citizens and companies. A good collection of essays on that topic can be found in the series of blue books on non-traditional security sponsored by CASS. While the launch of the BRI further fueled the discourse on the need to combine diplomatic and military instruments to protect China's overseas interests (SIRPA Think Tank Task Force 2015; Wu and Dong 2015), the best

---

[19] In Chinese: 和平崛起 (Hépíng juéqǐ).
[20] In Chinese: 创新介入 (Chuàngxīn jièrù) and 建设性介入 (Jiànshè xìng jièrù).

And Sun Degang

description of how China's military presence abroad should look was put forward by the Middle Eastern affairs expert Sun Degang (2014). His idea of a "soft military presence" envisioned Chinese troops and warships being smartly deployed through multilateral channels, especially the United Nations, to limit the diplomatic and economic costs associated with missions overseas while making the most out of the PLA's limited power-projection capabilities to contribute to regional stability and, therefore, to the protection of Chinese interests.[21]

Although it is difficult to assess how much the debate among scholars influenced the government, Chinese scholars believe that pressure from the academic community does play a role in the decision-making process (Chen 2016). Hence, we can speculate that the most likely scenario is that the debate about China's engagement in international security affairs and the protection of its overseas interests was already taking place within the government. This created room for scholars to discuss, and even be critical of, official policies, albeit in a moderate way. The strong position expressed by the majority of scholars, and the affiliation of the most prominent ones with influential universities and think tanks provided the intellectual support needed by those in the leadership and the ministries who believed in the necessity of a more proactive foreign policy. After all, as argued by Henry R. Nau (2012, ebook position 230–83):

> bureaucrats base their policy actions on expertise, and expertise is developed through the application and testing of ideas against practical realities.... Even if decisions are made for purely material reasons, such as protecting budgets and bureaucratic turf, bureaucracies perform specific functions or roles, and those roles reflect intellectual orientations.

Conclusion

Almost no one saw the Arab Spring coming, so Chinese diplomats and scholars can hardly be blamed for not having been able to warn policymakers in Zhongnanhai about that specific event. Against this background, this chapter has shown how the MFA can rely on a seasoned and skilled group of officials who know the Middle East and North Africa well. It is thus very likely that the diplomats mentioned in Chapter 3 were not the only ones to be aware

[21] In Chinese: 柔性军事存在 (Róuxìng jūnshì cúnzài).

of the threats brewing in those faraway regions, and that a number of cadres within the MFA, especially in the WANA Affairs Department, were not totally surprised by what happened in 2011, or by the scale of the damage suffered by Chinese companies. Rather, "inner circle" and "outer circle" experts faced different challenges that probably prevented them from warning the Chinese government and only allowed them to try to manage (or push the government to manage) the problem of defending its interests overseas when it had already become apparent.

While it is an exaggeration to talk about marginalization, the MFA had to deal with the presence of numerous other actors that could shape the environment in which Chinese diplomats work abroad, as well as the channels of communication between the ministry and the top policymakers. This was especially true in the years before and immediately after the emergence of China's interest frontiers in North Africa and the Middle East. Yang Jiechi's promotion to the CCP Politburo and Wang Yi's to the rank of state councilor should help the MFA to (re)assert its position within the Chinese foreign policy machine in a way that was not possible before. Nonetheless, given the importance of investments and other economic activities in countries included in the BRI, which are mostly developing countries, there is little reason to believe that the NDRC or the MOFCOM have lost any substantial amount of influence in shaping China's foreign economic engagement and, consequently, human presence abroad. The China International Development Cooperation Agency, whose explicit mission is to support the BRI through international aid, might not have the same influence as the MFA, the NDRC, and MOFCOM, but it too is a new competitor for skilled personnel and resources from the Ministry of Finance.

It is also important to keep in mind that the presence of Wang Qishan and other presidential special envoys means that the number of people who act on the behalf of the Chinese top leadership has grown. This can have an impact on the influence of the two diplomats, Yang Jiechi and Wang Yi, when, as in the case of Wang, the envoys have close personal relations with the top decision-maker. As the People's Daily noted, and Wang's recent trip to Israel shows, Xi Jinping's envoys seem to be playing a role in shoring up security cooperation in countries and regions where Chinese interests are threatened. It is impossible to measure clearly how much all these elements have impacted on the securitization of non-traditional threats against Chinese interest frontiers. Yet there is little doubt that they all contributed to making it more difficult for the voice of the experienced and skillful diplomats who serve in the Middle East and North Africa to be heard by the central leadership, thereby affecting the securitization process to some extent.

When it comes to actors in the "outer circle," the analysis indicates that they probably played a role in pushing China toward accepting the use of the military abroad to defend its citizens and companies' interests. They did so, however, in an indirect and reactive way. On the one hand, they mostly floated general ideas about whether and how to change some of the key principles of Chinese foreign policy, thereby providing the intellectual foundations upon which like-minded government officials could build and try to formulate new policies. Chinese scholars, at least according to the publicly available material, did not specify what "creative intervention" or "constructive intervention" might mean. On the other hand, the debate advanced because scholars saw the number of incidents abroad growing, not because they could read the local dynamics behind them. Indeed, not only is the community of Middle Eastern and North African affairs specialists still largely lacking the analytical tools to explore these local dynamics, but its development also suffers from the fact that international relations generalists, like those who pushed for a more active foreign policy, dominate the scene in Chinese academia. Chapter 5 moves the focus of the analysis further away from the "inner circle" in order to see whether and how Chinese public opinion played a role in the formation of China's policies relating to its interest frontiers.

Bibliography

Al-Sudairi, Mohammed. 2019. "Transnational Shi'ism in Southern China and the Party-State's 'Hawza' Diplomacy." Middle East Institute. November 5. Accessed November 7, 2019. https://www.mei.edu/publications/transnational-shiism-southern-china-and-party-states-hawza-diplomacy.

Chen, Qi, and Yuxing Huang. 2009. "国际干涉的规范维度 [Reconstructing Norms of International Interventions]." *World Economics and Politics* (4): 6–15.

Chen, Zheng. 2016. "China Debates the Non-Interference Principle." *The Chinese Journal of International Politics* 9 (3): 349–74.

Cheng, Hong. 2010. "中国的中东研究文献六十年综述 [Summary of Sixty Years of Publications of Middle Eastern Studies in China]." *West Asia and Africa* 4: 71–5.

Corkin, Lucy. 2011. "Redefining Foreign Policy Impulses toward Africa: The Roles of the MFA, the MOFCOM and China Exim Bank." *Journal of Current Chinese Affairs* 40 (1): 61–90.

Deegan, Michael, and Joel Keralis. 2017. "China." In Robert Hutchings and Jeremi Suri (eds), *Developing Diplomats: Comparing Form and Culture across Diplomatic Services*, 40–58. Austin, TX: University of Texas at Austin.

Dong, Zuozhuang. 2016. "中国外交转型中的外交投入 [Diplomatic Input amid Chinese Diplomatic Transformation]." *The Journal of International Studies* 4: 26–43.

Eisenman, Joshua. 2018. "Comrades-In-Arms: The Chinese Communist Party's Relations with African Political Organisations in the Mao Era, 1949–76." *Cold War History* 18 (4): 429–55.

Fan, Hongda. 2013. "中东变局背景下中国的中东研究 [An Analysis of Middle Eastern Studies in China against the Background of Upheaval in the Middle East]." *West Asia and Africa* 6: 146–57.

Fu, Mengzi. 1999. "从经济安全角度谈对"非传统安全"的看法 [Some Views on Non-Traditional Security from the Perspective of Economic Security]." *Contemporary International Relations* 3: 1–5.

Glaser, Bonnie. 2012. "Chinese Foreign Policy Research Institutes and the Practice of Influence." In Gilbert Rozman (ed.), *China Foreign Policy: Who Makes It, and How Is It Made?*, 87–124. New York: Palgrave.

Gong, Li, Honghua Men, and Dongfang Sun. 2009. "中国外交决策机制变迁研究 (1949-2009年) [China's Diplomatic Decision-Making Mechanism: Changes and Evolution since 1949]." *World Economics and Politics* 11: 44–54.

Gurtov, Melvin. 1969. "The Foreign Ministry and Foreign Affairs during the Cultural Revolution." *China Quarterly* 40: 65–102.

International Herald Leader. 2015. "大外交呼唤'小语种' [Big Diplomacy Needs 'Small Languages']." *Xinhua—International Herald Leader*. April 14. Accessed February 21, 2018. http://www.xinhuanet.com/herald/2015–04/14/c_134146931.htm.

Jakobson, Linda, and Ryan Manuel. 2016. "How Are Foreign Policy Decisions Made in China?" *Asia & the Pacific Policy Studies* 3 (1): 101–10.

Jia, Yue. 2015. "记者观察：30多位 '习近平主席特使' 的'特殊任务' [Journalist's Observations: The 'Special Duty' of More than Thirty 'Special Envoys' of President Xi Jinping]." *People's Daily*. July 10. Accessed March 21, 2019. http://politics.people.com.cn/n/2015/0710/c1001-27286924.html.

Lampton, David M., ed. 2001. *The Making of Chinese Foreign and Security Policy in the Era of Reform, 1978–2000*. Stanford, CA: Stanford University Press.

Li, Cheng. 2009. "China's New Think Tanks: Where Officials, Entrepreneurs, and Scholars Interact." *China Leadership Monitor* (26). Accessed October 14, 2020. https://www.hoover.org/research/chinas-new-think-tanks-where-officials-entrepreneurs-and-scholars-interact.

Li, Cheng. 2016. *Chinese Politics in the Xi Jinping Era*. Washington DC: Brookings Institution Press.

Li, Wentao. 2018. "中非军事安全合作向深层次迈进 [China-Africa Military Security Cooperation Is Moving to a Deeper Level]." *World Affairs* 15: 58–9.

Lin, Fengmin. 2012. "中东研究的立场问题 [Stand on Mideast Study]." *Journal of Northwest University for Nationalities* 1: 9–13.

Liu, Chang. 2018. "中国的外交危机决策机制与过程分析—以1999年'炸馆'事件为例 [Analysis of the System and the Process of China's Crisis Foreign Policymaking—The 1999 'Bombing of the Embassy' as a Case Study]." *China Institute of International Studies.* May 21. Accessed July 2, 2018. http://www.ciis.org.cn/chinese/2018–05/21/content_40346504.htm.

Liu, Xiaohong. 2001. *Chinese Ambassadors: The Rise of Diplomatic Professionalism since 1949.* Seattle, WA: University of Washington Press.

Loh, Dylan M. H. 2019. "Diplomatic Control, Foreign Policy, and Change under Xi Jinping: A Field-Theoretic Account." *Journal of Current Chinese Affairs* 47 (3): 111–45.

Lu, Ning. 1997. *The Dynamics of Foreign-Policy Decisionmaking in China.* Oxford: Westview Press.

Men, Honghua, and Feiteng Zhong. 2009. "中国海外利益研究的历程、现状与前瞻 [The History, the Actual Situation and the Future of the Research on China's Overseas Interests]." *Foreign Affairs Review* 5: 56–71.

Nau, Henry R. 2012. "Domestic Voices of Aspiring Powers." In Henry R. Nau and Deepa M. Ollapally (eds), *Worldviews of Aspiring Powers*, ebook position 142–756. New York: Oxford University Press.

People's Daily. 2005. "外交部公务员招考纳入统考体系 [The Entry Test of the MFA Is Included in the Unified Exam System]." *People's Daily.* October 19. Accessed January 21, 2019. http://politics.people.com.cn/GB/1027/3781775.html.

PRC NPC. 2009a. "关于驻外外交人员法草案总则—分组审议驻外外交人员法草案发言摘登（二）[Discussion about the General Rules of the Draft of the Law on Diplomatic Personnel Stationed Abroad—Published Extracts of the Comments about the Draft of the Law on Diplomatic Personnel Stationed Abroad (Two)]." PRC National People's Congress. July 6. Accessed March 3, 2019. http://www.npc.gov.cn/huiyi/lfzt/wjryf/2009–07/06/content_1509401.htm.

PRC NPC. 2009b. "关于驻外外交人员的职责、条件、义务和权利—分组审议驻外外交人员法草案发言摘登（三）[Discussion about the Responsibilities, Requirements, and Rights of Diplomats Abroad—Published Extracts of the Comments about the Draft of Law on Diplomatic Personnel Stationed Abroad (Three)]." PRC National People's Congress. July 6. Accessed March 4, 2019. http://www.npc.gov.cn/huiyi/lfzt/wjryf/2009–07/06/content_1509402.htm.

PRC NPC. 2011. "Law of the People's Republic of China on Diplomatic Personnel Stationed Abroad." *PRC National People's Congress.* February 16. Accessed March 3, 2019. http://www.npc.gov.cn/englishnpc/Law/2011–02/16/content_1620759.htm.

Pu, Yao, and Tian Li. 2018. "21 世纪以来中国中东研究述评 (2000–2016) [A Review of Middle East Studies from 2000 to 2016 in China]." *Journal of Strategy and Decision-Making* 4: 82–104.

Qiu, Zhibo. 2017. "China's Outdated Foreign Service Needs Rebooting for the Age of Trump." *Foreign Affairs*. January 23. Accessed December 15, 2018. http://foreign-policy.com/2017/01/23/reboot-chinas-foreign-service-for-the-age-of-trump/.

Ruo, Zhuo. 2014. "副部级大使是怎样炼成的 [How Does One Become an Ambassador with Vice-Ministerial Rank?]." *Shanghai Observer*. September 24. Accessed May 23, 2019. https://web.shobserver.com/wx/detail.do?id=255.

Shichor, Yitzhak. 1979. *The Middle East in China's Foreign Policy, 1949–1977*. Cambridge: Cambridge University Press.

Shirk, Susan L. 2007. *China Fragile Superpower*. Oxford: Oxford University Press.

SIRPA Think Tank Task Force. 2015. "安全，发展与国际共进 [Security, Development and Co-Prosperity]." *Journal of International Security Studies* 1: 45–77.

Su, Changhe. 2009. "论中国海外利益 [On China's Overseas Interests]." *World Economics and Politics* 8: 13–20.

Sun, Degang. 2014. "论新时期中国在中东的柔性军事存在 [About the New Era of Chinese Soft Military Presence in the Middle East." *World Economics and Politics* 8: 4–29.

Sun, Jing. 2017. "Growing Diplomacy, Retreating Diplomats—How the Chinese Foreign Ministry Has Been Marginalized in Foreign Policymaking." *Journal of Contemporary China* 105: 419–33.

Sutter, Robert G. 2012. *Chinese Foreign Relations: Power and Policy since the Cold War*. New York: Rowman & Littlefield.

Tretiak, Daniel. 1980. "Political Movements and Institutional Continuity in the Chinese Ministry of Foreign Affairs, 1966–1979." *Asian Survey* 20 (9): 943–63.

Wang, Tiezheng. 2010. "新中国的中东历史研究 [Study on the Middle East History on New China]." *West Asia and Africa* 4: 40–3.

Wang, Yizhou. 1998. "论综合安全 [On Comprehensive Security]." *World Economics and Politics* 4: 5–14.

Wang, Yizhou. 2011. 创造性介入:中国外交新取向 [*Creative Involvement A New Direction in China's Diplomacy*]. Beijing: Peking University Press.

Wang, Yizhou, and Xinda Li. 2017. "中国外交能力建设新课题: 以外交官人数的历史变迁为案例 [A New Lesson about the Construction of China's Diplomatic Capabilities: The Changes in the Number of Diplomats as an Example]." *Contemporary World* 9: 16–19.

Wang, Yong. 1999. "论中国的新安全观 [On China's New Security Concept]." *World Economics and Politics* 1: 42–5.

Wu, Zhicheng, and Zuozhuang Dong. 2015. ""一带一路"战略实施中的中国海外利益维护 [The Protection of Overseas Interests within the Framework of the One Belt One Road Strategy]." *Tianjin Social Sciences* 6: 69–75.

Xue, Li. 2012. "China's Foreign Policy Decision-Making Mechanism and 'One Belt One Road' Strategy." *Journal of Contemporary East Asia* 5 (2): 23–5.

Yang, Xingli. 2010. "中国的伊朗研究六十年 [Sixty-Year Study on Iran in China]." *West Asia and Africa* 4: 63–7.

Yu, Jie. 2018. "The Belt and Road Initiative: Domestic Interests, Bureaucratic Politics and the EU-China Relations." *Asia Europe Journal* 16 (3): 223–36.

Zha, Daojiong. 2006. "中国在非洲的石油利益:国际政治课题 [China's Oil Interests in Africa: A Topic of Discussion in International Politics]." *The Journal of International Studies* 4: 53–67.

Zhai, Kun. 2003. "关于非传统安全问题 [About Non-Traditional Security Issues]." *Party Building Research* 9: 58–9.

Zhang, Dongdong. 2016. "The Making and Implementation of the Belt and Road Policy." *EABER Working Paper Series* (126).

Zhang, Ji. 2013. "中国外交决策的基本过程 [The Basic Process of Chinese Foreign Policymaking]." *Aisixiang.* March 18. Accessed October 19, 2017. http://www.aisixiang.com/data/62213.html.

Zhang, Ji, and Shanshan Zhao. 2011. "'中国外交体制、运作创新与中国外交研究创新'研讨会综述 [Summary of the Workshop 'Innovation in China's Diplomatic System and Practice and Innovation in the Research about China's Diplomacy]." *Foreign Affairs Review* 1: 155–8.

Zhang, Ji, and Yusheng Fang. 2018. "中国外交安全智库国际话语权分析 [Analysis of the International Discourse Power of Chinese Foreign and Security Policy Think Tanks]." *Global Review* 5: 75–97, 160.

Zhang, Shuguang. 2009. "国家海外利益:风险的外交管理 [Managing the Risk of Overseas National Interests through Diplomacy]." *World Economics and Politics* 8: 6–12.

Zhang, Yun. 2017. "区域研究与国际政治学的对话与融合一兼论'一带一路'倡议的智力支持建构 [Dialogue and Integration of Regional Studies and International Politics—On the Construction of Intellectual Support for the 'Belt and Road Initiative']." *Foreign Affairs Review* 5: 141–56.

Zhao, Baoxu. 2005. "关于加强外国问题研究的一点史料—2004 年 6月5日在中国人民大学国际关系学院40周年庆典上的发言 [Historical Material on Strengthening the Study of Foreign Issues—Speech on June 5, 2004, at the 40th Anniversary Celebration of the School of International Studies, Renmin University of China]." *Aisixiang.* January 24. Accessed October 2, 2018. http://www.aisixiang.com/data/5561.html.

Zhao, Huasheng. 2011. "不干涉内政与建设性介入-吉尔吉斯斯坦动荡后对中国政策的思考 [Noninterference in Internal Affairs and Constructive Intervention—Reflection on Chinese Policy after the Unrest in Kyrgyzstan]." *Journal of Xinjiang Normal University* 32 (1): 23–9.

Zhao, Lei. 2007. "'为和平而来'—解析中国参与非洲维和行动 ['Come for Peace'—Analysis of China's Peacekeeping Operations in Africa]." *Foreign Affairs Review* 12: 29–36.

Zhao, Mingwei. 2016. "吴建民、胡锡进'鹰鸽' 之争反思：中国需要什么样的外交官？ [Wu Jianmin, Hu Xijin, and the 'Battle between Hawks and Doves': What Kind of Diplomats Does China Need?]." *The Paper*. April 8. Accessed January 2, 2019. https://www.thepaper.cn/newsDetail_forward_1453910.

Zhao, Quansheng. 1992. "Domestic Factors of Chinese Foreign Policy: From Vertical to Horizontal Authoritarianism." *American Academy of Political and Social Science* 519: 158–75.

Zhao, Quansheng. 2012. "Moving between the "Inner Circle" and the "Outer Circle": The Limited Impact of Think Tanks on Policy Making in China." In Gilbert Rozman (ed.), *China's Foreign Policy: Who Makes It, and How Is It Made?*, 125–49. New York: Palgrave.

Zheng, Jiancheng, and Xiangyang Long. 2011. "1949–1964 年中国外交部涉非地区司的三次调整 [Three Times Adjustment of Chinese Foreign Ministry's Regional Bureau Related to Africa Countries from 1949–1964]." *Contemporary China History Studies* 18 (5): 82–5.

Zhou, Lie. 2010. "新中国的阿拉伯语教学与研究 [Teaching and Research of Arabic in the New China]." *West Asia and Africa* 4: 59–62.

Zhu, Feng. 2004. ""非传统安全' 解析 [Analysis of 'Non-Traditional Security']." *Social Sciences in China* 4: 139–46.

Zhu, Xufeng, and Lan Xue. 2007. "Think Tanks in a Transitional China." *Public Administration and Development* 27: 452–64.

5

Chinese Public Opinion and the Interest Frontiers

Public opinion is another important functional actor with the ability to shape the securitization process. The lack of revolutionary credentials, intra-elite tensions, and intra-elite divisions are usually identified as key variables that can make Chinese leaders more receptive to what their citizens think (Hao and Lin 2007, 52-4). Those three elements were present when the war in Libya broke out. As shown in Chapter 1, the Hu administration, which emerged from the Youth League of the Chinese Communist Party (CCP) rather than from the ranks of China's "red nobility," has had concerns about the protection of China's interests abroad for a number of years. Moreover, while the People's Liberation Army (PLA) seemed reluctant to toe the line in its role overseas up until mid-2011 (Chapter 2), the incoming Xi Jinping leadership needed to project an image of strength and control in order to consolidate its authority in the aftermath of the 18th Party Congress of late 2012. As pointed out by Fewsmith and Rosen (2001, 155), "Chinese public opinion tends not to be effective as an independent force, but it can have an impact when joined with the concerns or interests of those higher in the system." Andrew Chubb (2018) too argues that there is little reason to believe that specific policies of the Chinese government might be the result of pressure from public opinion alone. Instead, the government can highlight or de-emphasize its role and/or the saliency of an issue in order to boost its legitimacy or avoid angering public opinion.

However, it is important to keep in mind that the protection of the country's interest frontiers is an extremely new problem in Chinese politics. Therefore, it differs from other security and foreign policy issues, such as Sino-American relations or maritime disputes, which are usually taken as cases for assessing the (possible) impact of public opinion on Chinese decision-making. First, it is not part of China's "core interests" (yet). That means that failing to protect companies and citizens abroad can hardly lead to the collapse of the regime, although it would damage its legitimacy. Therefore, there is more room for debate among the public as well as in intellectual circles, as Chapter 4 showed.

Protecting China's Interests Overseas: Securitization and Foreign Policy. Andrea Ghiselli,
Oxford University Press (2021). © Andrea Ghiselli.
DOI: 10.1093/oso/9780198867395.001.0001

Second, both the government and, especially, the ordinary citizen are far less familiar with events in faraway regions than those happening in Asia. This was especially the case before 2011. Hence, a serious crisis in North Africa and the Middle East could not but attract significant attention due to its novelty. Third, failing to prevent the loss of life or assets of many Chinese nationals in an incident overseas would certainly anger the Chinese public, but it is very unlikely to undermine the leading position of the CCP in the way that it might, for example, in the case of a defeat in a war against the United States. Actually, the government can easily and cheaply score political points with its domestic audience simply by inflating a threat and/or the effectiveness of any military assets deployed to tackle it.

Given the relatively greater space for discussion, one should not overlook the fact that popular attention for certain issues and the backing of public opinion for certain policies can further bolster the determination of the leadership (or some within it) around the necessity of implementing them. This chapter shows that this has indeed happened in the case of the defense of China's interest frontiers, as Chinese public opinion has long been in favor of a more muscular foreign policy. The first section of this chapter focuses on the debate in the media and social media. The second section revolves around how three recent popular movies—*Operation Mekong* (OM), *Wolf Warrior 2* (WW2), and *Operation Red Sea* (ORS)—were produced and inspired, respectively, by the murder of Chinese citizens on a boat on the Mekong River, the evacuation from Libya in 2011, and the evacuation from Yemen in 2015.[1] The reader can find some important considerations and caveats regarding the study of Chinese public opinion, the use of movies as case studies for understanding foreign policy and international relations, as well as a summary of all the information regarding the production and the stories narrated by the three movies in Appendix 7.

The Defense of the Interest Frontiers through the Lens of the Chinese Internet

The debate on the protection of Chinese overseas interests has mostly been influenced by events in Africa and the Middle East, rather than in Asia. This is evident from the level of attention paid by the Chinese people to different

---

[1] In Chinese: 湄公河行动 (Méigōnghé xíngdòng), 战狼 2 (Zhàn láng 2), and 红海行动 (Hónghǎi xíngdòng).

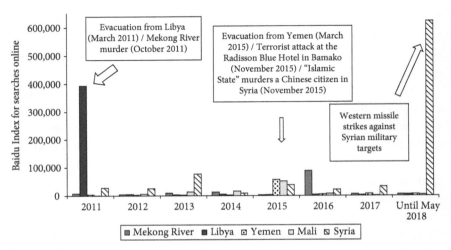

Figure 23 The Chinese Internet and crises overseas

Note: Baidu has not made public how its index is calculated, but only that there is a direct and positive correlation between number of searches and the value of the index.

Source: Baidu Index. Compiled by the author.

events abroad (Figure 23). Indeed, all the peaks in the searches for "Mali," "Yemen," "Syria," and "Libya" in the Chinese search engine Baidu correspond to days with incidents involving Chinese nationals. Even in the case of Syria, although the war there caught the attention of Chinese Internet users many times, the Baidu Index shows that the peak in searches in 2015 happened in the days following the killing of Fan Jinghui, a Chinese national. On the other hand, searches for the word "Mekong River" were more numerous in 2014 and, especially, 2016, when the highly successful *The Mekong River Case* TV series and OM were produced than when the murder of the thirteen Chinese citizens on the Mekong River actually took place in 2011.[2]

There are four likely interconnected reasons that can explain the lack of search activity on the Mekong case. First, although the incident on the Mekong River was bloodier than the evacuation from Libya, the sheer number of people involved (36,000 people) made the Libyan crisis a unique event in Chinese modern history. Second, Chinese people are, in general, much more familiar with what happens in Asia, especially in areas on the Chinese border, than events in faraway places like the Middle East and North Africa. Third, the Mekong River incident was not a one-time shock but a "long" event that stretched from the finding of the corpses in October 2011 to the capture and

---

[2] In Chinese: 湄公河 (Méigōnghé) and 湄公河大案 (Méigōnghé dà àn).

conviction of the criminals involved in March 2013. Fourth, the Chinese state acted through its police force and judicial system to solve the problem of the Mekong River. The PLA was not involved, as far as is publicly known. Although diplomatic maneuvering was clearly needed to establish a cooperation platform with Thailand, Laos, and Myanmar, this event was mainly presented as an issue under the control of domestic authorities, and as a case of international law enforcement, rather than as a purely international operation.

The first known signs of a link between the government and public opinion regarding the security of Chinese citizens and assets abroad started to appear in late 2008. It all began when the *Tianyu 8*—a Hong Kong-flagged ship—was attacked and its crew kidnapped on November 13 by Somali pirates off the coast of Kenya (Li 2008). In December of the same year, pictures of the Chinese sailors of the *Zhenhua 4* repelling the pirate attack by throwing rudimentary Molotov cocktails appeared on the Internet and in reports on Chinese state television (Global Times 2008). While such events were condemned by the Ministry of Foreign Affairs (MFA), two positions emerged on the Chinese Internet. On the one hand, the majority was in favor of the government's decision to join international efforts against piracy by regularly dispatching naval task forces. Indeed, the results of an online survey published by Sohu.com showed that up to 86 percent of responders online supported the mission to protect Chinese ships (Sohu 2008). In another survey with more than 17,000 participants, support reached 90 percent (People's Daily 2008). On the other hand, Chinese media report that other Internet users were against the deployment of the PLA navy for a variety of reasons (Sun 2008; Huang 2009, 171-2). Some thought that a military response to the problem of piracy was not effective. Moreover, they also argued that piracy was just another of the products of American foreign policy in the Middle East and, therefore, "Why should China go to clean up the mess created by the United States? We should just mind our own business and that is enough." Also, some feared it was possible that the United States could seize the opportunity to do something against China as soon as its most advanced ships had left Asia. Others were not only concerned that the PLA navy was not capable of carrying out the operation, but also argued that the cost of sending warships so far away should not have been ignored.

Interestingly, while journalists and military commentators put great emphasis on both the diplomatic importance of sending the warships to Somali waters and their role in protecting Chinese interests, Internet users appeared far less interested in discussing what other countries might or might not think about China. This is probably why there is no trace of a similarly heated debate regarding peacekeeping missions in the Chinese media and social media. Since China deployed its peacekeepers in Sudan in late 2007, this is a rather important fact to keep in mind. Only ninety-one people participated in an online survey on peacekeeping operations and, in any case, only one-fourth of them were in favor of the deployments of combat troops for peacekeeping operations (People's Daily 2010).

Margaret Roberts (2018) pointed out that Chinese Internet users tend to spend more time and effort on overcoming the obstacles created by what she defines as Chinese "porous" censorship and finding censored or hard-to-find information when a high-profile crisis takes place. Hence, this lack of interest from Internet users probably contributed to making the government less inclined to discuss an issue that is potentially riskier in political terms. Indeed, Chinese peacekeepers are sent to far more dangerous places than the Gulf of Aden. For example, even Chinese media reported that Sudanese warlords had been making explicit threats to the Chinese contingent, even before its arrival, and that the attack against the facilities of a Chinese oil company in December 2008, less than a month after the first Chinese soldiers arrived, was an act of retaliation against the Chinese military presence (*China Daily* 2008). In October 2008, five Chinese employees of the China National Petroleum Corporation were killed in Sudan. Only negative news, like the killing of a peacekeeper, could have caught the attention of an otherwise uninterested Chinese public, as it happened later.

In his work on the relationship between public opinion and Chinese foreign policy, Andrew Chubb (2018) argues that one should expect wide coverage of the Chinese government's actions in the media with both implicit and explicit claims of credit whenever the government is forced to act under pressure from public opinion. This was certainly the case in the evacuations from Libya in 2011. As mentioned before, there had already been instances of Chinese nationals being kidnapped or attacked in the Middle East and North Africa, with some of them having had to be evacuated. However, the evacuation of so many was simply unprecedented. Besides the sheer number of people, the evacuation was carried out under dramatic and, for many Chinese who had never seen their country involved in major crises outside Asia, unexpected conditions: with a raging civil war and Western military intervention under way.

As Figure 23 shows, Chinese Internet users avidly searched on Baidu for news about and from Libya in the days of the evacuation. Certainly many must have read the complaints about the service of the hotline set up by the MFA that were posted on *Weibo* by some Chinese nationals in Libya who were waiting to being evacuated (Chin 2011). A *Weibo* commentator with more than one million followers highlighted the fact that state-controlled CCTV was continuing to broadcast information about an earthquake in New Zealand even as the clashes in Libya were intensifying. Chinese companies were abruptly ordered to evacuate, and Chinese nationals were asking for help through *Weibo* and other social media platforms (Weibo 2011).

The government's response was threefold, massively employing what has been defined as "friction" and "flooding" techniques (Roberts 2018).[3] First, *Weibo* was heavily censored, and today it is extremely difficult to find comments about that event. Second, attempts were made to minimize the losses suffered by Chinese companies, as discussed in Chapter 3. Third, the propaganda machine was fully mobilized to report the efforts being made by the government to evacuate Chinese nationals from the North African country. The symbol of that media campaign is a volume published in March 2011, only a few weeks after the last Chinese nationals left Libya, by the People's Daily Press (Ma 2011). The book, unsurprisingly, focuses narrowly on the evacuation, without adding much information regarding the reason for so many Chinese nationals to be in Libya or, for example, the causes of the upheaval. The evacuation is described as a "national operation" directly overseen by Hu Jintao and other members of the CCP Politburo Standing Committee.[4] Their resoluteness and love for their compatriots guided them, narrates the book. The book also presents a series of articles, interviews, and, in theory, real comments passed on to journalists by Chinese Internet users and evacuees celebrating the success of the operation and the love of the motherland for its people. The bulk of the evacuation was carried out with chartered flights and ferryboats, but it is the role of the PLA that stands out in those pages. After all, especially in the light of the doubts expressed a few years earlier about the capabilities of the navy, it was important to show that years of double-digit increases in the military budget could translate into increased security when needed.

Chinese nationals continued to be the target of attacks in North Africa and the Middle East in the years that followed. For example, twenty-nine workers

---

[3] The government can create "friction" for Internet users trying to access information by increasing the cost of accessing it. That can happen, for example, by deleting blog posts, comments on social media, and articles in the media, so as to make it more difficult for Internet users to find information about a certain event. As for "flooding," it refers to the production of large quantities of news about topics different from the one the government wants to make less eye-catching, or about the same topic but framing in different, more government-friendly ways. By creating and spreading a vast amount of easily accessible information, the government creates a media environment where it is almost impossible not to be exposed and, at least to some extent, socialized to its point of view.

[4] In Chinese: 国家行动 (Guójiā xíngdòng).

of Sinohydro were kidnapped in Sudan in early 2012. The same happened to twenty-five employees of the Tianjin Cement Industry Design and Research Institute in Egypt at about the same time. In 2013, four were kidnapped in Sudan. In every case, Chinese Internet users on *Weibo* wished for the quick release of their unlucky compatriots and, at the same time, expressed their surprise that Chinese companies kept on operating in dangerous countries where similar incidents had already taken place. Many called for the deployment of special forces or private security companies in comparison to what, according to Chinese Internet users, the United States would do in the same situation. While it is extremely unlikely that those comments could put any pressure on the government, it is important to notice that it seems that reports about attacks on Chinese workers received more attention after 2011 than before. For example, while the post published by *Toutiao News*—one of the most popular news and information content platforms in China with more than fifty-seven million followers on *Weibo*—regarding the attack on two PetroChina workers in Yemen in 2010 was shared and commented on by Chinese Internet users only fifty-nine and twenty-four times, respectively (Toutiao 2010), those about the incidents in Egypt and Sudan received hundreds of comments and were shared even more times (Toutiao 2012, 2013).

The actions of the government were commented upon much more positively in 2015, when almost 600 Chinese nationals were evacuated from Yemen by using naval warships, thanks to the quick and efficient work done by Chinese diplomats in Aden. The evacuation from Yemen was much smaller than the one from Libya; the PLA navy already had warships in the Gulf of Aden for antipiracy patrols, and the Chinese embassies surely had learnt the lesson about being prepared to evacuate after Libya. These three factors made the evacuation smooth, and the government did its best to show its effectiveness to its domestic audience. In particular, state media made a comparison between China, the United States, and India. Great emphasis was put on the fact that the United States "does not have the capability to evacuate its citizens" while China clearly did (Wang 2015). As for India, "it was not a coincidence" that China performed better in evacuating its citizens (Global Times 2015). Chinese Internet users too were very positive in their comments, as they praised both the rapidity of the action and the decision to help foreign citizens (Toutiao 2015a, 2015b). Yet others also pointed out that, unlike the United States and other countries, China had not warned its citizens to leave the country earlier (Zhihu 2015a). Hence, considering too that most of the Chinese in Yemen were employees of state-owned enterprises, another Internet user argued that the government would had been "insulted to death" if it had not sent the PLA navy for this evacuation (Zhihu 2015b). The political costs would had been significant.

Yet Beijing could do nothing in November of the same year when Fan Jinghui, a Chinese national, was killed by so-called Islamic State in Syria, and three senior managers of the China Railway Construction Corporation died in a terrorist assault on the Radisson Blu Hotel in Bamako, Mali. Chinese Internet users were divided. In the case of Fan Jinghui, many pointed out that a military intervention would have been extremely risky and, to some extent like when China decided to send its warships into the Gulf of Aden, the fight against terrorism in the Middle East was not China's business (Toutiao 2015c). It was the fault of the United States if organizations like Islamic State exist. Moreover, there was the possibility that China could become the main target of terrorism. At the same time, however, there was significant dissatisfaction with the MFA's "strong condemnation" of the murder (Zhihu 2015c).[5] The issue of whether China should send troops was greatly debated, and many were in favor of doing so. This can be deduced from the fact that a great number of the most-liked comments on news relating to Fan Jinghui's murder revolved around this issue. Many of those comments are extremely critical of the so-called "keyboard warriors" who supported a military response, although it is extremely difficult to find any of these comments supporting a military response.[6] Clearly, many had been deleted and the remaining few pushed to the bottom of the list of comments in another kind of information "friction" and "flooding."

As for the attack in Bamako, it took place on November 21, just a week after *Xinhua* reported the presence of famous PLA units among the ranks of the peacekeeping contingent deployed with the United Nations (UN) Multidimensional Integrated Stabilization Mission in Mali in Gao (Zhang 2015). Therefore, it is not surprising that the questions "Why did the government not send our troops to save our fellow countrymen?" and, when French commandos intervened, "Why could France do it?" were asked repeatedly online (Observer 2015). The day after the attack, Chinese official media widely reposted an article that was tellingly entitled "The media explain the incidents involving Chinese citizens in Mali, why the peacekeepers did not go to save them" that specifically addressed the "friends online" who raised those questions (Xinhua 2015a).[7] On November 23, the same media

---

[5] In Chinese: 强烈谴责 (Qiángliè qiǎnzé).
[6] In Chinese: 键盘侠 (Jiànpán xiá).
[7] In Chinese: 媒体释疑中国公民马里遇害 维和部队为何未救 (Méitǐ shìyí zhōngguó gōngmín mǎlǐ yùhài wéihé bùduì wèihé wèi jiù) and 网友 (Wǎngyǒu).

outlets published pictures of an "emergency anti-terrorism exercise" held by Chinese peacekeepers in Mali where they appeared ready to shoot at the enemy while running out of their camp with assault rifles, body armor, and armored vehicles (Xinhua 2015b).[8] The government was on the defensive to explain through the media why sending elite combat troops abroad did not actually translate into a higher level of protection for the country's overseas interests.

In summer 2016, Chinese peacekeepers in Mali and South Sudan were victims of deadly attacks. Understandably, Chinese Internet users showed their support for the families of the dead soldiers and paid tribute to them. Nonetheless, it is clear that those deaths made many wonder why Chinese soldiers had to be there in the first place, and if their sacrifice was worthwhile. For example, while some wrote that the soldiers gave their lives only for the government's desire to create a "great power image," others pointed out that Mali and South Sudan are countries where the situation is too desperate and, therefore, the risks to Chinese peacekeepers were too high relative to what they could do to help (Toutiao 2016).[9] As in the case of the death of Fan Jinghui, some Internet users complained that "strongly condemning" it was all the government could do. An Internet user who claimed to be a former soldier argued that the problem was that the commanding officers of the peacekeepers were well trained in political thought but not in dealing with combat situations (Zhihu 2016). Moreover, others argued that the soldiers were killed because their armored personnel carrier was not of good quality. While it is impossible to say whether the Internet users' concerns were well-founded or not, China Military Web TV (2016), an Internet TV channel controlled by the PLA, tellingly produced two videos to explain that Chinese-produced vehicles are as safe as those of other countries and why China had not sent tanks.

It is important to point out that Chinese Internet users seem being more interested in events in which Chinese civilians are among the victims than those in which the victims are soldiers. This is clearly demonstrated in Figure 24, which shows the Baidu Index data regarding searches online for the words "Mali," "South Sudan," "Yemen," and "Libya." The number of searches for "South Sudan" and "Mali" when the Chinese peacekeepers were killed in 2016 is far smaller than when high-profile incidents like those in Libya, Yemen, and Mali happened. News related to military deployments, such as the decision to send combat troops to join the peacekeeping missions in Mali and South Sudan,

---

[8] In Chinese: 应急反恐演练 (Yìngjí fǎnkǒng yǎnliàn).
[9] In Chinese: 大国形象 (Dàguó xíngxiàng).

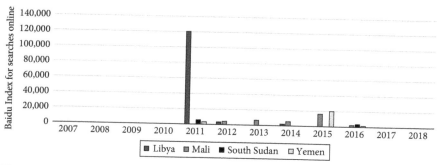

Figure 24 Different crises and different levels of attention online

Note: Baidu has not made public how its index is calculated, but only that there is a direct and positive correlation between the number of searches and the value of the index.

Source: Baidu Index. Compiled by the author.

received little attention. For example, in 2013, the peak of searches on Baidu took place in January, when France intervened in Mali and not when China announced that it was sending a contingent of peacekeepers. South Sudan received even less attention despite the widely publicized deployment of combat troops.

Real Traumas and Imagined Foreign Policy

Overseas operations carried out by the PLA and the Chinese People's Armed Police have been a popular subject for movies and TV series in China. Indeed, besides OM, WW2, and ORS, *Extraordinary Mission* and *Sky Hunter* were also screened in Chinese movie theaters in 2017.[10] However, they do not directly address the issue of the protection of Chinese citizens abroad. They are much more similar to generic action and police movies. *Sky Hunter*, despite its far less engaging story, was meant to be a powerful commercial for the Chinese air force, as *Top Gun* was for the American air force. Among the numerous TV series produced in China, *Peacekeeping Infantry Battalion*, and *Moon of Gulf of Aden* also put Chinese military presence abroad at the center of their plots.[11] Like OM, WW2, and ORS, they also mix real and fictional events. For example, the evacuation from Libya really took place but, unlike what is shown in *Peacekeeping Infantry Battalion*, no Chinese peacekeeper or infantry soldier was involved in it at any time.

---

[10] In Chinese: 非凡任务 (Fēifán rènwù) and 空天猎 (Kōng tiān liè).
[11] In Chinese: 维和步兵营 (Wéihé bùbīng yíng) and 舰在亚丁湾 (Jiàn zài yàdīng wān).

Apart from WW2, all the other movies and TV series have been produced and/or heavily sponsored by state ministries, such as the Ministry of Public Security (MPS) in the case of OM, and the PLA. Hence, it is clear that the Chinese government has been actively promoting the creation of a narrative about China's military engagement abroad and how successful it has also been in protecting Chinese interests overseas. However, it is the analysis of OM, WW2, and ORS that reveals the most about the success or failure of those attempts. There are a number of reasons why these three movies are of interest in this regard. First, they are not only based on real events (the killing of Chinese citizens in the Mekong River for OM, the Libyan crisis for WW2, and the evacuation from Yemen for ORS) but, as is described further below, they also feature scenes containing messages for the audience directly addressing the problem of the protection of overseas interests. Second, their commercial success was undeniable in comparison with the other two movies mentioned above: a sign of a preference for movies that, to some extent, are about real events that so caught the public's attention (Figure 25). Third, they have become common references in the media in discussing the government's measures to protect overseas interests. For example, WW2 and ORS are often mentioned in interviews with officials, even by Foreign Minister Wang Yi (Chen 2017; Xinhua 2018). In an interview with the *Global Times* (2017), the commander of the frigate stationed outside Libyan waters during the 2011 evacuation declared that the navy could act more quickly and effectively than people saw in the movie theaters. Fourth, they were not all produced or sponsored by the state/PLA. Indeed, WW2 was not only the most successful movie among them in commercial terms but also the only one that could be

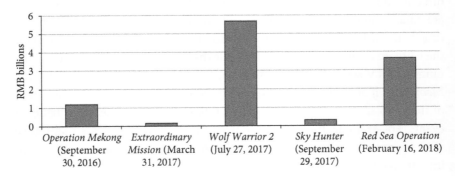

Figure 25 Commercial success of movies on crises overseas
Source: China Box Office. Compiled by the author.

considered a private production. Its plot was, of course, vetted by the censors and, therefore, it is in line with the state's preferences. However, there is a key opportunity here to observe the difference in terms of plot and commercial success between a narrative mostly aimed at communicating the message of the government and one primarily meant to appeal to moviegoers. Fifth, OM and ORS are similar as they are both state-sponsored and were directed by the same director, but they emphasize different elements in their plots. This is an especially important fact, since WW2 was screened after OM and before ORS. Therefore, these changes can offer precious insights into how the state adapted its message as the debate moved on in movie theaters and reverberated in the media and online.

Operation Mekong: We Will Always Protect You

On the morning of October 5, 2011, two Chinese cargo ships were attacked on a stretch of the Mekong River in the Golden Triangle region on the borders of Myanmar and Thailand. Thirteen Chinese sailors were killed. The Chinese MPS formed a task force to hunt down the main suspect, drug lord Naw Kham, and stationed over 200 officers in Laos, Myanmar, and Thailand. The ministry reportedly even contemplated the use of drones to kill him. On October 28, 2011, Thai authorities arrested nine soldiers from the elite anti-drug Pha Muang Task Force, who were accused of cooperating with the drug traffickers. Shortly afterwards, the Chinese government summoned the diplomatic representatives of Laos, Myanmar, and Thailand, and the four countries approved the "Joint Statement on Law Enforcement Cooperation along the Mekong River" and launched joint patrols that are still carried out today. Naw Kham and three subordinates were eventually extradited to China in 2012 and their death sentences were carried out and broadcast live on television in March 2013.

OM is not only inspired by these events, but, compared to WW2 and ORS, is also the movie which is most faithful to the facts. Given the success of the measures taken, the MPS—which was the main sponsor of the movie—and the state had good reason to represent the events in a semi-realistic way and to use OM to emphasize the message that they have always protected Chinese interests abroad. They did so by writing (in Chinese) the following message against the background of pictures of different places around the world before the end credits of the movie:

The conclusion of the Mekong River case did not only avenge the death of the 13 victims, but it also further proved the will of the state to defend the country's territorial integrity and people. Today, China's economic interests are global and its people everywhere. Protecting each of them is a crucial and long-term duty.

The MPS also produced the extremely successful TV series, *The Mekong River Case*, earlier in 2014 and, probably aiming at fully capitalizing again on the success of the Mekong River issue, played a key role in the production of OM as well.[12] According to news reports, the movie cost some USD 31 million. While it is unknown how much the government invested in it, the MPS at least ensured extensive access to officers involved in the real operation, equipment, training for the actors, and the quick approval of the script. When it arrived in movie theaters, there was another state-backed production already being screened, *My War*, with a less popular cast.[13] In comparison to OM, *My War*'s plot is a much more traditional one about the Korean War. Moreover, the direction of OM was entrusted to Dante Lam, a famous director of action movies, in order to make OM more appealing to a young and modern audience. Unsurprisingly, these elements greatly favored OM, which sold three times more tickets than its competitor.

The state is represented as strong and decisive. Its actions fill the gap of what ordinary people know about what happened between the moment the bodies were found and the conviction of Naw Kham. Its frontline representatives, that is, the MPS officers, are highly trained and skilled so that they can carry out the entire operation almost alone, either by compelling other countries to cooperate or by prevailing in intense fights with the drug traffickers. China appears as a force to be feared by those who wrong its citizens. As one of Naw Kham's associates says, China "is too big for us." China, therefore, is implicitly different from the neighboring countries involved in this incident. Although one of the main characters dies, it is clear that he is a martyr of the Chinese state for the safety of the citizens. While the Chinese are strong and righteous, their foreign counterparts are shown as weak and corrupt. This is best represented in the character of "Boss." Although his nationality is not made explicit, he is clearly a corrupt, high-ranking Thai military official.

---

[12] According to the data collected by CSM Media Research and reported on *Baidu Encyclopedia*, *The Mekong River Case* was much more successful than *Peacekeeping Infantry Battalion* and *Moon of Gulf of Aden*.

[13] In Chinese: 我的战争 (Wǒ de zhànzhēng).

To sum up, after the *The Mekong River Case* TV series, and less than a year after the incidents in Mali and Syria, the Chinese government decided to capitalize, once again, on the success gained in finding and punishing those responsible for the death of Chinese nationals seven years earlier. Although there are evident exaggerations and invented sequences, OM is the most realistic movie of the three considered in this chapter in terms of how its plot revolves around real events. It repeats the message that China is diplomatically and militarily stronger than its neighbors in order to lend credibility to the final message mentioned above, attempting to erase the Middle Eastern traumas in its narrative. Hence, it can be said that OM promotes a virtual continuity between the pre-2011 and the post-2011 situations. The movie's message is that the state has protected and will always protect its citizens, and that China's rise has not been disrupted by incidents overseas. Yet, with the arrival of WW2 in Chinese theaters in summer 2017, it became clear that such continuity does not exist.

Wolf Warrior 2: The Hero that the Chinese Nation Needs

While OM emphasized the continuity of state action, WW2 focused on the disruptive effect of overseas crises. This is a subject that, as shown above, appears to be of much greater interest to the public. Moreover, whereas OM added invented elements in the gaps of a true story, WW2 does the contrary and profoundly reinvents history. Although Wu Jing, who was both the producer and main actor of WW2, declared that the movie's script was inspired by the Libyan evacuation, the Chinese overseas crisis par excellence, the similarities with that event are extremely limited. First, the country where the story unfolds is an invented African country that borders the sea, like Libya. Second, the PLA is only a peripheral actor, both in the plot and in the production of the movie, as it was in the 2011 evacuation. Yet it could be said that WW2 was more accurate in describing the emotional trauma of the Libyan crisis than OM. Indeed, the connection between the movie and that event is crucial to understanding the attitude of the Chinese public.

Wu Jing received little support from private and public investors. He had to offer his own house as a guarantee to finance almost half the production and only the former Nanjing Military Region provided him with some training and material support. After all, the official propaganda machine was already fully engaged in the production and promotion of *Founding of an Army*, the final part of the *Founding of New China* movie trilogy, narrating the story of the foundation of the PLA.[14] Yet the comparison between the movies' box office revenues speaks volumes about the preference of Chinese audiences: *Founding of an Army* made USD 63 million, while WW2 made USD 896 million (USD 710 million more than OM). WW2 was the highest-grossing movie in China in 2017 and was watched hundreds of millions of times on popular streaming websites like Youku, Iqiyi, and QQ. "The hearts of the Chinese people were like dry brushwood, I am only the spark that set them on fire," Wu Jing declared when asked about the success of WW2 (Bai and Shi 2017). Tellingly, Figure 26 suggests that there is a connection between the level of attention that Chinese Internet users paid to different crises and the success of the movies inspired by them. The success of WW2, therefore, indicates not only that Libya had a deep and long-lasting impact on how Chinese people think about the protection of China's interests overseas, but also that for many overcoming that challenge is an issue of national pride.

This is why it is important to look at the narrative put forward in WW2. In it, defeat becomes victory and China is transformed into a great power respected by the populations of developing countries and is placed on a par with the United States. Such a change in the plot, however, takes place alongside an even more radical one: the protagonist of the movie is a hero who acts on behalf of the Chinese people in order to make up for the deficiencies of the Chinese state. The main character, Leng Feng, is a former member of the PLA Special Operations Forces, stripped of his rank and working in Africa as a private

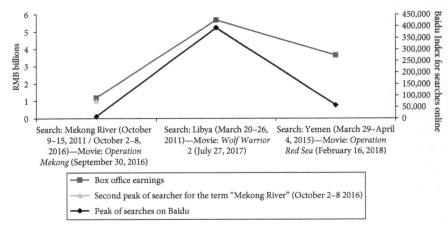

Figure 26 The relationship between real and imagined crises overseas

Note: Baidu has not made public how its index is calculated, but only that there is a direct and positive correlation between number of searches and the value of the index.

Source: Baidu Index and China Box Office. Compiled by the author.

[14] In Chinese: 建军大业 (Jiàn jūn dàyè) and 建国三部曲 (Jiànguó sān bù qǔ).

security contractor. He is entrusted with a mission to save an important Chinese doctor and other Chinese nationals because the PLA Navy is not authorized to intervene when civil war breaks out. The PLA is represented by warships and peacekeepers at the beginning and at the end of the movie that appear only as supporters of Leng Feng. It, essentially, remains at the margins of the story and, tellingly, acts only after Chinese nationals start being killed.

Foreigners play a crucial role in defining what China is in WW2. On the one hand, as even some Internet users pointed out (Douban 2017b), the description of local people is consistent with the stereotypical one that can be usually found in the Chinese media: poor Africans governed by corrupt and weak leaders. China and its people are represented as a righteous and powerful nation, admired by the developing world. Leng Feng embodies all these virtues and, naturally, succeeds despite being severely wounded several times while saving, and even flirting with, an American doctor of Chinese origin. On the other hand, Chinese actions are implicitly compared with those of Western countries and people, who, in different forms, appear evil, selfish, and incapable of protecting their fellow citizens in danger. For example, Western warships are shown abandoning the African country at the beginning of the movie and the American consulate is helpless and closes down. The UN also appears in the movie in association with the Chinese government: Chinese soldiers and warships are present in the African country because they are operating under the UN mandate and, at the same time, it is because of the UN that the Chinese government cannot intervene in a timely fashion.

The movie wants to reassure Chinese moviegoers that they are citizens of a great power that poor countries look up to and that developed ones, the United States in particular, cannot compete with anymore. Wu Jing has stated on many occasions that the proudest part of the movie for him is when a modified version of the Chinese passport appears before the final credits with a statement reminding Chinese citizens that the motherland will bring them home from wherever they are if they are in danger (Bai and Shi 2017). While WW2 is far from being a protest movie, the comparison between WW2 and OM clearly shows the differences that exist between the bottom-up narrative in response to a problem widely acknowledged by society, and the traditional top-down one aimed at strengthening the legitimacy of the ruling elites. While commercial success does not mean that all those who watched WW2 were interested in politics or were particularly nationalist, it still means that they were all exposed to the narrative put forward in it.

Hence, it is not surprising that state media tried to tone down the role of the individual hero and to emphasize the support that he received from the state. Wu Jing himself declared that even a hero like Leng Feng needs a strong country behind him (Sohu 2017). Later, the *People's Daily* (2017) endorsed such a message. However, WW2 was seen by the public as a hero movie rather than a war movie. A person is at the center of the story, not the state. Although some Internet users commented that this focus on a single person was an exaggeration (Douban 2017a), the commercial success of WW2 speaks clearly of the support for the Leng Feng-type of hero and its message after the Libyan crisis.

Operation Red Sea: Common Efforts and Common Sacrifice

While the above-mentioned article from the *People's Daily* can be seen as a reactive measure to popular pressure, ORS is a proactive attempt to shape and guide the narrative about what the state does, and should do, to protect its citizens abroad. ORS, unlike OM, does not downplay the problem of how to protect Chinese people abroad. On the contrary, it emphasizes it, and shows that there is not much that can be done. This means that, while OM's message was that the state always protects its citizens, ORS tells the viewer that the state will always do its best within the limits set by objective difficulties. This is further stressed by showing, at the end of the movie, a number that Chinese citizens can call in case of emergency abroad, which is a much less emphatic and much more sober message compared to those at the end of OM and WW2.

In keeping with the relaxation of the message, ORS's story draws on real events more than WW2 does, but less so than OM. Essentially, while the first part of the movie is to some extent similar to what happened in Yemen in 2015 (Chinese warships docked in Aden with Chinese soldiers establishing a security perimeter in the area where the evacuees gathered), the rest (firefights between Chinese soldiers and local insurgents, the pursuit of enemies in the desert, the rescue of a Chinese national being held hostage, the presence of a dirty bomb, and the use of tanks and drones) is invented. However, the movie does try to remain relatively realistic, even in the invented parts of the story.

The PLA is the pillar of ORS in every way. ORS is a product of the PLA Navy Political Department's Television Arts Center. Dante Lam, the same Hong Kong director responsible for OM, declared that his crew and he received vast support from the Chinese navy in terms of access to facilities, equipment, and officers present in Yemen in 2015. ORS's budget was also more than three times that of WW2 and more than double that of OM. Besides, no other state-sponsored, potential competitor movie was on in theaters when ORS came out. The PLA is also central to the story, as the main characters belong to its elite forces. The Chinese military is presented as a powerful, modern, and professional fighting force that is ready both to work with local partners and to fight alone, overcoming all obstacles to defend China's interests. According to Dante Lam, the great support from the PLA translated into significant realism in how the PLA acts in the movie. More importantly, he also declared that one important goal of the movie was to show the audience that war is a horrific thing (Zhao and Li 2018). For that reason, scenes in the movie containing realistic representations of death (to the extent that half of the Chinese elite soldiers are killed) and severe injuries are abundant.

Although ORS was less successful than WW2, about USD 200 million less in tickets sold, its message was received clearly by the many who watched it. Both in media articles and in online forums, the mainstream opinion was that ORS is a "real" war movie. It is "real" in three ways. First, all the characters are made of flesh and blood. They are not superhumans, immune to explosions and bullets like WW2's Leng Feng. As one commentator wrote, ORS "makes the audience cool down and think again about desiring war" (NewSeed 2018). The comment with most likes in *Douban* (2018a) points to a very important difference between ORS and WW2: in ORS "there is nothing to laugh about." Second, ORS shows in detail the PLA's drones, warships, rifles, and elite units. While some commented on the fact that the uniforms and the weapons used by the Chinese soldiers in the movie look too Western, others started a debate on the actual differences between Chinese and American capabilities (Baidu Zhidao 2018). Third, ORS is not an idealistic movie. While the main character in WW2 manages to save both the Chinese citizens and their local friends/partners, the leader of the Chinese soldiers in ORS tells a Chinese journalist they had just saved that "This country is such a mess, we can only complete our mission." In other words, they could only take care of Chinese nationals; there was no time and no way for the Chinese soldiers to solve the problems of other countries. According to one commentator, this is a crucial difference between WW2 and ORS, which echoes what many Chinese think about the Middle East and Africa (Observer 2018).

Although the majority found Ridley Scott's *Black Hawk Down* superior in terms of realism and narration style, many compared ORS favorably with it because of the bloody details and the sense of the chaos typical of wars fought in the Middle East (Douban 2018b; Zhihu 2018). Realism, not necessarily reality, is extremely important because it provides the opportunity for the narrator to de-emphasize the shortcomings of the state and government, and to highlight the external challenges. The Chinese government is not new to this propaganda strategy (He 2018). Chinese soldiers are not just heroes but martyrs in the face of the terrible challenges they have to overcome. If one believes that China is being portrayed realistically, then the problem faced is no longer the ineffectiveness of state actions. After all, the Chinese soldiers in the movie act like and use the same weapons as their American counterparts. They, therefore, are strong because they look like the strongest army in the world. The enemies and the challenges the PLA has to deal with also look real and frightening to the audience—men with long black beards and AK-47 rifles such as ordinary people are accustomed to seeing on the news. It is not the fault of the Chinese government if the world is so dangerous. Indeed, ORS reminds the audience that the problem of protecting overseas interests is far more complex than many would think after watching WW2, and it is in relation to such problems that the government is presented as being the only defender of the nation. The problem with protecting China's overseas interests in ORS originates in the complexity of the threat. The fact that eight fully geared special forces soldiers suffered heavy casualties only to save a few Chinese nationals makes it clear that no Leng Feng could have survived and completed the mission. As in OM, international organizations have no significant role. China is capable of acting alone.

Conclusion

Public opinion probably played a role in encouraging and providing popular support to the top leadership about the need to think about China's security strategy beyond traditional national defense and to pay attention to the protection of its interest frontiers. There is little doubt that the always alert Chinese government noticed how their citizens talked about this issue online and how much they liked the movies and shows on it, as well as how deeply the Libyan evacuation had shaped the attitude of the people. Although it is unlikely that public opinion was crucial in the securitization process, its influence should not be overlooked, as it made it increasingly difficult to justify the relative lack of involvement of the PLA in the protection of China's interests overseas.

At least in the late 2000s, the strong reaction of the Chinese people to incidents involving their compatriots abroad, especially in North Africa and the Middle East, was probably met positively by the leaders in Zhongnanhai, who were already leaning toward having a larger military engagement abroad and, beginning with Hu Jintao, having an increasingly populist agenda. In a way, the Chinese government was lucky that a major foreign policy initiative like the deployment of naval warships in the Gulf of Aden could be carried out with the approval of the international community and, in particular, with the apparently overwhelming support of their domestic audience.

Yet it is unlikely that public opinion determined this part of Chinese foreign policy. Even after Libya, Hu Jintao and Xi Jinping did not accelerate the securitization of non-traditional threats against the country's overseas interests because they were forced against their will. They did so, rather, because Chinese civilian and military leaders are as Chinese and nationalist as their fellow citizens. Moreover, while the missions of the PLA Navy against pirates and during the evacuations from Libya and Yemen easily caught the eye of both domestic and international observers, it is China's engagement in peacekeeping operations—which did not seem very interesting to the Chinese public—that has evolved the most over the years (see Chapter 7). The relationship between public opinion and policy change, therefore, appears weak.

While the influence of public opinion remains difficult to assess, it is much clearer that the government actively attempted to shape the mindset of its citizens. Past studies on episodes of virulent Chinese nationalism and its impact on foreign policy show that suppression and censorship (Gries 2004, 125–34), not drastic foreign policy variations, ensue when bottom-up narratives begin to challenge the party's role as supreme representative of the nation. Moreover, it is unlikely that Chinese citizens expect their government to solve the problem of terrorism and instability in other countries in the way that they do in the case of the reunification of the Chinese mainland and Taiwan, which they have been promised repeatedly since 1949. Hence, while the pressure from Internet users has been growing, Chinese policymakers have not been subject to extreme levels of public criticism while they at least *appeared* to be putting efforts into the protection of China's overseas interests.

Given the importance of appearance, it is not surprising that the government did its best to engage its citizens through a variety of media, from *Weibo* to newspapers, social media, movies, and TV series, not only to address the concerns of "friends online," but also to co-opt them into its own narrative. The comparison with other countries, both in state media and in OM and ORS, speaks clearly to the fact that Chinese leaders saw an opportunity to boost their image and legitimacy as the best guides for the country's journey to attaining the status of a superpower.

The Chinese government, however, had to guide public opinion not only in order to maximize political gains, but also to minimize losses. Indeed, it seems that the "strong condemnations" of the MFA and the emphasis that the government puts on the complexity of fighting against non-traditional security threats abroad did not make the Chinese public significantly less inclined to support a military response when they saw compatriots abroad in danger. The constant criticism and apparent censorship of the so-called "keyboard warriors" are symptomatic of the fact that, regardless of the rationality of calling for military intervention in places like the Middle East and North Africa, the desire for a more muscular defense of China's interest frontiers is quite diffuse. Moreover, the launch of antipiracy operations probably convinced many that the government is moving in that direction. As the attention paid by Chinese Internet users to incidents overseas increased after Libya, it has also become clear that, while the government tried to blur the lines between becoming a great power, military diplomacy, and defending overseas interests, Internet users apparently pay more attention to incidents where civilians are involved than when the victims are soldiers deployed for peacekeeping missions.

Hence, after the commercial success of WW2 showed that the Chinese public was highly interested in the protection of interests overseas, the government decided to adopt a co-optation strategy. While the seriousness and complexity of the threat are much more emphasized in ORS than in OM and WW2, the changes made in its plot correspond to the preferences of a public that wanted to be assured of protection provided by its government. The apparent adaptation of the government's narrative to a position closer to that preferred by the public is an important element. Indeed, regardless of whether it was only a superficial response to the demand of the public, or symptomatic of a deeper change in policy terms, it probably created an expectation in the Chinese public to know about the capabilities that the state can deploy and its will to do so. While that is an issue that is discussed at the end of this book, Chapter 6 focuses on the institutional and doctrinal changes that took place within China's foreign and security policy machine as the securitization process progressed.

Bibliography

Bai, Ying, and Jingan Shi. 2017. "专访吴京：我只是点燃了一根火柴 [Special Interview with Wu Jing: I Just Lit up a Match]." *Xinhua.* August 15. Accessed September 19, 2018. http://www.xinhuanet.com/politics/2017–08/15/c_11214 85858.htm.

Baidu Zhidao. 2018. "红海行动中国蛟龙特种部队与美国特种部队比较谁更厉害 [Who Is the Stronger between the Chinese Jiaolong Team in 'Operation

Red Sea' and the American Special Forces]." *Baidu Zhidao*. Accessed January 25, 2019. https://zhidao.baidu.com/question/1772335501846988620.html.

Chen, Yuping. 2017. "《战狼2》背后的真问题：海外遇到事，谁来保护你 [The Real Problem behind Wolf Warrior 2: Who Will Protect You in Case of Problems Abroad?]." *The Paper*. August 30. Accessed April 2, 2019. https://www.thepaper.cn/newsDetail_forward_1779302.

Chin, Josh. 2011. "China's Other Problem with Protests Abroad." *The Wallstreet Journal*. February 23. Accessed May 13, 2017. http://blogs.wsj.com/chinarealtime/2011/02/23/chinas-other-problem-with-protests-abroad/.

China Daily. 2008. "恐吓中国维和部队的苏丹军阀 [Sudanese Warlord Threatens Chinese Peacekeepers]." *China Daily*. January 1. Accessed November 4, 2018. http://www.chinadaily.com.cn/hqzx/2008–01/01/content_6362799.htm.

China Military Web TV. 2016. 中国军视网 [*China Military Web TV*]. July 22. Accessed February 2, 2019. https://weibo.com/u/5461853682?profile_ftype=1&is_all=1&is_search=1&key_word=%E6%88%91%E9%A9%BB%E5%8D%97%E8%8B%8F%E4%B8%B9%E7%BB%B4%E5%92%8C%E9%83%A8%E9%98%9F%E9%81%87%E8%A2%AD%E4%BC%A4%E4%BA%A1%E4%BA%8B%E4%BB%B6%E5%90%8E#1543644538987.

Chubb, Andrew. 2018. "Assessing Public Opinion's Influence on Foreign Policy: The Case of China's Assertive Maritime Behavior." *Asian Security*. doi:https://doi.org/10.1080/14799855.2018.1437723.

Douban. 2017a. "如何看待《战狼 2》中的爱国情怀？[How to Look at Wolf Warrior 2's Patriotism?]." *Douban*. Accessed November 20, 2018. https://www.douban.com/gallery/topic/1414/.

Douban. 2017b. "很遗憾，你在《战狼 2》中看到的不是真的非洲 [It Is a Pity, What You See in Wolf Warrior 2 Is Not the Real Africa]." *Douban*. August 12. Accessed May 23, 2019. https://movie.douban.com/review/8744774/.

Douban. 2018a. "红海行动的影评 [The Comments on Operation Red Sea]." *Douban*. Accessed February 21, 2019. https://movie.douban.com/subject/26861685/reviews.

Douban. 2018b. "红海行动与黑鹰坠落 [Operation Red Sea and Black Hawk Down]." *Douban*. March 10. Accessed December 27, 2018. https://movie.douban.com/review/9214488/.

Fewsmith, Joseph, and Stanley Rosen. 2001. "The Domestic Context of Chinese Foreign Policy: Does 'Public Opinion' Matter?" In David M. Lampton (ed.), *The Making of Chinese Foreign and Security Policy in the Reform Era: 1978–2000*, 151–90. Stanford, CA: Stanford University Press.

Global Times. 2008. "中国船员用自制燃烧弹击退索马里海盗 [Chinese Sailors Use Molotov Cocktailsto Fight Pirates]." *Sina*. December 18. Accessed May 25, 2018. http://mil.news.sina.com.cn/p/2008-12-18/1417535489.html.

Global Times. 2015. "社评： 中印从也门撤侨的差距不是偶然的 [Opinion: The Difference between China's Evacuation Operation and India's One Is Not a Coincidence]." *Global Times*. April 1. Accessed February 24, 2019. http://opinion.huanqiu.com/editorial/2015–04/6064101.html.

Global Times. 2017. "利比亚撤侨舰长谈《战狼 2：'中国海军不会像电影中那样反应迟缓！' [Navy Commander during the Libyan Evacuation Discusses 'Wolf Warrior 2': The Chinese Navy Would Not React so Slowly as It Does in the Movie!]." *Global Times*. August 8. Accessed November 30, 2018. http://world.huanqiu.com/article/2017–08/11093686.html.

Gries, Peter Hays. 2004. *China's New Nationalism: Pride, Politics, and Diplomacy*. Berkeley, CA: University of California Press.

Hao, Yufan, and Su Lin. 2007. 中国外交决策：开放与多元的社会因素分析 [*Chinese Foreign Policymaking: An Analysis of Societal Forces*]. Beijing: PRC, Social Sciences Academic Press.

He, Yinan. 2018. "Domestic Troubles, National Identity Discourse, and China's Attitude towards the West, 2003–2012." *Nations and Nationalistm* 24 (3): 741–66.

Huang, Li. 2009. 剑指亚丁湾 [*Sword Aimed at the Gulf of Aden: The Chinese Navy's Bright Far Oceans Sword*]. Guangzhou, PRC: Zhongshan University Press.

Li, Xiaokun. 2008. "Beijing Ready to Combat Pirates." *Xinhua*. November 20. Accessed May 14, 2018. http://www.chinadaily.com.cn/cndy/2008–11/20/content_7221920.htm.

Ma, Li, ed. 2011. 国家行动：利比亚大撤离 [*National Operation: The Great Evacuation from Libya*]. Beijing: People's Daily Press.

NewSeed. 2018. "《红海行动》逆袭：'爱国' 成瘾、'反战' 母题和博纳式主旋律的新 '样板' [Operation Red Sea Surprises: The New 'Model' of 'Patriotism,' 'Anti-War,' and Bona-Style Movies]." *NewSeed*. February 22. Accessed Decmber 4, 2018. https://news.newseed.cn/p/1343075.

Observer. 2015. "马里恐袭3名中国人遇害 中国维和部队为什么不去救？ [Three Chinese Killed dDuring a Terrorist Attack in Mali, Why Did the Chinese Peacekeepers Not Go to Save Them?]." *The Observer*. November 21. Accessed September 30, 2018. https://www.guancha.cn/Third-World/2015_11_21_342088.shtml.

Observer. 2018. "吴京应该感谢《红海行动》，林超贤也应该感谢《战狼 2》 [Wu Jing Should Thank Operation Red Sea, Dante Lam Should Thank Wolf Warrior 2]." *The Observer*. February 19. Accessed March 1, 2019. https://user.guancha.cn/main/content?id=5680.

People's Daily. 2008. "网友:支持中国海军护航 树起大国形象 [Netizens: Support Chinese Naval Escorts Establishing the Image of a Great Power]." *People's Daily*. December 24. Accessed November 23, 2018. military.people.com.cn/GB/42970/8570300.html.

People's Daily. 2010. "网友调查：中国是否应该派作战部队参与国际维和？ [Online Survey: Should China Send Combat Troops to Join Peacekeeping Missions?]." *People's Daily.* January 23. Accessed September 16, 2019. http://military.people.com.cn/GB/42970/10829577.html.

People's Daily. 2017. "吴京反驳《战狼2》太个人英雄主义：有些人被洋人欺负惯了 [Wu Jing Rejects the Comments about Too Much Individual Heroism in Wolf Warrior: Some People Have Become Accustomed to Being Mistreated by Foreigners]." *People's Daily.* August 6. Accessed November 1, 2018. http://fj.people.com.cn/n2/2017/0806/c181466-30575126.html.

Roberts, Margaret E. 2018. *Censored: Distraction and Diversion inside China's Great Firewall.* Princeton, NJ: Princeton University Press.

Sohu. 2008. "中国海军远征索马里揭秘：速射炮最适合打海盗 [Uncovering the Secrets of the Chinese Navy's Long-Distance Operations in Somalia: Rapid-Fire Assault Is the Most Suitable Way to Fight Pirates]." *Sohu.* December 26. Accessed October 2, 2018. mil.sohu.com/20081226/n261430151.shtml.

Sohu. 2017. "《战狼2》太过宣扬个人英雄主义？吴京这样说… [Does Wolf Warrior 2 Promote Too Much the Figure of the Individual Hero? Wu Jing Says…]." *Sohu.* August 8. Accessed February 2, 2019. http://www.sohu.com/a/163094671_485090.

Sun, Li. 2008. "中广网独家报道：金一南少将建议我国出动海军打击索马里海盗 [Exclusive Report of China Information Broadcast Network: Major General Jin Yinan Suggests Our Country to Send the Navy to Fight Somali Pirates]." *China Information Broadcast Network.* November 28. Accessed November 27, 2018. http://www.cnr.cn/military/luntan/200811/t20081128_505163506.html.

Toutiao. 2010. "中国石油工人在也门遭绑架 [CNCP Workers Kidnapped in Yemen]." *Weibo.* May 17. Accessed November 23, 2018. https://weibo.com/1618051664/k4Cih7lRR?refer_flag=1001030103_&type=comment.

Toutiao. 2012. "新华网快讯 [*Xinhua Newsletter*]." *Weibo.* January 29. Accessed January 23, 2019. https://weibo.com/1618051664/y31KXt64s?type=comment#_rnd1543568276195.

Toutiao. 2013. "3名中国工人在苏丹被劫持 另有1名工程师失踪 [3 Chinese Workers Kidnapped in Sudan and 1 Engineer Missing]." *Weibo.* January 13. Accessed January 2, 2019. https://www.weibo.com/1618051664/zejAlFvqy?type=comment#1358254990221.

Toutiao. 2015a. "大国担当 [Responsible like a Great Power]." *Weibo.* April 4. Accessed January 13, 2019. https://weibo.com/1618051664/CbHG8iciu?type=comment#_rnd1543578764023.

Toutiao. 2015b. "我国启动从也门撤侨准备工作 590人待撤 [Our Country Started the Evacuation Operation from Yemen, 590 People Are Waiting to

Leave the Country]." *Weibo.* April 29. Accessed May 3, 2018. https://weibo.com/1618051664/CaOlsAjCT?type=comment#_rnd1543578489362.

Toutiao. 2015c. "IS杀害中国人质 中方：一定要将罪犯绳之以法 [IS Killed Chinese Hostage, China: Those Responsible Must Be Brought to Justice]." *Weibo.* November 19. Accessed January 12, 2019. https://weibo.com/1618051664/D4xTVnUhg?type=comment#_rnd1543590856592.

Toutiao. 2016. 南苏丹内讧交火 中国维和人员1死多伤 [*Clashes in South Sudan, One Chinese Peacekeeper Dead and Others Injured*]. July 11. Accessed January 29, 2019. https://weibo.com/1618051664/DEgX2reAI?type=comment#_rnd1543636470811.

Wang, Lilan. 2015. "也门：美承认无力撤侨 望美民众乘外国船只离开 [Yemen: The United States Admits It Is Not Capable of Evacuating Its Citizens and Hope They Can Leave on Foreign Boats]." *Global Times.* April 7. Accessed October 16, 2018. http://world.huanqiu.com/exclusive/2015-04/6110420.html

Weibo. 2011. "Search for '头条新闻 利比亚 公民." *Weibo.* February 22. Accessed November 16, 2018. https://s.weibo.com/weibo?q=%E5%A4%B4%E6%9D%A1%E6%96%B0%E9%97%BB%20%E5%88%A9%E6%AF%94%E4%BA%9A%20%E5%85%AC%E6%B0%91&wvr=6&b=1&Refer=SWeibo_box&page=2.

Xinhua. 2015a. "媒体释疑中国公民马里遇害 维和部队为何未救 [The Media Explain the Incidents Involving Chinese Citizens in Mali and Why the Peacekeepers Did Not Go to Save Them]." *Xinhua.* November 22. Accessed November 29, 2017. http://www.xinhuanet.com/overseas/2015-11/22/c_128454584.htm.

Xinhua. 2015b. "中国第三批赴马里维和部队组织应急反恐演练（组图）[The Third Batch of Peacekeepers Deployed in Mali Held an Emergency Antiterrorism Exercise (Pictures)]." *Xinhua.* November 22. Accessed January 24, 2019. http://www.xinhuanet.com/world/2015-11/22/c_128454935_2.htm.

Xinhua. 2018. "王毅：做好领保工作是义不容辞的责任 有三个利民好消息 [Wang Yi: Consular Protection Work Is Our Utmost Duty, Three Pieces of Good News for Citizens]." *China Daily.* March 8. Accessed October 23, 2018. http://cn.chinadaily.com.cn/2018-03/08/content_35811569.htm.

Zhang, Man. 2015. "'钢铁七连 维和先锋'—记在西非马里维和的"钢七连" ['The Seventh Gangtie Company, Pioneers of Peacekeeping'—Records of the Seventh Gangtie Company in the Peacekeeping Operation in Mali]." *Xinhua.* November 14. Accessed November 14, 2017. http://www.xinhuanet.com/mil/2015-11/14/c_128428200.htm.

Zhao, Meng, and Yan Li. 2018. "林超贤'揭秘'《红海行动》如何与中国海军协调合作 [Dante Lam Reveals What It Was Like Cooperating with the Chinese Navy on Operation Red Sea]." *Beijing Youth Daily.* April 5. Accessed April 23, 2018. http://epaper.ynet.com/html/2018-03/05/content_280395.htm?div=-1.

Zhihu. 2015a. "也门撤侨事件中美国宣称无力撤侨的真正原因是什么？ [What Is the Real Reason the United States Declared It Could Not Evacuate Its Citizens from Yemen?]." *Zhihu*. Accessed December 29, 2018. https://www. zhihu.com/question/29386079.

Zhihu. 2015b. "如何评价美国在也门的不撤侨政策？ [How to Evaluate the US Policy of Not Evacuating Its Citizens?]." *Zhihu*. Accessed January 7, 2019. https://www.zhihu.com/question/29286535.

Zhihu. 2015c. "为什么中国外交部每次对于各种反恐行为都回应强烈谴责？ [Why Does the Chinese Ministry of Foreign Affairs Always Strongly Condemn All Kinds of Terrorism?]." *Zhihu*. Accessed Februuary 13, 2019. https://www.zhihu.com/question/37650277.

Zhihu. 2016. "装甲车被击穿？苏丹维和的装甲车那么脆皮吗？ [Has The Armored Vehicle Been Destroyed? Is the Armor of the Armored Personnel Carriers so Fragile?]." *Zhihu*. Accessed October 14, 2018. https://www.zhihu. com/question/48372415.

Zhihu. 2018. "《红海行动》和《黑鹰坠落》哪个好看？ [Operation Red Sea and Black Hawk Down, Which One Is Better?]." *Zhihu*. Accessed December 3, 2018. https://www.zhihu.com/question/267277406.

6

Diverse Threats, Diverse Responses

The first outcome of a successful securitization process is the adoption of regulatory tools. They have two functions. The first is to make the use of the resources and capabilities already at the disposal of the state more efficient and effective against new threats. The second is to lay the foundations for the eventual creation and employment of capacity tools. This chapter, therefore, looks at the regulatory tools that the Chinese government deployed to counter threats to the lives and assets of Chinese citizens and companies.

The first section of the chapter shows how the main institutions involved in the formulation and implementation of China's strategy to protect its interests overseas evolved and, in certain cases, were created as a result of the dynamics identified earlier in this book. This process is studied chronologically, showing how the Ministry of Foreign Affairs (MFA) was the first to react to threats to Chinese interests. In particular, its consular protection system was reformed and strengthened in the early and mid-2000s. As the securitization process advanced, certain institutions within the Chinese People's Liberation Army (PLA) also started to change following patterns similar to those identified in Chapter 2. The creation of the Central National Security Commission (CNSC) of the Chinese Communist Party (CCP) and the attempted push from China's developing domestic private security industry are also presented as the most recent effects of the response to non-traditional security threats overseas in the foreign and security policy debate among Chinese elites.

The translation of words into action is never easy, even when the securitizing actor successfully convinces its empowering audience. This is particularly true when the matter at hand is the use of force abroad by an organization as large and as lacking in relevant experience as the Chinese military. To shed light on this specific issue of the securitization process, the second section of the chapter is dedicated to the analysis of debate on the concept of Military Operations Other Than War (MOOTW) within the PLA. It shows how military scholars, including those belonging to the Chinese People's Armed Police (PAP), approached the issue of operating

Protecting China's Interests Overseas: Securitization and Foreign Policy. Andrea Ghiselli,
Oxford University Press (2021). © Andrea Ghiselli.
DOI: 10.1093/oso/9780198867395.001.0001

overseas, from discussing the capabilities required to debating the legal and, especially, strategic problems that have to be resolved in order to expand the geographical scope of Chinese military deployments and, in particular, the effective use of force when necessary.[1]

Laws and Institutions

Although some of the same principles can be found in the Constitution of 1954, three statements contained in the Chinese Constitution since its 1982 edition was issued provide the legal foundations upon which the state and armed forces have built as they reacted to the growth of new non-traditional security threats overseas (PRC NPC 1982). The first is the twelfth paragraph of the "Preamble," which states that China:

> consistently opposes imperialism, hegemonism and colonialism, works to strengthen unity with the people of other countries, supports the oppressed nations and the developing countries in their just struggle to win and preserve national independence and develop their national economies, and strives to safeguard world peace and promote the cause of human progress.

The second is Article 29, which calls on the armed forces "to strengthen national defense, resist aggression, defend the motherland, safeguard the people's peaceful labor, participate in national reconstruction, and work hard to serve the people." The third is Article 50, which reads: "The People's Republic of China protects the legitimate rights and interests of Chinese nationals residing abroad and protects the lawful rights and interests of returned overseas Chinese and of the family members of Chinese nationals residing abroad."

Despite their common origin in the Constitution, laws and institutions aimed at protecting the lives and assets of Chinese citizens abroad and those related to the deployment of Chinese soldiers for overseas operations have long developed separately. As shown in Chapter 1, the MFA was the first institution to be called upon to defend Chinese citizens and companies abroad. Chinese experts seem to agree on the fact that the golden age of institutional development for the consular protection system of the MFA was during the 2000s (Xu 2016; Xiang 2017). In general, they highlight the close

---

[1] The interested reader can find a discussion of the sources used in the second section of this chapter in Appendix 1.

relationship existing between Hu Jintao's idea of Governing for the People and the development of laws, regulations, and institutions aimed at protecting Chinese citizens and companies abroad (X. Li 2011; H. Li 2012). The main steps in building that framework were taken after the evacuation of Chinese citizens from Iraq and Kuwait was carried out by the State Council through the adoption of ad hoc measures. Those events made it clear that a more systematic approach was needed (Xiang 2017). In particular, the most important development was the publication of the *Guide to Consular Protection and Services outside Chinese Territory* in 2003. The term "consular protection" started being used officially in China from that point.[2]

The following year, the MFA established a coordination mechanism that brings together twenty-six ministries and state agencies in case of emergency, through the emergency room of its general office. Similar interagency efforts are behind the legal and regulatory work that, as mentioned in Chapter 3 and listed in Appendix 2, the MFA, MOFCOM, and other ministries and agencies have been carrying out since 2005, when the pivotal National Overseas Emergency Response Law was issued by the State Council. It is also important to mention that the MFA and MOFCOM have published a number of manuals for Chinese companies, such as the *Guide to Chinese Consular Protection and Assistance for Chinese Companies* and the *Guidelines for the Safety Management of Institutions and Personnel of Overseas Chinese-Funded Enterprises*, about how to improve their safety abroad since 2007.

Moreover, in 2006, the MFA set up the Consular Protection Division under the Department of Consular Affairs to handle cases pertaining to the safety of Chinese citizens and companies abroad. The division was upgraded with the inauguration of the Consular Protection Center in August 2007. These two institutions—the MFA General Office and the Consular Protection Center—and the Department of External Security Affairs are the three organs within the MFA that are officially in charge of both monitoring the evolution of the situation abroad and leading the management of sudden crises. Diplomats abroad play a key role in both activities by reporting any problem that might arise, and by contributing to the yearly report on the situation in foreign countries that the MFA has been issuing since 2008. Moreover, since 2011, MOFCOM officers abroad are also involved in the approval process for Chinese contractors who want to put in bids for projects abroad worth USD 5 million or more (PRC MOFCOM 2015). They

---

[2] In Chinese: 领事保护 (Lǐngshì bǎohù).

are asked to include a security assessment of the country where the project will be carried out.

Despite such progress, both Chinese scholars and diplomats have remained critical of the mostly reactive logic behind the institutionalization of their country's consular protection system (Xiang 2017). Institutional fragmentation has also been identified as a problem, especially in countries in Africa and the Middle East where China's economic diplomacy is essentially economics-driven. Indeed, one of the by products of the efforts to strengthen the state's ability to support Chinese nationals abroad in the mid-2000s was that the departments in charge of international cooperation and exchange within the different ministries also started to take responsibility for the security of different categories of Chinese citizens abroad (Li 2011, 130). For example, the Ministry of Education monitors the situation of Chinese students overseas, and MOFCOM looks after Chinese workers sent abroad for labor services and other types of contracts. This division of labor entails that, in countries where workers constitute the vast majority of the Chinese community, it is the representative of MOFCOM who usually deals with the problems of Chinese laborers, rather than the officials in charge of consular affairs (H. Li 2012, 114). As mentioned in Chapter 3, in emergencies MFA officials are told about the situation.

This means that the MFA might find itself having to manage urgent problems without having much information about the general situation. Even after Chinese diplomats are called into action, the lack of inter agency coordination risks undermining the effectiveness of their work. According to Xia Liping (2015), indeed, the MFA was unprepared to deal with the crisis in Libya, as the ministry knew of only 6,000 (one-sixth of the total of the evacuees) Chinese nationals—those registered in the ministry's official list—in Libya when the unrest began. Another Chinese scholar reported that MOFCOM sent a department-level delegation to Libya looking for new projects for Chinese companies shortly after the main armed clashes were over without consulting with the MFA (Z. Li 2012, 103). Reportedly, the Chinese top leadership is now trying to solve this problem through new regulations introduced in February 2018. Chinese officials interviewed by *Bloomberg* declared that Chinese ambassadors have been given total control over officials of other ministries and agencies working at the embassies and consulates abroad (Martin, Zhai, and Shi 2018).

At the same time, the consular protection system has been one of the main victims of the growing gap between resources allocated and tasks to perform, as described in Chapter 4. The number of cases of Chinese citizens who require the assistance of the MFA has been increasing every year, in terms of both the sheer number and the variety of the problems, from relatively small incidents, like robberies, to much more serious ones, like kidnappings and evacuations. For example, in 2015 the MFA had to deal with more than 80,000 cases; these included the evacuation of more than 6,000 people due to political unrest and natural disasters, and the kidnapping of more than fifty Chinese nationals abroad. In comparison, the total number of cases in 2004 was 20,000. The MFA is also under growing pressure from the unrealisitic expectations of Chinese citizens relating to what diplomats can do (Xia 2016). MFA officials, indeed, have even gone on record to complain about the situation. For example, an anonymous diplomat told the Chinese media that, even in 2004, threats against Chinese nationals abroad were more than the newly established Department of External Security Affairs could deal with effectively (Legal Daily 2004). The same year, Luo Tianguang, the then director of the Department of Consular Affairs, declared that the MFA was experiencing serious financial difficulties in the face of increasingly complex and numerous emergencies (Chinanews.com 2004).

The consular protection system has had its own budget since 2005. A diplomat declared that it was less than RMB 30 million (around USD 4.3 million) in 2015 (Xia 2016, 18). Embassies and consulates abroad too have their own small emergency budget. The MFA used almost its entire annual emergency budget in 2011 on the Libya evacuation and, as a Chinese scholar pointed out, that event revealed the excessively overstretched state of China's consular protection system (Li 2016, 14). Moreover, there is also a limit in terms of diplomats assigned to deal with overseas emergencies. The number of officers working in the Consular Protection Center is between fifteen and twenty and, even when the top leadership gave the order to evacuate Chinese citizens from Libya, the number never surpassed thirty (Xia 2016, 21). As of 2013, fewer than 300 diplomats overseas were specifically in charge of dealing with problems encountered by Chinese nationals, and even then, this was in addition to carrying out a number of other bureaucratic tasks, such as issuing passports and other documents (Yang 2013, 18). In 2011, the number of diplomats in charge of consular affairs abroad was the same as in 1994, but the number of Chinese nationals going abroad every year, and of cases handled by the consular affairs offices, was ten and seventy times higher, respectively (Lai 2012).

While the MFA began responding to the securitization process in the 2000s, the PLA did so later. The earliest law that provides the foundation for Chinese troops to go abroad is the National Defense Law of 1997

(PRC NPC 1997a). Articles 8, 65, and 67 contain all the key principles, from aiming at protecting world peace to non-intervention in other countries' internal affairs, that shape China's participation in international peacekeeping operations, as well as other forms of military cooperation with other countries. Since military operations overseas were originally conceived as a means of boosting China's international image, it is not surprising that the first signs of institutional development within the Chinese military machine took place in the Ministry of National Defense (MOD), which has always been "a shadowy organization that mainly functions as a window to the world outside the PLA" (Allen et al. 2015, 121).

The MOD is the lead organization under the State Council and the CCP Central Military Commission (CMC) that represents China in coordinating with the United Nations (UN) on peacekeeping operations, although the troops and assets actually deployed fall under the Office for International Military Cooperation of the CCP CMC. In keeping with the leading role of the MOD in the management of peacekeeping operations, the first institution related to the deployment of Chinese troops abroad was the Peacekeeping Affairs Office, which was established within the ministry. Created in 2001, this office is staffed with some fifty officers with previous overseas experience and fluency in foreign languages. It was upgraded to a bureau-level organization between 2002 and 2003. The director of this bureau has usually been one of the deputy directors of the former PLA General Staff Department's Second Department, the one in charge of military intelligence that is now part of the Joint Staff Department of the CCP CMC (Allen et al. 2015, 116).

A new round of institutional innovation happened between 2007 and 2009. The first change was the creation of an MOD spokesperson. The decision to do so was taken in December 2007 and the establishment of the Information Department within the MOD was officially announced in January 2008. According to Chinese media, "this department would provide information services for both domestic and foreign media" (Fan 2008). Hence, the MOD spokesperson's statements have always played an important role in creating the right media environment for military leaders to announce important events, from the coming release of a defense white paper to the deployment of warships to the Gulf of Aden, as well as explaining the PLA's point of view on specific issues and incidents (Boswell 2009).

At the same time, the PLA began to establish MOOTW-specialized institutions and to issue new regulations. However, it seems that the Chinese armed forces were mostly focusing on peacekeeping operations and domestic disaster relief. The first institution was the MOOTW Teaching and Research Office, opened in the Shijiazhuang Mechanized Infantry Academy and staffed with six professors. According to the Party Committee of the academy, the earthquake in Sichuan showed that non-traditional security cannot be neglected and, therefore, it was necessary to carry out better research pertaining to MOOTW (Global Times 2008). The second is the Huairou Peacekeeping Center, which was opened on June 25, 2009. It cost USD 29 million and comprises twenty different areas for training and teaching (Allen et al. 2015, 117). Besides providing the necessary facilities to strengthen the capabilities of Chinese peacekeepers, the center is also the venue for meetings with foreign pre-deployment experts that the PLA has been conducting since 2004 (Zhang 2007).

Against this background, new regulations were being issued between 2008 and 2010 (Zheng 2013, 13). They too appear to put significant emphasis on domestic operations rather than those overseas. This is clearly the case with the Opinions about Strengthening the Political Work in MOOTW, which describes how Chinese soldiers should relate to the domestic media when performing MOOTW in China. At the same time, the CCP CMC approved the Plan for the Development of MOOTW Capabilities, which describes the training, equipment, and capabilities necessary to carry out antiterrorism operations, "protection of rights and interests," international peacekeeping, surveillance, and international and domestic disaster relief operations.[3] The plan also updated the Regulations for the Armed Forces to Participate in Disaster Relief Operations that were issued in 2005. Finally, the CCP CMC issued a new regulation for domestic MOOTW in 2010. The Rules for the Command of the Armed Forces to Handle Sudden Events aimed at regulating the use of force and the chain of command in cases where the armed forces have to quell social unrest.

The first real upgrade of the intellectual resources invested in the preparation of MOOTW overseas took place only after the Libya evacuation. Indeed, in late 2011, the PLA Academy of Military Science (AMS) established the MOOTW Research Center, staffed with twenty-eight experts from state organizations, the CCP CMC, the PLA, the PAP, and public security institutions. The center specializes in antiterrorism and social unrest, domestic and international disaster relief, interest and rights protection, surveillance, international peacekeeping, and international exercises. The relationship between

---

[3] In Chinese: 权益保护 (Quányì bǎohù).

non-traditional security threats and military operations is also a topic of research at the center (Tian 2011). At the same time, new MOOTW-related regulations were approved in 2012. The most important ones are the Provisions for the Participation of the PLA in UN Peacekeeping Missions. According to *Xinhua* (CCP CMC 2012), this document sheds light on the duties, procedures for deployment and withdrawal, training, and legal arrangements for peace-keepers abroad. The financial aspects of MOOTW, like the administration of the budget for those operations, were clarified in another set of regulations issued by the then PLA Logistic Department (Bai 2012).

In late 2015, further major developments took place. First, the Standing Committee of the National People's Congress issued two important laws. After China's top legislative bodies started to work on it in late December 2014, the new National Security Law was approved in July 2015. Among the different issues it touches upon, this law clearly includes UN-led peacekeeping operations, international disaster relief, maritime escorts, and military operations to protect China's overseas interests among the duties of the Chinese state (PRC NPC 2015a). The law was seen as a breakthrough. In a rare interview, the officer in charge of the CCP CMC's Legal Affairs Bureau emphasized that this was the first time that a Chinese law explicitly allowed the PLA to operate overseas to carry out these kinds of operations (Mao 2015). According to him, the new law summarized the experience and the lessons learned by the Chinese military during the operations carried out in the previous years.

The second major MOOTW-related law was approved on December 27, 2015, four years after Chinese legislators had started to discuss the necessity of strengthening and consolidating China's antiterrorism legislation into one single law. The National Antiterrorism Law added antiterrorism operations to those that Chinese soldiers, especially those of the PAP, could carry out abroad (PRC NPC 2015b). At the same time, the law mandates the MFA and civilian security agencies to establish risk-assessment units and to send their officials overseas for missions related to the protection of Chinese interests abroad against terrorist attacks. However, the main target of the law was prob-ably domestic terrorism. According to Su Zelin, the deputy director of the Commission for Legislative Affairs of the National People's Congress Standing Committee, events at home and abroad both contributed to turning past pro-posals into effective legislation (China Daily 2015).

Although it was less eye-catching, it is important to also highlight the approval of the National Defense Transportation Law, which came into force on January 1, 2017 (PRC NPC 2016). While the PLA has long had the authority

178 PROTECTING CHINA'S INTERESTS OVERSEAS

to assume control over civilian assets for military purposes (Kennedy 2019, 2), this law specifically commands all Chinese institutions overseas, especially embassies, consulates, and companies operating in the international logistic sector, to provide facilities, supplies, and personnel whenever the PLA requires them to do so, including for peacekeeping and operations to defend Chinese nationals and assets. It is important to point out that this development took place after a number of Chinese civilian airlines were selected in 2013 to create "strategic projection air support fleets" to conduct missions such as transporting troops, evacuating casualties, and the rapid delivery of materials and equipment (Kennedy 2019, 19–20).[4] PLA scholars praised this law as an important pillar for the construction of a Chinese strategic power projection system, which they argued should be continued by boosting civil-military integration and developing the necessary means, such as long-range transport aircraft, that would allow the PLA to operate independently (Zhong et al. 2017).

The deployment of soldiers overseas was also influenced by reforms of the armed forces outlined in the CCP CMC-issued Opinions on Deepening Reforms of National Defense and Armed Forces, which aimed at making the PLA a world-class military by 2020 (CCP CMC 2016). The main casualty of these structural reforms was the PLA General Staff Department, whose departments were transferred to the new CCP CMC Joint Staff Department or transformed into stand-alone departments of the CCP CMC or had their functions assigned to the different services, including the new PLA Strategic Support Force. It is against this background that the CCP CMC established the Overseas Operations Office, whose existence was revealed for the first time in early 2016. This organization operates under the Operations Bureau of the CCP CMC Joint Staff Department.

PLA officers interviewed by Joel Wuthnow and Phillip C. Saunders (2017, 25–6) declared that the office is meant to oversee both wartime and peacetime operations. In the case of long-standing operations, like those in the Gulf of Aden, however, it might only play a coordinating role, while the military services involved would take care of the specific preparations and execution of the mission. Moreover, the office might be involved in establishing coordination mechanisms with foreign militaries and security forces in order to support the PLA's overseas operations. According to Major General Dai Shaoan, a former military attaché to the Chinese embassy in Cairo, this is necessary to push forward the normalization of military operations abroad by both

---

[4] In Chinese: 战略投送支援机队 (Zhànlüè tóu sòng zhīyuán jī duì).

negotiating agreements with other countries and improving the regulatory work in China (Guo 2016).

While the MFA and the PLA moved to upgrade their ability to better respond to threats against China's interest frontiers, the CCP focused on boosting interagency coordination by establishing the CCP CNSC in 2013, and upgrading the CCP Foreign Affairs Leading Small Group (FALSG) into the CCP Central Foreign Affairs Commission in 2018. However, while the CCP Central Foreign Affairs Commission is, essentially, an upgraded version of the leading small group that it replaced thanks to the presence of a member of the CCP Polituburo (Yang Jiechi) as the leader of its general office, the CCP CNSC is an almost entirely new institution. The establishment of the CCP CNSC came after previous attempts by Jiang Zemin and Hu Jintao to create an institution similar to the American National Security Council failed. Instead, China had a CCP National Security Leading Small Group that was created in September 2000 based on the blueprint of the CCP FALSG and probably did not prove fit to deal in a timely manner with security crises (Erickson and Liff 2016, 207–8).

Today, Chinese civilian and military scholars seem to agree on the fact that the CCP CNSC will play a key role in formulating a comprehensive national security strategy that includes both civilian and military actions (Liu 2013; Hu 2015). Experts from a number of Chinese universities argued that the CCP CNSC is structured according to the "small core, large scope management model," thereby centralizing both the policymaking process and the flow of information while having authority over a vast number of issues (Xue, Peng, and Tao 2015).[5] At least when it comes to crises abroad, the CCP CNSC probably has the most determining role against non-traditional security threats. Indeed, according to the director of the Political Work Teaching and Research Office of the PLA National Defense University (NDU), Gong Fangbin (2014), it was established in order to better coordinate the response to those kinds of threats. After all, he maintained, the CCP CMC is more than capable of dealing with traditional threats. Similarly, Zhi Binyou (2013), the director of the Emergency Response Training Center of the Chinese Academy of Governance, argued that the main functions of the CCP CNSC will be to coordinate military activities in peacetime regarding non-traditional security issues.

---

[5] In Chinese: 小核心、大外围的成员管理模式 (Xiǎo héxīn, dà wàiwéi de chéngyuán guǎnlǐ móshì).

Figure 27 Chinese economic presence overseas and the development of the Chinese market for private security services
Source: Andrea Ghiselli (2018), translated from *Phoenix International Think Tank* (2016).

Against this background of profound transformation within key institutions in Beijing, Chinese companies abroad tried to improve the security of their employees and assets, especially after 2011. As Figure 27 shows, the Chinese market for private security has been growing faster since that year, which indicates that the perceived mismatch between demand and supply of protection provided by the state had widened. It has already been pointed out in Chapter 3 that the state itself pushed Chinese companies to take responsibility for their employees' protection. Given the large sums of money that they could spend, and the size of their presence in unstable countries, it is the SOEs that not only began spending the most on security but also lobbied central government to reform the domestic private security industry.

China National Petroleum Corporation (CNPC), one of the Chinese energy giants, spends up to 3–5 percent of the capital destined for investment in risky countries on security-related activities and preparation. In places where the security conditions are extremely precarious, such as Iraq, this can rise to 20 percent. According to estimates made by *China Economic Weekly*, CNPC spent at least USD 3.3 billion on security over the last twenty-four years (Jia 2017). CNPC, Sinopec, and the China National Offshore Oil Corporation spent more than USD 2 billion in 2015. It is common practice for Chinese SOEs operating in dangerous places to defend themselves by asking local governments for protection, developing in-house risk-assessment capabilities, and outsourcing tasks that require additional resources—such as armed guards. For example, in 2007, CNPC established an antiterrorism and overseas emergency center staffed by 160 analysts. As of 2013, it employed roughly 1,300 security guards to protect its projects overseas (Nanguo Zaobao 2013). In comparison, small businesses spend much less. As a Chinese consultant lamented, those companies often underestimate the risks abroad and prioritize cutting costs over the quality of the services that they purchase (Deng 2015). They usually dedicate only 1 percent of their budget to security.

Companies like Control Risk and G4S dominate the Chinese private security market thanks to their global presence, highly trained personnel, and wide range of services on offer. At the same time, local security contractors in countries where Chinese companies invest offer cheap services and the advantage of reducing any friction between foreign investors and local communities. While big foreign firms are usually contracted by Chinese SOEs, local private security companies (PSCs) often attract smaller clients because of their low prices. Chinese customers can also choose Chinese PSCs. According to the *Financial Times*, there were 3,200 Chinese private guards abroad in 2016, more than the number of Chinese peacekeepers deployed in the same year (Clover 2017). They are usually hired only to guard areas within compounds and construction sites. In the case of Iraq, for example, the outermost ring of security was guaranteed by American or Iraqi soldiers. Local armed guards made up the second layer of protection outside the homes and workplaces of CNPC and other Chinese companies workers (Global Times 2014). The first Chinese PSC to offer services targeting companies investing abroad, in Iraq in particular, only started doing so in 2010 (Beijing Daily 2010). In keeping with the logic of supply and demand, Chinese PSCs that offer overseas services have taken note of the growing security threats to the operations of rich SOEs in Middle Eastern and African countries and have decided to establish offices there (Phoenix International Think Tank 2016).

Recently, Chinese PSCs and international insurance companies have also started exploring cooperation with foreign PSCs (Arduino 2018, 136). However, Chinese PSCs suffer seriously from both high- and low-end competition because the range and quality of the services they can offer is limited. Although most of the employees of Chinese PSCs are former soldiers, mostly from PLA and PAP special forces units, their scant knowledge of foreign languages and culture, coupled with far less operational experience than their foreign counterparts, further affects the competitiveness of China's domestic security industry even in the area of non-armed services (Chen 2016).

However, the main problem is that Chinese citizens cannot carry and use firearms abroad, and this undermines the attractiveness of Chinese PSCs for customers who have interests in dangerous parts of the world. As a Chinese scholar put it, since domestic PSCs offering overseas services are regulated by the Ministry of Public Security, which mostly focuses on domestic law enforcement, this is a source of uncertainty (Cao 2018). Although this ministry is an extremely powerful institution within Chinese borders, it lacks the ability to control the activities of Chinese PSCs abroad. Moreover, these types of PSCs inhabit a gray area of Chinese law. The current law on private security, which came into force in 2010, allows for the existence of two kinds of PSCs—"security companies" and "security companies that provide armed escorting services"—but it makes no specific reference to their possible activities in other countries (PRC State Council 2009).[6]

Moreover, Chinese law on gun control is ambiguous with regard to the use of firearms abroad. While the punishment for offenses involving the possession or use of guns in China ranges from a minimum of three years' imprisonment to the death penalty, crimes committed abroad, whose maximum punishment is a period of three years in prison, might not be prosecuted (PRC NPC 1997b). Chinese PSCs have tried to escape this legal gray zone by working with Chinese SOEs through ad hoc agreements. For example, the first time a Chinese PSC provided armed services abroad was through a partnership with the giant Chinese shipping company, COSCO in 2012. Similarly, the Macao-registered Hua Wei Security Group's website suggests that its guards are allowed to carry guns, at least on board Macao-flagged vessels, as part of an agreement with the Macao authorities.

There is also a case of attempted bottom-up reform, which was initiated by one of the top managers of an SOE—Han Fangming—who has been serving as deputy chairman of the Foreign Affairs Committee of the Chinese People's Political Consultative Conference since 2008, and founded the Charhar Institute, the Chinese think tank that has written the most detailed report on China's private security market so far (Charhar Institute 2015). Han was also holding a top managerial position at Sinohydro in 2012 when twenty-nine workers of the company were kidnapped in Sudan. When the kidnapping took place, he did not just declare to the media that China needed to have firms like the infamous Blackwater, but also drafted a law proposal with other members of his committee in the Chinese People's Political Consultative Conference requiring Chinese embassies abroad to publish reports on local security situations, calling for the creation of a database of Chinese citizens overseas, the expansion of the mandatory security

---

[6] In Chinese: 保安服务公司 (Bǎo'ān fúwù gōngsī) and 从事武装守护押运服务的保安服务公司 (Cóngshì wǔzhuāng shǒuhù yāyùn fúwù de bǎo'ān fúwù gōngsī).

measures that companies investing abroad have to implement, and, most importantly, supporting the regulation of the activities of Chinese PSCs abroad (Sheng 2012). However, the last part of the proposal was eliminated from the final draft (Zhang 2012).

At the time of writing, there is no sign that other attempts to reform the Chinese security industry have been undertaken. One of the possible reasons for this is that allowing Chinese companies to become like their foreign counterparts would not necessarily improve the protection of Chinese companies, especially small ones. According to scholars at Tsinghua University, a reform in that direction would be useful only if it could give access to armed security to medium-sized and small companies at reasonable prices (Zhao and Li 2015). Otherwise, they argue, the diplomatic and political risks originating from the presence of armed Chinese citizens abroad would far outweigh the potential advantages gained by the hiring of domestic armed PSCs by the large SOEs.

The Evolution of Chinese Military Operations Other Than War

Although Roy D. Kamphausen (2013, 1) stated that "the PLA does not consider all 'non-war' activities to be MOOTW," the Chinese concept of MOOTW, in fact, includes almost all military operations short of war. The term MOOTW appeared in one of China's defense white papers for the first time in 2008. According to a text published by the PLA AMS, however, it has been in use since the publication of the 2001 edition of the *Outline of Military Training and Evaluation* (Zheng 2013, 13). The same text shows how it has changed from the original concept imported from the 1995 US Army's *JP3-07 Joint Doctrine for Military Operations Other Than War*, where the concept of MOOTW was enunciated for the first time, to that outlined in the 2011 *Chinese People's Liberation Army Terminology* (hereafter *Terminology*). According to the *Terminology*, MOOTW are:

military operations that are carried out to protect national security and national development interests and that do not constitute an act of war. They include anti-terrorism, disaster relief, protection of rights and interests, surveillance, international peacekeeping, international disaster relief, etcetera.

(Zheng 2013, 1–2)

Although it elaborates more on the content of MOOTW in China's military doctrine, *The Science of Military Strategy* also refers to the definition given in the 2011 *Terminology* (PLA AMS 2013, 158).

Despite its American origin, Chinese scholars argue in *The Science of Military Strategy* that the PLA has extensive experience in carrying out MOOTW because its soldiers have always had to deal with a variety of tasks other than war, from building roads to disaster relief, already during the war against the Japanese and the nationalist forces (PLA AMS 2013, 155–6). Nonetheless, many books published by Chinese military scholars, mostly through the PLA AMS and the PLA NDU, highlight the fact that, as in the West, the rise of new non-traditional security threats after the end of the Cold War is the main factor that pushed the Chinese military to explore the concept of MOOTW (Wang et al. 2006; Xiao 2009; Shou and Xu 2009; Zheng 2013). The authors of *The Science of Military Strategy* even argued that it is the combination of rising non-traditional security threats and expanding overseas interests that made MOOTW important for the PLA (PLA AMS 2013, 86).

Yet, especially up to 2008, the concept of MOOTW not only was not considered important, but it was also understood in so many different ways that some doubted that it could be effectively developed and used by the Chinese military (Liu and Chen 2007). For example, some clearly saw MOOTW as indissolubly connected to war, either before or after a full-scale conflict (Wang 2005). The line between MOOTW and war operations is almost non-existent, since the transition from one to the other is meant to be seamless. Another commentator argued that MOOTW have become a substitute for expensive wars. Others, instead, claimed that MOOTW are an important way for a country to display military prowess and deter or coerce enemies (Zhang 2006). Otherwise, MOOTW can boost China's soft power through military cooperation with other countries (Wang and Wu 2007). Apparently, no one looked at overseas MOOTW as operations meant to neutralize non-traditional security threats.

The idea of developing new MOOTW-specific capabilities cannot be found in the debate in *China Military Science* or other PLA-published journals and magazines during those years. It is quite clear that all the resources available to the Chinese military machine had to be aimed at the improvement of traditional national defense capabilities. Another element that shows the superficiality of the debate is that Chinese military scholars did not discuss the geographic scope of MOOTW (Are they domestic operations or is the PLA going to perform them abroad as well?) or the relationship between MOOTW and the principle of noninterference. Although, in the case of peacekeeping, it

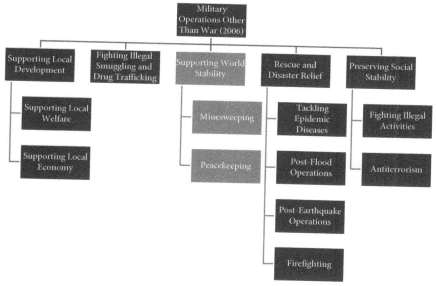

Figure 28 Military Operations Other Than War in Chinese military doctrine in 2006

Note: Light-colored boxes refer to international operations.

Source: Wang, Chang, Xu, and Zhang (2006). Compiled by the author.

is implicit that the PLA is operating abroad, none of the articles, for example, examines what "international" in "international cooperation" actually means in terms of where and how those operations should be carried out. A book published by the PLA NDU Press in 2006 indicates only peacekeeping and minesweeping as being clearly overseas operations (Figure 28). Given the lack of conceptual focus, it is natural that virtually none of the scholars and officers discussed practical issues, such as what kind of legal framework was necessary. The superficiality of the debate is rather remarkable if one considers the fact that the civilian leadership introduced the New Historic Missions of the PLA already in the 2004 defense white paper (PRC State Council's Information Office 2004).

The 2008–11 period was a pivotal one. The number of articles published on MOOTW increased significantly and, consequently, the debate suddenly became extremely spirited and much more sophisticated than before (Figure 29). In early 2009, the white paper, *China's Defense in 2008*, featured the term "MOOTW" for the first time, firmly enshrining it in Chinese defense policy (PRC State Council's Information Office 2009). However, it seems that it was the earthquake in Sichuan Province in May 2008, which resulted in

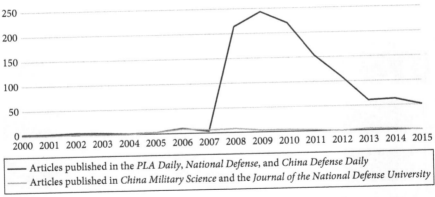

Figure 29   Articles on Military Operations Other Than War in Chinese military publications
Compiled by the author.

thousands of people losing their lives, that prompted the PLA to pay more attention to MOOTW. Thereafter, the debate took two main directions. On the one hand, the majority—the Cadre Department of the former PLA General Political Department (2008) among them—focused on the single case of the Wenchuan earthquake. The main outcome seems to have been that it was seen to be necessary to improve the political work related to domestic MOOTW, to guide both domestic and international public opinion, and to strengthen the bond between the army and the people. As pointed out already, the regulations approved in that period aimed at addressing that problem. Further, some found that it was necessary to boost the "fighting capability" of the PLA when performing MOOTW.[7] To do so, better training and equipment had to be provided to Chinese troops in order to improve their performance in disaster relief operations (Wang 2008).

On the other hand, the debate moved to analyzing the American concept of MOOTW in relation to China's national security policies and the capabilities of the PLA. These commentators, in particular, started to look at MOOTW as missions that could be performed outside China's border, beyond peacekeeping. Zhang Wei (2008), a scholar at the PLA AMS, argued that the idea of MOOTW was a still-developing concept and needed to be expanded in order to overcome the obstacles the that had led the American military to drop it in 2006. As China's external security environment was changing, it was necessary to think about a larger number of operations that could also be

---

[7] In Chinese: 能战度 (Néngzhàn dù).

carried out abroad, and even to contemplate the use of a certain degree of force in case of emergency (H. Zhang 2008; Chen 2009).

The legal aspects of operating overseas also began to be discussed. For example, a PLA legal expert found several issues that needed to be urgently addressed, from the rules concerning the use of force during MOOTW to the relationship between Chinese and foreign soldiers in an international context (Xie 2008). In order to solve or at least mitigate these problems, different commentators suggested a twofold approach. On the one hand, China could rely on international law, which offers a framework accepted by every country (Li and Ou 2008). On the other hand, the embryonic legal framework created in 2007 for a joint exercise in Russia could be further developed by drawing on the experience of other countries, especially that of the United States (Peng and Xiao 2008).

Nonetheless, many kept on interpreting the concept of MOOTW overseas through the lens of traditional security, or as operations aimed at cementing China's international image. Senior Colonel Lin Dong (2009) saw the concept of MOOTW as a driver for doctrinal and strategic innovation. Lin argued that it was necessary to break the static vision of the alternation between war and peace because interdependence made the great powers fear wars with each other and created a "new space for strategic bargaining."[8] Within such a space, military confrontation has been reduced to crisis management and MOOTW, intended either as deterrence or as defense cooperation, are important new tools in the state's hands. Otherwise, overseas MOOTW were mainly seen as political operations aimed at improving China's image (Liu 2008). A growing number of scholars and officers started to appreciate the diplomatic cover provided by greater engagement in MOOTW, especially for the development of power projection capabilities and other capabilities that could be useful for winning a war against another country (Huang 2009; Li 2009). The fact that these officers found MOOTW somehow useful did not mean that the development of MOOTW-specific capabilities was necessary. The better performance of the PLA during the May 2010 Yushu earthquake relief operations probably further cemented this belief (Mulvenon 2010).

In general, while Chinese scholars were showing much more interest in MOOTW overseas than before, they remained deeply divided over what direction to take with the development of that concept. A text published by the PLA NDU Press in 2009 lists a large number of MOOTW that the PLA had already carried out, or intended to carry out, but many of them could

---

[8] In Chinese: 战略博弈新空间 (Zhànlüè bóyì xīn kōngjiān).

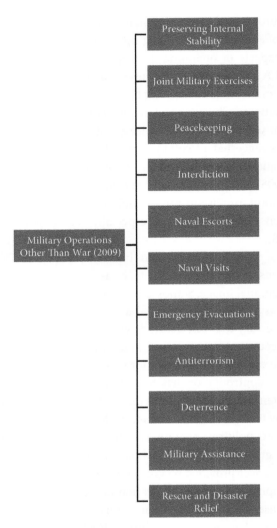

Figure 30 Military Operations Other Than War in Chinese military doctrine in 2009
Source: Xiao (2009: 41–73). Compiled by the author.

only take place during a confrontation against another country, rather than in order to confront a non-traditional security threat (Figure 30). This ambivalence caused several officers to call for more work to avoid overstretching the concept of MOOTW (Wang and Guo 2010). A commentary published in the *People's Liberation Army Daily* in August 2010 warned that the concept had become too broad without having been tested at an operational level (Yang 2010).

While still present in the 2015 defense white paper "China's Military Strategy" (PRC State Council's Information Office 2015), the term "MOOTW" has started to disappear from the debate from 2011. However, that does not mean that the PLA has lost interest in these operations. On the contrary, the quantitative decrease in the publications seems to correlate positively with the increase in their quality. Chapter 2 shows that the PLA embraced a holistic understanding of security, thereby creating a bridge between war operations and MOOTW. The first signs of this development can be found in the 2013 edition of *The Science of Military Strategy*, which, for the first time, treats MOOTW as a category of operations that is separate from deterrence. It categorizes MOOTW according to their nature into "confrontational" MOOTW (antiterrorism and antipiracy operations), "law enforcement" MOOTW (international peacekeeping and internal martial law enforcement), "rescue" MOOTW (disaster relief and non-combatant evacuation operations), and "cooperative" MOOTW (international joint exercises).[9] The same year, the PLA AMS published a text explicitly intended for use in military classrooms to train Chinese officers. As Figure 31 shows, the number and variety of missions included in the concept of MOOTW significantly expanded to include a roughly equal number of domestic and overseas operations aimed at both traditional and non-traditional security threats. A clue as to what kind of capabilities the PLA now needs to develop can be found in a recent study on all domain operations (Yue 2015). The author lists power projection, joint maneuvering, and high mobility among the key capabilities necessary for carrying out "diversified military tasks" assigned to the PLA by Hu Jintao in 2013. Indeed, he also points out that the development of those capabilities could help to bridge the gap between what is needed for fighting a war and for fulfilling the New Historic Missions.

The Chinese armed forces, including both the PLA and the PAP, started to consider the use of force abroad in the case of non-traditional security threats as a real possibility. For example, although engaging in peacekeeping still remains, to quote the officer in charge of the MOD Peacekeeping Office of China, an "important diplomatic operation," other PLA scholars published a detailed study on the possible use of force by Chinese peacekeepers and the variables at play in that situation (Liu and Duan 2016). According to them,

[9] In Chinese: 对抗性 (Duìkàng xìng), 执法性 (Zhífǎ xìng), 救助性 (Jiùzhù xìng), and 合作性 (Hézuò xìng).

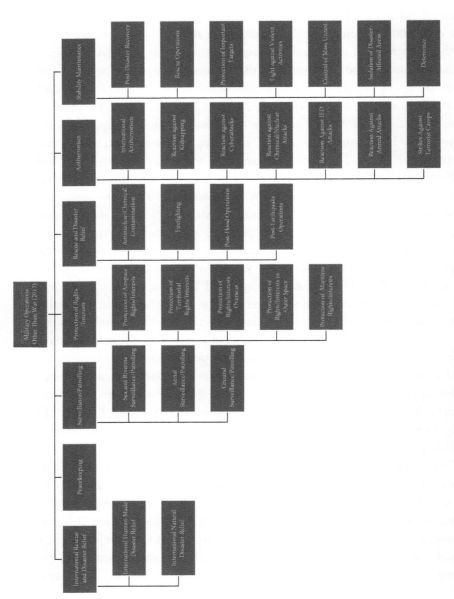

Figure 31 Military Operations Other Than War in Chinese military doctrine in 2013

Source: Zheng (2013, 3). Compiled by the author.

there are a number of issues that must be clarified before Chinese peace-keepers will be able and/or allowed to fire their weapons. First, the relationship between Chinese diplomacy and international peacekeeping must be clarified. Indeed, they argue that, if participating in peacekeeping operations is also meant to protect Chinese overseas interests, a more flexible attitude toward these is necessary. Both new laws and a proper "peacekeeping strategy" must be crafted.[10] Second, the chain of command must be clarified and strengthened because the MOD Peacekeeping Affairs Bureau does not have the authority or the ability to oversee a more proactive use of force by Chinese peacekeepers. Third, intelligence gathering must become a regular and key part of the activities of Chinese peacekeepers, supported by and supporting other Chinese institutions abroad and at home. Fourth, Chinese soldiers need more training in order to be ready to use their weapons in an effective and controlled way. Fifth, the weapons and equipment used by the peacekeepers must be further developed to become more resistant to the different climatic conditions and the type of threat typical of the places where the peacekeepers are deployed. At the same time, an adequate quantity of ammunition and spare parts must be given to the peacekeepers to ensure that they can use their weapons in an effective manner in every situation. Similarly, officers of the PAP began to study how antiterrorism operations overseas should be conducted. According to Senior Colonel Qin Tian (2017), the PAP's main instrument against terrorists overseas is its special forces units, equipped and trained to carry out decapitation strikes and raids against enemies who threaten Chinese interests. Interestingly, Qin lists almost the same problems, from developing the right equipment to strengthening the legal framework and clarifying the chain of command.

These two extremely interesting studies are part of a larger number of articles written by PLA scholars about the need to strengthen the legal and regulatory aspects of MOOTW overseas. Many seem to take it for granted that Chinese MOOTW will soon include the use of force, which will thereby create the need to define the legal relation between Chinese soldiers, Chinese and foreign civilians, and foreign militaries. Moreover, it is far from clear what kind of legal protection Chinese soldiers can rely on in the case of an incident. For example, two articles in *National Defense* discuss the following deficiencies (Lui and Liu 2013; Song and Li 2014). First, Chinese laws are too vague when it comes to providing the legal foundations for MOOTW overseas.

---

[10] In Chinese: 维和战略 (Wéihé zhànlüè).

Second, some of the existing laws, such as the National Overseas Emergency Response Law, pay little attention to the armed forces and, for example, do not specify under which conditions the deployment of troops is permissible and/or necessary. Third, there is no law or regulation that regulates key aspects of MOOTW, from the use of force to the identification of what information regarding MOOTW can and cannot be reported by the media. Fourth, since most of the MOOTW require the PLA to work with other domestic and international agencies, for example, in the case of international disaster relief, it is necessary to clarify what institutions are in charge of commanding the troops and coordinating with third actors. It is important to point out that these issues are far from being confined to the journals and newspapers of the PLA. Indeed, Chinese media report that a delegation from the former Nanjing Military Region submitted a bill for the establishment of a MOOTW-specific law to the National People's Congress both in 2015 and in 2016 (PLA Daily 2018).

Conclusion

As the securitization of non-traditional security issues abroad gathered steam, no institution in the Chinese foreign and security policy machine was left untouched by its tremendous transformative effects. In general, all the organizations taken into consideration in this chapter promoted the development of the necessary tools for improving their ability to defend China's interest frontiers, although even Chinese analysts recognize that there are still important problems that must be addressed.

Being already the main organization in charge of protecting the rights and interests of Chinese passport holders abroad, the MFA was the first to adapt to the evolving situation. On the one hand, it bolstered its in-house institutions while also publishing new documents and regulations aimed at regulating the consular protection system and the relationship between the ministry and Chinese nationals abroad. On the other hand, the ministry also tried to transform its general office into the "cockpit" of China's emergency first-response system. Nonetheless, as the complaints of senior cadres and analysts close to the ministry clearly indicate, the MFA has been overstretched both before and after the protection of China's interest frontiers, especially in the Middle East and North Africa, became an important issue in the country's foreign policy agenda.

A more radical transformation took place within Chinese companies, especially the SOEs. Under pressure to take care of the security side of their operations abroad, they began to buy security services from foreign and—to a far lesser extent—domestic PSCs. At the same time, the companies with the necessary resources also developed their own in-house capabilities, thereby adjusting themselves to the changes in the regulations issued by the MFA, MOFCOM, and the National Development and Reform Commission discussed in Chapter 3. International PSCs and security contractors based in the countries where Chinese companies invest have become the main solution to inevitable security problems there, as they provide a range of services, especially armed protection, that Chinese PSCs cannot offer.

The change of attitude of Chinese companies was so radical that at least one top SOE manager tried to influence Chinese legislation on the domestic private security industry so that Chinese PSCs could become a flexible substitute for the regular armed forces. This initiative was met by a veto from the government. However, the most likely motivations of this decision can be easily identified. On the one hand, the mix of local, domestic, and international PSCs provides Chinese investors in risky regions with the possibility of buying all the services they need and can afford. On the other hand, the priority of the government is to push Chinese companies to become more self-sufficient in terms of security and not to increase the profits of Chinese PSCs ultimately at the expense of Chinese diplomacy.

As for the PLA, it is evident that the evolution of its institutions, as well as its doctrine, has mirrored the patterns highlighted in Chapter 2. It is possible to say that, at least with regard to the defense of China's interest frontiers, the transformation of the PLA has often lagged behind in the missions it has been set by top civilian leaders. An example of this is the opening of the Huairou training center, which took place years after concerns voiced by both military and civilian experts about the scarcity of well-trained troops for peacekeeping missions began to circulate in English- and Chinese-language publications (Tang 2002; Pang 2005). The fact that MOOTW-specialized training and research centers existed only at the service level until 2011 clearly shows the lack of importance attached to those operations when they occurred in an international context. At the same time, however, it would be unfair to blame this situation on the different preferences and mindsets of Chinese soldiers alone. Indeed, the more PLA experts considered the deployment and use of force abroad as a real possibility, even in times of peace, the more they found that significant obstacles stood in their way. While training and equipment are issues that the PLA alone could improve, the real limits to what Chinese soldiers are allowed to do abroad can only be removed through significant changes in Chinese diplomacy, laws, and decision-making institutions.

The recent approval of laws to strengthen the regulation of different aspects of overseas operations and the creation of the CCP CNSC seem to indicate that the central government is trying to address those problems. However, the timing of these legal and institutional developments, and the concerns voiced by PLA scholars about their incompleteness, reveal the slowness (or the difficulties) of the government in matching words with actions, despite the urgency perceived in the aftermath of the Libyan crisis. It is not possible to explain this delay with absolute certainty but, after all, even top Chinese leaders are not immune to the logic of the vast bureaucracy beneath them. This is particularly true when other urgent issues demand their attention. Moreover, the kind of reform that seems necessary entails not just restructuring key organizations like the PLA and the ministries of the State Council, but also revising the pillars of Chinese diplomacy against a background of growing fears of appearing to the outside world as an aggressive nation and pressure from the Chinese public to adopt a more resolute approach to the defense of the lives and assets of Chinese nationals and companies abroad. Chapter 7, therefore, explores how the military presence on China's interest frontiers has slowly changed as a result of the drastic and sometimes contradictory evolution of the regulatory tools in the hands of Beijing.

Bibliography

Allen, Kenneth W., Christopher M. Clarke, John F. Corbett, and Connie D. Henley. 2015. "China's Defense Minister and Ministry of National Defense." In Kevin Pollpeter and Kenneth W. Allen (eds), *The PLA as Organization v2.0*, 100–34. Vienna: Defense Group Inc.

Arduino, Alessandro. 2018. *China's Private Army*. Singapore: Palgrave.

Bai, Shuo. 2012. "总后勤部印发 '军队非战争军事行动财务保障办法' 和 '军队战时财务保障规定' [The PLA Logistic Department Issues the 'Measures for the Financial Security of MOOTW' and 'Measures for the Financial Security of the Armed Forces in Time of War']." *PLA Daily*. March 21. Accessed December 30, 2017. http://www.81.cn/jwzb/2012–03/21/content_5567794.htm.

Beijing Daily. 2010. "中国保安将赴海外中企提供安保 [Chinese Security Company Will Provide Security to Chinese Companies Abroad]." *Sina.* October 28. Accessed December 21, 2017. http://news.sina.com.cn/c/ 2010-10-28/032818295559s.shtml.

Boswell, Mathew. 2009. "Media Relations in China's Military: The Case of the Ministry of National Defence Information Office." *Asia Policy* 8: 97–120.

Cadre Department of the Former PLA General Political Department. 2008. "关于做好非战争军事行动干部工作的研究与思考 [A Study and Analysis of Improving Cadres' Work in Nonmilitary Operations]." *China Military Science* 5: 71–6.

Cao, Ruiqi. 2018. "中国私营安保公司海外业务监管相关问题对策分析 [Analysis of the Problems and Solutions Related to the Supervision of Overseas Operations of China's Private Security Companies]." *China Market* 8: 211–13.

CCP CMC. 2012. "胡锦涛签署命令发布施行 '中国人民解放军参加联合国维持和平行动条例（试行）' [Hu Jintao Signs the Order to Issue the 'Regulations for the PLA to Participate in UN Peacekeeping Missions (Draft)']." *Xinhua.* March 22. Accessed March 2, 2018. http://news.xinhuanet.com/politics/ 2012–03/22/c_111691498.htm.

CCP CMC. 2016. "中央军委关于深化国防和军队改革的意见 [Opinions on Deepening Reforms of National Defense and Armed Forces]." *China Daily.* November 25. Accessed May 17, 2018. http://china.chinadaily.com.cn/ 2016–11/25/content_27487634.htm.

Charhar Institute. 2015. "私营安保公司：中国海外安全的供给侧改革 [Private Security Companies: The Supply-Side Reform of Chinese Overseas Security]." Charhar Institute. December 3. Accessed December 3, 2017. http://www. charhar.org.cn/newsinfo.aspx?newsid=10203.

Chen, Jing. 2016. "护航：中国安保企业海外试水 [Maritime Escort: Chinese Security Industry Tests the Waters Abroad]." *China Youth Daily.* May 27. Accessed May 24, 2018. http://zqb.cyol.com/html/2016–05/27/nw.D110000 zgqnb_20160527_1-05.htm.

Chen, Zhou. 2009. "试论新形势下中国防御性国防政策的发展 [On the Development of China's National Defense]." *China Military Science* 6: 63–71.

China Daily. 2015. "Lawmakers Weigh in on China's Draft Anti-Terrorism Law." *China Daily.* February 25. Accessed March 21, 2017. http://www.chinadaily. com.cn/china/2015–02/25/content_19653472.htm.

Chinanews.com. 2004. "港报：中国领事保护 '三板斧' 应对涉外危机 [Hong Kong Media: The 'Three Aces' of China's Consular Protection System to Deal with Crises]." *Chinanews.com.* December 8. Accessed May 21, 2018. http:// www.chinanews.com/news/2004/2004-12-08/26/514541.shtml.

Clover, Charles. 2017. "Chinese Private Security Companies Go Global." *Financial Times.* February 26. Accessed March 2, 2017. https://www.ft.com/content/ 2a1ce1c8-fa7c-11e6-9516-2d969e0d3b65.

Deng, Yancai. 2015. "中国民营安保公司 '出海' 记 [Memories of a Chinese Security Company Abroad]." *Xinhua—International Leader Herald*. December 2. Accessed April 23, 2018. http://www.xinhuanet.com//herald/2015-12/02/c_134877677.htm.

Erickson, Andrew S., and Adam P. Liff. 2016. "Installing a Safety on the 'Loaded Gun'? China's Institutional Reforms, National Security Commission and Sino-Japanese Crisis (In)Stability." *Journal of Contemporary China* 25 (98): 197–215.

Fan, Junmei. 2008. "Earthquake Pushes Early Debut of MOD Spokesperson." 中国网 [*China.org*]. May 28. Accessed November 6, 2017. http://www.china.org.cn/government/central_government/2008-05/29/content_15542040.htm.

Ghiselli, Andrea. 2018. "Market Opportunities and Political Responsibilities: The Difficult Development of Chinese Private Security Companies Abroad." *Armed Forces & Society*. doi:https://doi.org/10.1177%2F0095327X18806517.

Global Times. 2008. "建"非战争军事行动教研室"在中国军校引发争论 [The Creation of the MOOTW Teaching and Research Office in a Chinese Military School Sparks Debate]." *Global Times*. October 31. Accessed November 26, 2017. http://mil.huanqiu.com/china/2008-10/269035.html.

Global Times. 2014. "详解中国在伊拉克安保团队　多为退役王牌特种兵 [Shedding Light on Chinese Security Teams in Iraq, Most of Them Are Former Special Forces Soldiers]." *Sina*. June 23. Accessed November 18, 2017. http://mil.news.sina.com.cn/2014-06-23/0854786359.html.

Gong, Fangbin. 2014. "国家安全委员会设立后的安全管理 [The Management of Security after the Establishment of the National Security Commission]." *Study Times*. January 13. Accessed January 2, 2018. http://www.studytimes.com.cn/shtml/xxsb/20140113/3722.shtml.

Guo, Yuandan. 2016. "揭秘解放军 '海外行动处' 强化境外快反职能 [The PLA 'Overseas Operation Unit' to Strengthen Overseas Rapid Reaction Capabilities]." *Global Times*. March 25. Accessed March 28, 2018. http://mil.huanqiu.com/china/2016-03/8768818.html.

Hu, Weixing. 2015. "Xi Jinping's 'Big Power Diplomacy' and China's Central National Security Commission (CNSC)." *Journal of Contemporary China* 25 (98): 163–77.

Huang, Kunlun. 2009. "从亚丁湾护航看履行我军新使命 [Looking at the New Missions of Our Army from the Perspective of the Naval Escorts in the Gulf of Aden]." *PLA Daily*. January 4.

Jia, Wei. 2017. "中企海外安保需要多少 '吴京' [How Many 'Wu Jings' Do Chinese Companies Need?]." *China Economic Weekly*. August 28. Accessed September 30, 2017. http://www.ceweekly.cn/2017/0828/203229.shtml.

Kamphausen, Roy. 2013. "China's Military Operations Other Than War: the Military Legacy of Hu Jintao." *The Hu Jintao Decade in China's Foreign and Security Policy (2002–2012): Assessments and Implications*. Stockholm:

SIPRI. Accessed October 14, 2020. https://silo.tips/download/china-s-military-operations-other-than-war-the-military-legacy-of-hu-jintao.

Kennedy, Conor M. 2019. "Civil Transport in PLA Power Projection." *CMSI China Maritime Reports* 4.

Lai, Jingchao. 2012. "外交部副司长：部分海外公民对政府提无理要求 [Deputy Director of the MFA: Some Overseas Citizens Make Unreasonable Demands on the Government]." *Chinanews.com*. April 25. Accessed November 21, 2018. http://www.chinanews.com/gn/2012/04-25/3843849.shtml.

Legal Daily. 2004. "海外华人屡遭安全威胁 中国领事制度面临挑战 [Overseas Chinese Are Repeatedly Threatened by Security Threats, China's Consular System Is Facing Challenges]." *Legal Daily*. December 12. Accessed November 9, 2017. http://www.china.com.cn/chinese/2004/Dec/726769.htm.

Li, Haibo. 2012. *海外中国公民领事保护问题研究 (1978–2011)* [*Research on the Consular Protection of Chinese Citizens Abroad (1978–2011)*]. Guangzhou Jinan University Press.

Li, Haibo. 2016. "中国领事保护可持续发展探析 [Analysis of the Sustainable Development of the Chinese Consular Protection System]." *Contemporary International Relations* 6: 9–14.

Li, Jie. 2009. "航母不仅能打仗 [An Aircraft Carrier Can Do More than Fight]." *China National Defense Daily*. February 17.

Li, Xiaodong, and Can Ou. 2008. "部队走出国门 法律如何保障 [The Armed Forces Go Abroad, How Does the Law Protect Them?]." *PLA Daily*. April 15.

Li, Xiaomin. 2011. *非传统安全威胁下中国公民海外安全分析* [*Analysis of the Safety of Chinese Citizens Abroad Threatened by Non-Traditional Security Threats*]. Beijing: People's Publishing House.

Li, Zhongmin. 2012. "中国海外经济利益保护战略刍论 [China's Overseas Economic Interests Protection: A Strategic Analysis]." *World Economics and Politics* 8: 92–106.

Lin, Dong. 2009. "以战略创新引领军事转型 [Guide Military Transformation with Strategic Innovation]." *China Military Strategy* 4: 65–9.

Liu, Kun. 2013. "专家：国家安全委员会负责人应是最高领导人 [Experts: The People in Charge of the National Security Commission Should Be the Highest Leaders]." *Beijing Youth Daily*. November 13. Accessed June 4, 2018. http://mil.huanqiu.com/china/2013-11/4558366.html.

Liu, Shuai, and Hua Liu. 2013. "非战争军事行动法规体系建设探微 [Exploring the Construction of a Legal Framework for MOOTW]." *National Defense* 8: 58–60.

Liu, Xiangyang. 2008. "非战争军事行动探要 [A Study of Non-War Operations]." *China Military Science* 3: 1–6.

Liu, Xiaolian, and Youxian Chen. 2007. "论非战争军事行动的本质特点 [Discussing the Essential Characteristics of MOOTW]." *Journal of the National Defense University* 10: 23–5.

Liu, Zhao, and Jianwei Duan. 2016. "我军参与联合国维和行动中的武力使用问题研究 [A Study of China's Armed Forces in the Use of Force in UN Peace-Keeping Operations]." *China Military Science* 3: 149–56.

Mao, Jun. 2015. "依法履行维护国家安全的使命任务—中央军委法制局负责人答记者问 [Performing the Mission of Safeguarding National Security in Accordance with the Law—Interview with Officer in Charge of the Legal Affairs Bureau of the Central Military Commission]." *PLA Daily.* July 15. Accessed April 29, 2018. http://www.81.cn/jfjbmap/content/2015–07/15/content_117221.htm.

Martin, Peter, Keith Zhai, and Ting Shi. 2018. "As U.S. Culls Diplomats, China Is Empowering Its Ambassadors." *Bloomberg.* February 8. Accessed March 1, 2018. https://www.bloomberg.com/news/articles/2018-02-07/as-u-s-culls-diplomats-china-is-empowering-its-ambassadors.

Mulvenon, James. 2010. "Party-Military Coordination of the Yushu Earthquake Response." *China Leadership Monitor* 33.

Nanguo Zaobao. 2013. "中国安保企业在海外有诸多优势 [Chinese Private Security Companies Have Many Advantages]." *Sohu.* February 2. Accessed December 25, 2017. http://m.sohu.com/n/365357298/.

Pang, Zhongying. 2005. "China's Changing Attitude to UN Peacekeeping." *International Peacekeeping* 12 (1): 87–104.

Peng, Junhua, and Feng Xiao. 2008. "加快非战争军事行动的立法 [Accelerating the Regulation of MOOTW]." *PLA Daily.* October 28.

Phoenix International Think Tank. 2016. "'一带一路' 是中国保险经纪重要发展机遇—2016中国企业海外安全管理报告 [The 'Belt and Road Initiative' Is an Important Development Opportunity for China's Insurance Brokers—2016 China Enterprises Overseas Safety Management Report]." *Phoenix International Think Tank.* March 30. Accessed March 1, 2017. https://pit.ifeng.com/event/special/haiwaianquanguanlibaogao/chapter1.shtml.

PLA AMS. 2013. 战略学 [*The Science of Military Strategy*]. Beijing: Military Science Press.

PLA Daily. 2018. "细察兵心民意 情系国防民生 [Inspecting the Minds and Hearts of the People]." *Global Times.* March 6. Accessed December 28, 2018. http://sd.people.com.cn/n2/2018/0306/c172839-31313863.html.

PRC MOFCOM. 2015. "商务部办公厅关于印发 '关于驻外经商机构为企业办理对外承包工程项目投标（议标）核准意见的暂行规定' 的通知 [Notice of the General Office of MOFCOM on Printing and Distributing the 'Interim Provisions on the Opinions for the Approval of Companies' Bids (or Negotiations)

for Overseas Contracted Projects by Economic and Trade Institutions Abroad']."
PRC MOFCOM. October 10. Accessed January 23, 2020. http://hzs.mofcom.gov.
cn/article/zcfb/a/201612/20161202110143.shtml.

PRC NPC. 1982. "Constitution of People's Republic of China." PRC
NPC. December 4. Accessed May 4, 2018. http://www.npc.gov.cn/englishnpc/
Constitution/node_2830.htm.

PRC NPC. 1997a. "中华人民共和国国防法 [PRC National Defense Law]." PRC
NPC. April 14. Accessed January 15, 2018. http://www.npc.gov.cn/wxzl/gong-
bao/2000–12/05/content_5004681.htm.

PRC NPC. 1997b. "刑法 [Criminal Code]." PRC NPC. July 1. Accessed March 26,
2018. http://www.npc.gov.cn/wxzl/gongbao/2000–12/17/content_5004680.htm.

PRC NPC. 2015a. "中华人民共和国反恐怖主义法 [PRC National Anti-
terrorism Law]." PRC NPC. December 27. Accessed March 21, 2018. http://
www.npc.gov.cn/npc/xinwen/2015–12/28/content_1957401.htm.

PRC NPC. 2015b. "中华人民共和国国家安全法 [PRC National Security Law]."
PRC NPC. July 1. Accessed April 24, 2017. http://www.npc.gov.cn/npc/xin-
wen/2015–07/07/content_1941161.htm.

PRC NPC. 2016. "中华人民共和国国防交通法 [PRC National Defense
Transportation Law]." PRC NPC. September 3. Accessed April 21, 2018. http://
www.npc.gov.cn/npc/xinwen/2016–09/03/content_1996764.htm.

PRC State Council. 2009. "保安服务管理条例 [Regulation on the Management
of Security Services]." PRC Central Goverment. October 23. Accessed
November 26, 2017. http://www.gov.cn/zwgk/2009–10/19/content_1443395.
htm.

PRC State Council's Information Office. 2004. "2004 年中国的国防 [China's
Defense in 2004]." PRC State Council's Information Office. December 27.
Accessed September 2, 2017. http://www.scio.gov.cn/zfbps/ndhf/2004/Document/
307905/307905.htm.

PRC State Council's Information Office. 2009. "China's National Defense in 2008."
China.org. January 20. Accessed January 17, 2018. http://www.china.org.cn/
government/whitepaper/node_7060059.htm.

PRC State Council's Information Office. 2015. "China's Military Strategy." PRC
Ministry of National Defence. May 2017. Accessed 30 October. http://www.
mod.gov.cn/auth/2015–05/26/content_4586723.htm.

Qin, Tian. 2017. "武警部队出境反恐问题研究 [A Study of Overseas Counter-
terrorism Operations by the People's Armed Police]." China Military Science
1: 82–7.

Sheng, Yuan. 2012. "政协外事委副主任韩方明：探讨建立中国黑水公司
[Deputy Chairman of the Foreign Affairs Committee of the Chinese People's

Peolitical Consultative Conference Han Fangming: Discussing the Establishment of a Chinese Blackwater]." 中国政协新闻网 [*China Consultatie Conference News*]. February 3. Accessed June 23, 2018. http://cppcc.people.com.cn/GB/35377/17010201.html.

Shou, Xiaosong, and Jingnian Xu. 2009. 军队与非传统安全 [*Study of Military Response to Non-Traditional Security Threats*]. Beijing: Military Science Press.

Song, Wei, and Jian Li. 2014. "我军遂行海外非战争军事行动法律保障体系建设问题浅议 [Discussion on the Establishment of the Legal Guarantees for Overseas Non-War Military Operations]." *National Defense* 8: 58–9.

Tang, Yongsheng. 2002. "中国与联合国维和行动 [China and United Nations Peacekeeping Operations]." *World Economics and Politics* 9: 39–44.

Tian, Yiwei. 2011. "中国军方成立非战争军事行动研究中心 [The AMS MOOTW Research Center Has Been Established]." *Chinanews.com*. December 13. Accessed October 19, 2017. http://www.chinanews.com/gn/2011/12–12/3526428.shtml.

Wang, Mingwu, Yongzhi Chang, Ge Xu, and Nan Zhang. 2006. 非战争军事行动 [*Military Operations Other Than War*]. Beijing: PLA National Defense University Press.

Wang, Ping. 2005. "陆军战役军团应对边境非战争行动应遵循的原则 [Principles That the Army Groups Should Observe for Non-War Operations along the Borders]." *Journal of the National Defense University* 1: 45–6.

Wang, Xin. 2008. "在破解 '瓶颈' 中提高非战争军事行动能力 [Breaking the Bottleneck and Strengthening MOOTW Capabilities]." *China National Defense Daily*. August 28.

Wang, Xingsheng, and Zhizhong Wu. 2007. "论军事软实力建设 [On Building Soft Military Power]." *China Military Science* 1: 92–9.

Wang, Yubao, and Jinfa Guo. 2010. "厘清非战争军事行动的五个基本问题 [Shedding Light on Five Basic Problems Related to MOOTW]." *China National Defense Daily*. July 29.

Wuthnow, Joel, and Phillip C. Saunders. 2017. "Chinese Military Reforms in the Age of Xi Jinping: Drivers, Challenges, and Implications." National Defense University Press. March 21. Accessed July 23, 2018. http://ndupress.ndu.edu/Media/News/Article/1125539/chinese-military-reforms-in-the-age-of-xi-jinping-drivers-challenges-and-implic/.

Xia, Liping. 2015. "十八大以来 '外交为民' 理念与实践的新发展 [Practice and Development of 'Diplomacy for the People' since the 18th Party Congress]." *People's Daily*. February 6. Accessed February 23, 2018. http://cpc.people.com.cn/n/2015/0206/c187710-26521276.html.

Xia, Liping. 2016. "中国领事保护需求与外交投入的矛盾及解决方式 [On the Contradiction of the Chinese Consular Protection Service and Diplomatic Input and Its Solutions]." *The Journal of International Studies* 4: 10–25.

Xiang, Wenhui. 2017. "中国的海外公民保护—战略实施、制约因素及策略应对 [The Protection of Chinese Citizens Abroad: Strategic Measures, Constraints, and Policy Responses]." *Global Review* 4: 87–103.

Xiao, Tianliang. 2009. *军事力量的非战争运用* [*The Non-War Use of Military Force*]. Beijing: PLA National Defense Universiy Press.

Xie, Zhou. 2008. "非战争军事行动诸干法律问题初探 [Discussion on the Legal Issues of Non-War Military Operations]." *China Military Science* 3: 19–24.

Xu, Yuhong. 2016. "'一带一路' 与外交领事保护问题 [The 'Belt and Road' and the Problem of Consular Protection]." *China Law Review* 2: 46–9.

Xue, Wei, Long Peng, and Peng Tao. 2015. "国家安全委员会制度的国际比较及其对我国的启示 [Comparison between Different Foreign Models of National Security Commission and Lessons for China]." *Chinese Public Administration* 1: 146–51.

Yang, Guoxin. 2010. "美军缘何停用 '非战争军事行动' [Why Did the US Military Stop Using 'MOOTW'?]." *PLA Daily*. August 5.

Yang, Yang. 2013. "中国领事保护中存在的问题及对策 [The Problems of China's Consular Protection System and Solutions]." *The Journal of International Studies* 2: 17–29.

Yue, Guiyun. 2015. "论全域机动作战 [On All-Domain Maneuvers]." *China Military Science* 4: 118–25.

Zhang, Haiming. 2006. "浅析非战争军事行动的源起 [Analyzing the Origin of MOOTW]." *China National Defense Daily*. March 30.

Zhang, Haizhou. 2012. "更好保护海外公民和财产安全的建议 [Suggestions on How to Better Protect Chinese Citizens and Assets Abroad]." Charhar Institute. March 9. Accessed January 29, 2018. http://www.charhar.org.cn/newsinfo. aspx?newsid=4244.

Zhang, Hui. 2008. "国际恐怖主义威胁与军队的新职责 [International Terrorist Threat and New Missions of the Armed Forces]." *China Military Science* 3: 14–24.

Zhang, Ping. 2007. "Remarks on the People's Liberation Army's Participation in UN Peacekeeping." Speech delivered at the "Multi-Dimensional and Integrated Peace Operations: Trends and Challenges" conference, Beijing. March 26–27.

Zhang, Wei. 2008. "美军非战争军事行动理论的兴起和中止 [Growth and 'Termination' of the American Theory of Non-War Military Operations]." *China Military Science* 3: 31–41.

Zhao, Kejin, and Shaojie Li. 2015. "探索中国海外安全治理市场化 [On the Privatization of China's Overseas Security System]." *World Economics and Politics* 10: 133–55.

Zheng, Shouhua, ed. 2013. *非战争军事行动教程* [*MOOTW Teaching Material*]. Beijing: Military Science Press.

Zhi, Binyou. 2013. "国家安全委员会设立后的应急管理 [Emergency Response after the Establishment of the National Security Commission]." *Study Times.* December 18. Accessed October 1, 2018. http://www.studytimes.cn/shtml/xxsb/20131216/3264.shtml.

Zhong, Fei, Yao Xu, Yun Qi, and Yalei Cao. 2017. "战略投送体系研究问题 [A Study of the Building of Strategic Projection System]." *China Military Science* 3: 102–10.

7

Guarding the Interest Frontiers

While Chapter 6 explored the tumultuous transformation of China's regulatory tools, this chapter revolves around the much slower evolution of China's capability tools: its military presence on its interest frontiers. Besides the slow and complex mechanics that shaped and probably slowed down the process of adaptation of the Chinese foreign and security policy machine, there is another factor that has always been in the background and that has been mentioned more or less explicitly in the previous chapters as foreign policy experts and military officers called for a revision of the principles of their country's foreign policy: the principle of noninterference.

China has long said its decisions on foreign policy questions are taken according to the Five Principles of Peaceful Coexistence: mutual respect for sovereignty and territorial integrity; mutual nonaggression; noninterference in each other's internal affairs; equality and mutual benefit; and peaceful co-existence. The Chinese leadership originally spelled out these principles in 1954, when China was trying to reach out to non-Communist countries in Asia. They were later incorporated into the Ten Principles of Bandung, which were issued in April 1955 at the historic Asian-African Conference in Bandung, Indonesia. While China has been increasingly bending the noninterference principle in a variety of more or less benign ways, from playing a more active role inside the United Nations (UN) to the use of informal embargoes to pressure foreign government into friendlier positions, it has always been extremely cautious in doing so. On the one hand, whenever Chinese diplomats have voted in favor of resolutions of the UN Security Council (UNSC), they have carefully evaluated not only the impact on Chinese interests, but also the degree of diplomatic support voting in one way or the other could receive from other great powers and regional actors (Wuthnow 2013; Fung 2019). For example, the former Special Envoy of the Chinese Government to the Middle East, Wu Sike (2019), declared that he had to fly to the Gulf immediately after China vetoed resolutions that would have paved the way for military intervention against the Syrian regime. According to him, the goal of his mission was to explain that China was defending the principle of noninterference in other countries'

Protecting China's Interests Overseas: Securitization and Foreign Policy. Andrea Ghiselli,
Oxford University Press (2021). © Andrea Ghiselli.
DOI: 10.1093/oso/9780198867395.001.0001

internal affairs, especially militarily, rather than President Assad per se. On the other hand, the most obvious cases of Chinese intervention in the domestic affairs of other countries have never included a military component comparable to that of Western or Russian military actions around the world.

Since 1990, soldiers of the Chinese People's Liberation Army (PLA) have been deployed abroad for a variety of reasons, from regional exercises with other countries to peacekeeping and international disaster relief missions. As of November 2018, more than 38,000 Chinese soldiers have participated in twenty-four different UN peacekeeping operations (Xinhua 2018a). The PLA has also joined at least thirty-six disaster relief operations, twenty-eight joint exercises, and thirty-four joint training sessions abroad. The PLA Navy has been operating in the Gulf of Aden since early 2009 and contributed in different degrees to the evacuations from Libya and Yemen in 2011 and 2015, respectively. The PLA Navy's hospital ship *Peace Ark* has been on several goodwill cruises since 2008. The PLA Air Force too has flown outside China's national borders, albeit much less than the PLA Ground Forces and PLA Navy. Even the Chinese People's Armed Police (PAP) has a minimal presence abroad. Virtually all those deployments are related to non-traditional security threats. Even the exercises organized by the Shanghai Cooperation Organization are officially depicted as aiming at boosting the antiterrorism capabilities of the participating countries (Hartnett 2012a). The participation of the PLA Air Force in the NATO-sponsored Anatolian Eagle Exercise in early October 2010 is, for example, a rare outlying case.

Although many inside and outside China have highlighted the gradual but steady shift from "keeping a low profile" to "actively doing something"—the two components of the eight-character foreign policy mantra laid down by late patriarch Deng Xiaoping in the early 1990s—China's military presence overseas remains very much shaped by the idea of keeping a low profile by acting through the UN or with its blessing (Foot 2014).[1] The domestic factors pushing for the protection of China's interest frontiers and the choice of the UN as the only channel of action combine with each other following the patterns of what Cohen, March, and Olsen (1972) called the Garbage Can Model. According to it, solutions, or inherently preferred policies, may exist prior to, and independently of, any problem. The advocates of particular solutions will try to attach them to any problem and opportunity that could serve as a vehicle for the policy's adoption. The linking of problems and solutions is determined more by "temporal sorting"—in which problems and solutions

---

[1] In Chinese: 韬光养晦 (Tāoguāng yǎnghuì) and 积极有所作为 (Jījí yǒu suǒ zuòwéi).

that arise at the same time become linked in choice opportunities provided by the platform of international organizations through which a government decides to act—rather than by a rational fitting of solutions to problems. This means that changes in the policy preferences of the Chinese leadership related to the defense of China's interest frontiers can only manifest when and where it is possible to do so through the UN, potentially, with a lag of a few years.

Against this background, this chapter looks at the creeping effects of securitization that started to appear in the operations and deployments of the Chinese armed forces overseas. The first section of the chapter focuses on the evolution of the quantity and quality of Chinese "boots on the ground," including the PAP, as the importance of protecting Chinese interests pushed the focus of their deployments toward the Middle East and North Africa. The second section of the chapter considers the maritime and air components of China's overseas military presence as they began to integrate with those of the ground presence along China's interest frontiers.

Boots on the Ground: From Asia to the Interest Frontiers

After some decades of a hostile attitude toward UN peacekeeping missions, the evolution of Chinese peacekeeping can be broken down into different periods (Figure 32). The first, from 1989 to 2002, was characterized by a low quantitative and qualitative engagement aimed essentially at shoring up China's international image. During the second phase, from 2002 to 2011, China's contribution of troops grew exponentially. In the third phase, after 2011, Chinese combat troops started to be deployed for the first time.

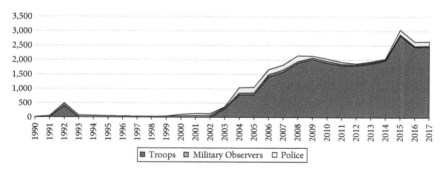

Figure 32 China's contribution to UN peacekeeping missions
Source: United Nations peacekeeping statistics. Compiled by the author.

In the early 2000s, the PLA expert on peacekeeping affairs, Tang Yongsheng, argued that China should have the choice whether or not to engage in peace-keeping operations (2002, 44). Joining them was not something that should be taken for granted. After all, as pointed out in Chapter 6, sufficiently well-trained troops were scarce back then and the situation was even worse in the 1990s. Hence, the leaders in Zhongnanhai had to make every soldier, observer, and police officer deployed in UN peacekeeping operations count. This is why China's involvement in international peacekeeping largely focused on deploy-ments in Asia throughout the 1990s. During those years of timid and rigid participation in peacekeeping and other activities under the banner of inter-national governmental organizations (Fravel 1996), China mostly contributed military observers in Asia, as well as some in Kuwait and Palestine.

The only exceptions were Cambodia and, to a lesser extent, East Timor. Indeed, the participation of two 400-strong batches of military engineering troops and some fifty military observers in the UN Transitional Authority of Cambodia (UNTAC) between 1992 and 1993 is extremely telling if one con-siders that China again sent a comparable number of troops abroad only ten years later to join the UN Mission in Liberia. As for the UN Transitional Administration in East Timor (UNTAET), Beijing sent police units there for the first time. Bates Gill (2007, 124) reports that PLA observers were also meant to join the mission, but a lack of bureaucratic coordination under-mined this intention. The exceptional nature of those deployments, rather than their overall size, reflects the importance of UNTAC and UNTAET for China's involvement in UN peacekeeping.

There was a risk that failed states would emerge in China's neighborhood, in the case of both Cambodia and East Timor, a consideration that probably played a role in Beijing's decisions (Gill 2007, 134). However, China also faced tremendous diplomatic pressure immediately after the events of Tiananmen Square, and the risk was extremely high that the domestic economy could fail if economic ties were not restored with other Asian countries and the rest of the world. The 1995-6 Taiwan Strait crisis and NATO's intervention in Kosovo further contributed to increasing the Chinese sense of vulnerability. As Pan Zhongying (2005, 88) argued:

> central to Chinese concerns is the changing nature and context of peace operations—with the potential for mission creep and the move to "coalitions of the willing"—and the implications this would have for international involvement in China's key internal affairs relating, for example, to Taiwan, Tibet and Xinjiang.

Hence, in keeping with the argument in Chapter 1, the Chinese government seized the opportunity that non-traditional security problems had created in order to boost the chances of survival of the Chinese state and the Communist regime.

From this point of view, the decision to authorize UNTAC and UNTAET and to contribute represented China's response to its own fear that the UN could be sidelined by Western powers, especially in countries on its doorstep (Masuda 2011, 9–11). Indeed, while China's peacekeeping charm offensive was successful in Cambodia (Hirono 2011), Chinese efforts were also rewarded in East Timor. Xanana Gusmão labeled China a "reliable friend" and committed East Timor to the One China policy even before officially becoming president of the new country (Storey 2006). In order to further strengthen its position there, China was the first country to establish diplomatic relations with the Democratic Republic of Timor-Leste when it gained formal independence on May 20, 2002, and immediately pledged USD 6 million in aid.

After having signaled its intention to join the UN's standby arrangements for peacekeeping operations in 1997, China formally joined the Class-A standby arrangements system in January 2002 and offered an engineering battalion (525 troops), a medical unit (thirty-five troops), and transport companies (160 troops in total) deployable within ninety days of a request from the UN (China Daily 2002). Before that moment, an engineering brigade located in Beijing had been identified as the primary unit for peacekeeping missions (Blasko 2016). This decision was taken while three crucial changes were under way inside and outside China, thereby bringing the first exploratory phase of Chinese participation in UN peacekeeping missions to an end. First, becoming a member in the World Trade Organization and the beginning of the War on Terror created the favorable environment that China needed, and both its economy and its diplomatic standing were significantly strengthened. Crucially, the International Olympic Committee awarded the 2008 summer games to Beijing in 2001. Second, China's economic and human footprint greatly expanded outside Asia, which thereby, as Chapter 3 showed, created the preconditions for the emergence of China's interest frontiers a decade later. Third, the conditions for the return of UN "blue helmets" to Africa fully materialized after a number of attempts by regional actors to bring stability to the continent failed in the mid-1990s because of a lack of logistical and financial support and the growing divergence in the political and economic agendas of African countries (Adebajo and Landsberg 2000).

Hence, during this 2002–11 phase, China's participation in peacekeeping missions grew remarkably. While the average annual number of Chinese participants was 111 (including military observers, police officers, and troops) until 2002, it grew to 1,763 in the years that followed. At the same time, the center of gravity of the presence of Chinese ground troops abroad steadily moved outside Asia and closer to where today's interest frontiers lay. Those years were characterized by both continuity and important changes. The clearest sign of continuity is the fact that China kept on deploying only engineering and medical units. Moreover, participation in peacekeeping missions remained mainly a diplomatic issue, and the consent of the host country was an unchanged condition for China's support of and participation in a peacekeeping mission. Yet the changes outlined above were also starting to shape the motivations behind Chinese peacekeeping. By then, showing the international community that it was a "responsible great power," a concept that had been fully absorbed in Chinese diplomatic language, had become a key factor (Suzuki 2008; Li 2011).[2] Hence, good relations with many African governments and growing demand for peacekeepers provided a number of opportunities for China to deploy its troops. At the same time, the presence of Chinese companies and workers in the host countries slowly started to be a new factor in the peacekeeping equation, albeit not yet as the main referent object of the securitization promoted by the Chinese civilian leadership.

The most significant deployment of Chinese peacekeepers in those years was in the UN Mission in Liberia (China was part of the mission from its launch in 2003); the UN Organization Mission in the Democratic Republic of Congo (China joined in 2003); the UN Organization Stabilization Mission in the Democratic Republic of Congo; the UN Interim Force in Lebanon (China joined in 2007); the UN Mission in Sudan (UNMIS; China was part of the mission since its launch in 2005); the UN Mission in South Sudan (UNMISS, which took over UNMIS in 2011); and the UN-African Union Hybrid Operation in Darfur (UNAMID; China was part of the mission from its launch in 2007). China had some interest in Congo and Sudan but the consent of the host government was the real necessary condition for China to join all those missions (Cho 2018). However, it is in Sudan—the only country among those hosting Chinese peacekeepers that was identified in Chapter 3 as a pillar of China's interest frontiers—that China's actions took an unexpected course, with the launch of UNAMID.

UNAMID was not the first UN mission in Sudan. UNMIS was established in 2005 as part of the Comprehensive Peace Agreement signed in Nairobi by the government of Sudan and the Sudan People's Liberation

---

[2] In Chinese: 负责任大国 (Fù zérèn dàguó).

Movement/Army, which was the main constituent of the government of the then semi-autonomous South Sudan. Given the explicit consent of local powerholders and the close ties with the ruling National Congress Party, which controlled key institutions like the Ministry of Energy and Mining, China joined UNMIS and sent more than 400 engineering troops, together with a few military observers and police. Stationed in southern Sudan, however, these contingents were isolated from the western Darfur region, where the situation was rapidly worsening.

The UNSC Resolution (1706/2006) "invited" the Sudanese government to give its consent to the deployment of the peacekeepers in the Darfur region, but that invitation was turned down. China then started to voice its support for the mission and put increasing pressure on the Sudanese government to change its position. Hu Jintao intervened personally as a broker to convince the Sudanese government to accept UN intervention (China Daily 2007). Once the Sudanese President Bashir consented to the peacekeeping mission, China promised to send a 315-strong engineering unit to Darfur. In 2012, a spokesperson of the Ministry of National Defense (MOD) revealed that, given the dangerous environment, a "self-defense security unit" was established as part of the engineering unit (Xinhua 2012). The first 140 Chinese peacekeepers arrived in Darfur in November 2007. They were the first non-African UN peacekeeping force to enter Darfur. According some analysts (Hirono and Lanteigne 2011), China was learning how to act like a great power and trying to strengthen its status in international politics from norm-taker to norm-maker.

However, one could argue easily that China did not have much choice. Chapter 3 identified Sudan as one of the five pillars of China's interest frontiers and, as such, instability in that country was bound to trigger a Chinese response. Given its low sulfur content, Sudanese oil is well suited to Chinese refineries. Thus, it is not surprising that, just in the upstream part, Chinese investment in Sudan's energy industry totaled USD 4.3 billion, making up some 43 percent of total foreign direct investment in that part of the Sudanese economy between 1996 and 2007 (Suliman and Badawi 2010). Outside the oil sector, the presence of Chinese construction companies was also significant. The number of Chinese workers in the country steadily grew from slightly more than 3,600 in 2002 to 20,000 in 2008 (Figure 33).

Yet, while it is true that China acted because of its significant presence in Sudan, it would be equally wrong to assume that it acted primarily to defend its interests there. As pointed out by Yitzhak Shichor (2007) and Courtney Fung (2016), economic concerns make for only a partial explanation as to why Beijing intervened in Sudan. Indeed, it seems that the risks to Chinese

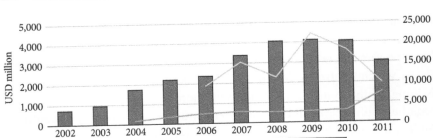

Figure 33 Chinese economic and human presence in Sudan

Source: PRC MOFCOM, National Bureau of Statistics of China, and PRC State Administration of Foreign Exchange (various years) and Department of Trade and External Economic Relations Statistics, National Bureau of Statistics of China (various years). Compiled by the author.

companies and workers increased with increasing intervention by China in the Darfur crisis. Sudanese warlords made explicit threats against Chinese soldiers even before their arrival, and Chinese companies were attacked in October and December 2007, shortly before and shortly after the deployment of the first part of the Chinese contingent (China Daily 2008). Five employees of the China National Petroleum Corporation were killed in those attacks.

In those years, China's understanding of security had already begun to change as Hu Jintao pressed for a more people-centric approach to policy-making. However, the attacks on Chinese interests in Sudan were no different from those that had taken place in previous years in other countries. From a certain point of view, thus, they hardly made for an emergency situation. The real problem for Beijing was not the economic damage of instability in Sudan, buts the dependency of the Sudanese economy on China, especially in terms of oil revenues (Figure 34). As the Sudanese state became increasingly reliant on oil revenues and the crisis in Darfur worsened, the Chinese purchase of Sudanese oil increasingly became a political and diplomatic liability for China. Chinese diplomats had previously attempted to delink military inter-vention from the concept of responsibility to protect in order to "avoid some of the image costs of obstructing the UN effort to prevent and respond to atrocities, without ceding ground on its core peacekeeping policies and pri-orities" (Teitt 2011, 299).

However, as the 2008 Beijing Olympic Games—which *The Economist* (2006) defined as China's coming out party—came closer, a harsh campaign that linked the killing in Darfur with the games was mounted in Western media. The pressure further escalated when Amnesty International (2007)

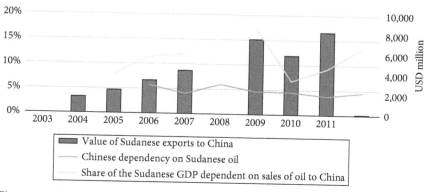

Figure 34 The Sino-Sudanese energy relationship
Source: IHS Markit, World Bank, and ITC Trademap. Compiled by the author.

published a report blaming China for the failure of the arms embargo on the Sudanese government. At the same time, a regional consensus about the necessity of a UN intervention in Darfur had emerged clearly. Some Western heads of state even threatened to boycott the opening ceremony of the games in Beijing. Although China's survival was not at stake, what its governments had worked hard to achieve since 1989 was seriously imperiled. Hence, Chinese leaders took the unprecedented step of mediating personally in the crisis. From this point of view, Chinese peacekeepers, who constituted less than 1.7 percent of the military personnel authorized in July 2007 by UNSC Resolution 1769 (UNSC 2007, 3), represent the tip of the spear of Chinese diplomacy rather than a tool to defend China's interest frontiers. The games of 2008 were a success and the French president, Nicolas Sarkozy, attended them despite his previous threats not to.

Although it is often overlooked, PAP troops also began to be deployed abroad in those years. The PAP soldiers who are deployed abroad come from the Snow Leopard Commando Unit.[3] This unit, which is the 3rd Group of the 13th Detachment of the PAP Beijing General Corps (Sinodefense 2008), was established in 2002 and its existence remained a secret until 2007. According to Chinese media, each of the soldiers is estimated to be outfitted with RMB 300,000 (approximately USD 43,500) worth of equipment, including body armor and communications equipment (China.org 2011). The candidates come from all active service units of the PAP and have to go through eight months of a specialized training and selection process before joining the 400-strong Snow Leopard Commando Unit (Xinhua 2016).

[3] In Chinese: 雪豹突击队 (Xuěbào tújí duì).

Besides the protection of the Olympic torchbearer abroad in 2008, some of those soldiers have been deployed to protect the Chinese embassy and diplomats in Iraq since 2004. Since then, the Snow Leopard Commando Unit has also been assigned to the protection of embassies in Somalia, Yemen, Syria, and Afghanistan. Usually, every embassy hosts ten commandos who remain there for one year before a new team arrives (Qilu Evening News 2015). Their duty is to protect the embassies and the diplomats when they attend events and meetings in those countries. Despite their limited presence, soldiers of the Snow Leopard Commando Unit have been the victims of the dangers on China's interest frontiers. In July 2015, one of them was killed and three others injured in a terrorist attack in Mogadishu at the Jazeera Palace Hotel, where the Chinese embassy and a number of other foreign diplomatic representations were located. The Somali militant Islamist group al-Shabab claimed responsibility for the attack.

The third phase of Chinese engagement in peacekeeping began in 2012. Although it is important to note that the number of peacekeepers deployed has continued to grow, it is the qualitative change in the Chinese contribution and approach to peacekeeping that deserves particular attention. Already in 2009 and 2010, two deputy directors of the MOD Peacekeeping Affairs Bureau stated that it would not have been unthinkable for China to send combat troops under the UN aegis (Cheng 2010). However, as one of them suggested, considerations about the response of the international community as well as concerns about the capabilities of Chinese soldiers impeded such a move. Nonetheless, the first sign of change happened in 2012, when a platoon of "guard units" was deployed in South Sudan to provide protection exclusively to the Chinese peacekeepers already there.[4]

Like the self-defense unit established in 2007 by the Chinese contingent in Darfur, they had no other role within the framework of UNMISS and, for this reason, they were not officially considered as representing China's first combat troops operating under the UN aegis. Those troops, nevertheless, set an important precedent for the deployment of combat troops, following a clear shift in China's attitude to the use of force in peacetime highlighted in the 2013 Chinese defense white paper. Indeed, while it is not clear what kind of troops are part of the self-defense unit in Sudan, those in South Sudan are from an elite rapid reaction unit of the Chinese armed forces (Hartnett 2012b). The fact that their presence was revealed immediately, and

[4] In Chinese: 警卫部队 (Jǐngwèi bùduì).

not years later, is also telling about China's attitude. Probably, as Courtney Fung (2020) points out, Chinese officials needed some time to assess the performance of the self-defense unit in Darfur and the general attitude of foreign countries to China's engagement in peacekeeping operations. Since 2012, the PLA has deployed similar troops, both in the UN Multidimensional Integrated Stabilization Mission in Mali (MINUSMA) in 2013 and UNMISS in 2015.

These troops differ significantly from the average PLA infantry. While the standard equipment issued to the PLA troops is still relatively outdated and cheap (Zhang 2014), the combat troops deployed in Mali and South Sudan can boast full body armor, new weapons, drones, and modern armored personnel carriers (Zhang 2015). Moreover, a good proportion of the soldiers sent abroad had already been deployed on the same mission or others. For example, almost a hundred of the 396 soldiers who left Jinan in April 2018 had already participated in peacekeeping missions twice (Qiu 2018). At least before the most recent reforms that replaced the military regions with theater commands, the PLA tended to assign a peacekeeping mission to particular military regions (Blasko 2007, 341).

So far, the combat troops in South Sudan and Mali have been provided, repectively, by the former Jinan and Shenyang Military Regions, which now form part of the central and northern theater commands. Chinese peacekeepers are usually deployed in multiple sequential batches via commercial aircraft. They use commercial ships to transport heavy equipment, such as armored personnel carriers and bulldozers and earth movers (Blasko 2016). There are, however, qualitative and quantitative differences between the deployments in the two countries which reflect their importance in the context of China's attempts to defend its interest frontiers.

China does not have significant economic interests in Mali, though the value of Chinese assets in that country has steadily grown over time, from USD 12 million in 2003 to USD 394 million at the end of 2017. Mali is also not a key country in terms of contracts awarded to Chinese companies and, accordingly, the number of Chinese workers there is extremely limited (the peak was slightly more than 1,400 in 2011). The main Chinese activities in the country are related to the construction and maintenance of Trans-African Highway 5. As Cobus van Staden (2018) noted, that highway is the only one of all the Trans-African highways to be completed, but parts of the highway and railroad components either are in bad condition or need to be upgraded from narrow to standard gauge. The China Railway Construction Corporation is part of this plan and is active in many countries, including Mali. The Chinese nationals killed in November 2015 in Bamako, Mali's capital, were managers of that company. In September 2014, Mali signed a USD 11 billion agreement with China to support the construction of the railroad connecting Bamako to Guinea's port capital, Conakry, in the east, and the upgrade of the railroad linking the Malian capital with the Senegalese capital, Dakar, in the west (Railway Technology 2014).

Yet the situation changes if one looks north to Algeria, one of the countries identified in Chapter 3 as critical in terms of Chinese human and economic presence (Figure 35). Most likely because of the North African country's market for engineering projects, the community of Chinese working in Algeria has grown steadily to become the largest one in North Africa and the Middle East. There are also Chinese assets worth around USD 2 billion there. It is important to remember that these are conservative estimates. Hence, Mali per se is not important for China, but ensuring its stability has significant implications for China's interest frontiers.

China's deployment of peacekeepers in Mali resembles that in UNTAC and UNAMID in terms of both the relationship between what its soldiers (can) do and their being the tip of the spear of Chinese foreign policy. On the one hand, the Chinese contingent, in spite of the presence of combat troops, is too small and its role is too limited to have a significant impact on the ground. Even including medical and engineering troops, China's 400 soldiers make up only 3.5 percent of MINUSMA's total military strength of 11,200 troops.

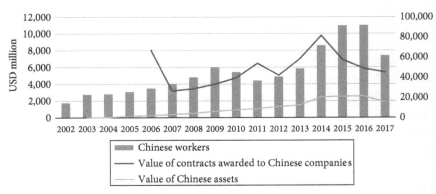

Figure 35 Chinese economic and human presence in Algeria

Source: PRC MOFCOM, National Bureau of Statistics of China, and PRC State Administration of Foreign Exchange (various years), and Department of Trade and External Economic Relations Statistics, National Bureau of Statistics of China (various years). Compiled by the author.

The main duty of the Chinese "guard units" is to guard the Super Camp of Sector East in Gao, where African and Asian troops live and work. They are not involved in operations directly aimed at stabilizing Mali, although, as the deaths and injuries suffered by Chinese peacekeepers in July 2016 clearly prove, their task is far from being risk-free. MINUSMA is the deadliest ongoing UN peacekeeping operation.

Although it has been reported that special forces are enmeshed with regular troops in the Chinese contingent (van der Putten 2015, 9), open-source research, at most, reveals that the "guard units" are from mechanized divisions of the PLA. For example, the "Steel" 7th Company, which was deployed as part of the third Chinese contingent of peacekeepers to Mali, is part of the former 39th Army Group, which was the first in the PLA to complete the process of mechanization.[5] That company also has a reputation in the history of the PLA and, as mentioned in Chapter 5, Chinese media reported its presence with pride just before the terrorist attack in Bamako in 2015.

However, the assessment of the performance of Chinese peacekeepers is not unanimously agreed. Indeed, although they have been praised a number of times by UN authorities, European officials present in Mali have highlighted several problems (van der Putten 2015; Albrecht, Cold-Ravnkilde, and Haugegaard 2017). For example, many Chinese peacekeepers lack the skills to communicate with other nationalities, which impedes the building of solid personal relationships with either locals or fellow soldiers from other countries. This issue is not an obstacle when it comes to simply carrying out their tasks, but it certainly undermines attempts to generate soft power as well as gathering precious intelligence. It has also been pointed out that the Chinese-run hospital does not meet the standards of European militaries and, at least in the initial phases of the missions, Chinese troops have not provided the same level of protection to the Super Camp that European troops have in Camp Castor, which accommodates MINUSMA's special forces, helicopters, and intelligence units. These reports, therefore, indicate that some of the best peacekeepers that China can field have the same difficulties that other soldiers from developing countries have.

On the other hand, however, there is no doubt that the deployment of Chinese combat troops in Mali is the clearest manifestation of China's changing attitude to the role of peacekeeping as a result of the country's securitization process. MINUSMA has been labeled as "the first UN

---

[5] In Chinese: 钢铁七连 (Gāngtiě qī lián).

counter-terrorism operation" because its mandates have increasingly reflected the debate over the role of the UN in international antiterrorism that has been going on for more than ten years (Karlsrud 2017). While it was not one of the initiators of this change, China not only did not oppose it but, in fact, supported it to some extent against the resistance of the UN bureaucracy (Andersen 2018). The UN has also always been identified by China as the only actor allowed to take the lead in global antiterrorism activities. At the same time, a more pragmatic Chinese approach to terrorism in the region, which identifies the causes of terrorism in local instability caused by both Western interventionism and economic underdevelopment, has started to emerge (Liu 2014).

Moreover, the limit of a softer approach to peacekeeping as a way to protect China's interests overseas had already become evident. Indeed, in January 2012, Chinese troops in UNMIS asked to join the search operations to rescue the twenty-nine employees of Sinohydro who had been kidnapped by local insurgents. However, their commander turned down their request because the UN chain of command and the mandate of the mission did not allow them to abandon their position for that purpose (Wu and Cui 2012). Hence, the criticisms of the initial French intervention in Mali in 2012 were mostly due to the fear that, after the disaster in Libya, France was trying to exploit the UN and international law again to protect its interests in the former colony rather than because there was disagreement over the need to fight terrorists (He 2013).[6] This is why China and the other members of the UNSC mandated the peacekeepers of MINUSMA to adopt an increasingly robust posture to "deter threats and take active steps to prevent the return of armed elements" as part of the efforts to help the Malian government to regain control over the country's territory (UNSC 2013a, 2016).

Chinese support for MINUSMA and the deployment of troops not only allows China to strengthen the authority of the UN against what it perceives as unilateral Western actions, as it aimed at doing in UNTAC, and to build its image as a "responsible great power," as was the case in UNAMID, but also contributes to shaping the role of the UN in tackling issues—terrorism and political instability in other countries—that have increasingly been securitized in its domestic debate in relation to its overseas interests. Against this background, it is important to point out that a few weeks before approving

---

[6] France acted in response to a direct invitation from the Malian government when the insurgents in the north of Mali began their attack before the African-led International Support Mission to Mali could deploy.

the establishment of MINUSMA, China also voted in favor of UNSC Resolution 2098. This resolution approved the creation of the first-ever "offensive" combat force within the UN Organization Stabilization Mission in the Democratic Republic of Congo, intended to carry out targeted operations to neutralize and disarm the notorious 23 March Movement, as well as other Congolese rebels and foreign armed groups in the strife-riven African country (UNSC 2013b). The scale of Chinese investments, the value of the Democratic Republic of Congo market for Chinese companies, and the number of Chinese workers were not significant when China joined the peacekeeping mission. However, the value of all those three parameters increased significantly in the early 2010s. Not only did Chinese companies sign contracts worth billions of US dollars, but the value of Chinese assets and the number of Chinese workers grew steeply from USD 0.24 million in 2003 to USD 1 billion in 2013 and USD 2 billion in 2014, and from just over 300 workers in 2004 to 10,600 in 2013 and 14,400 in 2014. China surely did not approve this exceptional measure specifically to protect its interests but, nonetheless, its vote conforms with the idea that Beijing's approach to UN-authorized use of force changed along with growing concerns regarding the security of its overseas interests.

The presence of Chinese combat troops in the guise of peacekeepers along the perimeter of China's interest frontiers is the manifestation of its growing commitment to the UN as an organization that can both guarantee the legitimacy of China's security engagement with the world and, increasingly, protect its interests. This is further evident in China's decision in late 2014 to send an infantry battalion to join UNMISS. UNMISS essentially took over UNMIS in July 2011, as its founding resolution was approved the same day the mandate of UNMIS ended. Much of UNMIS's personnel and equipment, including that of China, was transferred to UNMISS in South Sudan. As mentioned in Chapter 3, South Sudan is one of the most sensitive countries for the stability of China's interest frontiers and it shares a border with Ethiopia. Ethiopia is a country that is becoming of great importance for China in economic terms and, like Algeria in the case of Chinese participation in MINUSMA, it has problems with what happens on the border with its unstable neighbors.

Despite hopes for the stabilization of the newly born South Sudan, the situation quickly deteriorated and, by 2013, most of the oilfields had been closed by the government due to security concerns (Vasselier 2016). As of January 2014, some of the largest oilfields operated by Chinese state-owned enterprises were under the control of militias backed by Riek Machar, the

South Sudanese vice president until he was sacked in July 2013 (Wu 2014). Originally, the mandate of UNMISS did not include the protection of specific places, but it was expanded when the UNSC met in May 2014 and approved UNSC Resolution 2155 (UNSC 2014). China seized the opportunity that general support for robust peacekeeping provided. Indeed, Beijing tried, and partially succeeded, in shaping the mandate of UNMISS in its favor. The UNSC Resolution document urges the peacekeepers to protect, among other facilities, oil installations, by all means necessary. Reportedly, China not only proposed the inclusion of those objectives in the mandate but asked to have its own soldiers there as well, although it was also open to deploying them in other areas as long as the mandate included the protection of the oilfields (Lynch 2014). Other countries supported China's proposal regarding the protection of oil installations on the grounds that oil revenues are the main source of wealth for this otherwise failing state. China also backed its interests with a significant increase in terms of peacekeepers contributed by offering an infantry battalion.

The arrival of 700 infantry, double the number of medical and engineering units, in early 2015 placed China in the top ten of contributors to UNMISS. According to the Chinese MOD (2015), the size of the battalion exceeded the PLA standard and "has three affiliated battle companies and one affiliated support company, covering a number of Army corps such as infantry, armored forces, special operation forces, artillery forces, communication troops and medical troops." There are now 1,050 Chinese military personnel, or 11.9 percent, out of 12,500 authorized by the UNSC. Under the command of the UNMISS Regional Protection Force, the Chinese infantry operates from the UNMISS headquarters in Juba, which was established in 2016 to provide protection to key facilities and the main routes into and out of the city, as well as to strengthen UN security in protecting civilian sites and other UN premises. The engineering troops are located in Kaucjok, Rumbek, and Wau, where there is also a level-two hospital operated by Chinese officers. Chinese media also emphasize that these places, in addition to being dangerous, frequently lack fresh water and fresh food supplies.

The troops deployed to South Sudan deserve particular attention. For instance, they are:

> equipped with weapons and equipment such as wheeled infantry combat vehicles, armored troop carriers, anti-tank rocket projectiles, unmanned aerial vehicles, mortars and heavy machine guns. Of the 108 sets of individual equipment, the protective equipment is especially worth mentioning, because

it not only protects important positions such as the heart, but also protects the crotch and neck. It is substantially superior to the "vests" used by other Chinese peacekeeping forces in terms of protective area or protective ability.

(PRC MOD 2015)

Moreover, the majority of the infantry troops deployed to South Sudan belong to motorized divisions (mechanized in the case of the second batch of peace-keepers) of the former 54th, 20th, and 26th Army Groups of the former Jinan Military Region, whose troops are the most used to long-distance operations and train in different climatic conditions (Blasko 2012, 182–5).

The 162nd Motorized Infantry Division of the 54th Army Group is one of the oldest rapid-reaction units of the PLA, and they were already present in South Sudan as part of the small detachment deployed in 2012 (Hartnett 2012b). The 26th and 54th Army Groups are among those with organic heli-copter assets and their soldiers train more frequently with them (Hwang 1997). This might be an important element, as China has also been deploying helicopters in UNMISS since 2017, although they have been provided by the 81st Army Group of the Central Theater Command so far (Yu 2018). As far as we know, therefore, the Chinese contribution of combat troops to UNMISS is not only superior in terms of quantity to that in Mali, but, to a certain extent, is also superior from a qualitative point of view.

Their performance, as far as public reports have made it possible to know, has had both successes and failures, although the latter were not entirely their fault. During the clashes in Juba that resulted in the death of two Chinese peacekeepers and more than 300 civilians on July 8–11, 2016, UN forces were accused of ignoring a call for help from local and foreign civilians who were being attacked, raped, and killed by both government forces loyal to Salva Kiir Mayardit and supporters of Riek Machar, the former vice president turned rebel leader. The findings of the UN investigation into the events backed the claims of aid workers that UN troops refused to respond when government soldiers attacked an international aid compound in Juba. The report found that serious problems in the chain of command impeded the response of the four troop contingents from China, Ethiopia, Nepal, and India (1,800 soldiers in total). The leader of the Chinese battalion was the incident commander, a position which gave him control over all the troops present, but he was given contradictory orders by the force commander, the Kenyan Lieutenant General Johnson Mogoa Kimani Ondieki. The report argued that a "confused arrangement, in combination with the lack of leadership on the ground, contributed to incidents of poor performance among the military and police contingents at UN House" (UN 2016, 3). Chinese peacekeepers abandoned their positions at least twice, and Nepalese peacekeepers failed to stop looting inside the UN compound. While the force commander was forced to resign, together with the UN Mission Chief, Ellen Margrethe Loj, there is no mention of punishment inflicted on the Chinese soldiers. As two of them died in the clashes on those days, they too were victims of the situation.

The deaths of the two Chinese soldiers prompted the reopening of the debate among Chinese policymakers, especially within the PLA, regarding whether or not to deploy combat troops in peacekeeping operations (Fung 2020). Yet China continued to participate in UNMISS and the performance of Chinese soldiers was much improved almost two years later in the same location as where the 2016 incident took place. Armed men entered the restricted zone of the UN compound in Juba that the Chinese peacekeepers were tasked with guarding. Fifteen Chinese soldiers rushed to confront them and, although they were quickly outnumbered and guns aimed at them, they successfully negotiated a retreat by the insurgents without resorting to violence (Huang 2018). Besides these episodes, Chinese soldiers in South Sudan probably have the same communication problems with locals and other foreign soldiers that have been highlighted with their comrades in Mali. It is also important to note that in 2014 the Chinese media reported that Chinese peacekeepers were coordinating with the Chinese embassy, Chinese businesses, and local South Sudanese authorities to help Chinese nationals in danger (PRC Central Government 2014). However, they do so only if the emergency happens near their base.

At Sea, in the Air, and Toward the Land

Even when allowed by international law, the PLA Navy and, in particular, the PLA Air Force have had a limited role in the defense of China's interest frontiers so far. This is mostly because of the lack of the necessary capabilities. Therefore, the changes that were clearly visible in China's peacekeeping missions are more difficult to see at sea and in the air. Nonetheless, the change from a diplomacy-first approach to that of diplomacy-and-security as result of the securitization of non-traditional security issues overseas can still be observed. The establishment of the first overseas military base in Djibouti in 2015 is the most visible sign of this.

The myriad reports about the growth of the Chinese defense budget or the launch of new warships might induce an observer to take the Chinese presence in those waters for granted. Between 2008 and 2018, the Chinese navy has sent out 26,000 officers and soldiers, escorted 6,595 ships, and successfully rescued or aided more than sixty Chinese and foreign ships in the Gulf of Aden (Xinhua 2018b). However, the PLA Navy did not have the capacity to carry out operations outside of Asia until the early 2000s. When a PLA Navy task force visited Pearl Harbor in 1996, many observers noticed that the ships had no systems to desalinate water and that the foreign components they relied on were not designed to work with Chinese components (Yung et al. 2010). A few years later, in 2002, during the ambitious world tour at sea, the diesel engine of the *Qingdao* destroyer broke, and German technicians had to be flown in to repair it. Similar episodes were not uncommon in those years (Grubb 2008, 32-3). It seems, therefore, that the concerns raised by Chinese Internet users mentioned in Chapter 5 were not completely without foundation. In order to avoid such embarrassments, the PLA Navy deployed only its best ships to the Gulf of Aden.

Between late 2008 and 2012, the PLA Navy deployed ten task forces, each composed of a supply ship and two surface combatants, mostly frigates and destroyers. They carried two helicopters and a crew of more than 700, which included a team of special forces operators. Among the thirty ships sent to the Gulf of Aden, the three supply ships had been deployed multiple times. The *Weishanhu* and the *Qiandaohu* supply ships alone supported the antipiracy missions for almost four years. Similarly, the same ten surface combatants from different fleets had been rotated continuously during those years. The reason behind this is that between 2005 and 2010 the PLA Navy had fewer than six Type 54 frigates and four Type 52 destroyers available (O'Rourke 2017, 30-4). Those two kinds of ships are among the first modern warships produced by Chinese shipyards that can also provide decent living conditions for their sailors and carry a helicopter. Only after the departure from Qingdao of the 11th task force did the number of rotations per ship decline. From then on, almost all the surface combatants deployed participated in only one expedition.

The PLA Navy could not count on receiving solid logistics support in those years. While, today, the *People's Daily* confirms that the Chinese Beidou navigation system has surpassed the American GPS in terms of performance (Zhang 2017), Chinese experts in 2009 admitted that the PLA Navy had to rely on the American system because the Beidou system still had too many problems and shortcomings that made it unfit for military use (Beijing Youth Daily 2009). The PLA Navy managed to find a partially sustainable arrangement through port calls in the region and the support of Chinese embassies, consulates, and companies. Thanks to this solution, the duration of every deployment was extended from four to six months from the arrival of the fourth task force between 2009 and 2010. Nonetheless, complaints about the inadequacies of this system have not disappeared (Erickson and Strange 2015, 182).

By looking at the list of records broken by the first task force, it also emerges quite clearly that operating in the Gulf of Aden for the PLA Navy was much more about overcoming the challenge of simply being there than fighting pirates (Sun and Zhu 2017). For example, it was the first time the PLA Navy conducted maintenance at sea. Most of the activities described are about testing things like the take-off and landing of helicopters at sea, and verifying the resistance of the equipment. Therefore, it is not surprising that the rules of engagement of the Chinese flotillas were more conservative than those established by the UN for the mission.

What the Chinese media described as the first and only time a Chinese task force used force against pirates, who had already left by the time the Chinese soldiers arrived, was to liberate the merchant ship *Taiankou* in November 2010 (Guo 2018). Usually, the Chinese fire warning shots and do not pursue the pirates ashore (Erickson and Strange 2013, 98–103). The first known arrest of a pirate by the Chinese navy took place only in early 2017 (Dong 2017). Moreover, they originally provided protection only to Chinese and foreign ships that made this request within the 550 nautical mile-long corridor that goes from a point that is 100 nautical miles north of the island of Socotra and another that is 75 nautical miles southwest of the port of Aden. The PLA Navy, therefore, escorted ships within a certain area, while Western navies both patroled and responded to any distress calls.

As Chinese media and commentators pointed out, all these limitations emerged on October 19, 2009. That day, the Chinese-flagged bulk carrier *Dexinhai* and its twenty-five Chinese sailors were captured by pirates 19,350 nautical miles northeast of the Seychelles and 700 nautical miles off the east coast of Somalia. Like the *Tianyu 8*—the first Chinese ship attacked by Somali pirates—the *Dexinhai* was captured outside of waters patrolled by PLA Navy warships. When the news broke, the Chinese warships were reported to be steaming toward the last known location of the *Dexinhai*—1,080 nautical miles away from where they had been patrolling. They would have needed almost two days to get there. Moreover, it seems that the Type 54 frigate, *Zhoushan*, risked running out of fuel before arriving due to the increased fuel consumption needed to maintain maximum speed for such a long time (News163 2009). In any case, the *Dexinhai* was released after the Chinese government transferred USD 3.5 million to the pirates.

While there is no doubt that military action might have increased the danger to the hostages, it is also true that the PLA Navy was not in a position to engage in this way in any case. Indeed, the pirates could attack ships within a much wider area than that then patrolled by Chinese warships, as pointed out by a PLA officer (Sina 2009). He also suggested improving Chinese coordination with other foreign navies in the area in order to try and solve any similar future incidents through negotiation, as well as paying the ransom if needed. Another commentator argued that China was still lacking the necessary intelligence-gathering and rapid-reaction capabilities (Hai 2009).

Against this background, in 2010 China announced it would change the coordinates of the corridor patrolled by its ships to make it overlap with the International Recommended Transit Corridor of NATO and the European Union, thereby increasing international coordination and cooperation. At the same time, following a pattern already highlighted in Chapter 3, the Ministry of Transportation instructed Chinese shipping companies and their vessels and crews "to strengthen self-protective measures in an effort to prevent hijack by pirates" (Xinhua 2009).

When the Libyan evacuation took place, the PLA Navy had the same problems that it faced in the rescue of the *Dexinhai* in 2009. The order to evacuate Chinese nationals from Libya arrived at the Chinese embassy in Tripoli on the evening of February 21, 2011. Two days later, the Chinese top leadership ordered the *Xuzhou* frigate to leave the antipiracy task force and head for Libya. The commander of the *Xuzhou* ordered its crew to prepare for emergency medical operations and to study all the documents available about sea routes and ports in the Mediterranean Sea. However, as he later told Chinese media, they had no clear information about the actual situation they were going into (Guo 2017). Was the port of Tripoli safe? Was there a threat of armed attack in Libyan waters? How many Chinese citizens needed to be evacuated? They did not know. Reportedly, the PLA Navy started to experiment with the use of small scout drones only in March 2019 and one, curiously, lost control near Benghazi in Libya (Africa Intelligence 2019).

In general, despite the media campaign mounted by the government (see Chapter 5), the main difference between 2011 and 2009 is, as an article published by *Xinhua* points out (Xinhua 2011), a "an element of 'chance.'"[7] By coincidence the naval task force in the Gulf of Aden was near a port where it could quickly complete refueling, which allowed the *Xuzhou* to leave immediately after the

---

[7] In Chinese: 一个"偶然"因素 (Yīgè "ǒurán" yīnsù).

order arrived. In any case, the *Xuzhou* remained outside Libyan territorial waters between March 1 and March 4, only flying its helicopter over the ships that were carrying the Chinese evacuees away from the North African country. The vast majority of the Chinese citizens were evacuated by commercial ships and charter flights. In comparison, the PLA Air Force as detailed further below, played a more direct role.

Chapter 6 showed that, when China announced that it would join the antipiracy operations, the securitization of non-traditional security issues was already under way. In the case of the antipiracy missions, the concerns of the civilian leadership were backed by the fact that a fifth of the Chinese ships transiting through the Gulf of Aden were victims of pirates in one way or another (Wu and Peng 2008). At the same time, pressure to act from the ministries of the State Council was probably growing. On the one hand, costs sustained by Chinese shipping companies were increasing as a grow-ing number of ships started to take a longer route around the Cape of Good Hope in order to avoid passing through Somali waters (Erickson 2010, 310). In addition to the Ministry of Foreign Affairs (MFA), the State-Owned Assets Supervision and Administration Commission, which owns the main Chinese shipping companies was also probably concerned about the situation. On the other hand, by December 2008, all the UNSC members had already announced they would be participating in the antipiracy missions. India's warships also arrived in the Gulf of Aden in October. Not participating in those missions would have put the Chinese government in an extremely awkward position, both on the international stage and at home, where many were eager to see the navy in action (see Chapter 5). Other scholars, indeed, have argued that the initial deployments to the Gulf of Aden probably were mostly motivated by diplomatic concerns rather than security ones (Lin-Greenberg 2010).

It seems that, originally, the Chinese military was not enthusiastic about of this shift. First, the ground forces-centric PLA was not convinced of the importance of Military Operations Other Than War (MOOTW) and, in any case, the investments made were for peacekeeping-related preparations (see Chapter 6). Second, PLA Navy officers were keen to promote the expansion of the role of the navy, but it seems that they looked at the possibility mostly in traditional security terms, to boost investment in the modernization of their own service (see Chapter 2). Third, confidence in carrying out overseas MOOTW was undermined by the acknowledgment that doing so required overcoming an entirely new set of challenges well beyond a simple modern-ization of the armed forces (see Chapter 6).

This mix of concerns about the feasibility of overseas operations and the lack of interest in them might well explain why it took two months for the MFA to convince the PLA to give the green light to the antipiracy operations in the Gulf of Aden in late 2008 (International Crisis Group 2009, 26). The fact that the PLA Navy initially followed its own rules of engagement, escorting only the ships that made that request, and patrolling an area different from that of other international actors, is also consistent with the fact that the PLA obeys the country's leadership but is also able to influence the implementation of any orders to suit itself. With this in mind, the first task forces deployed by the PLA Navy had the same function as the self-defense unit established in 2007 within the Chinese peacekeeping contingent in Darfur: to test the capabilities of Chinese soldiers and the reaction of international public opinion.

As the defense of China's interest frontiers emerged as a priority after 2011, however, the situation changed. On the one hand, the PLA itself had gained confidence in its capabilities thanks to the experience it had accumulated over the years. Furthermore, the growing availability of modern ships meant that the costs of deployments off Somalia decreased in terms of resources diverted from traditional national defense. On the other hand, as shown in Chapter 2, consensus about the need to engage as a result of non-traditional security threats not only allowed the full integration of the antipiracy missions within the general modernization process of the PLA, but also made Chinese officers think seriously about the next step: establishing a long-term military presence overseas.

The fact that in mid-2013 the then member of the Central Military Commission and leader of the former PLA General Logistics Department, Zhao Keshi, was writing in *China Military Science* about the necessity of exploring possible ways to establish military outposts overseas is a strong indication that the PLA top brass had already agreed on that move (Zhao 2013). Indeed, in 2011 the PLA and the provincial government of Henan Province started discussing the establishment of a "civil-military fusion strategic projection base" in Zhengzhou to study how to integrate rail and road services with airports for rapid troop, equipment, and materials loading onto aircraft (Kennedy 2019, 28).[8] These critical changes within the PLA certainly helped to translate into action the urgent orders coming from the civilian leadership, which, as Chapter 1 argued, was already looking at defending the country's overseas interests and not just its development interests at sea. Hence, although the piracy threat in the Gulf

---

[8] In Chinese: 军民融合战略投送基地 (Jūnmín rónghé zhànlüè tóu sòng jīdì).

of Aden sharply decreased after 2011 (Prins, Daxecker, and Phayal 2017), China's naval presence remained constant.

In March 2015, the PLA Navy was again called on to support the evacuation of Chinese nationals, this time from Yemen. That month, the frigates *Linyi* and *Weifang* entered the ports of Aden and Hodeida to evacuate over 600 Chinese and around 200 foreign evacuees. The supply ship *Weishanhu* evacuated a handful of people from Socotra to the port of Salalah in Oman. Reportedly, the *Linyi* had its weapon systems and helicopter ready to open fire because of the uncertain security conditions. The evacuation began immediately after a brief ceasefire between the warring parties was agreed on March 29, three days after the Saudi-led coalition forces launched air strikes in Yemen against the Shiite Houthi group. There are a number of elements that made it possible for the PLA Navy to play a more active role here than in Libya. First, there were fewer evacuees in 2015 than in 2011. Second, the PLA Navy ships were already near Yemen, and the destination port, Djibouti, was very close. Third, the PLA Navy was much more familiar with Yemen, or at least the port of Aden, because its Chinese warships frequently went there to resupply. Using the PLA, therefore, was the most effective solution.

Nonetheless, it is important to highlight that this was the first time that Chinese warships had entered the territorial waters of another country for operations other than resupplying or port calls. Reportedly, given the feasibility of a PLA-led evacuation, the Chinese government established an ad hoc working group to ensure legal foundations for the operations were in place (Sina 2017). International customary law guaranteed the legitimacy of China's evacuations in Libya as well, as in Yemen as there was no other reliable means of protecting its citizens. Hence, given the better conditions in Yemen, the existence of that working group is symptomatic of both Beijing's caution and, at the same time, its growing commitment to learning how to use military assets to protect its interest frontiers when needed.

The evacuation from Yemen took place against the background of the final stages of the negotiations between the Chinese government and its Djiboutian counterpart to establish China's first military base overseas. On November 26, 2015, the MOD spokesperson, Wu Qian, confirmed that the two countries were defining the terms of the agreement. By then, the PLA had also gained some experience of how to operate a base thanks to its base in Zhengzhou, which was opened in 2014, as well as to its increased knowledge about Djibouti.[9] Indeed, Djibouti's President Ismail Omar Guelleh visited

---

[9] As of 2018, the base in Zhengzhou has provided airlifts for the deployment of Chinese peace-keepers abroad, delivery assistance to Myanmar and Afghanistan, and support for cross-regional

Beijing for the 2012 Forum on China-Africa Cooperation. In those days, the two sides signed agreements for the establishment of a bilateral joint ministerial commission and a deepening of civil, naval, and military ties (Styan 2019). China sent its first military attaché to the African country shortly afterwards.

In the years preceding the conclusion of the negotiations over the base, a number of factors contributed to making Djibouti the best choice. First, the war in Yemen made both Yemen and Oman too risky in both security and diplomatic terms. Second, a military base in Saudi Arabia would not only have caused concern in the United States, but would also have been read as a sign of Chinese support for the Saudi rulers and policies by other countries in the region, thereby undermining the image of neutrality that China has long cultivated. In particular, as the sanctions against the Iranian nuclear program were on the way to being lifted, China would have risked losing its position as the primary economic and diplomatic partner of Tehran without gaining any real improvement in its position in Riyadh. Third, Djibouti not only had the most-visited port in the region by the PLA Navy (Figure 36), but is also a country that hosts military bases for a number of other countries. Djibouti, therefore, suits the preferences of both the PLA and, most likely, the MFA. Fourth, Djibouti's neighbor, Ethiopia, is one of the countries in which China's economic and human footprint has expanded the most in recent years (see Chapter 3). The base in Djibouti, therefore, could also strengthen China's ability to support regional stability through its peacekeeping missions in the neighboring Sudan and South Sudan.

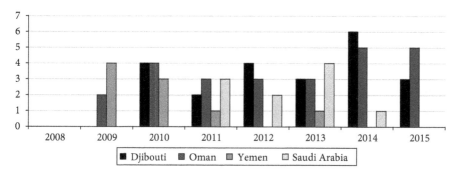

Figure 36 PLA Navy's logistic stops between 2008 and 2015
Source: Chinese media reports. Compiled by the author.

exercises carried out by Chinese police (Lu, Hao, and Li 2018). In total, the base has supported the transportation of more than 9,000 men and 600 tons of materials to other countries and regions of China.

Against this background, the establishment of the military facilities also brought massive investment in infrastructure aimed at improving Djibouti's connection with its neighbors, especially Ethiopia and the rest of the region. For example, the China Railway Engineering Corporation and China Civil Engineering Construction Corporation completed the 756-kilometer railroad connecting Djibouti with Addis Ababa thanks to the financial backing of the China ExIm Bank and the Ethiopian government. The Chinese bank provided 70 percent of the USD 3.5 billion needed to build the 650-kilometer Ethiopian part of the project. The railroad aims to enhance regional economic integration in the Horn of Africa and will provide a maritime outlet to Ethiopia's burgeoning industrial zones, which are partly designed, financed, and occupied by Chinese investors and companies producing for a global market. The China Civil Engineering Construction Corporation is also involved in the construction of two new international airports in Ali-Sabieh. China Merchants Port has also contributed a large share of the USD 590 million investment needed to upgrade the Doraleh multipurpose port. Finally, the Poly-GCL Petroleum Group is in charge of a project that includes a liquefaction plant and a 767-kilometer natural gas pipeline connecting Ethiopia's Ogaden Basin to an export terminal to be located in Damerjog, near Djibouti's border with Somalia. Poly's project is part of a broader plan to develop the Ethiopian natural gas and oil industry that began in 2013 with a deal with Ethiopia's Mines Ministry.

Although Chinese media initially only mentioned the need to improve the logistics support to the Chinese soldiers engaged in peacekeeping and antipiracy missions in the region (People's Daily 2015), Chinese commentators close to the PLA were already making explicit references to a potential base in Djibouti and its role in boosting the defense of Chinese overseas interests before the MOD confirmed what was happening between China and the African country (Song 2015). According to some analysts (Bhat 2017), the satellite images of the base—which was officially inaugurated on the symbolic date of August 1, 2017,[10] with the arrival of the first detachment of soldiers and ZBL-08 and ZTL-11 armored vehicles—suggest that it can accommodate over one brigade, has a four-layered security ring, and can handle a dozen helicopters. According to the same sources, the base should have "at least 10 storage barracks, ammunition point, storage, office complex and a heliport. The base also has a huge underground air-conditioning plant, which may possibly include a water filtration (reverse osmosis) and ice-making plants."

---

[10] The first day of August is the anniversary of the foundation of the PLA.

Some in the Chinese media, drawing from a Russian magazine, speculate that there are some 2,000 soldiers on the base (Sina.com 2018). However, it is still unknown how many soldiers are or can be hosted there. The Chinese base is about 0.5 square kilometers, much smaller than Camp Lemonnier, the American base also in Djibouti, which supports approximately 4,000 American and allied forces military and civilian personnel and defense contractors. China's base is situated near the Doraleh multipurpose port area of Djibouti. The base also includes a pier that should allow for the docking of at least a four-ship flotilla, including China's new generation Type 901 supply ships, destroyers, and frigates, as well as amphibious assault ships. The changes in Djibouti have been taking place along with the transformation of the PLA Navy-Marine Corps, whose size and position within the PLA navy command structure, as well as the scope of its training, were significantly expanded in 2017, arguably to transform them into a real expeditionary force (Peck 2018).

China and Djibouti signed a ten-year lease for the land where the base is located at the cost of USD 20 million per year in rent.[11] Over that period, it will not be surprising to see the PLA Air Force too making an appearance on a regular basis. As of today, besides international joint exercises and deliveries of humanitarian aid, the only operation of the PLA Air Force outside Asia has been the evacuation of Chinese citizens from Libya. On February 27, 2011, four Ilyushin Il-76s of the 13th Transport Division started the necessary preparations to leave Diwopu International Airport in Urumqi as soon as possible. They took off the next day for Sabha, in east-central Libya. Before returning to China on April 3, they transported 1,655 Chinese citizens to Khartoum in Sudan and the remaining 287 back to Beijing Nanyuan Airport. The four Il-76s flew around 10,000 km, crossing five countries (Ma 2011, 27-9). Both the lack of a significant number of long-range heavy transport military aircraft and the absence of a "perch" have long prevented the Chinese air force from flying outside Asia, which has consequently delayed its transformation "from an aviation force into an integrated air and space force, from a mechanized air force into an informatized air force and from a supporting air force into a strategic leading force" (PLA AMS 2013, 218).

A recent report published by the RAND Corporation indicates that the Chinese air force in 2016 relied on three Y-20 and twenty Il-76 heavy-transport aircraft to support the operations of the 13th Transport Division and,

[11] For Camp Lemonnier, the United States pays about USD 60 million per year.

sometimes, the 15th Airborne Corps (Garafola and Heath 2017, 8-11). However, the lack of complete technical information and the scarcity of spare parts for the fleet of Russian-made Il-76s have added to other technical problems that made the frequent use of these aircraft impossible (Garafola and Heath 2017, 28-9). These issues are behind the efforts led by the Xi'an Aircraft Industrial Corporation to develop the Y-20, which came into service on July 6, 2016. On May 8, 2018, a Y-20 conducted its first paratrooper and cargo parachute drop in Sichuan. This aircraft, in theory, should be able to carry a Type 99 tank as well as a variety of other vehicles, supplies, or a large number of troops. Currently the Y-20 uses four Russian-made Soloviev D-30 turbofan engines, although the PLA Air Force plans to replace them with Chinese-made Shenyang WS-20 turbofans by 2020. This should give the aircraft short take-off capabilities and a greater range. As to the "perch," while the 400-meter airstrip on the base in Djibouti is too short to allow the landing of fighter jets and heavy-transport aircraft, there is little doubt that the PLA Air Force would be granted the use of the main airport in Djibouti if and when necessary, thereby completing the construction of security infrastructure centered on this base and capable of providing military protection to China's interest frontiers via land, sea, and air.

Conclusion

The difficulties of acting through the UN and technical and legal uncertainties were (and still are) serious problems for China's defense of its interest frontiers. While the importance of achieving diplomatic goals, from breaking the post-1989 isolation to establishing an image of a "great responsible power," never decreased, the effects of the securitization of non-traditional security slowly but steadily began to shape Chinese military operations in North Africa and the Middle East in three interconnected ways over the years.

First, China's military presence changed from being country- to sub-region-focused and from single-purpose- to multipurpose-oriented. The pre-2011 period was characterized by an attempt to tackle specific problems in a specific area, such as the pirates in the Gulf of Aden and instability in Sudan. Accordingly, an analysis of the operations initiated in those years reveals the crisis-driven nature of Chinese actions. After all, the precise nature of the threat was not clear, even to the top civilian leadership, and the PLA's focus on traditional security threats probably did not help the working-out of a long-term strategy. Moreover, it seems that concerns regarding its own capabilities made the PLA more cautious about engaging in operations overseas.

From this point of view, the problems encountered by the MFA that were described in Chapters 4 and 6 become even more evident: the ministry had not only to take responsibility for the protection of Chinese nationals abroad with its limited resources, but also to convince a seemingly reluctant PLA to become more involved overseas. The situation changed drastically after the Libyan evacuation, as both the civilian and the military leadership began to think about a more strategic and long-term approach to the defense of the country's interest frontiers. With more assertive behavior within the UNSC coupled with the deployment of combat troops in South Sudan and Mali and the establishment of the first overseas base in Djibouti, China has begun to build a security infrastructure that does not target specific threats in a specific place anymore, but aims at stabilizing subregions composed of the countries identified in Chapter 3 and their neighbors.

Second, China's military presence has gradually expanded from a land-only dimension to include the sea surrounding and, to a lesser extent, the air above its interest frontiers. This process took place in an uncoordinated fashion in its initial phases. Chapter 6 showed that, by the time the PLA Navy was preparing to send its first task force to the Gulf of Aden, the PLA was investing in improving the peacekeeping capabilities of its soldiers. The shortcomings of this approach quickly became evident. For example, the PLA Navy alone could not do much more than what it had done to rescue the *Dexinhai* in 2009 and the Chinese nationals in Libya in 2011. The PLA Ground Forces operating only under the command of the UN could not help the Chinese citizens in Sudan and Mali. Paradoxically, it was the PLA Air Force that was the quickest and, despite its limited resources, the most efficient in its single intervention in Libya. However, the joint efforts of the civilian and military leadership to find a way to ease the pressure on China's interest frontiers led to negotiations for the opening of the base in Djibouti. The opening of the base was clearly done with much more in mind than simply improving the logistics of the ongoing peacekeeping and antipiracy operations. Indeed, the base has enabled China to develop a multidimensional presence on land, at sea, and in the air.

Third, while the UN remains the preferred venue for China to frame its military presence abroad because it provides an effective burden-sharing and diplomatically unassailable platform, there are signs that the explicit blessing of the UN might not be necessary as long as bilateral agreements and international law can justify military action. This is an apparently small change that the extremely low intensity of Chinse operations has further managed to obfuscate. However, while the UN limits when, where, and how Chinese troops can act, international treaties like the Vienna Convention on Consular Relations, which was rightly invoked by China during the evacuations from Libya and Yemen, allow much more room to maneuver as long as Chinese troops are sent to protect its citizens. The two other changes mentioned above indicate that post-2011 China has indeed been preparing for a more active use of its armed forces inside and, to a lesser extent, outside the UN, even though, as shown by the great attention paid to the legal side of the evacuation from Yemen, it is always careful to avoid being perceived as taking unilateral action.

Bibliography

Adebajo, Adekeye, and Chris Landsberg. 2000. "Back to the Future: UN Peacekeeping in Africa." *International Peacekeeping* 7 (4): 161–88.

Africa Intelligence. 2019. "The Chinese Army Loses Its First Drone in Libya." *Africa Intelligence*. September 9. Accessed October 5, 2019. https://www.africaintelligence.com/mce/corridors-of-power/2019/09/05/the-chinese-army-loses-its-first-drone-in-libya,108371106-eve.

Albrecht, Peter, Signe Marie Cold-Ravnkilde, and Rikke Haugegaard. 2017. "African Peacekeepers in Mali." Danish Institute for International Studies. Accessed February 2, 2019. https://www.passblue.com/wp-content/uploads/2017/06/DIIS-Report-02-African-Peacekeepers-in-Mali_FINAL.pdf.

Amnesty International. 2007. "Sudan Arms Continuing To Fuel Serious Human Rights Violations In Darfur." Amnesty International. Accessed August 23, 2017. https://www.amnesty.org/download/Documents/60000/afr540192007en.pdf.

Andersen, Louise Riis. 2018. "The Hippo in the Room: The Pragmatic Push-Back from the UN Peace Bureaucracy against the Militarization of UN Peacekeeping." *International Affairs* 94 (2): 343–61.

Beijing Youth Daily. 2009. "Expert: First Generation of Beidou Still Has Many Shortcomings, Cannot Be Used by the Military." *Beijing Youth Daily*. March 25. Accessed August 3, 2018. http://military.china.com/zh_cn/important/64/20090325/15394974.html.

Bhat, Vinayak. 2017. "China's Mega Fortress in Djibouti Could Be Model for Its Bases in Pakistan." *The Print*. September 27. Accessed December 20, 2017. https://theprint.in/security/china-mega-fortress-djibouti-pakistan/11031/.

Blasko, Dennis J. 2007. "PLA Ground Force Modernization and Mission Diversification: Underway in All Military Regions." *Right Sizing the People's*

Liberation Army: Exploring the Contours of China's Military, 281–374. Carlisle, PA: US Army War College Press.

Blasko, Dennis J. 2012. "Clarity of Intentions: People's Liberation Army Transregional Exercises to Defend China's Border." In Roy Kamphausen, David Lai, and Trevis Tanner (eds), *Learning by Doing: The PLA Trains at Home and Abroad*, 171–212. Carlisle, PA: US Army War College Press.

Blasko, Dennis J. 2016. "China's Contribution to Peacekeeping Operations: Understanding the Numbers." *China Brief* 16 (18): 3–7.

Cheng, Guangjing. 2010. "Chinese Combat Troops 'Can Join UN Peacekeeping'" *China Daily*. July 7. Accessed May 23, 2018. http://www.chinadaily.com.cn/china/2010–07/07/content_10073171.htm.

China Daily. 2002. "UN Praises China for Role in Peacekeeping." *China Daily*. August 22. Accessed May 4, 2018. http://www.chinadaily.com.cn/en/doc/2002–08/22/content_133184.htm.

China Daily. 2007. "Hu Puts Forward Principle on Darfur Issue." *China Daily*. February 5. Accessed July 30, 2018. http://www.chinadaily.com.cn/china/2007–02/05/content_801393.htm.

China Daily. 2008. "恐吓中国维和部队的苏丹军阀 [Sudanese Warlord Threatens Chinese Peacekeepers]." *China Daily*. January 1. Accessed March 7, 2019. http://www.chinadaily.com.cn/hqzx/2008–01/01/content_6362799.htm.

China.org. 2011. "China's Snow Leopard Commando Unit." China.org. May 4. Accessed October 6, 2017. http://www.china.org.cn/world/2011–05/04/content_22493737.htm.

Cho, Sunghee. 2018. "China's Participation in UN Peacekeeping Operations since the 2000s." *Journal of Contemporary China* 28 (117): 482–98.

Cohen, Michael D., James G. March, and Johan P. Olsen. 1972. "A Garbage Can Model of Organizational Choice." *Administrative Science Quarterly* 17 (1): 1–25.

Department of Trade and External Economic Relations Statistics, National Bureau of Statistics of China. Various years. 中国贸易外径统计年鉴 [*China Trade and External Economic Statistical Yearbook*]. Beijing: China Statistics Press.

Dong, Zhuhong. 2017. "检徽在亚丁湾闪耀 [The Badge of the Procurator Shines in the Gulf of Aden]." *Procurator Daily*. August 1. Accessed September 25, 2017. http://newspaper.jcrb.com/2017/20170801/20170801_004/20170801_004_1.htm.

Economist. 2006. "Coming Out." The Economist. March 23. Accessed March 9, 2018. https://www.economist.com/special-report/2006/03/23/coming-out.

Erickson, Andrew S. 2010. "Chinese Sea Power in Action: The Counter Piracy Mission in the Gulf of Aden and Beyond." In Roy D. Kamphausen, David Lai, and Andrew Scobell (eds), *The PLA at Home and Abroad: Assessing the*

Operational Capabilities of China's Military, 295–376. Carlisle, PA: US Army War College Press.

Erickson, Andrew S., and Austin M. Strange. 2013. "No Substitute for Experience: Chinese Antipiracy Operations in the Gulf of Aden." *U.S. Naval War College China Maritime Studies* 10.

Erickson, Andrew S., and Austin M. Strange. 2015. *Six Years at Sea...And Counting: Gulf of Aden Anti-Piracy and China's Maritime Commons Presence.* Washington DC: Jamestown Foundation.

Foot, Rosemary. 2014. "'Doing Some Things' in the Xi Jinping Era: The United Nations as China's Venue of Choice." *International Affairs* 90 (5): 1086–100.

Fravel, M. Taylor. 1996. "China's Attitude toward U.N. Peacekeeping Operations since 1989." *Asian Survey* 36 (11): 1102–21.

Fung, Courtney J. 2016. "What Explains China's Deployment to UN Peacekeeping Operations?" *International Relations of the Asia-Pacific* 16: 409–41.

Fung, Courtney J. 2019. *China and Intervention at the UN Security Council.* New York: Oxford University Press.

Fung, Courtney J. 2020. "Providing for Global Security: Implications of China's Combat Troop Deployment to UN Peacekeeping." *Global Governance* 25 (4): 509–34.

Garafola, Cristina L., and Timothy R. Heath. 2017. *The Chinese Air Force's First Steps toward Becoming an Expeditionary Air Force.* Santa Monica, CA: RAND Corporation.

Gill, Bates. 2007. *Rising Star.* Washington DC: Brookings Institution Press.

Grubb, Michael C. 2008. "A Comprehensive Survey of China's Dynamic Shipbuilding Industry." *China Maritime Studies* 1.

Guo, Yuandan. 2017. "利比亚撤侨海军舰长：海军具备全球遂行任务能力 [The Commander of the Warship of the Evacuation from Libya: The Navy Has the Capabilities to Perform Globally]." *Global Times.* August 8. Accessed February 3, 2018. http://mil.huanqiu.com/china/2017–08/11093856.html.

Guo, Yuandan. 2018. "中国海军解救商船 美军舰以挑剔目光在旁围观 [The Chinese Navy Rescues a Merchant Ship, American Warship Watches at Close Distance]." *Global Times.* December 27. Accessed December 27, 2018. http://mil.huanqiu.com/world/2018–12/13908898.html?agt=81.

Hai, Tao. 2009. "学者：'德新海'敲警钟 中国需要'远洋存在' [Scholar: The Case of the Dexinhai Sounds the Alarm, China Neds a 'Far-Seas Presence']." *Phoenix.* October 28. Accessed December 17, 2017. http://news.ifeng.com/mil/special/antipirates/comment/detail_2009_10/28/450444_0.shtml.

Hartnett, Daniel M. 2012a. "Looking Good on Paper: PLA Participation in the Peace Mission 2010 Multilateral Exercise." In Roy Kamphausen, David Lai, and Travis Tanner (eds), *Learning by Doing: The PLA Trains at Home and Abroad,* 213–58. Carlisle, PA: U.S. Army War College Press.

Hartnett, Daniel M. 2012b. "China's First Deployment of Combat Forces to a UN Peacekeeping Mission—South Sudan." U.S.-China Economic and Security Review Commission. March 13. Accessed November 27, 2017. http://www.uscc.gov/sites/default/files/Research/MEMO-PLA-PKO_final.pdf.

He, Wenping. 2013. "贺文萍：警惕'新干涉主义'在非洲合法化 [He Wenping: Attention! The 'New Interventionism' in Africa Is Being Legalized]." *Global Times*. January 18. Accessed February 3, 2019. http://opinion.huanqiu.com/opinion_world/2013-01/3523918.html.

Hirono, Miwa. 2011. "China's Charm Offensive and Peacekeeping: The Lessons of Cambodia—What Now for Sudan?" *International Peacekeeping* 18 (3): 328–43.

Hirono, Miwa, and Marc Lanteigne. 2011. "Introduction: China and UN Peacekeeping." *International Peacekeeping* 18 (3): 243–56.

Huang, Kristin. 2018. "Chinese Peacekeepers in Tense Stand-Off with Armed Militants in South Sudan." *South China Morning Post*. July 20. Accessed July 28, 2018. https://beta.scmp.com/news/china/diplomacy-defence/article/2127140/chinese-peacekeepers-tense-stand-armed-militants-south.

Hwang, Byong-Moo. 1997. "Changing Military Doctrines of the PRC: The Interaction between the People's War and Technology." *The Journal of East Asian Affairs* 11 (1): 221–66.

International Crisis Group. 2009. "China's Growing Role in Peacekeeping." International Crisis Group. April 17. Accessed Noverber 23, 2019. https://d2071andvip0wj.cloudfront.net/166-china-s-growing-role-in-un-peacekeeping.pdf.

Karlsrud, John. 2017. "Towards UN Counter-Terrorism Operations?" *Third World Quarterly* 38 (6): 1215–31.

Kennedy, Conor M. 2019. "Civil Transport in PLA Power Projection." *CMSI China Maritime Reports* 4.

Li, Chien-Pin. 2011. "Norm Entrepreneur or Interest Maximiser? China's Participation in UN Peacekeeping Operations, 2001–2010." *China: An International Journal* 9 (2): 313–27.

Lin-Greenberg, Erik. 2010. "Dragon Boats: Assessing China's Anti-Piracy Operations in the Gulf of Aden." *Defense & Security Analysis* 26 (2): 213–30.

Liu, Zhongmin. 2014. "中东变局以来中东恐怖主义的新发展及其根源 [The New Development of Terrorism in the Middle East and Its Root Causes]." *West Asia and Africa* (6): 4–18.

Lu, Wei, Qingjie Hao, and Na Li. 2018. "聚力打造军民融合战略投送保障劲旅 [Coming Together to Create Elite Civil-Military Fusion Strategic Projection Support]." *Civil-Military Integration* 2. Accessed December 7, 2019. https://www.xuehua.us/2018/08/10/%E8%81%9A%E5%8A%9B%E6%89%93%E9%80%A0%E5%86%9B%E6%B0%91%E8%9E%8D%E5%90%88%E6%88%98%E7%95%A5%E6%8A%95%E9%80%81%E4%BF%9D%E9%9A%9C%E5%8A%B2%E6%97%85/zh-hk/.

Lynch, Colum. 2014. "U.N. Peacekeepers to Protect China's Oil Interests in South Sudan." *Foreign Policy*. June 16. Accessed December 21, 2017. http://www.bbc.com/news/world-africa-25654155.

Ma, Li, ed. 2011. 国家行动: 利比亚大撤离 [*National Operation: The Great Evacuation from Libya*]. Beijing: People's Daily Press.

Masuda, Masayuki. 2011. "China's Peacekeeping Diplomacy and Troop Dispatch: A New Avenue for Engagement with the International Community." *NIDS Journal of Defense and Security* 12: 3–26.

News163. 2009. "德新海号被劫凸显索马里护航困境 [The Pirating of the Dexinhai Shows the Difficulties of Antipiracy Operations in Somalia]." *News163*. Accessed October 26, 2017. http://war.163.com/special/00013RNI/SomaliPiratesHijackChineseShipDeXinHai.html.

O'Rourke, Ronald. 2017. "China Naval Modernization: Implications for U.S. Navy Capabilities." *Congressional Research Service*. September 18. Accessed January 5, 2018. https://www.fas.org/sgp/crs/row/RL33153.pdf.

Pang, Zhongying. 2005. "China's Changing Attitude to UN Peacekeeping." *International Peacekeeping* 12 (1): 87–104.

Peck, Michael. 2018. "China Is Tripling the Size of Its Marine Corps." *The National Interest*. August 29. Accessed September 2, 2018. https://nationalinterest.org/blog/buzz/china-tripling-size-its-marine-corps-29942.

People's Daily. 2015. "中国将在吉布提建设后勤保障设施 [China Builds Logistic Facilities in Djibouti]." *People's Daily*. November 26. Accessed November 26, 2018. http://world.people.com.cn/n/2015/1126/c157278-27860707.html.

PLA AMS. 2013. 战略学 [*The Science of Military Strategy*]. Beijing: Military Science Press.

PRC Central Government. 2014. "中国维和部队积极应对南苏丹紧张局势履行维和义务 [Chinese Peacekeepers Actively Respond to Emergency Situations in South Sudan and Fulfil Their Duties]." *Xinhua*. January 3. Accessed September 21, 2018. http://www.gov.cn/jrzg/2014–01/03/content_2559512.htm.

PRC MOD. 2015. "A Look into Chinese Peacekeeping Infantry Battalion." PRC Ministry of National Defense. April 10. Accessed January 21, 2019. http://eng.mod.gov.cn/DefenseNews/2015–04/10/content_4579404.htm.

PRC MOFCOM, National Bureau of Statistics of China, PRC State Administration of Foreign Exchange. Various years. "中国对外直接投资统计公报 [Statistical Bulletin of China's Outward Foreign Direct Investment]." Beijing. http://hzs.mofcom.gov.cn/article/date/201512/20151201223578.shtml.

Prins, Brandon, Ursula Daxecker, and Anup Phayal. 2017. "Somali Pirates Just Hijacked an Oil Tanker. Here's What Pirates Want—and Where They Strike."

The Washington Post. March 14. Accessed October 11, 2017. https://www.washingtonpost.com/news/monkey-cage/wp/2017/01/25/what-do-pirates-want-to-steal-riches-at-sea-so-they-can-pay-for-wars-on-land/?utm_term=.178ce33ed621.

Qilu Evening News. 2015. "战乱中的中国驻外使馆 [Chinese Embassies in the Midst of War]." *Qilu Evening News*. August 21. Accessed March 9, 2018. http://dubaocankao.com/html/news/hqlw/2015/0821/6310.html.

Qiu, Chengliang. 2018. "中国第六批赴马里维和部队正式组建 [The Sixth Batch of Peacekeepers to Mali Is Officially Assembled]." *Xinhua*. April 18. Accessed May 19, 2018. http://www.xinhuanet.com/world/2018–04/18/c_129853363.htm.

Railway Technology. 2014. "Mali Signs $11bn Agreements with China for New Rail Projects." *Railway Technology*. September 16. Accessed May 21, 2018. https://www.railway-technology.com/uncategorised/newsmali-signs-agreements-with-china-for-new-rail-projects-4375202/.

Shichor, Yitzhak. 2007. "China's Darfur Policy." *China Brief* 7.

Sina.com. 2009. "我护航编队前往营救被劫货轮 [Our Naval Escort Goes to Rescue the Pirated Cargo]." *Sina.com*. October 21. Accessed October 23, 2018. http://news.sina.com.cn/o/2009-10-21/022716470497s.shtml.

Sina.com. 2017. "回忆海外撤侨死里逃生：'军舰来了 祖国万岁' [Recalling the Overseas Evacuation of Overseas Chinese: 'The Warship Is Coming, Long Live the Motherland']." *Sina.com*. November 26. Accessed January 3, 2018. http://news.sina.com.cn/c/nd/2017-11-26/doc-ifypathz6007582.shtml.

Sinodefense. 2008. "People's Armed Police Beijing General Corps." *Web.archive*. February 4. Accessed January 3, 2019. https://web.archive.org/web/20080410195836/http://www.sinodefence.com/organisation/armedpolice/beijing-gc.asp.

Song, Zhongping. 2015. "中国海外基地的梦想与现实 [The Dream and the Reality of China's Military Base Overseas]." *International Herald Leader*. June 17. Accessed May 28, 2018. http://www.xinhuanet.com/herald/2015–06/17/c_134335194.htm.

Storey, Ian. 2006. "China and East Timor: Good, but Not Best Friends." *China Brief* 6 (14).

Styan, David. 2019. "China's Maritime Silk Road and Small States: Lessons from the Case of Djibouti." *Journal of Contemporary China*. doi:https://doi.org/10.1080/10670564.2019.1637567.

Suliman, Kabbashi M., and Ahmed A. A. Badawi. 2010. "An Assessment of the Impact of China's Investments in Sudan." *Africa Portal*. Accessed November 21, 2017. http://dspace.africaportal.org/jspui/bitstream/123456789/32436/1/Sudan-China-FDI-relations.pdf?1.

Sun, Yanxin, and Hongliang Zhu. 2017. "第一批护航编队：开创中国海军史上多项第一 [The First Chinese Naval Taskforce Breaks Multiple Records in the History of the Chinese People's Navy]." *Xinhua*. August 17. Accessed March 4, 2018. http://www.xinhuanet.com/2017–08/17/c_1121500917.htm.

Suzuki, Shogo. 2008. "Seeking 'Legitimate' Great Power Status in Post-Cold War International Society: China's and Japan's Participation in UNPKO." *International Relations* 22 (1): 45–63.

Tang, Yongsheng. 2002. "中国与联合国维和行动 [China and United Nations Peacekeeping Operations]." *World Economics and Politics* 9: 39–44.

Teitt, Sarah. 2011. "The Responsibility to Protect and China's Peacekeeping Policy." *International Peacekeeping* 18 (3): 298–312.

UN. 2016. "Executive Summary of the Independent Special Investigation into the Violence Which Occurred in Juba in 2016 and UNMISS Response." United Nations. November 1. Accessed November 9, 2017. http://www.un.org/News/dh/infocus/sudan/Public_Executive_Summary_on_the_Special_Investigation_Report_1_Nov_2016.pdf.

UNSC. 2007. "Resolution 1769 (2007)." UN Security Council. July 31. Accessed November 25, 2017. http://www.un.org/ga/search/view_doc.asp?symbol=S/RES/1769(2007).

UNSC. 2013a. "Resolution 2100 (2013)." UN Security Council. April 25. Accessed April 26, 2019. https://www.securitycouncilreport.org/wp-content/uploads/s_res_2100.pdf.

UNSC. 2013b. "Resolution 2098 (2013)." United Nations. March 28. Accessed November 25, 2017. https://undocs.org/S/RES/2098(2013).

UNSC. 2014. "Security Council, Adopting Resolution 2155 (2014), Extends Mandate of Mission in South Sudan, Bolstering Its Strength to Quell Surging Violence." United Nations. May 27. Accessed November 25, 2017. https://www.un.org/press/en/2014/sc11414.doc.htm.

UNSC. 2016. "Resolution 2295 (2016)." UN Security Council. June 29. Accessed November 26, 2017. https://www.securitycouncilreport.org/wp-content/uploads/s_res_2295.pdf.

van der Putten, Frans Paul. 2015. "China's Evolving Role in Peacekeeping and African Security." Clingendael Report. September 14. Accessed December 21, 2018.https://www.clingendael.org/publication/chinas-evolving-role-peacekeeping-and-african-security.

van Staden, Cobus. 2018. "Can China Realize Africa's Dream of an East-West Transport Link?" *China Brief* 18 (6): 9–12.

Vasselier, Abigaël. 2016. "Chinese Foreign Policy in South Sudan: The View from the Ground." *China Brief* 16 (12): 15–19.

Wu, Jiao, and Kuang Peng. 2008. "Sailing to Strengthen Global Security." *Xinhua*. December 26. Accessed September 2, 2017. http://www.chinadaily.com.cn/china/2008–12/26/content_7342612.htm.

Wu, Sike. 2019. "中东特使吴思科：捍卫正义，中国连续三次动用安理会否决权 [Special Envoy to the Middle East Wu Sike: Protecting Justice and China's Three Vetoes at the United Nations]." *Beijing Daily*. September 21. Accessed October 13, 2019. http://www.bjd.com.cn/a/201909/21/WS5d8570f9e4b0081bfdf29bd4.html.

Wu, Wenbin, and Tongchen Cui. 2012. "中国驻苏维和部队官兵辩证看待华工被劫事件 [Chinese Peacekeepers in Sudan Look at the Kidnapping of Chinese Workers Dialectically]." *Jiangsu Daily*. February 6. Accessed March 21, 2018. http://js.people.com.cn/html/2012/02/06/75416.html.

Wu, Yuwen. 2014. "China's Oil Fears over South Sudan Fighting." *BBC News*. January 8. Accessed March 26, 2019. http://www.bbc.com/news/world-africa-25654155.

Wuthnow, Joel. 2013. *Chinese Diplomacy and the UN Security Council*. London: Routledge.

Xinhua. 2009. "Hijacked Chinese Bulk Carrier Rescued." *China Daily*. December 28. Accessed November 25, 2017. http://www.chinadaily.com.cn/china/2009–12/28/content_9235846.htm.

Xinhua. 2011. "大撤侨也凸显中国软肋：徐州号上阵存在偶然因素 [The Evacuation of Chinese Highlights China's Weakness: There Is an Accidental Factor in the Operation of the Xuzhou]." *Phoenix*. March 7. Accessed February 5, 2019. http://news.ifeng.com/mil/4/detail_2011_03/07/5012988_0.shtml.

Xinhua. 2012. "China Values Self-Defense in Peacekeeping Operations." *China. org*. February 23. Accessed November 23, 2017. http://www.china.org.cn/world/2012–02/23/content_24715382.htm.

Xinhua. 2016. "外交官也是人，谁来保护他们的安全？ [The Diplomats Are Human, Who Protects Them?]." *Xinhua*. December 21. Accessed October 25, 2018. http://www.xinhuanet.com/world/2016–12/21/c_129413954_2.htm.

Xinhua. 2018a. "Facts & Figures: China's Overseas Peacekeeping Operations." *China Daily*. August 1. Accessed September 19, 2018. http://www.chinadaily.com.cn/china/2017–08/01/content_30320744.htm.

Xinhua. 2018b. "China Sends New Naval Fleet for Escort Mission." *China Daily*. December 9. Accessed September 1, 2018. http://usa.chinadaily.com.cn/a/201812/09/WS5c0cf250a310eff30328feef.html.

Yu, Lei. 2018. "中国首支维和直升机分队完成轮换交接 [The First Peacekeeping Helicopter Unit Completes the Handover]." *Xinhua*. August 28. Accessed September 1, 2018. http://www.xinhuanet.com/world/2018–08/28/c_1123342289.htm.

Yung, Cristopher D., Ross Rustici, Isaac Kardon, and Joshua Wisema. 2010. "China's Out of Area Naval Operations: Case Studies, Trajectories, Obstacles, and Potential Solutions." *China Strategic Perspectives*. https://ndupress.ndu. edu/Portals/68/Documents/stratperspective/china/ChinaPerspectives-3.pdf.

Zhang, Huan. 2017. "Expert Says China's Self-Developed Beidou System Performs Better than GPS." *People's Daily*. September 23. Accessed March 18, 2019. http://en.people.cn/n3/2017/0928/c90000-9274508.html.

Zhang, Qian. 2014. "How Much Does PLA Soldier's Individual Equipment Cost?" *People's Daily*. December 6. Accessed January 30, 2017. http://en.people. cn/n/2014/1206/c90000-8819167.html.

Zhang, Tao. 2015. "China's Peacekeeping Equipment Questioned." PRC Ministry of National Defense. January 4. Accessed March 2, 2018. http://eng.mod.gov. cn/DefenseNews/2015–01/04/content_4561933.htm.

Zhao, Keshi. 2013. "新形势下加快我军后勤现代化的战略思考 [Strategic Thoughts on Accelerating Modernization of PLA Logistics in the New Situation]." *China Military Science* 4: 1–10.

Conclusion

The perception that other states are more centralized and better organized than they actually are, as Robert Jervis (1976, 319–42) pointed out in his classic *Perception and Misperception in International Politics*, is a common phenomenon in international relations. Today, one of the most widely shared myths about China is how its political model is unique because it has succeeded in completing large-scale projects, from building the longest bridge in the world to lifting hundreds of millions of people out of poverty, in a quick and effective way. Dazzled by those achievements, regardless of their actual success, both supporters and detractors often take them as evidence of China's capacity to play the long game, to work out and execute complex strategies. After all, when so much time has been spent, so many sacrifices made, so many resources consumed, there must be a plan. Every headline, every announcement, every statement about the next big project reinforces this myth. Myths like this appear useful and are easily accepted because they help us to simplify reality and justify our actions. They conveniently spare us having to look at what lies beneath the surface. This is why they are created and why they are dangerous when they are used as foundations for political arguments at times of growing tensions in international affairs.

Especially outside of China, contemporary perceptions of Chinese intentions are that Beijing is aiming to replace the West, the United States in particular, at the top of the international system. While discussing the veracity of this argument is well beyond the scope of this study, the aim of this book is to contribute to the discussion of Chinese foreign policy, at least in relation to its military presence outside Asia, and to make it more nuanced in two ways. First, the argument presented here is that the deployment of Chinese soldiers in critical regions like the Middle East and North Africa is not symbolic but, at least until today, it has not been motivated by the desire to erode American supremacy in those regions either. The argument linking it to a Sino-American struggle in Asia is feeble too. Rather, the process that led Chinese policymakers to opt for a more flexible use of the armed forces beyond traditional territorial defense was related to the need to manage non-traditional security issues abroad. This is because, either through international cooperation or by protecting Chinese nationals and assets abroad, doing so was, and certainly still is, beneficial in boosting the chances of survival of the regime. Second, as a Chinese saying goes, "Every story is made of coincidences," and the one narrated in this book is no exception.[1] The vast majority of the events related to China's interest frontiers were hardly the result of a well-thought-out plan. As in other countries, all the actors involved in the formulation and implementation of the response to the threats against Chinese citizens and companies abroad had their own interests, preferences, and ways to further these. This final chapter, therefore, comments on the main feature of this tortuous process and, finally, examines the implications for how we understand and deal with China.

The Power of Crises

Chinese policymakers have long focused on how to solve problems within China while paying less attention to the repercussions of these decisions outside the country. This is what Edward Luttwak (2012) labeled "great-state autism." As he puts it:

> in all great states there is so much internal activity that leaders and opinion-makers cannot focus seriously on foreign affairs as well, except in particular times of crisis. They do not have the constant situational awareness of the world around them.
>
> (Luttwak 2012, 13)

While in Luttwak's analysis, the problem lies in the lack of attention to the points of view of external observers, in the case of China's interest frontiers it was a partial lack of awareness regarding the situation of Chinese nationals and companies abroad. Interestingly, it seems that the problem was made worse by the risk-accepting behavior of those who suffered the most because of it, that is, Chinese investors and contractors abroad.

This issue can be observed to different degrees in a number of cases. As highlighted in Chapter 1, the first case is that of how civilian elites have been managing non-traditional security issues since the 1990s. It began with a legitimacy crisis at home and abroad in the wake of the events in Tiananmen Square in 1989, which was further aggravated by the implosion of the Soviet

---

[1] In Chinese: 无巧不成书 (Wú qiǎo bù chéng shū).

Union in 1991. Non-traditional security became one of the pillars of the bridge that China built with its neighbors first, and the wider world later on. By the mid-2000s, the Hu Jintao administration was beginning to worry about the security implications of the expansion of Chinese economic activities abroad and, consequently, terms like "development interest" and "new historic missions" appeared in documents published in those years. At the same time, the Ministry of Foreign Affairs (MFA) was commanded to improve its response to incidents involving Chinese nationals abroad that were by then starting to become frequent. Yet the real catalyst behind the militarization of China's response to non-traditional security threats was the evacuation of almost 36,000 Chinese nationals from Libya in 2011. Taking place at a delicate moment in Chinese political life, the Libyan incident disrupted the formulation of China's security strategy and significantly contributed to the identification of Chinese nationals and assets abroad as the main referent object of the securitization act. Hence, it was a crisis that, once again, increased the sensibility of Chinese decision-makers about non-traditional security issues, provoking a change in Chinese foreign policy.

The second example, as Chapter 4 shows, is the limited influence that the community of foreign policy experts had, at least before 2011, in a period during which the top Chinese leadership did not travel to the regions where China's interest frontiers first emerged. The information gathered and analyzed by Chinese diplomats abroad and area studies experts in China probably hit a number of obstacles on its way to the desks of the top decision-makers. Since the Arab Spring was not foreseen by the vast majority of experts around the world, it is unlikely that the events analyzed in this book would have been significantly different, even in the case of better communication between the Chinese policymakers and the foreign policy community. However, while the precise moment and place of the emergence of China's interest frontiers was impossible to predict, even Chinese media reported that the unpreparedness of Chinese companies in North Africa and the Middle East to face large-scale security crises was a well-known fact, at least within the MFA. As for the community of regional experts in universities and think tanks, it is still in the early stages of development and its influence and capabilities are relatively limited. After 2011, the situation began to improve thanks to a mix of concerns among policymakers, growing interest among better-connected international relations scholars, and increasing attention paid by public opinion to the security of Chinese interests overseas.

The third case that one can list among the effects of "great-state autism" is the continuity in the intensity of political support for policies aimed at making

Chinese companies "go global." Economic necessities motivated the formulation of Deng Xiaoping's reform, Jiang Zemin's Go Global strategy, and Xi Jinping's Belt and Road Initiative (BRI). Hu Jintao, too, promoted these kinds of policies. Although there is no documentation publicly available, it is probable that the incidents regarding Chinese companies and citizens abroad were not numerous when Deng and Jiang were thinking about the need for Chinese companies to invest abroad as part of the effort to strengthen ties between China and the world economy. Hu Jintao and, especially, Xi Jinping had to face a significantly different situation. Yet the intensity of the promotion of Chinese economic overseas activities grew in parallel with the clarification of the nature and scope of the challenges of China's interest frontiers, that is, a growing awareness of threats overseas. Moreover, Xi Jinping's BRI mostly targets developing countries, many with well-known security problems. The relative easing of the procedures to carry out investments abroad discussed in Chapter 3 further indicates that, despite the emphasis on making the companies responsible for the security of their economic operations, economic considerations apparently still trump security ones. At the same time, the leading role assigned to the state-owned enterprises (SOEs), regardless of their self-protection capabilities, continues to make China's economic and human presence in unstable regions of the globe more dependent on domestic political considerations than solely risk-assessment calculations, as would be the case for private companies.

Coordination in Policymaking

As pointed out by Sebastian Heilmann (2017), Chinese policymaking is characterized by cycles of decentralization, during which different institutions and organizations are able to pursue their own interests, and reassertion of the authority of the central leadership through anticorruption and institutional reorganization campaigns. The emergence of the problem of China's interest frontiers occurred between the end of a period of decentralization/fragmentation and the dawn of one of strong recentralization of power, with the arrival of Xi Jinping. To some extent, it even contributed to accelerating it. This can be seen at three different levels: civil-military relations, inter-ministerial relations, and, to a lesser extent, party-state relations.

A good analyst should always be careful not to misinterpret the normally intricate and non-linear patterns of interaction between large organizations as political clashes between them (Freedman 1976). Moreover, the matter at hand can hardly be seen as a reason for a serious fracture between civilians and soldiers in China. However, as far as the available sources mentioned in Chapter 2 can tell us, it seems that, for some years, civilian leaders and the armed forces have had different opinions about the need to have the Chinese People's Liberation Army (PLA) involved in operations abroad. The difference between their opinions, as hypothesized by scholars, became evident as soon as one looked beyond the traditional cases discussed by foreign observers, such as the territorial defense of China and its reunification with Taiwan, over which civilian and military elites have long shared the same or extremely close opinions. The PLA's behavior confirmed Stephen D. Krasner's argument (1972) that organizational interests are more influential when it comes to the implementation of new policies than during the making of them.

As the literature on organizational processes and foreign policy tells us, it is usually in moments of crisis that this kind of problem emerges. Hence, "failure and civilian intervention go hand in hand," wrote Barry R. Posen (1984, 57). This is what appears to best explain the sudden and radical change in position and actions of the PLA after 2011. The PLA's role before and during the evacuation from Libya was not as pivotal as the media portrayed it, although the air force did make a substantial contribution. At the same time, the evolution of civil-military relations under Hu Jintao, reportedly, was cause for concern for Xi Jinping, and rumors of corruption were widespread (Li 2017). Against this background, it is not difficult to imagine that, motivated by the fear that another Libya-like crisis could take place and result in the deaths of Chinese nationals, the civilian leadership intervened in the doctrinal affairs of the PLA, as part of a vast reorganization and anticorruption campaign launched by Xi Jinping shortly after he took power. Meanwhile, of course, it is likely that many within the PLA favored change because the purpose of the organization is to protect Chinese citizens.

At the same time, while the MFA remains the chief agency for monitoring and protecting Chinese citizens abroad, it seems that the human, economic, and political resources at its disposal have not grown in proportion to the tasks assigned to it. As mentioned in Chapter 6, the evacuation from Libya almost exhausted the emergency budget of the MFA and put a strain on its personnel. Moreover, it is important to keep in mind the Ministry of Commerce (MOFCOM)'s leading role in Chinese economic foreign policy, which is likely to influence the MFA's operations in countries where China's human footprint mostly consists of laborers. For example, while there was no certainty around the number of evacuees in 2011, MOFCOM apparently did not coordinate with the MFA in sending its delegations to look for business opportunities in Libya, despite the dangerous situation. Therefore, it is not so surprising that the commander of the frigate *Xuzhou* later declared that he had not received sufficient information to play a larger role during the evacuation.

The recent promotions of senior figures like Wang Yi and Yang Jiechi within the foreign policy institutions of the State Council and Chinese Communist Party (CCP), respectively, should decisively increase the ability of the foreign affairs apparatus to provide information to the top leadership and oversee the operations of other ministries so that they do not undermine China's foreign policy and security. Moreover, the recent reforms of the agencies and ministries of the State Council, the upgrade of the CCP Central Foreign Affairs Leading Small Group into a Commission, and the establishment of the CCP Central National Security Commission (CNSC) should help to solve the problems of top-down interagency coordination. However, the creation of the China International Development Cooperation Agency, and the looming presence of the National Development and Reform Commission risk limiting the MFA's input in the management and protection of Chinese economic activities abroad in the context of the BRI, thereby further restricting the ability of its officials to prevent the emergence of new problems.

Finally, as the party began to expand its already long reach beyond policy-making to policy implementation, the autonomy of state institutions decreased. In particular, it did so in two ways after 2011. First, the creation of the CCP CNSC and the CCP Leading Small Group for Advancing the Development of the One Belt One Road has increased the number of party organizations with authority over foreign policy. Although their focus is different, they overlap to some extent in terms of competencies as well as members shared with the CCP Central Foreign Affairs Commission. While the CCP CNSC is meant to be a highly influential and permanent body, the CCP Leading Small Group for Advancing the Development of the One Belt One Road is simply task-oriented and, therefore, less influential than the commission.

Second, the control of the party over the actions of SOEs has been strengthened via the CCP Central Commission for Discipline Inspection to fight corruption and prevent the creation of powerful interest groups within the state-owned economy. The stronger role of the party in the management of the career paths of top managers of SOEs is clearly aimed at problems other than the misbehavior of those companies abroad, although there is no reason to believe that the CCP Central Commission for Discipline Inspection would not intervene in the case of a serious diplomatic incident. Nonetheless, the strengthening of the control of the party over the activities of ministries and agencies of the State Council is not a simple translation of ideology into practice. Rather, these developments seem to underscore the need for Chinese leaders to find better ways to control the vast bureaucracy of the party, state, and armed forces beneath them.

Old and New Problems, Old and New Solutions

In 2012, Henry Kissinger wrote that:

> China's recent military build-up is not in itself an exceptional phenomenon: the more unusual outcome would be if the world's second-largest economy and largest importer of natural resources did not translate its economic power into some increased military capacity.
>
> (Kissinger 2012, 48)

Although he made this observation in the context of Sino-American relations, it can also fit easily into the story of China's turbulent interest frontiers. Indeed, it would have been surprising if China did not have problems with the protection of its expanding interests overseas. It would have been surprising too if the consensus on the need to develop and employ military means to deal with those problems had not emerged. China, therefore, does not seem different from other great powers in history: it too has to face the problem of "turbulent frontiers" and is looking at its armed forces to do so.

For the moment, it might seem that China has found a good compromise between what is necessary and what it can do. The analysis in Chapters 6 and 7 offer a good example of this. Chinese policymakers have seemingly behaved in the way Jack Snyder's unitary executive model (1993) predicted: they have been cautious in not over-expanding the country's military footprint abroad while checking, or at least doing their best to check, against both parochial and diffuse interests whenever necessary. Over the years, a number of Chinese nationals have lost their lives, while many more have lost their jobs or their assets. Yet those losses, however tragic and economically significant, represent an extremely small fraction of the hundreds of thousands of Chinese people and of the billions of RMB invested in dangerous places around the globe.

From this point of view, China has not done badly, especially if one considers its minimal military investment. Moreover, there is also another issue that is worth considering and that contributes to a positive assessment of Chinese actions. Not only are the so-called "wars amongst the people" extremely painful for those who fight them and for those who live in the countries they are fought in (Smith 2007), but military interventions against/in a foreign country to protect or boost economic interests usually achieve the opposite outcome (Zachary, Deloughery, and Downes 2017). Hence, since the main threat to Chinese interests originates from the host country's inability to provide a safe environment, and a total military occupation seems very far from being Beijing's favorite option, helping local governments, instead of changing them, is probably the least bad solution in economic terms. China did this through its participation in and support of United Nations-mandated operations, which is another commendable decision, given the lack of well-trained and well-equipped troops that plagues international peacekeeping.

The problem, however, is that this innovative solution might not be politically sustainable in the long run, especially from a domestic point of view. This is where new solutions cannot solve an old problem. While the superior cost-effectiveness of peacekeeping operations is well known in comparison to unilateral interventions in solving the kinds of problems that China has on its interest frontiers, a soft and rather passive approach like that adopted by Beijing is difficult to sell domestically in a country where military modernization is an important part of government propaganda (Ross 2009). Chapter 5 showed that, while Chinese Internet users might rally around the flag when soldiers are victims of attacks or accused of misconduct by UN reports or Western media, they are more critical when Chinese nationals are in danger in countries where Chinese soldiers are deployed. This is especially true now that the PLA is not simply looking more capable of operating overseas, but is in fact really becoming so.

The domestic narrative about the defense of interests overseas is largely composed of implicit and explicit comparisons between China and other countries, especially the United States. The mimicking of the symbols of American power in movies and official media cannot but raise the expectations of the public and the armed forces. At the same time, even Chinese military scholars have pointed out that a substantial reformation of the principles that have long guided foreign policy is necessary if China wants to be serious about the use of military tools in protecting its interest frontiers. Therefore, the government will have to be increasingly careful in choosing between the costs associated with an unsatisfied public and those related to a dramatic change in its foreign policy and international orientation.

As some scholars argue, it is too early for China to talk about strategic overstretch as long as its material power grows and the government is able to define its goals clearly (Pu and Wang 2018). China, a Chinese expert commented, must be ready to pay a price for its military presence in peacekeeping operations that contribute to the stability of dangerous regions of the world (Ma 2016). However, while domestic public opinion and policymakers might be prepared, and willing, to pay an even higher price to protect their compatriots, every hint as well as every real step toward a more proactive use of the PLA outside China is met, and will keep being met, with suspicion by other countries. While the literature on Chinese Military Operations Other Than War outlined in the Introduction of this book indicates that the Western academic community is inclined to interpret those operations in a negative way, other studies have shown how military operations ostensibly aimed at addressing common non-traditional security threats have not been conducive to cooperation in Asia. On the contrary, they have become a new platform for competing countries to show off their military prowess (Lin-Greenberg 2018). Regardless of what Chinese policymakers decide, the protection of their interest frontiers will remain a thorny issue for years to come and they will have, one way or another, to spend significant amounts of political capital to solve it.

Final Considerations

Besides the specific issue of China's military footprint abroad, especially to defend its interests overseas against non-traditional security threats, this book aims to offer as clear a picture as possible of the intricacies and factors that make Chinese foreign policymaking a phenomenon that is both difficult to study and easy to get wrong. The Chinese political system remains as opaque as its values are different from those in the West. Understanding this does not mean eliminating the problems that exist; however, it greatly helps to avoid new ones.

Hence, policymakers who happen to read this book are advised to avoid simplifications and thinking that every Chinese move is aimed at achieving some sort of grand (vicious) goal. Like many other governments, especially in large countries, the Chinese government is constantly preoccupied with domestic issues and with the control of the vast bureaucracy beneath it. The problem of protecting Chinese interest frontiers is fueling the need for a Chinese military presence in regions that are also of great interest to the United States and its allies. While China is mostly an economic competitor in those regions, its military presence is far from being as threatening as, for example, Russia's is. Given the cautious approach of Chinese policymakers to the protection of their country's interests overseas, Beijing is unlikely to want to become a threat in any way, as this would represent an enormous political, diplomatic, and military gamble.

Yet Western military operations have, as in Libya, damaged Chinese interests in certain cases. As China's capacity to deploy military assets outside Asia develops, it would not be strange if they were also to be used to impede

Western actions that do not take China's preferences into consideration. China has been very careful so far in avoiding getting involved in thorny issues in the Middle East or elsewhere outside Asia. However, given the domestic attitude to the protection of their interest frontiers, perceived provocations might not go without a response in the future. Even without a direct confrontation, China has the resources to signal its resolve and increase the costs for Western countries' actions. For example, joint deployments of Chinese and Russian forces, or similar actions in support of regional partners, would be hard to ignore and could significantly complicate the situation for Western and local decision-makers. This eventuality should not be overlooked, and China's interests should not be ignored.

From this point of view, scholars and analysts can play a critical role. Abandoning the belief that China is a monolith is both necessary and possible. Much of the argument of this book is based on an analysis of the growing number of publicly available Chinese sources—many of which can be easily accessed online and are updated regularly by the various agencies of the Chinese government. These sources reveal the reasoning of the different branches of the Chinese policymaking system. Many of the dynamics that regulate their behavior are similar to those in the West. As discussed in the Appendices of this book, much of what comes out in Chinese journals and databases ought to be taken with a grain of salt. However, as long as scholars are able to find the appropriate sources and willing to spend time doing that, there is every reason to believe that the fruits of that labor will be highly valued by both the academic and the policy community.

Finally, it is important to point out that there are numerous other areas of Chinese politics where deeply ingrained assumptions held by external observers have created limits to our understanding. This book simply focuses on one of the most relevant, but least studied cases. China changes quickly; we should be ready to follow it.

Bibliography

Freedman, Lawrence. 1976. "Logic, Politics and Foreign Policy Processes: A Critique of the Bureaucratic Politics Model." *Foreign Affairs* 52 (3): 434–49.

Heilmann, Sebastian. 2017. "China's Core Executive: Pursuing National Agendas in a Fragmented Polity." In Vivienne Shue and Patricia M. Thornton (eds), *To Govern China: Evolving Practices of Power*, 107–48. New York: Cambridge University Press.

Jervis, Robert. 1976. *Perception and Misperception in International Politics*. II. Princeton, NJ: Princeton University Press.

Kissinger, Henry A. 2012. "The Future of U.S.-Chinese Relations: Conflict Is a Choice, Not a Necessity." *Foreign Affairs* 91 (2): 44–55.

Krasner, Stephen D. 1972. "Are Bureaucracies Important? (Or Allison Wonderland)." *Foreign Policy* 7: 159–79.

Li, Xiaoting. 2017. "Cronyism and Military Corruption in the Post-Deng Xiaoping Era: Rethinking the Party-Commands-the-Gun Model." *Journal of Contemporary China* 26 (107): 696–710.

Lin-Greenberg, Erik. 2018. "Non-Traditional Security Dilemmas: Can Military Operations Other Than War Intensify Security Competition in Asia?" *Asian Security* 14 (3): 282–302.

Luttwak, Edward. 2012. *The Rise of China vs. the Logic of Strategy*. Cambridge, MA: Belknap Press of Harvard University Press.

Ma, Xiaolin. 2016. "马晓霖: 中国参与维和的冷思考 [Ma Xiaolin: A Cold Assessment of China's Participation in Peacekeeping Operations]." *Beijing Youth Daily*. June 4. Accessed March 29, 2018. http://epaper.ynet.com/html/2016-06/04/content_201565.htm?div=-1.

Posen, Barry R. 1984. *The Sources of Military Doctrine: France, Britain, and Germany between the World Wars*. Ithaca, NY: Cornell University Press.

Pu, Xiaoyu, and Chengli Wang. 2018. "Rethinking China's Rise: Chinese Scholars Debate Strategic Overstretch." *International Affairs* 94 (5): 1019–35.

Ross, Robert S. 2009. "China's Naval Nationalism: Sources, Prospects, and the U.S. Response." *International Security* 34 (2): 46–81.

Smith, Rupert. 2007. *The Utility of Force: The Art of War in the Modern World*. New York: Random House.

Snyder, Jack. 1993. *Myths of Empire: Domestic Politics and International Ambition*. Ithaca, NY: Cornell University Press.

Zachary, Paul, Kathleen Deloughery, and Alexander B. Downes. 2017. "No Business Like FIRC Business: Foreign-Imposed Regime Change and Bilateral Trade." *British Journal of Political Science* 47 (4): 749–82.

Appendices

APPENDIX 1

List of Countries and Comments on Sources

Countries included in the definition of the Middle East: Bahrain, Egypt, Iran, Iraq, Israel, Jordan, Kuwait, Lebanon, Oman, Palestine/West Bank and Gaza, Qatar, Saudi Arabia, Syria, Turkey, United Arab Emirates, and Yemen.

Countries included in the definition of North Africa: Algeria, Djibouti, Eritrea, Ethiopia, Libya, Mali, Morocco, Somalia, South Sudan, Sudan, and Tunisia.

The bulk of the analysis in Chapter 1 is based on the analysis of five kinds of sources: the *Selected Works* compiled by the Central Literature Editing Committee of the Chinese Communist Party (CCP) and published by the People's Publishing House, reports on the work of the government, the speeches of leaders and high-ranking officials published by Chinese media, and defense white papers.[1] Finally, despite their much lower level of authoritativeness, the analysis has to include assessments by Chinese and foreign scholars of the changes in China's foreign and security policy in order to better interpret the words of the civilian leadership.

Including defense white papers might be seen as controversial, and it is therefore important to explain this. Behind the drafting of defense white papers, there are usually uniformed officers from the National Defense Policy Center of the Chinese People's Liberation Army (PLA) Academy of Military Science (AMS). Major General Chen Zhou, the director of the center, for example, was the leader of the team from the PLA AMS that worked on the latest defense white papers. The white paper is then approved by the Central Military Commission (CMC) of the CCP, the State Council, and the Ministry of National Defense. Since the Ministry of National Defense has no real authority and the State Council has very little influence in the drafting of the documents, the white papers might seem predominantly military documents that should not be relied on to extrapolate the position of civilians.

Nonetheless, as Timothy R. Heath (2015, 21–2) has written, documents like these are largely built on how civilians define the concepts of national security and national defense, and the role the PLA has to play. PLA officers, then, "may add detail and expand on the direction provided by the central leadership, but they may not undermine or contradict the national level decision." Hence, despite the heavy military participation in the writing process, the defense white papers ought to be considered primarily as a civilian documents. The white papers, thanks to their English translation, have an important communicative role in response to calls from the international community for greater transparency about military affairs. They, therefore, can hardly be seen as proper military-strategic documents, but more like a political/diplomatic message from China's top leadership to Chinese citizens and other countries. To sum up, the defense white papers are the military platform for the civilian

---

[1] In the case of Xi Jinping, the books taken into consideration are *The Governance of China* (CCP Central Policy Research Office 2014) and *Excerpts of Xi Jinping's Discussions Related to the Comprehensive National Security Concept* (CCP Central Literature Research Center 2018).

leaders to express their thoughts about security, while those on other issues are conveyed through other white papers and reports on the work of the government.

As for Chapters 2 and 6, the analysis focuses on the relationship between the PLA and non-traditional security issues in foreign policy. The best publicly accessible place to observe trends in Chinese military thinking consistently is the publications of the PLA AMS and the PLA National Defense University (NDU), the two most important institutions of the Chinese professional military education system. The PLA AMS, China's foremost military think tank, is an institution under the command of the CCP CMC. Founded in 1958, and modeled on the Soviet General Staff Academy, the PLA AMS conducts research on all aspects of military affairs and doctrine, including foreign militaries, campaign tactics, military organization, strategy, theory of war, and military history. The PLA AMS publishes important texts, like *The Science of Military Strategy* and *The Science of Campaigns*, and its officers are involved in the drafting of China's biannual defense white papers as well as other speeches and documents for PLA leaders.[2] As for the PLA NDU, it was established in 1985 to become the PLA's top institution for the training of senior officers. Commanding officers go there prior to their promotion (Shambaugh 2002, 178).

The PLA AMS publishes *China Military Science*, which is the most important publicly available journal on military affairs in China.[3] A variety of important figures from the PLA, including military scholars, regional commanders, top-ranking officers, and even members of the powerful CCP CMC, engage in a broad variety of topics related to military affairs. From time to time, officers from the Chinese People's Armed Police (PAP) and civilian scholars also publish in *China Military Science*. The main publication of the PLA NDU is the *Journal of the National Defense University*.[4] The different functions of the two institutions are reflected in the content of their publications. *China Military Science* and the texts published by the PLA AMS tend to focus less on specific operational issues and revolve around broader and more general topics, from doctrinal affairs to ancient military history and studies on foreign militaries. Both the PLA AMS and the PLA NDU, however, publish texts intended to be used to teach Chinese military officers.

In addition to *China Military Science* and the *Journal of the National Defense University*, Chapters 2 and 6 also draw on articles by Chinese military officers published in the *Chinese People's Liberation Army Daily* and *China National Defense Daily*, both of which are published under the auspices of the Political Work Department of the CCP CMC, which was known as the PLA General Political Department until 2016.[5] Some could argue that the articles taken into consideration here do not fully represent the opinions of "the PLA" (assuming that it is possible to look at it as a unitary actor). However, since the authors are military officers and scholars belonging to a variety of PLA institutions and their ranks vary from colonel to major general, their articles offer at least a good sample of what the PLA "thinks." Moreover, even if someone in the PLA disagrees with what their comrade(s) wrote, they must be part of a minority that is not powerful enough for their view to be considered.

---

[2] In Chinese: 战略学 (Zhànlüè xué) and 战役学 (Zhànyì xué).
[3] In Chinese: 中国军事科学 (Zhōngguó jūnshì kēxué).
[4] In Chinese: 国防大学学报 (Guófáng dàxué xuébào).
[5] In Chinese: 解放军日报 (Jiěfàngjūn rìbào) and 中国国防报 (Zhōngguó guófáng bào).

APPENDIX 2

Regulations and Policy Documents Related to the Expansion of Chinese Overseas Interests Issued between January 2001 and December 2017

This is not a complete list. Although some websites, such as that of MOFCOM, offer the option to navigate through the measures approved by their institution, others do not. Moreover, even those websites do not include all the regulations.

2001

- Notice on Printing and Distributing the Detailed Rules for the Implementation of the Measures for Administration of International Market Developing Funds of Small and Medium-Sized Enterprises (PRC MOFTEC and PRC MOF).

2002

- Interim Measures for Joint Annual Inspection of Overseas Investment (PRC MOFTEC and PRC SAFE)
- Overseas Investments Statistical System (PRC MOFTEC and PRC NBS)
- Measures for Comprehensive Performance Evaluation of Overseas Investment (PRC MOFTEC)
- Notice on Issues Concerning the Clearance of Foreign Investment Repatriation Profit Margin (PRC SAFE).

2003

- Notice on the Pilot Work Concerning the Examination and Approval of Overseas Investments (PRC MOFCOM)
- China's Policy on Mineral Resources (PRC State Council)
- Notice on Issues Relating to Simplifying the Examination and Approval Procedures for the Projects of Overseas Processing Trade and Delegating the Authority (PRC MOFCOM and PRC SAFE).

2004

- Interim Measures for the Administration of Examination and Approval of the Overseas Investment Projects (PRC NDRC)

- Notice on Distributing the Guide Catalogue of Countries and Industries for Investment Abroad 1 (PRC MOFCOM and PRC MFA)
- Decision on Reforming Investment System (PRC State Council)
- Notice on Distributing the Industrial Guidance Catalogue of Investment to Foreign Countries (PRC MOFCOM and PRC MFA)
- Notice on Supportive Credit Policy on Key Overseas Investment Project Encouraged by the State (PRC NDRC and China ExIm Bank)
- Notice on the Reporting System for Investment Obstacles in Different Countries (PRC MOFCOM)
- Supplementary Notice on the Support of the Prior Period Expenses of Overseas Investments in Resource and Foreign Economic Cooperation Projects (PRC MOFCOM and PRC MOF)
- Internal Accounting Control Specification—Foreign Investment (For Trial Implementation) (PRC MOF)
- Measures for the Examination and Approval of Investment to Run Enterprises Abroad (PRC MOFCOM).

2005

- National Foreign Emergency Response Law (PRC State Council)
- Notice on Promoting Development of Export Name Brands with Help of Export Credit Insurance (PRC MOFCOM and PRC SINOSURE)
- Notice on Implementing Export Credit Insurance (PRC MOFCOM and PRC SINOSURE)
- Notice on Further Strengthening the Financial and Insurance Support for Key Overseas Projects (PRC NDRC and CDB)
- Detailed Measures for the Examination and Approval of Investments to Open and Operate Enterprises Abroad (PRC MOFCOM)
- Notice on Using and Managing Special Funds for Foreign Economic Cooperation (PRC MOFCOM and PRC MOF)
- Registration System for Overseas Chinese-Invested Enterprises (Organizations) (PRC MOFCOM)
- Supplementary Notice on the Support of the Prior Period Expenses of Overseas Investments in Resource and Foreign Economic Cooperation Projects in 2004 (PRC MOFCOM)
- Policies for Development of Iron and Steel Industry (PRC State Council and PRC NDRC)
- Notice on the Relative Issues on Enlarging Pilot Reform of Foreign Exchange Administration Concerning Overseas Investments (PRC SAFE)
- Notice on Revision of Certain Foreign Exchange Control Policies for Overseas Investments (PRC SAFE)
- Opinion on Strengthening the Safety Protection of Chinese Enterprises and Personnel in Overseas Chinese Enterprises (PRC MOFCOM, PRC SASAC, and PRC MFA)

- Notice on the Establishment of Risk Guarantee Mechanism for Key Projects for Overseas Investment (PRC NDRC, and SINOSURE)
- Notice on Distributing the Guide Catalogue of Countries and Industries for Investment Abroad 2 (PRC MOFCOM, PRC SASAC, and PRC MFA).

2006

- Nine Principles on Encouraging and Standardizing Outward Investment (State Council)
- Circular on Relevant Issues Concerning Financial Interest Subsidy to Loans for Foreign Contracted Projects in 2005 (PRC MOFCOM and PRC MOF)
- Encouraging and Supporting "Go-Global" of Privately Owned Enterprises (Draft) (MOFCOM)
- Outward Investment Sector Direction Policy (PRC NDRC, PRC MOFCOM, PRC SAFE, PRC SAT, PRC MFA, PRC MOF, and PRC GAC)
- Urgent Notice on Strengthening the Statistical Work of China's Outward Foreign Direct Investment (PRC MOFCOM)
- Interim Measures for Chinese Enterprises' Overseas Business Complaint Service (PRC MOFCOM)
- Notice on Further Strengthening the Support for Financial and Insurance Support for Key Overseas Projects (CDB and SINOSURE).

2007

- Opinion of the State Administration of Taxation upon Doing Well in the Taxation Service and Management for the Overseas Investments of Chinese Enterprises (PRC SAT)
- Adjusting the Relevant Matters on the Examination and Approval of Overseas Investment (PRC MOFCOM)
- China's Energy Conditions and Policies (PRC State Council)
- Notice on the Statistical System of Direct Overseas Investments (PRC MOFCOM and PRC NBS)
- Notice of MOFCOM and MFA of Distributing Guide Catalogue of Countries and Industries for Investment Abroad 3 (PRC MOFCOM, PRC SASAC, and PRC MFA)
- Interim Measures for the Administration of Overseas Investment of Insurance Funds (PRC SAFE, POBC, and PRC CIRC)
- Notice on the Proof of the Registration of Overseas Investment Projects (PRC NDRC).

2008

- Administrative Measures on Contracting Foreign Projects (PRC State Council)
- Notice on the Strengthening Administration over the Foreign Investment Activities of Central Enterprises (PRC SASAC).

2009

- Measures for Overseas Investment Management (PRC MOFCOM)
- Notice on Issues Concerning Foreign Exchange Administration of Overseas Lending Granted by Domestic Enterprises (PRC SAFE)
- Notice on Issues Concerning Administration of Overseas Organizations' Foreign Exchange Accounts in China (PRC SAFE)
- Notice on Issuing the Provisions on the Foreign Exchange Administration of the Overseas Direct Investment of Domestic Institutions (PRC SAFE)
- Notice on Improving Issues Concerning the Management of Overseas Investment Projects (PRC NDRC)
- Notice on Matters Related to the Joint Annual Inspection of Overseas Investment (PRC MOFCOM and PRC SAFE)
- Notice on Further Clarifying the Relevant Issues Concerning Submitting Tax Certificates for Foreign Payments under Trade in Services and Other Items (PRC SAFE and PRC SAT)
- Notice on Issues Concerning Corporate Income Tax Credits (PRC MOF and PRC SAT)
- Notice on Issues Concerning Foreign Exchange Administration of Overseas Enterprises' Loans for Domestic Enterprises (PRC SAFE)
- Notice on the Administration of Foreign Exchange for Overseas Direct Investment by Domestic Institutions (PRC SAFE).

2010

- Notice on Printing and Distributing the Measures for Administration of Special Venture Capital for the Exploration of Overseas Mineral Resources (PRC MOF and PRC MLR)
- Measures on Safety Management of Overseas Chinese-Funded Enterprises and Their Employees (PRC MOFCOM, PRC SASAC, PRC MFA, PRC MPS, PRC NDRC, SAWF, and ACFIC)
- Notice on Issues Concerning Foreign Exchange Administration of Overseas Direct Investments by Domestic Banks (PRC SAFE)
- Notice on Adjusting the Examination and Approval Power for Some Foreign Exchange Businesses under Capital Accounts (PRC SAFE)
- Notice on the Administration of External Guarantees Provided by Domestic Institutions (PRC SAFE)
- Notice on Issuing the Overseas Security Risk Early Warning and Information Release System of Foreign Investment Cooperation (PRC MOFCOM)
- Notice on Regulating Issues Concerning Individuals Holding Shares in Overseas Investment of State-Owned Enterprises (PRC MOF)
- Opinions on Further Improving the Taxation Service and Management of "Going Out" Enterprises (PRC MOF)
- Notice on the Adjustment of Insurance Fund Investment Policy (SINOSURE).

2011

- Notice on the Special Fund for Foreign Economic and Technological Cooperation in 2011 (PRC MOF and PRC MOFCOM)
- Notice of Application of the 2011 Special Funds of Foreign Economic and Technology Cooperation (PRC MOF and PRC MOFCOM)
- Interim Measures for the Pilot Program of RMB Settlement for Overseas Direct Investment (POBC)
- Interim Measures for the Supervision and Administration of Foreign Assets in Central Enterprises (PRC SASAC)
- Guide for Investments in Foreign Countries (PRC MOFCOM, PRC SASAC, and PRC MFA)
- Notice Improving the Decentralization for the Approval of Overseas Investment Projects (PRC NDRC)
- Interim Measures for the Administration of Foreign Property Rights in Central Enterprises (PRC SASAC)
- White Paper on China's Foreign Aid (PRC State Council)
- Notice on Issues Concerning the Income Tax Credit of Oil (Gas) Resources Exploited by Chinese Petroleum Enterprises Abroad (PRC MOF and PRC SAT)
- Notice of the Capital Account Management Department of the State Administration of Foreign Exchange on the Relevant Issues Concerning Doing a Good Job in the Foreign Exchange Registration of Overseas Investment Projects (PRC SAFE).

2012

- Guide for the Safety Management of Institutions and Personnel of Chinese-Funded Enterprises Abroad (PRC MOFCOM)
- Notice on Printing and Distributing the Detailed Rules for the Implementation of the Interim Measures for the Administration of Overseas Investment of Insurance Funds (PRC CIRC)
- China's Energy Policy (PRC State Council)
- Interim Measures for the Supervision and Administration of Overseas Investment of Central Enterprises (PRC SASAC)
- Measures for the Supervision and Administration of Overseas Investments by Central Enterprises (PRC SASAC).

2013

- Notice of the China Insurance Regulatory Commission on Matters Related to the Risk of Investment in Insurance Institutions (PRC CIRC).

2014

- Measures for Foreign Investment Management (PRC MOFCOM)

- Administrative Measures for the Approval and Recordation of Foreign Investment Projects (PRC NDRC).

2015

- Notice on Relevant Policies on Adjusting Overseas Investment of Insurance Funds (PRC CIRC)
- Notice on Further Simplifying and Improving the Foreign Exchange Management Policy for Direct Investment (PRC SAFE).

2016

- —.

2017

- Measures for the Supervision and Administration of Overseas of Central Enterprises (PRC SASAC)
- Guiding Opinion on Strengthening the Prevention and Control of Integrity Risks of Central Enterprises (PRC CCDI and PRC SASAC)
- Measures for the Supervision and Administration of Overseas Investment by Central Enterprises (PRC SASAC)
- Measures for the Administration of Overseas Investment of Enterprises (PRC NDRC)
- Notice on Further Guiding and Regulating the Direction of Overseas Investment (PRC State Council, PRC MFA, POBC, PRC MOFCOM)
- Guiding Opinion on Regulating Banking Service Enterprises to Go Global and Strengthen Risk Prevention and Control (CBRC)
- Notice on Printing and Distributing the Measures for the Financial Management of Overseas Investment by State-Owned Enterprises (PRC MOFCOM).

APPENDIX 3

Chinese Statistics

Most of the data presented in this book come from the Ministry of Commerce (MOFCOM), the National Bureau of Statistics, the General Administration of Customs, and the State Administration of Foreign Exchange. These are the agencies that collect, process, and publish all the data related to China's foreign economic relations. The data are made available by those institutions either in the form of yearly reports and yearbooks or through the websites of international organizations like the United Nations Conference on Trade and Development and the World Bank.

Those data have both significant strong points and shortcomings. On the one hand, they are for a period that usually covers the last twenty years and stretches back to 1980 in some cases. They also allow an observer to gain important insights into the different aspects of Chinese economic relations with other countries, such as the number and value of contracts signed by Chinese companies abroad, the number of workers sent to foreign countries, China's imports and exports, and the value of Chinese assets abroad. On the other hand, as Kerry Brown (2008, 43) vividly pointed out, "Statistics in China is an area where the brave, the wise, the cowardly and the foolish all stand as equals." Indeed, not only is the way the numbers are processed not clear, as technical issues and political considerations can compromise their reliability, but some key data are simply not available. Country- and sector-specific Chinese data, which are also used by most international agencies, started to be published only in the early/mid-2000s and usually do not cover the years and decades before that. The same is true in the case of the data on Chinese investments overseas reported by MOFCOM, the National Bureau of Statistics, and the State Administration of Foreign Exchange.

In particular, there are two areas where the numbers shown should be seen more as indicators of general trends than as describing the situation precisely. The first is that, regardless of the concerns one might have about the way those data are gathered, Chinese data on outward direct investments (ODI) report only the annual flow and the stock of investments at the end of the year. We do not know how much capital actually flows out of China. Moreover, many investments are carried out through third countries. For example, the acquisition of a mine in Angola might well result in an increase in Chinese investments in Luxemburg, where the owner is hypothetically registered. Finally, there is the issue of "round-tripping," that is, the fact that many Chinese investors invest inside China by making their capital abroad first so that they can enjoy the fiscal benefits offered to foreign investors. According to a relatively old paper published by the Asian Development Bank (Xiao, 2004), up to 50 percent of Chinese ODI finds their way back to China.

The second problem concerns country-level data on the contracts signed by Chinese companies abroad. These data are crucially important for understanding the expansion of Chinese interests overseas, because Chinese companies today engage more in bidding for projects financed by foreign money, especially those coming from international organizations, than those financed by the Chinese government (Chen, Goldstein, and Orr 2009). Therefore, looking at Chinese ODI is not enough. MOFCOM divides those contracts into three different categories: contracts for labor services, contracts for design and consulting, and contracts for engineering projects (National Bureau of Statistics 2008, 801). The first is defined as "The provision and management of labor contracted for any project abroad" (ibid.). As for design and consulting, they include topographic surveying,

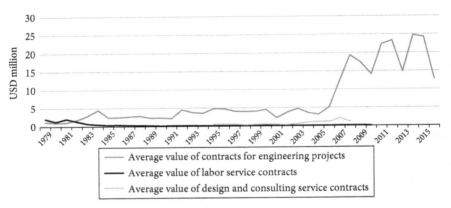

Figure 37 Average value of contracts signed by Chinese companies overseas

Source: Department of Trade and External Economic Relations Statistics, National Bureau of Statistics of China (various years). Compiled by the author.

geological prospecting, development zone programming, provision of documents, blueprints, materials on production process, technical consultation, project feasibility studies and evaluation, and personnel training. Engineering projects include the construction of bridges, railroads, ports, and any other infrastructure a Chinese company can be contracted to build.

Unfortunately, the data regarding the value of labor services and of design and consulting services, are available only until 2010 and 2008, respectively. Only those regarding engineering projects financed with both Chinese and foreign capital, including both aid and loans, and undertaken by Chinese contractors, are still updated every year. In any case, the contracts for engineering projects are far more lucrative than the others (Figure 37), and thus are a good indicator of the importance of a certain country as a market for big Chinese companies. At the same time, the data on the number of workers sent abroad for labor services and to complete engineering projects are available (Figure 38). It is important to emphasize that it is very likely that these data do not include workers and contracts signed by Chinese private companies. Indeed, it seems that private companies are not mandated to report those data to MOFCOM and, in any case, medium-sized and small private enterprises have a poor track record in following government directives when they operate abroad (PRC MOFCOM 2014, Gill and Reilly 2007).

Although these data are not enough to depict the scope of China's human and economic presence around the world precisely, they are still sufficient to describe the magnitude of Chinese interests in risky areas. Indeed, Chinese SOEs, like those of other countries (Bass and Chakrabarty 2014), tend to ignore risks in order to achieve the political mission granted to them and, in the specific Chinese case, the data and information available mostly refer to them rather than to private actors. Chinese private companies also invest in

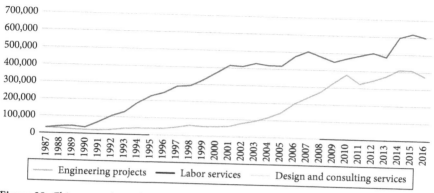

Figure 38 Chinese workers abroad

Source: Department of Trade and External Economic Relations Statistics, National Bureau of Statistics of China (various years). Compiled by the author.

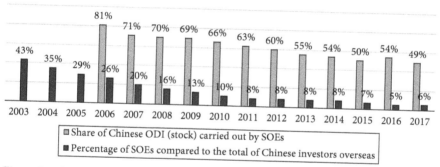

Figure 39 The weight of state-owned enterprises in Chinese investments overseas

Source: PRC MOFCOM, National Bureau of Statistics of China, and PRC State Administration of Foreign Exchange (various years). Compiled by the author.

resource-rich and sometimes unstable countries, but they tend to prefer high-income and stable countries that offer a large market and clear regulations (Amighini, Rabellotti, and Sanfilippo 2012). Moreover, despite a decline in recent years, SOEs still constitute about 50 percent of Chinese ODI (Figure 39) notwithstanding a steep increase in Chinese non-state-owned entities that decide to invest abroad year after year. Given the fact that the phenomenon of "round-tripping" is more common for private capital, that percentage of Chinese ODI carried out by SOEs is probably higher than what the data show. This means that the data for Chinese ODI in countries that are historically troubled by bad governance, are often involved in wars, and have a low per capita income mostly represent investments carried out by SOEs rather than private investors.

Chinese Diplomats

The data cover four generations of ambassadors posted to Europe, North Africa, and the Middle East from early 2000. On average the earliest group of ambassadors took up service in 2004. Unfortunately, it was impossible to go back further because of the serious lack of information available on the websites of China's Ministry of Foreign Affairs (MFA) and embassies, and the Wikipedia-like Baidu Baike. The data for some ambassadors were not available or were incomplete. Yet clear patterns do emerge. Considering that a diplomat reaches the rank of ambassador when he is around 50 years old, the figures include officials who joined the MFA from the late 1970s/early 1980s up to the mid-1990s.

The countries taken into consideration in Table 2 of Chapter 4 are those from the list in Appendix 1 in which the Chinese ambassadors belong to the Department of West Asian and North African Affairs and the Department of European Affairs of the MFA. San Marino, Monaco, and Lichtenstein are not considered, either because China's top diplomat there is a consul or because the relations with those countries are managed by the ambassadors in Italy and France. Unfortunately, information on the careers of Chinese consuls is unavailable.

Chinese Think Tanks

In 2009, the Shanghai Academy of Social Sciences (SASS) established the first national-level institute to monitor the development of Chinese think tanks and research institutions (see Tables 4–7). That center has been publishing annual reports on that topic since 2013, based on methods developed by James G. McGann and Donald Abelson. In those reports, SASS analysts rank the Chinese research centers according to how a number of invited scholars evaluate them depending on their perceived influence and sectorial expertise.

Table 4 Most influential research institutions in military and national defense affairs (2016)

Rank	Name
1	PLA National Defense University
2	PLA Academy of Military Science
3	China Institute of International Studies
4	Knowfar Institute for Strategic and Defense Studies
5	National Defense and Military Strategy Research Center, PLA National University of Defense Technology

Note: The Chinese Think Tanks Report 2017 does not include an updated ranking of Chinese research institutions working on military and national defense affairs.

Source: Chinese Think Tanks Report 2016, SASS. Compiled by the author.

Table 5 Most influential research institutions in policymaking (2017)

Rank	Name
1	Chinese Academy of Social Sciences (CASS)
2	Development Research Center of the State Council
3	Chinese Academy of Sciences
4	CCP Central Party School
5	Academy of Macroeconomic Research of the National Development and Reform Commission
6	China Institutes of Contemporary International Relations
7	Chinese Academy of Engineering
8	PLA Academy of Military Science
9	China Center for International Economic Exchanges
10	National Institute of International Strategy, CASS
11	China Development Institute
12	PLA National Defense University
13	China Institute of International Studies
14	Shanghai Academy of Social Sciences
15	China Center for Economic Research, Peking University

Source: Chinese Think Tanks Report 2017, SASS. Compiled by the author.

Table 6 Most influential research institutions in international affairs (2017)

Rank	Name
1	China Institutes of Contemporary International Relations
2	China Institute of International Studies
3	Shanghai Institute for International Studies
4	National Institute of International Strategy, CASS
5	National Institute for Global Strategy, CASS
6	China Institution for International Strategic Studies
7	Xinhua World Affairs Research Centre
8	Institute of International and Strategic Studies, Peking University
9	Center for China and Globalization
10	Center for American Studies, Fudan University

Source: Chinese Think Tanks Report 2017, SASS. Compiled by the author.

Table 7 Most influential research institutions for the BRI (2017)

Rank	Name
1	Development Research Center of the State Council
2	China Institutes of Contemporary International Relations
3	Chinese Academy of International Trade and Economic Cooperation, Ministry of Commerce
4	China Institute of International Studies
5	International Cooperation Center, National Development and Reform Commission
6	National Institute of International Strategy, CASS
7	China Center for International Economic Exchanges
8	China Center for Contemporary World Studies
9	National Institute for Global Strategy, CASS
10	Chongyang Institute for Financial Studies, Renmin University

Source: Chinese Think Tanks Report 2017, SASS. Compiled by the author.

APPENDIX 6

Research Projects Funded by the National Planning Office for Philosophy and Social Sciences

Since 1991, the National Planning Office for Philosophy and Social Sciences has been managing official funding of social science research in China on behalf of the Central Committee of the CCP. Its database is also quite complete and detailed when it comes to identifying the topics and the typologies of the studies that it funds. Hence, although there are other sources of funding for social scientists in China provided by the Ministry of Education and the Chinese Academy of Social Sciences, looking at the projects funded by the National Planning Office for Philosophy and Social Sciences can provide important insights into the interests of the Chinese leadership. (See Table 8.)

Table 8 Research projects per country supported by the National Planning Office for Philosophy and Social Sciences

	2000	2001	2002	2003	2004	2005	2006	2007	2008	2009	2010	2011	2012	2013	2014	2015	2016	2017
Egypt																		
Law																		
Religion														1				
World history									1									
Local literature						1			2		1	2		4	2		1	2
Local language																		1
Iran																		
International affairs					1													
World history											2				1			1
Religion								1	1					1	2	2		1
Iraq																		
International affairs																		1
World history							1											
Israel																		
World history				1														
Local literature						1					1	1					1	
Economic theory												1						
Religion															1			
Ethnic issues													1	1				
Saudi Arabia																		
World history																	1	
Local literature													1		1			

(Continued)

Table 8 (Continued)

	2000	2001	2002	2003	2004	2005	2006	2007	2008	2009	2010	2011	2012	2013	2014	2015	2016	2017
Syria																		
International affairs																1	1	
World history									2							1	1	
Turkey																		
Political science																	1	
Ethnic issues										1								
Religion									1							1	1	
World history			1										1					
Local language					1													
Libya																		
International affairs												1						
World history										1								
Somalia																		
Law										1								
World history																1		
Sudan and South Sudan																		
World history										1					1			
Religion							1											

Source: National Planning Office for Philosophy and Social Sciences. Compiled by the author.

APPENDIX 7

Studying Chinese Public Opinion and General Information about Movies

Chinese public opinion is represented by Chinese Internet users, or "friends online," as the media call them, and, to a lesser extent in the second part of Chapter 5, by Chinese moviegoers.[6] After all, as of December 2016, over half of the Chinese population has access to the Internet (731 million users). At least 614 million Chinese regularly access the Internet for their daily news. At the same time, Weibo (China's Twitter), Zhihu (China's Quora), Douban (China's Rotten Tomatoes), which were the main websites consulted for the analysis in Chapter 5, have more than 370 million, 160 million, and 160 million users, respectively. These numbers are important because those who use the Internet for reading news also tend to be more resistant to the government's message (Denmark and Chubb 2016). At the same time, the presence of social media with a vast number of users provides fertile ground for Internet users to express themselves as they prefer, especially as long as criticism of the state is not aimed at organizing any kind of collective action (Shen, et al. 2009, King, Pan and Roberts 2013). Although Internet users do not represent the entire Chinese population and cannot be seen as an accurate sample of Chinese society, they are those who are most likely to form, express, and spread their own ideas within an extremely large portion of the population.

Yet, in a country where power and citizens communicate in oblique and indirect ways, one should not ignore how the protection of China's interest frontiers has become an important subject for movies and TV series. Indeed, movies based on real events but with fictional characters, dialogue, and events are common "at moments when nations are undergoing some kind of cultural or political stress, change or upheaval" and are symptomatic of the attempt to "come to grips with a trauma" (Rosenstone 2006, 162). As the eighteenth-century novel helped in the creation of national identities by allowing individuals to imagine themselves as part of a larger group (Anderson 2006), movies and other cultural products today continue to "define and represent, or to construct" and "reproduce extant power relations" in domestic and international politics (Weldes 2003, 7; see also Ling and Nakamura 2019).

Fictional images, therefore, can be as powerful as real ones, as they allow their producers to create new narratives that give new meaning to the facts they are inspired from and, by changing the story where deemed necessary, they rewrite history, thereby legitimizing or delegitimizing the actions of the people and institutions involved in it (Mikalsky and Gow 2007, 219). Making comparisons with other countries and international actors can play an important role in this (Neumann 1999, 1–39). Fictional narratives can create real fears and expectations that influence how the public perceive reality and policymakers make the case for their decisions and policy proposals (Daniel III and Musgrave 2017). This is why cultural governance, that is, the management of how an individual imagines the national community he or she belongs to and its relationship with the state he or she is a citizen of, has greatly substituted purely coercive aspects of state control in most countries (Shapiro 2004, 31). The Chinese government, as Elizabeth J. Perry, (2017) highlighted, has a long tradition in doing so by adapting to the use of different technologies and symbols in order to bolster its legitimacy and manage the expectations of its subjects. Table 9 summarizes

---

[6] In Chinese: 网友 (Wǎngyǒu).

the key information about movies related to the defense of overseas interests taken into consideration in Chapter 5.

In any case, studying Chinese public opinion is like watching a shadow puppetry show with the light too strong and the puppets too far from the screen over which their shadow is projected. One can only hope that the light (government censorship) will dim for a moment, or that the puppets (the voices of citizens) will get a bit closer to the screen. The government employs more than two million people not only to censor but also to monitor and report to the leadership on the ideas and opinions that trend online (Hunt and Xu 2013). Known as the "Fifty-Cent Army," they write apparently spontaneous pro-regime comments and shape public opinion (Han 2015).[7] Spontaneous censorship and self-censorship also contribute to part of the difficulty. There are only a few instruments, like FreeWeibo, that allow some insights to be gained into what is censored online. However, that website was launched in 2012 and shows only a fraction of the posts deleted by censors.

In order to interpret the interests and attitude of Chinese public opinion, the analysis of Chapter 5 was carried out according to the following principles. First, the numbers of likes/comments/reposts were taken as indicative of the level of interest of both the public and the government because, while people usually use those tools to express their opinion about topics of interests rather than those deemed less important, state commentators are also more likely to intervene when antigovernment positions are numerous and, therefore, it is necessary to steer the development of the debate in the "right" direction. Those posts and comments, therefore, are the best sample available. Second, direct references to the "friends online" and other groups like the "keyboard warriors" on media and social media platforms are important evidence of the level of contestation of government policies and actions. Indeed, while the vast majority of critical comments are usually deleted, the fact that government-affiliated media refer explicitly to concerns expressed by online commentators, or that a vast number of similar pro-government/antigovernment comments appear below posts about incidents overseas, strongly suggests that there was a coordinated effort to neutralize criticism.

Obviously, everything must be taken with a grain of salt, especially when it comes to assessing whether a critical post online represents the point of view only of the person who posted it or whether it can be taken as an example of a more popular opinion. Although the risk of making a mistake is always present, the presence of other posts with a similar content—and/or the presence of vastly more numerous comments carrying the opposite message—is an indicator that the content of the post under consideration is not an isolated case of criticism of the policies/actions of the government. Additional specific caveats in the case of other online surveys and data from the Baidu Index can be found in the footnotes and in the main text of Chapter 5. (See Table 9.)

---

[7] In Chinese: 五毛军 (Wǔmáo jūn).

Table 9 Key information about movies related to the defense of overseas interests

Movie	State-sponsored competition in movie theaters	Support from the state / armed forces	Result at the box office	Role of the state / armed forces in the plot	Role of local people	Image of the West	Role of international organizations
Operation Mekong 30 September 2016	*My War*	Support from the MPS.	RMB 1.184 billion (USD 186 million).	The main characters are from the PAP.	No clear role of local people. Corrupt local officials are among the enemy.	Western countries are not involved.	International organizations are not involved. China is the leader of the diplomatic initiative aimed at improving the governance of the Golden Triangle region.
Wolf Warrior 2 27 July 2017	*Founding of an Army*	Limited support from the former Nanjing Military Region.	RMB 5.678 billion (USD 896 million).	Limited support toward the end of the movie.	Local people are victims of their weak government and civil war. They look up to China. The main character saves local people in danger.	The main enemy is a group of European mercenaries. The US government is represented as unwilling to help its citizens.	International organizations are important actors, and China does not act outside the UN mandate. Hence, the PLA does not intervene until the end. Chinese peacekeepers appear in the movie.
Operation Red Sea 16 February 2018	None	Produced by the PLA navy.	RMB 3.646 billion (USD 575 million).	The main characters belong to the PLA.	Local people are victims of war and terrorism. China cannot do much for them.	No Western country is involved. Non-local foreigners are among the evacuees saved by China.	The PLA seemingly acts within the boundaries of international law, but there is no clear reference to the UN or international law.

Source: Chinese media. Compiled by the author.

Bibliography

Amighini, Alessia, Roberta Rabellotti, and Marco Sanfilippo. 2012. "Do Chinese SOEs and Private Companies Differ in Their Foreign Location Strategies?" *EUI Working Paper* 27.

Anderson, Benedict. 2006. *Imagined Communities: Reflections on the Origin and Spread of Nationalism*. Rev. ed. London: Verso.

Bass, Eric, and Subrata Chakrabarty. 2014. "Resource Security: Competition for Global Resources, Strategic Intent, and Governments as Owners." *Journal of International Business Studies* 45: 961–79.

Brown, Kerry. 2008. *The Rise of the Dragon: Inward and Outward Investment in China in the Reform Period 1978–2007*. Oxford: Chandos Publishing.

CCP Central Literature Research Center. 2018. 习近平关于总体国家安全观论述摘编 [*Excerpts of Xi Jinping's Discussions Related to the Comprehensive National Security Concept*]. Beijing: Central Party Literature Press.

CCP Central Policy Research Office. 2014. *The Governance of China*. Vol. I. Beijing: Foreign Language Press.

Chen, Chuan, Andrea Goldstein, and Ryan J. Orr. 2009. "Local Operations of Chinese Construction Firms in Africa: An Empirical Survey." *International Journal of Construction Management* 9 (2): 75–89.

Daniel III, J. Furman, and Paul Musgrave. 2017. "Synthetic Experiences: How Popular Culture Matters for Images of International Relations." *International Studies Quarterly* 61 (3): 503–16.

Denmark, David, and Andrew Chubb. 2016. "Citizen Attitudes towards China's Maritime Territorial Disputes: Traditional Media and Internet Usage as Distinctive Conduits of Political Views in China." *Information, Communication & Society* 19 (1): 59–79.

Department of Trade and External Economic Relations Statistics, National Bureau of Statistics of China. Various years. 中国贸易外径统计年鉴 [*China Trade and External Economic Statistical Yearbook*]. Beijing: China Statistics Press.

Gill, Bates, and James Reilly. 2007. "The Tenuous Hold of China Inc. in Africa." *The Washington Quarterly* 30 (3): 37–52.

Han, Rongbin. 2015. "Manufacturing Consent in Cyberspace: China's 'Fifty-Cent Army'." *Journal of Contemporary Chinese Affairs* 44 (2): 105–34.

Heath, Timothy R. 2015. "An Overview of China's National Military Strategy." In Joe McReynolds (ed.), *China's Evolving Military Strategy*, 12–46. Washington DC: Jamestown Foundation.

Hunt, Katie, and Cy Xu. 2013. "China 'Employs 2 Million to Police Internet'." *CNN*. October 7. Accessed February 23, 2019. https://www.cnn.com/2013/10/07/world/asia/china-internet-monitors/.

King, Gary, Jennifer Pan, and Margaret E. Roberts. 2013. "How Censorship in China Allows Government Criticism but Silences Collective Expression." *American Political Science Review* 107 (2): 326–43.

Ling, L. H. M., and Mari Nakamura. 2019. "Popular Culture and Politics: Re-Narrating the Senkaku/Diaoyu Islands Dispute." *Cambridge Review of International Affairs* 32 (4): 541–58.

Mikalsky, Milena, and James Gow. 2007. *War, Image, and Legitimacy*. London: Routledge.

National Bureau of Statistics. 2008. 中国贸易外经统计年鉴 [*China Trade and External Economic Statistical Yearbook*]. Beijing: China Statistics Press.

Neumann, Iver B. 1999. *Uses of the Other: "The East" in European Identity Formation.* Minneapolis, MN: University of Minneapolis.

Perry, Elizabeth J. 2017. "Cultural Governance in Contemporary China: 'Re-Orienting' Party Propaganda." In Vivienne Shue and Patricia M. Thornton (eds), *To Govern China: Evolving Practices of Power*, 59–105. New York: Cambridge University Press.

PRC MOFCOM. 2014. "商务部关于 '对外承包工程业务统计制度》和《对外劳务合作业务统计制度' 公开征求意见的通知 [Notice of the Ministry of Finance on Issuing the 'Statistical System for Foreign Contracted Projects' and the 'Statistical System for Foreign Labor Cooperation']." PRC Ministry of Commerce. December 26. Accessed November 21, 2018. http://www.mofcom.gov.cn/article/b/g/201407/20140700674715.shtml.

Rosenstone, Robert A. 2006. *History on Film/Film on History.* Harlow: Pearson.

Shambaugh, David. 2002. *Modernizing China's Military: Progress, Problems, and Prospects.* Berkeley, CA: University of California Press.

Shapiro, Michael J. 2004. *Methods and Nations: Cultural Governance and the Indigenous Subject.* New York: Routledge.

Shen, Fei, Ning Wang, Zhongshi Guo, and Liang Guo. 2009. "Online Network Size, Efficacy, and Opinion Expression: Assessing the Impacts of Internet Use in China." *International Journal of Public Opinion Research* 21 (4): 451–76.

Weldes, Jutta. 2003. To Seek Out New Worlds: Science Fiction and World Politics. New York: Palgrave.

Xiao, Geng. 2004. "People's Republic of China's Round-Tripping FDI: Scale, Causes and Implications." *ADB Institute Discussion Paper 7.*

Index

Note: Tables, figures, and notes are indicated by an italic "*t*", "*f*," and "*n*" following the page number.